COUNTERPRESERVATION

signale
modern german letters, cultures, and thought

Series editor: Peter Uwe Hohendahl, Cornell University

Signale: Modern German Letters, Cultures, and Thought publishes new English-language books in literary studies, criticism, cultural studies, and intellectual history pertaining to the German-speaking world, as well as translations of important German-language works. *Signale* construes "modern" in the broadest terms: the series covers topics ranging from the early modern period to the present. *Signale* books are published under a joint imprint of Cornell University Press and Cornell University Library in electronic and print formats. Please see http://signale.cornell.edu/.

COUNTERPRESERVATION

Architectural Decay in Berlin since 1989

DANIELA SANDLER

A Signale Book

CORNELL UNIVERSITY PRESS AND CORNELL UNIVERSITY LIBRARY
ITHACA AND LONDON

Cornell University Press and Cornell University Library gratefully
acknowledge the College of Arts & Sciences, Cornell University, for
support of the Signale series.

First published 2016 by Cornell University Press and
Cornell University Library

Printed in the United States of America

Library of Congress Cataloging-in-Publication Data

Names: Sandler, Daniela, 1974– author.
Title: Counterpreservation : architectural decay in Berlin since 1989 /
    Daniela Sandler.
Other titles: Signale (Ithaca, N.Y.)
Description: Ithaca, New York : Cornell University Press : Cornell
    University Library, 2016. | Series: Signale : modern German letters,
    cultures, and thought | Includes bibliographical references and index.
Identifiers: LCCN 2016036451 | ISBN 9781501703164 (cloth : alk. paper) |
    ISBN 9781501703171 (pbk. : alk. paper)
Subjects: LCSH: Architecture—Germany—Berlin—History—
    20th century. | Architecture—Germany—Berlin—History—
    21st century. | Historic preservation—Germany—History—20th century. |
    Historic preservation—Germany—History—21st century. | Berlin
    (Germany)—Buildings, structures, etc. | Ruined buildings—Germany—
    Berlin. | Ruins, Modern—Germany—Berlin.
Classification: LCC NA1085 .S26 2016 | DDC 720.943/1550904—dc23
LC record available at https://lccn.loc.gov/2016036451

Cornell University Press strives to use environmentally responsible
suppliers and materials to the fullest extent possible in the publishing of
its books. Such materials include vegetable-based, low-VOC inks and
acid-free papers that are recycled, totally chlorine-free, or partly composed
of nonwood fibers. For further information, visit our website at
www.cornellpress.cornell.edu.

Supplementary materials are
available on the Signale website.

To my family

Contents

Illustrations

PREFACE

I was not looking for decay when I began this book. I arrived in Berlin in 2003 for a year of fieldwork, planning to study how preservation policies and practices embodied the ideological turmoils of German identity after unification. I lived in a tiny but smartly refurbished attic apartment in an *Altbau* (old building) in the unfashionable border between the western districts of Schöneberg and Wilmersdorf. The building was pristinely kept, its white façade graced by fluted columns and ample balconies, at the dead end of placid little Tharandter Straße.

Early on, I made a friend. She was a young student at the Freie Universität who helped me practice my German. She came to visit me and remarked upon what I thought was an unremarkable (if pretty) building: "But this doesn't look like Berlin!" The hallways, she meant, and the rug on the inner stairwell, and the façade and all the common spaces, and even the brass mailboxes . . . "It is all too . . . nice." It did not sound like a compliment.

I was intrigued. What was "too nice" about it, and why was that bad? In fact, although they were well kept, I did not find the building's spaces particularly striking; the dark wooden railings and floorboards even looked a bit dull to me. My friend explained that all of the people she knew in Berlin, including herself, lived in buildings whose common spaces, interiors, and exteriors were in much more precarious conditions.

I soon visited her apartment in fashionable Friedrichshain, which was then a very happening area, and saw for myself: the grimy façade, the worn-out steps, the state of decay and neglect of all the common spaces. I was surprised, though, to find that the apartment she shared with several roommates was perfectly well-appointed and maintained. Over the course of the next ten months this experience would be repeated. All my friends lived in similar buildings, slightly decrepit on the outside, where the stairwells and courtyards and halls looked abandoned; all in trendy areas: Prenzlauer Berg, Kreuzberg, Friedrichshain; but inside, their apartments looked just as "nice" as mine.

I found this very curious. I was born and raised in São Paulo, Brazil, where severe social inequalities are manifest quite visibly in the urban landscape through shantytowns, slums, homeless encampments. Dilapidation, grime, dirt, and neglect were all ingrained in my urban subconscious as signs of poverty and destitution, of an utter lack of alternatives. I had never heard of anyone voluntarily choosing to live in a decrepit building—much less people like my new acquaintances, who were students, artists, architects, and who appeared to have the means either to live somewhere else or to fix their abodes. The juxtaposition of crumbling façades with well-groomed apartments made everything all the more perplexing.

I continued to be intrigued by this—my own choice to live in a well-maintained building in a sleepy bourgeois neighborhood also a badge of my cultural biases and background. In my off time, I began to pursue examples of this voluntary embrace of decay. Eventually this personal curiosity found its way into my field research, as case studies; and then into my writing, initially as a single chapter on what I had begun to call counterpreservation. Then one day, having grown like untamed ivy let loose on the walls of a dilapidated building, counterpreservation took over, and became my whole project.

Acknowledgments

This book has been a long time in the making. I have a decade's worth of individuals and institutions to thank, over three continents and nine cities where the research and writing for this book were carried out. This book, like many, started with a doctoral dissertation, written in the Program in Visual and Cultural Studies at the University of Rochester. My main adviser, Andrés Nader, was unwaveringly supportive, open-minded, and stimulating. I cannot thank him enough for his scholarly guidance and inspiration. My other advisers were equally encouraging and helpful. Joan Saab was a thoughtful and perceptive reader. Out of a sea of too much information and too-broad writing plans, she helped me single out the one idea that ended up becoming the book. Douglas Crimp helped me become a more rigorous scholar and a more precise writer. He is the one who led me through the intellectual field of visual and cultural studies from the very beginning. Celia Applegate was a patient interlocutor, empathetic toward my subject and sensitively attuned to my writing style; she turned my attention to the voices behind the walls of the buildings.

For more than a decade, my friends and colleagues Margot Bouman, Jennie Hirsh, Derya Özkan, Roni Shapira, T'ai Smith, Lisa Uddin, Norman Vorano, and Catherine Zuromskis have read my work, held my hand, given me practical help and advice, and inspired me through example. You all have my gratitude and admiration, always. Very special thanks to Rosalyn Deutsche, whose work has inspired and informed my own, and who helped me find my way to graduate school.

During my studies, many professors and mentors introduced me to ideas, theorists, and works that inform this book, both at the University of Rochester and at the Faculdade de Arquitetura e Urbanismo at the University of São Paulo: Janet Berlo, Tom DiPiero, Paul Duro, Marta Dora Grostein, Elizabeth Grosz, Rachel Haidu, Randall Halle, Ricardo Marques de Azevedo, Lilia Moritz Schwarcz, Jorge Oseki, Vera Pallamin, Regina Prosperi Meyer, Rebeca Scherer, Catherine Soussloff, David Walsh, Sharon Willis, Erika Wolf, and Janet Wolff. Equally important were comments and support from my peers: Lucy Curzon, Renato Cymbalista, Margo Eastlund, Pedro Fiori Arantes, Mariana Fix, Leanne Gilbertson, Beth Hinderliter, Beatriz Kara José, April Miller, Silvana Olivieri, Renata Pereira Barbosa, Matt Reynolds, Renata Ursaia, and Amy Wlodarski. And I could not have finished this work without the swift, efficient, and brilliant help of two Berlin-based research assistants: Anne Doose in 2005 and Irene Hilden in 2015.

I was very lucky to find a rich intellectual home for this book in the Signale series. It is an honor to have as my editor Peter Hohendahl, who championed this project and steered it in the most productive direction. Signale managing editor, Kizer Walker, supported me through what was at points a nerve-wracking process. His insightful guidance and patience are much appreciated. I am forever indebted to the manuscript reviewers, who provided me with such attentive, detailed, generous, and helpful comments. They understood what I was trying to do, and helped me do it better. I also want to thank the entire Signale editorial board for supporting this project.

Along the years and across many institutions I have continued to meet scholars who each imparted something to this work. Martin Berger, Jennifer González, and Gary McDonogh were and continue to be terrific academic mentors who encouraged me and showed me the way to getting this published. Heinrich Hermann contributed very thoughtful advice on ideas, references, and the subtleties of the German language. Enrique Martínez gave me a provocative architect's perspective. For their feedback, support, and inspiration I also thank Monica Amor, Christopher Bardt, Mary Bergstein, Sara Blaylock, Julia Bryan-Wilson, Luis Carranza, Paola Demattè, Barbara von Eckardt, Daniel Harkett, Donna Haraway, Carola Hein, Leora Maltz-Leca, Barbara Miller Lane, Stella Nair, Daniel Peltz, Lisa Saltzman, Azade Seyhan, Elliot Shore, and Lynnette Widder.

At my current home, the University of Minnesota, I am deeply thankful for the intellectual companionship of Greg Donofrio and Lisa Hsieh. My colleague and mentor Katherine Solomonson not only cheered me up, but was also the most amazing reader and editor I could have hoped for. Jane Blocker helped me overcome one of the toughest challenges of this manuscript. Renée Cheng, Gail Dubrow, and Marc Swackhamer provided much-needed support and encouragement. I also thank Constance Severson, Martha McDonell, and Janaya Martin for their administrative help with various issues, and the students who took my classes at the same time that I was finishing this book for their understanding regarding grading delays and shorter office hours.

Institutional support was crucial for my research and writing. I am grateful for the funding I received from the Program in Visual and Cultural Studies, the Department of Modern Languages and Cultures, and the Friends of the Library, all at the University of Rochester; the Deutscher Akademischer Austauschdienst; the Rhode Island School of Design; the University of California, Santa Cruz; and the Imagine Fund at the University of Minnesota. I also relied on the resources, materials, archives, and professionals of the Freie Universität Berlin; the Staatsbibliothek zu Berlin; the Landesdenkmalamt Berlin; Studio Libeskind; raumlabor Berlin; the Haus Schwarzenberg; the Gedenkstätte und Museum Sachsenhausen; and the Fachhochschule Polizei Brandenburg. A heartfelt thank-you goes to the libraries and librarians at the University of Rochester (especially Stephanie Frontz); Bryn Mawr College (Iliana Chaleva); the Rhode Island School of Design; the University of California, Santa Cruz; and the University of Minnesota. I owe extra gratitude to the interlibrary loan offices at these institutions (with a special shout-out to the staff at the University of Minnesota).

My stays in Berlin were brightened by the friendship and hospitality of Rita Bakacs; Anke Lehmann and Guido Schmitz; Christine Schuster; Jörn Tessen; Paul Antonius, Lola Wagner, and Tillmann Wagner; and most especially Martin Bloem, who has continued to assist me for over a decade in all sorts of last-minute queries. In Berlin and elsewhere, I benefited from the patience and generosity of many professionals: Anne Albrecht, Helmut Bräutigam, Meike Danz, Ralf Dehne, Heinrich Dubel, Marcela Faé, Doris Fleischer, Benjamin Foerster-Baldenius, Esther Häring, Jörg Haspel, Andrej Holm, Annemargret Hein, Udo Hesse, Wolfgang Hiepen, Werner Kernebeck, Stephan König, Christian Kyelczynski, Daniel Libeskind, Günter Morsch, Anna Maria Odenthal, Philipp Oswalt, Jutta Ramien, Blase Rösch, Christian Röttele, Sibylle Schulz, Christian von Steffelin, Berthold Weidner, Henryk Weiffenbach, Saskia Wendland, Christian Wendland, Jutta Weitz, Petra Wilfert-Demirov, Ursula Wilms, and Henner Winkelmüller.

Finally, without my family, to whom this work is dedicated, there would have been no book. My parents, Ester and Paulo Sandler, have supported me emotionally, intellectually, and materially so that I could follow my dreams. They inspire me through their professional and intellectual example, their own books, writings, and ideas, and their ethics. They make the world a better place. My brother and my sister-in-law, Luiz and Carolina Sandler, and my niece, Beatriz, have lovingly cheered me on. My husband, Antoine Yoshinaka, has spurred me to see this work through, setting up deadlines, encouraging me to take action, sitting through crying sessions, and making it possible for me to finish this by taking care of our daughter and our house as I spent long hours in the office. Most of all, I thank my daughter, Clara, who has patiently waited through interminably busy, stressful, and in many ways painful months of book writing. This book is for you, my love.

Counterpreservation

INTRODUCTION

After the fall of the Wall in 1989, Berlin underwent a spectacular and much publicized face-lift. First came the sea of cranes, the scaffolding, the billboards, and the bulldozers. Then, gradually, the so-called New Berlin emerged: a sparkling new government district, glossy corporate developments, a constellation of memorials and gussied-up museums. Plus fresh coats of paint over block after block of historical buildings, now revamped as upscale rentals, condos, and trendy commerce. But even in the most gentrified neighborhoods there remained lively pockets of decay. Not picturesque ruins (although these exist), not soon-to-be-demolished remnants (although these too are there), but thriving ramshackle buildings and sites; decrepit, grimy, disintegrating—and teeming with social and cultural activities.

In popular views informed by North American perspectives, decay often equals urban blight, conjuring up associations with social and economic vicissitudes, disinvestment, unemployment, crime, homelessness, segregation, and depopulation. This is not necessarily so in Berlin. There, urban decay might be coupled with cooperative living initiatives, public interest projects, and thoughtful engagements with history. Many individuals and groups who could afford to be in refurbished or rehabilitated buildings choose instead decrepit ones. More than that—they choose to display and cultivate ruination.

Resourceful residents, who fix up their homes with their own hands in order to inhabit them, stop short of cleaning up façades and making things pretty, and instead encourage the ongoing weathering of their buildings. Exposed chunks of raw masonry, sooty walls, rotting window frames, and rusty railings form the backdrop for collective residential communities, art and cultural centers, and memorial sites. These groups and individuals have transformed decay into a vital part of the urban fabric; decay connects social and physical tissues instead of disrupting them. Communities thrive not *despite* architectural decay, but often *through* it.

This intentional incorporation of decay is a hallmark of Berlin. I call it *counterpreservation,* so as to indicate that while it runs counter to mainstream preservation, it is a purposeful social practice that should not be mistaken for neglect or destruction. In counterpreservation, decay is neither a contingency nor a handicap. Rather, decay is a choice. But why is architectural dilapidation appropriated, cultivated, and displayed consciously and pointedly in a city so full of opportunities for both new construction and historical restoration? How is dilapidation used, and what kinds of spaces does it produce? And what are its political, social, and cultural implications?

This book is an attempt to answer these questions through the examination of diverse case studies. They represent a range of social and spatial practices that respond to key issues, such as Berlin's official urban policies; gentrification; and past events that still shape the city, from the destruction of the imperial palace to the building of the Wall. The appropriation of decay is a meaningful social and aesthetic act, tied to the context of Berlin as a city with a strong countercultural lineage (and an equally strong legacy of top-down public and private developments that this counterculture has resisted). The case studies examined here are both iconoclastic and judicious in their approaches to history, using spatial and material dilapidation to highlight historic events and convey social and political meanings.

By turning my attention to the willful appropriation of decay, I want to stress not only the intentionality behind this practice, but also the value of space, architecture, and materiality as vital data. In other words, the architectural history of these spaces matters. By this I do not mean only a history of floor plans, designers, builders, and styles, but also a history that accounts for dilapidation as a meaningful and momentous stage in the life cycle of certain buildings. As an architectural historian, I am interested in the appropriation of decay as design: an act of material, spatial, and aesthetic creation; an intentional mark; a purposeful decision upon the world, which transforms (and is transformed by) a variety of contexts. Therefore one of my goals is to cast my net wide over a constellation of examples, not only spread across a large geographical area but also representative of a variety of motivations, circumstances, and architectural outcomes. These examples are valuable in their specificities, and in many ways they are not generalizable; but they all rely on acts of design in order to process, reshape, and exhibit architectural and urban decrepitude.

In this book, design appears not only in its familiar guise as architectural projects and urban plans, but also through informal instances. One of my premises is that collective and anonymous action, gradual and piecemeal interventions, everyday use (and misuse),[1] temporary changes, and conceptions and representations of space are all significant means of transforming buildings and urban spaces; they should be taken seriously both in their purposefulness and in their impact. Counterpreservation overlaps with the concepts of everyday urbanism and insurgent urbanism—umbrella terms that include both grassroots initiatives to transform or create urban and architectural spaces, and quotidian adaptations and appropriations born out of necessity and custom.[2] Everyday or insurgent urbanism is often opportunistic, taking advantage of available conditions and responding to specific circumstances. This does not mean that such urbanism cannot be proactive or premeditated, but that it is always tactical and contextual.

Similarly, appropriating decay in Berlin is, to some measure, a function of the availability of dilapidated sites and structures there. Berlin is still pockmarked by many poignant and picturesque ruins and fragments, stemming from World War II bombings, the building of the Wall, postwar neglect, and post-Wall shifting priorities: the Kaiser-Wilhelm-Gedächtniskirche; the Anhalter Bahnhof portal; the Franziskaner Klosterkirche; the blackened sculptures at the Martin-Gropius-Bau; the raw and unrestored surfaces incorporated in refurbished buildings such as the Reichstag, Parochialkirche, and Neues Museum; industrial structures at the margins of the River Spree; East German housing projects slated for demolition; and the deeply punctured façades of both anonymous and notorious buildings damaged by grenades and bullets in the Battle for Berlin (such as the stately Villa Parey, where the holes are marked with a transparent plaque naming them "Wunden der Erinnerung" or "wounds of memory").[3]

The notorious and pervasive presence of these ruins and signs of destruction in the landscape has continued to sustain a rough and ruinous image of the city even after extensive reconstruction, so that the mention of "ruins in Berlin" might not come off as much of a surprise. But what I argue here is that counterpreservation is

---

1. The misuse of space is a formulation proposed by Derya Özkan in her PhD dissertation, "The Misuse Value of Space: Spatial Practices and the Production of Space in Istanbul" (University of Rochester, Rochester, NY, 2008).

2. John Chase, Margaret Crawford, and John Kaliski's *Everyday Urbanism*, first published in 1999 and expanded in 2008 (New York: The Monacelli Press), is a pioneer in the field, along with Steven Harris and Deborah Berke, eds., *Architecture of the Everyday* (New York: Princeton Architectural Press, Yale Publications on Architecture, 1997). Since the early 2000s there has been a burst of publications: e.g., Jeffrey Hou, ed., *Insurgent Public Space: Guerrilla Urbanism and the Remaking of Contemporary Cities* (New York: Routledge, 2010); Marcos Rosa and Ute Weiland, *Handmade Urbanism: From Community Initiatives to Participatory Models* (Berlin: Jovis, 2013); Peter Bishop and Lesley Williams, *The Temporary City* (New York: Routledge, 2012); Philipp Oswalt, Klaus Overmeyer, and Philipp Misselwitz, *Urban Catalyst: The Power of Temporary Use* (Berlin: Dom Pub, 2013); Kristien Ring, *Self-Made City: Self-Initiated Urban Living and Architectural Interventions* (Berlin: Jovis, 2013); and Klaus Overmeyer, *Urban Pioneers: Temporary Use and Urban Development in Berlin* (Berlin: Jovis, 2007).

3. Senatsverwaltung für Stadtentwicklung und Umwelt, "Denkmaldatenbank," OBJ-Dok-Nr.: 09050289, http://www.stadtentwicklung.berlin.de/cgi-bin/hidaweb/getdoc.pl?DOK_TPL=lda_doc.tpl&KEY=obj%2009050289.

a distinct phenomenon that cannot be understood in the same terms—and which has not yet been fully teased out by scholars, with a few exceptions that broach the topic (which I discuss below in my review of recent literature). The phenomenon has, however, caught the attention of popular culture, being featured in blogs, travel guides, and news stories, signaling that it is a recognizable trope of Berlin.[4] Counterpreservation is not about ruins as such (even if some examples do include ruins); it is rather about ruination, about the state of decay, the process of becoming decrepit, dilapidation itself.

Ruins, after all, have been part of the repertoire of architecture and even preservation for a long time—from the artificial picturesque ruins of the eighteenth century to the debate over whether to preserve the ruins of the Heidelberg Castle as such instead of rebuilding it in the early twentieth century. Appropriating and reusing ruins, or leaving them as interactive ready-made installations (as in the Duisburg Industrial Landscape Park in Germany and the Gas Works Park in Seattle), is already an established practice—unlike the iconoclastic, still surprising, and for the most part intentionally shocking use of open-ended decay. The Duisburg Park and the Seattle Gas Works are finished designs, despite the possibility that their ruins might weather and change in what are often minor ways. These places are, in Phil Smith's evocative words, "ruins" as opposed to ruins:

> Ruins are different from 'ruins.' . . . 'Ruins' are what remain when ruination is temporarily and superficially removed from ruins—those strange places where the grass is mown in the moat, . . . where wooden walkways are constructed for apparent fear that folk may become infected by the thirteenth century.[5]

There is a certainty in the configuration of these "ruins" that is lacking in counterpreservation. The "ruins" described by Smith are composed as finite, delimited sites; they are ends in themselves. With counterpreservation, there is no end—or, at the end, there is a question mark.

Chapter Outline

This book begins with a conceptual discussion of counterpreservation, which defines the term in more detail and explores its connections with relevant theoretical and critical works (chapter 1). The rest of the book is divided thematically, grouping case studies together according to how they employ and in turn contribute to counterpreservation.

---

4. See, for instance, Paul Sullivan, "Berlin: City of Decay," *Slow Travel Berlin*, March 13, 2014, http://www.slowtravelberlin.com/berlin-city-of-decay/.

5. Phil Smith, "Sites of Dereliction: Beginnings and Allies of Performance," *Performance Research: A Journal of the Performing Arts* 20, no. 3 (2015): 67.

The first group of case studies corresponds to collective living projects, or *Haus-projekte*, housed in apartment buildings from the nineteenth and early twentieth centuries, often begun as squats and later legalized through lease contracts (chapter 2). After the fall of the Wall, many buildings sat empty and neglected in East Berlin as their property ownership was defined in court. Within a period of about a year, about 120 buildings were occupied illegally by political activists, artists, students, and *Autonomen* (social dropouts) in search of affordable housing and spaces where they could follow alternative lifestyles freely.[6] They were the current heirs in a long lineage of communal housing, dating back to the 1970s and 1980s in both East and West Berlin, which had similarly taken advantage of vacant and decayed buildings to carve out affordable spaces for collective and alternative living.[7]

The squatters of the 1970s and early 1980s had bound up their occupation of buildings (*Hausbesetzung*) with the self-organized restoration of these buildings (*Instandsetzung*), and the two concepts were fused in the neologism *Instandbesetzung* to indicate the dual character of their activity as an act of reclaiming and repair.[8] But of course things changed in 1989. The corollary of the dissolution of the Eastern Bloc after the end of the Cold War appeared to be the unavoidable dominance of capitalism, under the growing sign of globalization. Official plans for the newly unified capital of Germany—especially the government district and central corporate developments—painted a stark image of a gentrified, global, neoliberal future. The squatters of 1989 and 1990 were mindful of this, and they highlighted the weathered, aggressively deteriorated façades of their buildings as insignia of their political and cultural opposition to such glossy visions. There was a lot of *Besetzung*, but not necessarily as much *Instandsetzung*. Grimy walls and pockmarks were the architectural equivalent of ripped and worn-out clothes; graffiti and banners were flaunted as proudly as tattoos. The steady gentrification of central neighborhoods in what was formerly East Berlin only amplified these visual statements by contrast.

If *Hausprojekte* exemplify the spontaneous, bottom-up, collective, and often improvised character of counterpreservation, they do not tell the full story. Independent, nonprofit cultural and art centers are the second type of case studies in this book (chapter 3). Many, though not all, of them were founded in squatted buildings; and all of them, like *Hausprojekte*, claimed the right to affordable spaces in the center of the city through a combination of self-organization, cooperative

---

6. Andrej Holm and Armin Kuhn, "Squatting and Urban Renewal: The Interaction of Squatter Movements and Strategies of Urban Restructuring in Berlin," *International Journal of Urban and Regional Research* 35, no. 3 (May 2011): 650.

7. Armin Kuhn, *Vom Häuserkampf zur neoliberalen Stadt. Besetzungsbewegungen und Stadterneuerung in Berlin und Barcelona* (Münster: Westfälisches Dampfboot, 2014), 69–90; Alex Vasudevan, "Autonomous Urbanisms and the Right to the City: The Spatial Politics of Squatting in Berlin, 1968–2012," in *The City Is Ours: Squatting and Autonomous Movements in Europe from the 1970s to the Present*, ed. Bart van der Steen, Ask Katzeff, and Leendert van Hoogenhuijze (Oakland, CA: PM Press, 2014), 131–51. See also Lothar Schmid's photo essay *Häuserkampf in Berlin der 1980er* (Berlin: Berlin Story, 2013).

8. Kuhn, *Vom Häuserkampf zur neoliberalen Stadt*, 70.

management, and resistance to gentrification. Their character is more public, as they open up their doors and activities to a wide audience by operating art galleries, museums, cinemas, cafés, and bars and by organizing events, performances, and parties.

The artists, designers, and organizers behind these cultural centers make concerted efforts to plan and program their buildings—not only events and activities, but also spaces and their presentation. Cultural centers such as the Haus Schwarzenberg, Schokoladen, and the defunct Tacheles may look similar to *Hausprojekte* at first glance, with a juxtaposition of graffiti and posters over eroded walls, odd sculptures, architectural fragments, grime, and overgrown ivy. However, these spaces are composed with more forethought and coordination, and undergo significant (but selective) repairs, refurbishment, and even preservation measures. These cultural centers also articulate the meaning of their dilapidation clearly and self-consciously in pamphlets, websites, and interviews. They demonstrate that counterpreservation can be premeditated and self-reflective, and not just an ad hoc, opportunistic tactic.

Both *Hausprojekte* and cultural centers produce their spaces with varying degrees of informality, improvisation, and collective involvement. This might suggest that counterpreservation is limited to the fields of everyday architecture and insurgent urbanism mentioned above. Indeed counterpreservation has an affinity with the informal production of space through quotidian or tactical social practices, but it has also "trickled up" into official, top-down, centrally planned approaches.

One example is Daniel Libeskind's unbuilt proposal for the site of former SS barracks next to the Sachsenhausen Concentration Camp Memorial (chapter 4). This plan was commissioned by the local city government in the early 1990s. Unlike the piecemeal and localized character of the first two types of counterpreservation, the scale of this plan was very large both in size and in its potential socioeconomic impact. And while the spaces of *Hausprojekte* and cultural centers are conceived and transformed by diverse groups that may or may not include designers or architects (and in many cases, they do not), the Oranienburg plan was designed by an architect who was, by then, already a rising star, producing a finished, elaborate, and highly cohesive project. On the one hand, this means that the open-ended and participatory nature of *Hausprojekte* and alternative cultural centers is missing. On the other hand, the poetics of counterpreservation was articulated more sharply through the architect's authorial presence, in a daring and iconoclastic take on the treatment of historic ruins. The political commitments so visible in the *Hausprojekte* and cultural centers were also present in Libeskind's socially minded program.

To be clear, the project commission—a competition—did not call for a "counterpreservation" solution; this was a reaction of the architect to the original competition brief and site. Libeskind proposed to submerge under water the ruins of SS barracks and other structures that originally supported the adjacent Sachsenhausen Concentration Camp (preserved as a memorial site today). The submersion would have encouraged the further dissolution of these ruins, an idea counter to archaeological and historical approaches that treasure such remnants as molecular documents of the past and as physical evidence of wrongful deeds. Libeskind's ruin landscape would have been complemented by an area of new development where several buildings would provide spaces for education, rehabilitation, crafts, and other public-interest programs.

Libeskind's project spotlights memory as a fulcrum of counterpreservation, as the aquatic ruins would draw attention to the otherwise forgotten history of the site (this history is still, for the most part, suppressed; the plan was not built, and the site was turned into the Brandenburg Police Academy, with no public access and only minor marking of the Nazi past). Such entanglements of history, memory, representation, and forgetting are also present in the previous examples of counterpreservation, but they are not foregrounded with such intensity. Nor is Libeskind's plan the only one to incorporate an open ruin (and the ongoing process of ruination) into a memorial site.

By now the reader familiar with Berlin might be thinking of the Topography of Terror, an open-air exhibition and documentation center at the heart of the city where archaeological excavations of Gestapo structures once mingled with postwar ruins and debris (chapter 5). The Topography of Terror began as a temporary, guerrilla exhibition, and its helter-skelter quality earned it the nickname "open wound." The site proved to be charismatic enough for the temporary, grassroots exhibition to be made permanent and official; and it also inspired a trove of academic publications. In its first few incarnations, the Topography of Terror was exemplary of counterpreservation; these earlier incarnations are extensively discussed in published literature.[9] But the most influential analyses of the site were published before it was redesigned according to a more definitive and all-encompassing plan, in 2005. In this book, I do not reenact the many analyses of the Topography of Terror as open wound, although I do bring them up; rather, I look at the new configuration of the site, which is significantly different, and I probe whether it might be considered an example of counterpreservation—and conversely, whether counterpreservation is the most appropriate response for the site.

The final group of case studies in this book tests the concept of counterpreservation against two ruins of a more recent past: structures built by the German Democratic Republic (GDR), and called into question after unification (chapter 6). One of them, the now-demolished Palace of the Republic, exemplifies counterpreservation in a different form—not as the display of picturesquely crumbling façades, but as

9. Karen Till, *The New Berlin: Memory, Politics, Place* (Minneapolis: University of Minnesota Press, 2005); James Young, *The Texture of Memory: Holocaust Memorials and Meaning* (New Haven, CT: Yale University Press, 1993); Brian Ladd, *Ghosts of Berlin: Confronting German History in the Urban Landscape* (Chicago: University of Chicago Press, 1997); Jennifer Jordan, *Structures of Memory: Understanding Urban Change in Berlin and Beyond* (Stanford, CA: Stanford University Press, 2006).

new interventions and installations set into the gutted shell of a former Socialist civic center. The second structure is the Berlin Wall as it is preserved and memorialized in the Berlin Wall Memorial Grounds on Bernauer Straße, built between 2007 and 2014. The centerpiece of the memorial grounds (and the reason for their being there) is a long, decaying section of the Wall, complemented by a constellation of remains and archaeological findings related to the border fortifications. But the presence of ruins and fragments does not make the project—a tidy, tightly conceived, and interpretive new design—an example of counterpreservation. This final case study helps sharpen the concept of counterpreservation by contrast.

Scholarly Approaches

In order to discuss the relationship between the present book and existing scholarly approaches to the topic, it is important to restate the question at the heart of this research, so as to distinguish its inquiry from the very profuse collection of works on ruins, memory, Berlin history, and gentrification in general. If many books and articles have brushed the issue and the images of decay in Berlin, few have tackled this particular question: Why do people in Berlin want to live, work, perform, and play in decrepit buildings when they could either renovate their buildings with their own hands, or, in some cases, afford to be in renovated ones?[10] This is not usually the case elsewhere; and even in Berlin it is not always the case. Recall the self-built renovations carried out by the *Instandbesetzungen* of the 1970s and 1980s; in addition, many contemporary residential cooperatives and *Hausprojekte* do not embrace ruination.[11] The answer to the question does not lie only in an aesthetic or sensorial preference for ruinous atmospheres, although these certainly have a cachet among the contrarian subcultural communities of Berlin; and it does not lie only in the economic cycle of gentrification and the politics of urban activism, as

10. This was especially the case in the late 1990s and early 2000s, when a good number of buildings in Berlin had already been renovated, but rents and real estate values had not yet skyrocketed. Berlin in the early 2000s was a disappointment to developers who had bet on the city as a hot market. This situation changed over the last decade because of a variety of factors, including tourism, speculation, and a tight rental market. Today, one might not say so easily that individuals could afford to be in a renovated building in a central neighborhood. For an overview of Berlin's real estate market from the 1990s to the present from an investor's viewpoint, see Alberto Matta, "Berlin's Real Estate Is Hot Property, Says Optimum," *World Finance*, July 7, 2014, http://www.worldfinance.com/wealth-management/berlins-real-estate-is-hot-property-says-optimum. See also Janet Ward, "Berlin, the Virtual Global City," *Journal of Visual Culture* 3, no. 2 (2004): 239–56; and Kirsten Forkert, *Artistic Lives: A Study of Creativity in Two European Cities* (Farnham, UK: Ashgate, 2012).

11. See the following *Hausprojekte*: La Vida Verde (lavidaver.de), Jagowstr. 15, Hausprojekt Burge, Chuzpe Plietsch, and Bödi 9, among others. They do not all have their own websites, but the site of the Mietshäuser Syndikat, which aggregates *Hausprojekte* in Germany, has brief descriptions and images (http://www.syndikat.org/de/projekte/?land=Berlin). Residential cooperatives, while not the same as *Hausprojekte*, also offer an example of affordable living in self-restored central buildings. See *Das Selbst-Bau-Modell: Eine Mietergenossenschaft in Prenzlauer Berg*, published by Energiekontor GmbH; Architekten Kny & Weber; and S.T.E.R.N. GmbH (Berlin: Ch. Links, 1998).

these can manifest in a variety of forms other than crumbling nineteenth-century buildings. The latter approach is present in a glut of studies on the gentrification of neighborhoods in what was formerly East Berlin (discussed below); and the first approach guides the work of many cultural historians, anthropologists, and art historians who have poured over the poetics of ruins not only in Berlin but in many other areas (discussed in more detail in chapter 1). While both approaches are crucial to understanding counterpreservation, on their own they have failed not only to answer the question but even to pose it in the first place—because counterpreservation is constituted precisely from the encounter of these two realms, the practical and the symbolic, the economic and the aesthetic, the social and the atmospheric. So while previous works have brought up ruins, and even noted the use of ruination by alternative communities, they have not problematized it as other than a superficial and circumstantial instrument.

One exception is Greg Engle's PhD dissertation, evocatively titled "Ruinous Charm: The Culture and Politics of Redevelopment in Eastern Berlin" (University of Wisconsin, Madison, 2009). Engle is a cultural anthropologist, and set out to study activists in the neighborhood of Prenzlauer Berg who had rallied together to preserve and restore the Stadtbad Oderberger Straße (Oderberger Street City Bath) in the early 2000s.[12] As he integrated himself among the residents of the neighborhood, Engle realized he had to contend with two inescapable factors: one, the mythology of Prenzlauer Berg as a place of bohemian life, political resistance against the East German dictatorship, and artistic and social experimentation; and two, the attraction many residents felt to the "ruinous charm" ("morbide Charme" or "marode Charme") of decayed buildings.[13]

In reconstituting the history (and mythology) of Prenzlauer Berg through interviews, documents, and literary texts, Engle shows that the decrepitude of the dwellings, public buildings, and urban spaces was inextricably and sometimes contradictorily tied to the experiences of those who lived there: artists, writers, political oppositionists, social dropouts, students, young singles, and old retirees.[14] If the physical precariousness and the conspicuous public neglect of the neighborhood were felt as hardships, they were also turned into badges of honor and signs of freedom, resistance, and creativity. Life in Prenzlauer Berg then was rife with "contradictions and alternating fear, excitement, suspicion, resourcefulness, despair, and liberation."[15]

After 1989, and especially after unification in 1990, the neighborhood garnered intense interest from private developers, a process facilitated by public policies.

---

12. Greg Engle, "Ruinous Charm: The Culture and Politics of Redevelopment in Eastern Berlin" (PhD diss., University of Wisconsin, Madison, 2009), 13.
13. Ibid., 17–18.
14. Ibid., 35–36.
15. Ibid., 37.

Although the transitional early 1990s saw a burst of *Hausbesetzungen*, alternative nightlife, and art initiatives, the neighborhood soon became an upper-middle-class area for families (at some point nicknamed "Pregnancy Hill"),[16] dotted with pretty cafés and boutiques set against a background of smoothly painted, stucco-bejeweled, restored apartment buildings. Although the credence of the neighborhood as a hotbed of opposition waned even before the end of the GDR, "Prenzlauer Berg's legend as a bohemia in East Berlin would continue to grow" in inverse proportion to the bohemia itself, just as the ruinous charm of grimy, crumbling buildings became all the more prized because it was increasingly disappearing.[17]

Engle's work helps elucidate the myriad personal and collective motivations behind the attraction to ruinous charm. Significantly, Engle attaches the dynamic symbolism of decay to social practices, political goals, and lived experiences—one cannot be understood without the others. My concept of counterpreservation can be compared to Engle's exploration of ruinous charm—and ultimately, our work is complementary and convergent. But it also differs in important ways. Engle's dissertation is a focused study of one building, one group of activists, and one neighborhood (although he connects them to the larger context of Berlin). As I mentioned above, I purposefully defined my objects of study more broadly, so as to focus not on the *spirit of one place*, but rather on a *conception of space present in many places*. I address the issue as a question for architectural history, and not anthropology. Where Engle lingers on interviews and textual analyses, I attend to space, materials, programs, and designs. Ruinous charm is a cultural phenomenon; counterpreservation is a design concept that includes, but is not limited to, this cultural phenomenon.

As a result, my scope and methodology also differ from Engle's. Encompassing a large number of case studies was important for me to demonstrate the reach of counterpreservation beyond a few anecdotal or exceptional examples, and it was also important for testing the concept in diverse spatial, programmatic, and urban conditions. This wider reach meant that I had to sacrifice the deep focus on a single neighborhood that makes Engle's work so rich. My goal was not to rewrite the history of any single area in Berlin, but to give insight into a spatial practice that pops up across the city and even beyond it.

Another recent work of cultural anthropology has also turned its attention to ruins in Berlin: Hanna Katharina Göbel's *The Re-Use of Urban Ruins: Atmospheric Inquiries of the City* (New York: Routledge, 2015). Göbel's book is a thorough immersion in the ways in which a variety of individuals transformed, understood, and represented three buildings in Berlin: the Palace of the Republic, the Café Moskau

---

16. Julia Heilmann and Thomas Lindemann, "Angeblicher Babyboom: Die Kinder-Lüge vom Prenzlauer Berg," *Spiegel Online*, October 28, 2011, http://www.spiegel.de/panorama/gesellschaft/angeblicher-babyboom-die-kinder-luege-vom-prenzlauer-berg-a-793619.html.

17. Engle, "Ruinous Charm," 47–53.

(a GDR-era structure), and the E-Werk industrial ruin. Through extensive subject interviews, participant observation, and ethnographic visits, she provides a thick description of how a particular scene of cultural and design professionals and nightlife entrepreneurs targeted these three buildings, reshaped them through use and spatial interventions, and resignified them for their purposes.

Göbel seeks to redress what she sees as a scholarly blind spot on "the circle of gentrification." For Göbel, this blind spot corresponds to "the material and aesthetic agencies of built materials *qua* methodology,"[18] with particular attention to the ways in which these materials engage sensorial perception in space through the creation of atmospheres. She calls attention to the *"in-between* nature" of atmospheres:

> They are exclusively enacted in between the subject and object; they influence inner modes of the subjects and also "environmental qualities," but they do not belong to either. The accountability of atmospheres, thus, enjoys a nebulous status of being in between subject and object: constituted, shaped, and re-shaped by interobjective relationships.[19]

By considering atmospheres as in-between, she shifts the focus of analysis toward space itself without doing away with the groups and individuals who use and transform it. Space is not a mere stage set, a passive vessel for social processes, but also has its own relational agency; conversely, space cannot be understood separately from the actions, statements, language, and cultural values of those who inhabit it. Her attention to the in-between-ness of atmospheres, their "nebulous accountability," also means that the very concept of design is more flexible than its authored, controlled connotations might suggest: "Design is understood as a practical accomplishment and not as an intentionally directed task, a collaborative activity of stabilizing and de-stabilizing built objects."[20] In this way, both her work and mine align with the scholarship on everyday urbanism mentioned above.

There is, however, a deceptively subtle difference between Göbel's work on the one hand, and Engle's and my own research on the other. Göbel deals with buildings as ruins—dilapidated shells appropriated and recast as exceptional spaces such as art exhibitions, nightclubs, and even office space. While her take on atmospheres and her culturally minded ethnography are quite fresh, her treatment of buildings as ruins (however eloquent, labile, and ever-changing these spaces might be) is still akin to conventional literary and art-historical viewpoints of the ruin as an object or fixed site. This is different from my treatment of dilapidation as a process. Similarly, "ruinous charm" is more conceptual and dynamic than "the charm of ruins."

---

18. Hanna Katharina Göbel, *The Re-Use of Urban Ruins: Atmospheric Inquiries of the City* (New York: Routledge, 2015), 5.
19. Ibid., 10; Göbel's italics.
20. Ibid., 3.

If Engle and Göbel represent the perspective of cultural anthropology, another field has also addressed the deteriorated condition of buildings and neighborhoods in Berlin with relation to squatting and alternative cultures: the field of urban studies, which takes into account political and economic factors along with socio-cultural processes and historical data. This field is well represented by an ever-swelling collection of studies—notably, Andrej Holm's work on gentrification and resistance in former East Berlin after 1989; Alex Vasudevan's research on the history of squatting, which contributes not only historical documentation but also the conceptualization of squatting as an art form; Armin Kuhn's tracing of the interplay between the *Hausbesetzer* scene in West Berlin and official urban policies; Udo Grashoff's detailed study of illegal dwelling (*Schwarzwohnen*) in East Germany; Barbara Lang's pioneering study of Kreuzberg; and Margit Mayer's work on new social movements, urban activism, and neoliberalism, among others.[21]

These studies contribute immensely both to an analytical understanding of urban change through the prism of political and economic processes, and to a historical documentation of the squatter scene before and soon after the fall of the Wall. Alongside these works, there is also a complementary body of publications of a more historical or documentary nature: focused ethnographies, collections of testimonies and interviews, and chronicles: Anja Schwanhäußer on the techno-underground scene; Ulrich Gutmair on the nightclub, bar, and party scene; and a slew of publications on Prenzlauer Berg from before and after 1989.[22]

Heide Kolling's *Honig aus dem zweiten Stock: Berlin Hausprojekte erzählen* (Berlin: Assoziation A, 2008) is one of the few books to focus exclusively on post-Wall *Hausprojekte*. Kolling's book is an indispensable resource, as she literally lets the inhabitants of *Hausprojekte* tell their stories about everyday life, challenges, and peculiarities; she arranges these stories so as to highlight the "similarities among"

21. Andrej Holm, *Reclaim Berlin: Soziale Kämpfe in der neoliberalen Stadt* (Berlin: Assoziation A, 2014); Holm, *Die Restrukturierung des Raumes: Stadterneuerung der 90er Jahre in Ostberlin; Interessen und Machtverhältnisse* (Bielefeld: transcript, 2006), among others; Alex Vasudevan, *Metropolitan Preoccupations: The Spatial Politics of Squatting in Berlin* (Malden, MA: Wiley-Blackwell, 2015); Kuhn, *Vom Häuserkampf zur neoliberalen Stadt*; Udo Grashoff, *Schwarzwohnen: Die Unterwanderung der staatlichen Wohnraumlenkung in der DDR* (Göttingen: V&R unipress, 2011); Barbara Lang, *Mythos Kreuzberg: Ethnographie eines Stadtteils, 1961–1995* (New York and Frankfurt: Campus, 1998); Margit Mayer, *Social Movements in the (Post-) Neoliberal City* (London: Bedford Press, 2010). See also Andreas Suttner, *"Beton brennt": Hausbesetzer und Selbstverwaltung im Berlin, Wien und Zürich der 80er* (Vienna and Berlin: LIT, 2011); Thomas Dörfler, *Gentrification in Prenzlauer Berg? Milieuwandel eines Berliner Sozialraums seit 1989* (Bielefeld: transcript, 2010); Tanja Marquardt, *Käthes neue Kleider: Gentrifizierung am Berliner Kollwitzplatz in lebensweltlicher Perspektive* (Tübingen: Tübinger Vereinigung für Volkskunde, 2006); and Christian Krajewski, *Urbane Transformationsprozesse in zentrumsnahen Stadtquartieren: Gentrifizierung und innere Differenzierung am Beispiel der Spandauer Vorstadt und der Rosenthaler Vorstadt in Berlin* (Münster: Institut für Geographie der Westfälischen Wilhelms-Universität Münster, 2006).

22. Anja Schwanhäußer, *Kosmonauten des Underground: Ethnografie einer Berliner Szene* (New York and Frankfurt: Campus, 2010); Ulrich Gutmair, *Die ersten Tage von Berlin: Der Sound der Wende* (Stuttgart: Klett-Cotta, 2013); Bernt Roder and Bettina Tacke, eds., *Prenzlauer Berg im Wandel der Geschichte: Leben rund um den Helmholtzplatz* (Berlin: be.bra, 2004); Daniela Dahn, *Kunst und Kohle: Die "Szene" am Prenzlauer Berg, Berlin, DDR* (Darmstadt: Luchterhand, 1987).

Hausprojekte, both in their physical configuration and in their social dynamics.[23] The texts are presented alongside numerous photographs and facsimiles of handwritten notes. *Honig aus dem zweiten Stock* is a precious document of life in *Hausprojekte*, but it does not offer a critical analysis of its subject matter, nor does it place it within a broader theoretical or historical context.

Taken together, these studies—both the more theoretical and the more descriptive—form a thorough picture of the transformation of central Berlin from a haven of alternative cultures into a gentrified and neoliberal area, from the 1970s to the present. The reader who wants to understand the dynamics of *Hausbesetzungen*, their relationship to private development and public policies, and the cultural and symbolic milieu of housing activists and alternative cultures in Berlin needs to look no further than the studies listed above.

If, however, the reader hopes to gain insight into the particular seductions of architectural dilapidation and its connections not only to social activism, but to design and architectural thought, then these studies do not suffice, if only because they did not set out to examine this question as other than a background circumstance. The works mentioned above have looked *primarily* at gentrification, globalization, social activism, and political movements. These are their research entry points. Ruins and decay come up, of course, inevitably, because that was the environment where the other processes took place; but they are simply taken as the setting for the actions and decisions of the "real" protagonists—*Hausbesetzer*, artists, the government, private investors, designers; or they are brought up, unquestioningly, as intrinsically transgressive and alluring, as if these qualities were effluvia emanating naturally from decayed sites. Although the numerous studies above are invaluable sources for understanding contemporary Berlin, most of them (with the exception of Engle and Göbel) do not afford groundbreaking insight into the meanings of appropriated dilapidation. Even if the image of sooty Berlin façades might be familiar, it does not mean it has been understood.

Two early articles did at least open up the question. Kate Shaw's "The Place of Alternative Culture and the Politics of Its Protection in Berlin, Amsterdam, and Melbourne"[24] discusses alternative cultures with relation to private development and gentrification, and to conventional policies of historical conservation that end up displacing subcultures, artists, and other lower-income groups. Shaw dealt with dilapidation only briefly, as she focused on social, economic, and political processes, but she established a key link between decay and the survival of an alternative scene in her discussion of the now-extinct Tacheles art center, by noting that the space was "too dark and cold and strange" to allow for more mainstream or profitable

23. Heide Kolling, *Honig aus dem zweiten Stock: Berlin Hausprojekte erzählen* (Berlin: Assoziation A, 2008), [4].
24. Kate Shaw, "The Place of Alternative Culture and the Politics of Its Protection in Berlin, Amsterdam, and Melbourne," *Planning Theory & Practice* 6, no. 2 (June 2005): 149–69.

uses.[25] This connection between decay and urban activism is crucial to how I define counterpreservation, which otherwise might be explained away as a superficial aesthetic affectation.

Although Shaw noted the strong physical pull of the hulking Tacheles building, she stopped short of addressing the voluntary embrace of decay—an embrace as much symbolic as it was concrete—in which the building occupants and visitors engaged. This might imply that the connection between decay and activism was circumstantial, opportunistic—a contingency turned into an advantage. I maintain that it is much more than that. The tactical component is but one part of counter-preservation. The examples in my book demonstrate that appropriating decay is a meaningful, willful, laborsome gesture; one that *purposefully seeks* (and not merely *happens upon*) the particular materiality and symbolism of dilapidation. Thus appropriated, decay is architecturally eloquent, speaking not only through politics and banners but also through space itself.

The second article that points the way to a different understanding is Janet Stewart's "The Kunsthaus Tacheles: The Berlin Architecture Debate in Micro-Historical Context."[26] Stewart addresses dilemmas that loomed large in the early 1990s: to look to the future through new development, or to acknowledge the past; to make Berlin into a playground for contemporary architects, or to amend its fabric through preservation. These dilemmas were on everyone's lips then—architects, planners, visitors, residents, and academics. Many scholars, especially in the field of memory and memorial studies, argued against the dangers of burying Berlin's past too swiftly under new government buildings and corporate developments such as Potsdamer Platz: Andreas Huyssen in "After the War: Berlin as Palimpsest,"[27] James Young in "Daniel Libeskind's Jewish Museum in Berlin: The Uncanny Arts of Memorial Architecture,"[28] and Brian Ladd in *The Ghosts of Berlin*,[29] among many others.

Stewart comes at the dilemma from the standpoint of architectural debates, as architects like Rem Koolhaas grumbled about Berlin's strict zoning laws, which limited architectural creation.[30] In her words,

> On the one hand, there is the desire to create the space of global capitalism seen in the
> steel and glass skyscrapers, the shopping arcades . . . —signs of the dawning of the

---

25. Ibid., 159.

26. Janet Stewart, "The Kunsthaus Tacheles: The Berlin Architecture Debate in Micro-Historical Context," in *Recasting German Identity: Culture, Politics, and Literature in the Berlin Republic*, ed. Stuart Taberner and Frank Finlay (Rochester, NY: Camden House, 2002), 51–66.

27. Andreas Huyssen, *Present Pasts: Urban Palimpsests and the Politics of Memory* (Stanford, CA: Stanford University Press, 2002), 72–84.

28. James Young, "Daniel Libeskind's Jewish Museum in Berlin: The Uncanny Arts of Memorial Architecture," *Jewish Social Studies* 6, no. 2 (2000): 1–23.

29. This argument is especially clear in the chapter "Metropolis," in Ladd, *Ghosts of Berlin*, 83–125.

30. Rem Koolhaas, "Berlin: The Massacre of Ideas," *Frankfurter Allgemeine Zeitung*, October 16, 1991, 33.

"global city." On the other hand, there is the desire to create a metropolis at once new and old. "Critical reconstruction," a direction in urban planning development . . . sets out to ensure that new buildings in the city are designed according to existing patterns and plans.[31]

Stewart sees neither position as able to "provide an adequate exit from the impasse" on the appropriate architecture that could do justice to Berlin's complicated past; if visions of the global city seem most obviously amnesic, she suggests that Critical Reconstruction and historical restoration are nostalgic, idealized, and end up erasing cultural memories.[32]

Stewart zones in on the Tacheles art center as an example of a fruitful engagement with history through the ways in which artists occupied and transformed the structure while keeping its ruined character. She draws attention to the value of the ruin as such, not only as a multilayered embodiment of memory, but as a living structure capable of fostering diverse and inclusive social practices in the present. Memory, she posits, is better served by the unstable ruin than by an attempt to secure it.

Stewart's perspective is informed not only by architectural and urban history, but also by the field of visual culture. In analyzing the spaces and representations of the Tacheles as mutually constitutive, she delineates an interdisciplinary approach that brings together the material and the symbolic, the visual and the spatial, the focused scale of the building and the larger context of urban policies and architectural debates. This is how she comes to see the *"Kulturruine"* as "a paradigmatic signifier of the revolutionary hope of 1989, [and] also of the continuing tension between construction and reconstruction, art and global capitalism."[33] The interdisciplinary approach of visual culture allows Stewart to see the building as a signifier, to distill its meanings as representative of larger historic processes, and at the same time to take the building at its most concrete, spatial, and situated conditions.

Such is also my methodological approach and theoretical framework. My approach is based on the perspective of visual and cultural studies, which establishes a dynamic and dialogic set of disciplines (such as critical theory, art history, film studies, and comparative literature) to consider the meaning and sociopolitical uses of images, objects, spaces, sounds, and events in context. I draw from critical theory, memory studies, urban studies, and social theories of space in order to decode the meanings suggested or signified by buildings and sites. I also rely on my professional training as an architect and my academic practice as an architectural historian to observe, describe, and make inferences about the external and internal appearance of buildings, urban spaces, and plans, considering their programs, uses,

---

31. Stewart, "The Kunsthaus Tacheles," 52.
32. Ibid., 54, 55.
33. Ibid., 62.

patterns of circulation, materials, and urban context. The premise of my research, which is key to my choice of methods, is that buildings and sites are meaningful objects that not only convey social messages, but also transform cultural perceptions and spatial practices. They are not inert vessels, but participate in the dynamic and multidirectional production of both meaning and space. This means that the buildings and sites themselves are the main focus of both my field observations and interpretive analyses.

My approach relies on a contextual understanding of architectural space, which attends to the eloquence of the object—an eloquence in excess of, and sometimes in contradiction to, the intentions of the individuals responsible for shaping and presenting said object. This is not to say that these intentions do not matter, but that they are tempered by other factors, and sometimes they betray inadvertent or unconscious impulses. Interviews, testimonies, and public statements by architects, members of *Hausprojekte* or of alternative cultural centers, and institutional directors or representatives have served to inform my argument—variously confirming, directing, questioning, or correcting my hypotheses and my fieldwork. These interviews and statements have not, however, been taken as ultimate determinants. By this I do not mean to suggest I have ignored or overridden these perspectives, but rather that in some cases they could not be taken at face value, or they did not tell the whole story.

My research was informed by a combination of methods. First, I carried out direct observation of spaces, buildings, and sites under a variety of conditions (on regular days, during special events, etc.) and over a period of seven years, including a year-long research stay (2003–4) and several month-long periodical stays over the next six years. In my site visits, I took photographs to record visual information, in addition to writing field notes. This direct observation of architectural, urban, and phenomenological properties (including the observation of the ways in which these sites were used by residents and visitors) provides the raw matter for my analyses and interpretations.

In fact, these observations shaped my argument in the first place. I did not set out to study dilapidation from the start, nor did I have the term "counterpreservation" in mind a priori. I began this project as a study of historical preservation practices in general, but in the course of my immersion in the city I became intrigued by the intentionality and even pride associated with living or working in decrepit buildings. Eventually I began to follow this thread as the guide to selecting my case studies, many of which I discovered by combing the streets of particular neighborhoods on foot or by public transportation (especially the tram, which runs mostly in former East Berlin neighborhoods and affords a low-speed, panoramic view of the city).[34]

---

34. The case studies in this book are a selection of a much larger number of structures and sites investigated during fieldwork. The rationale for this selection is explained in the chapter overview.

Second, I collected as many primary materials in and around these sites as possible: flyers, posters, pamphlets, local newspapers, self-published books and documents, and images. In addition to these physical materials, I have also gathered their digital counterparts by printing or electronically archiving (as PDF files or via the Zotero tool for archiving digital sources) web pages maintained by *Hausprojekte*, cultural centers, museums, and memorials. These digital materials afford insight into the self-presentation of groups and institutions; in addition, much of their communication with other groups, advertising of events or spaces, and even political activism are carried out through websites, online forums, and social media, making digital documents an important and current source. These digital sources—especially the *Hausprojekte* web pages—were also valuable because they listed other similar projects, leading me to further case studies.

Third, I carried out a total of nineteen formal interviews with individuals, aiming for at least one individual associated with each case study in this book, whenever possible: residents of *Hausprojekte*; public-relations representatives for art centers, museums, and other institutions; directors of these institutions; and architects who designed buildings, memorials, sites, and plans.[35] These interviews served a few purposes. First, they provided oral histories of communities, projects, sites, and designs, imparting information not found elsewhere. Second, they filled in blanks and answered specific questions that were particularly relevant for my query. Third, they were useful for complementing, confirming, or amending information I had found elsewhere. (Conversely, the interviews themselves were cross-checked with documentary sources.) Finally, interviews often contained unexpected leads that further guided my research.[36]

A fourth component of my research was the collection of news stories from German and international newspapers during the period of study (2003–15). News stories documented several events and developments not recorded in other publications—for example, protests by urban activists, the eviction of *Hausprojekte*, and the changing status of official architectural competitions and plans. I tried to account for the bias of certain publications when discussing their stories; and I also tried to cross-check information by drawing from more than one source whenever possible. Newspapers and magazines also corroborated my field notes on social values, views, and trends. As a complement, I considered artistic and literary sources—exhibitions, installations, novels, fiction films, and so on. When relevant

---

35. Out of the nineteen interviews, I did eleven in person and five by e-mail. The remaining three interviews were done in person by my research assistants on two occasions when I could not be present in Germany and when an e-mail or phone interview was not possible (Anne Doose carried out two interviews in 2005, and Irene Hilden carried out another in 2015). Not all of these interviews are cited here; while they all helped inform my work, they were not all directly relevant to the final text.

36. Although I conducted interviews and direct observation, I did not undertake these as an ethnographic study. Such a study—although sorely needed for post-Wall *Hausprojekte*—would have been beyond the scope of my fieldwork, argument, and theoretical framework as delineated above.

and appropriate, I drew from them in order to highlight, support, or elucidate values and ideas suggested by my observations and interviews.

My main primary-source materials were the buildings and sites themselves. In addition, I consulted the archives of the Landesdenkmalamt Berlin (at the outset of my research, this required a physical visit; now, their database is publicly available online), and I obtained primary-source materials such as competition briefs, reports, and maps from institutions and individuals. I also relied on documentary films and footage, especially on *Hausprojekte*, most of which are publicly accessible online (although some had to be ordered from filmmakers). I analyzed all of the collected materials—field notes, photographs, interviews, documents—through the framework of visual and cultural studies as described above.

My research, while rooted in the analysis of case studies in Berlin since 1989, aims for a broader practical and theoretical reach. My investigation offers a framework for understanding examples of counterpreservation beyond Berlin, recognizing the particularities that distinguish disparate geographical and sociocultural contexts. Not every finding or insight from Berlin will apply to New York, Copenhagen, or Havana, and vice versa, but these sites can speak to each other in a fruitful dialogue through the analytical perspective proposed here.[37] In addition to comparative resonances with other places, which I will discuss in more detail in the next chapter, my work also offers a theoretical contribution to the disciplines of architectural preservation and memorial studies, proposing new ways of thinking about architectural heritage.

---

37. Jennifer Hosek's exploration of urban decay in Havana draws from my unpublished dissertation; see Hosek, "Transnational Cinema and the Ruins of Berlin and Havana: *Die neue Kunst, Ruinen zu bauen* [*The New Art of Making Ruins,* 2007] and *Suite Habana* (2003)," in *Spatial Turns: Space, Place, and Mobility in German Literary and Visual Culture,* ed. Barbara Mennel and Jaimey Fisher (Amsterdam: Rodopi, 2010), 211–31; see 212–13.

1

Counterpreservation as a Concept

I propose the term "counterpreservation" to understand the intentional use of architectural decay in the spatial, visual, and symbolic configuration of buildings.[1]
The word "counterpreservation" serves to identify, analyze, and aggregate tendencies present in a range of examples, indicating coincident social processes and convergent cultural meanings. While this book was born out of the observation of
Berlin's specific and unique circumstances, it holds value for the critical study of
architectural and urban heritage beyond the borders of Germany's capital city, as I
discuss below.

---

1. To the best of my knowledge, the term "counterpreservation" has not been explored in art and
architectural history other than in my own research, which was partially published (in abbreviated
form) as "Counterpreservation: Decrepitude and Memory in Post-Unification Berlin," *Third Text* 25,
no. 6 (November 2011): 687–97. The only example other than my research is a tangential, offhand mention in an article on New York tunnels by Ginger Nolan. Nolan uses the term in a similar way, to sig-
nify an interest in preservation that involves an aesthetics of decay: "In general, art and aesthetics played
a significant role in both the preservation of the underground and then, later, in the sort of counterpreservation [*sic*] stance that romanticized and aestheticized the tunnels and their inhabitants." Ginger
Nolan, "Film Monsters and Mole People: Exorcising New York's Underground," *Journal for the Arts,
Sciences, and Technology* 3, no. 10 (2005): 81. Nolan does not expand on what she means by "counterpreservation," nor does she relate the word to theories of heritage and memorials. For an overview of
recent approaches to the incorporation of decay and ruination, including my article on counterpreservation, see Caitlin DeSilvey and Tim Edensor, "Reckoning with Ruins," *Progress in Human Geography*
37, no. 4 (November 2012): 465–85.

In Berlin, counterpreservation is a response to three issues that have defined the city since 1989: gentrification, historical memory, and unification. Architects, artists, and activists use ruination consciously as a communicative gesture in the cityscape. In some cases the message of counterpreservation is overtly political, as in the antigentrification movement. In this case, the stakes are very tangible: affordable spaces for living and working in central areas. In other cases, the political dimension is symbolic, related to historical forgetting in narratives of unification, German division, and the Nazi era. In these cases ruination allows for the resurfacing of voices effaced by conventional architectural restoration.

As a spatial tactic, the intentional incorporation of decay had been a part of the urban landscape since the postwar era, especially from the 1960s on. Its reach and symbolism were, however, more limited then, partly because so much of the city looked decrepit that the effect was lessened by a background in which decay was an involuntary and pervasive circumstance. It was only in the first decade following unification that counterpreservation came into its own as a multivalent and politically powerful practice at the heart of the city. While the years since the first decade of the twenty-first century have curbed counterpreservation because of political, economic, and legal pressures, it continues to be a significant and strident presence in the material and symbolic life of Berlin. The case studies in this book trace the arc from the explosion of counterpreservation in the 1990s to its more limited and exceptional status in recent years. Thus the case studies evince larger transformations in urban planning, political orientation, and economic makeup, which relate not only to the particular history of Berlin as a national capital and tourist center, but also to its place in larger transnational processes of globalization, speculation, and urban competition.

The flowering and fading of counterpreservation also relate to changing tendencies in Germany's engagement with its history. The 1990s saw not only the reconstruction of a freshly unified country, but also the proliferation of memorials, self-made historians, institutional programs, and scholarly publications. Then, counterpreservation thrived as one of many possible responses that acknowledged a traumatic history in all its complexities. Now, almost two decades later, the "memory boom" has crystallized into a tourist attraction in its own right, while Berlin has found other vocations—creative city, media center, expat haven, trendy place. Instead of the "dig-where-you-stand" attitude that unsettled the ground of historically charged sites and left them open as urban wounds, as Karen Till recounts,[2] now the engagement with the past is contained in centralizing, polished, and grandiose structures such as Peter Eisenman's Memorial to the Murdered Jews of Europe, which by its very monumentality seems to offer a final, all-encompassing gesture. One may lay a wreath and pay respects, then head off to check out the

---

2. Karen Till, *The New Berlin: Memory, Politics, Place* (Minneapolis: University of Minnesota Press, 2005).

shops in nearby Potsdamer Platz. This comes close to the problematic attitude identified by Theodor Adorno as the "intention . . . to close the books on the past and, if possible, even remove it from memory."[3] In this context, counterpreservation survives as a pesky, uncomfortable proposition, dissonant in the increasingly slick city of tourism and real estate development.

The appropriation of decay for social practices and symbolic statements reveals an active public sphere for exercising the right to the city as Henri Lefebvre defined it: the right of socially, economically, and culturally diverse groups and individuals to use urban space for everyday life, personal and social development, and dialogue. When this right is not ensured by capitalist or technocratic regimes, Lefebvre suggests that city dwellers must employ alternative tactics, such as the reappropriation of space, its occupation, or its "diversion" (*détournement*).[4]

This attitude of collective engagement, which views the city as a labile medium for spatial and social transformations, is not exclusive to the case studies presented in this book, but connects to two larger phenomena. One is the culture of public dialogue and citizen participation characteristic of Berlin, manifest in grassroots initiatives (including the squatter movement and its heirs), in socially engaged planning philosophies (such as the idea of Careful Urban Renovation, or *Behutsame Stadterneuerung,* proposed in West Berlin in the 1980s), in the Stadtforum Berlin (an advisory board founded in 1991 that aimed to foster public debate about the planning and transformation of the city),[5] and in the antigentrification movement of the first two decades of the twenty-first century.

The second phenomenon is the rising tide of public demonstrations and occupations of urban space around the world since at least 2009: student protests in Tehran in 2009, political protests in Spain in 2011 and 2012, the Occupy movement that began in the United States in 2011 and spread internationally, the Arab Spring in 2010, the Gezi Park and Taksim Square protests in Turkey in 2013, the nationwide street demonstrations in Brazil also in 2013, and the political protests in Venezuela in 2014.[6] These larger social movements suggest a return to participatory forms of political action that take advantage of urban space as a platform for visibility and effectiveness, often including the city itself as the object and subject of demands (through issues such as affordable housing, public transportation, and green spaces).

---

3. Theodor Adorno, "The Meaning of Working through the Past," in *Critical Models: Interventions and Catchwords* (New York: Columbia University Press, 1998), 89.
4. Henri Lefebvre, *The Production of Space* (Malden, MA: Blackwell, 1991), 164–68. See also Lefebvre, *The Right to the City*, published in French as *Le droit a la ville* (Paris: Anthropos, 1968), and translated in English as the second section in Lefebvre, *Writings on Cities* (Malden, MA: Blackwell, 1996).
5. "Stadtforum 1991–2001," Senatsverwaltung für Stadtentwicklung und Umwelt, http://www.stadtentwicklung.berlin.de/planen/forum2020/index_stadtforum.shtml.
6. David Harvey, *Rebel Cities: From the Right to the City to the Urban Revolution* (London: Verso, 2012).

In connecting with these broader contexts, counterpreservation can be understood as one among many possible activist tactics that share common goals: affordable housing, access to public space, historical awareness, diversity, inclusiveness, and social justice. This connection with international movements also means that counterpreservation may be deployed in different places besides Berlin—and indeed it is—but in each place it will relate to specific conditions, values, and struggles. Therefore it will not look the same, or convey the same messages, everywhere.

However, counterpreservation is also unwillingly complicit in some of the very processes it seeks to critique or undo. The rebelliousness of Berlin's alternative culture has itself become a tourist attraction, and as it increases the city's desirability and cachet, it also increases its real estate prices—a well-documented phenomenon in gentrification, which I discuss in more detail in the following chapter. And while the multilayered, constantly changing spaces and materials of "counterpreserved" buildings offer a dynamic representation of history and memory, they also risk becoming a new cliché, a conventionalized signifier under a veneer of thoughtfulness that eventually might neither shock nor engage as it originally did.

Finally, the willing embrace of decay is a cultural luxury. Only those privileged with enough social, cultural, or material capital can afford to dwell so conspicuously, and so proudly, in the middle of shambles. They do not need to fear that their address and the look of their home might hurt job prospects, welfare rights, or their social life; or that the appearance of their business or place of work might repel customers. More than that, they can symbolically dissociate decay from misery in a way that others—ethnic minorities, recent migrants, or the very poor—cannot. I will address these shortcomings toward the end of this chapter. While they do not cancel out the positive potential of counterpreservation, they do limit it in important ways.

Decay Pride

Counterpreservation begins with the refusal to restore buildings and sites that are weathered, decrepit, or ruined. When groups and individuals first occupy these buildings, or consider them as part of designs and interventions, they encounter decay as an existing condition—a condition that is not necessarily sought out or artificially cultivated, but which is taken as an essential material and historical datum. They do not see decay as a vicissitude, as a temporary misfortune to be corrected so that one may reveal the "real building" beneath. Rather, decay is integral to the building, even if the ideas of decay and integrity might seem antithetical. The refusal to restore is parlayed into the appropriation of decay for symbolic purposes, along with the conspicuous display of features such as bullet pockmarks, grimy façades, crumbling walls, and precipitous holes (fig. 1). In addition, these groups might add new elements, such as murals, installations, and functional fixtures, that would not have been permitted by strict preservation guidelines. The buildings

Figure 1. Haus Schwarzenberg, street façade on Rosenthaler Straße 39 (2004).
© Daniela Sandler

are open not just to weathering, but also to present and future interventions. All of this represents, on the one hand, a departure from conventional restoration and conservation practices. On the other hand, counterpreservation retains a sense of contrivance and intentionality that distinguishes it from forgetfulness, inadvertent destruction, or intentional demolition.

Counterpreservation is not the same as passively letting a building decay. It is neither neglect nor active effacement. Even though the decay may have resulted from involuntary actions, in counterpreservation it is intentionally framed as a desirable feature, as an element to be displayed and noticed. Individuals, groups, and designers *reappropriate* decay—in the Lefebvrian sense mentioned above—and put it to good use, turning decay into a means of achieving affordable living and working spaces in prime neighborhoods. This reappropriation is not only concrete, but also symbolic, infusing decay with positive associations of social inclusiveness, freedom, and creativity.

In counterpreservation, decay is also seen as a way to represent the history of buildings and sites more truthfully than restoration. This particular view was recurrently voiced to me in interviews with the occupants of counterpreserved buildings. It is precisely because the building occupants (or designers, in some cases) are concerned with knowing and displaying history that they refuse to preserve or restore. This allows all of the diachronic transformations of the building to remain, synchronically, in the present, through the overlaying of traces, signs, ruptures, and additions.

There are plenty of buildings in Berlin and elsewhere that show signs of decay, but this does not mean that these signs are intentionally exhibited. They are contingent upon other circumstances—say, a landlord's neglect, or scarce financial resources. In these cases, the attractiveness of a weathered building may reside in literary or visual representations, in the way these buildings might have been captured in film or on paper, even becoming tourist attractions. Those who inhabit these run-down buildings, or their surroundings, would not necessarily concur that there is beauty in such decay: the romance is in the eye of the beholder.

Ruinenlust is the widely used German term to denote this lust for decay, which has been well recognized in art history and philosophy, and extensively studied with relation to neoclassicism, the picturesque, and romanticism.[7] *Ruinenlust* never really went away, despite the experiences of widespread destruction by war or natural disasters that produced vast ruined landscapes, and even vaster human losses, in the twentieth and twenty-first centuries. The subject cyclically recurs in popular and academic culture: for example, the Tate Britain in London organized a show in 2014 entitled Ruin Lust; in 1998, the Getty Center in Los Angeles had organized

---

7. Sophie Thomas, *Romanticism and Visuality: Fragments, History, Spectacle* (New York: Routledge, 2008), 48. See also DeSilvey and Edensor, "Reckoning with Ruins."

Irresistible Decay: Ruins Reclaimed.[8] Numerous recent publications attest to the continued fascination of ruins.[9]

A correlated, contemporary manifestation of *Ruinenlust* is "ruin porn." The term is attributed to Detroit-based photographer James Griffioen to describe the trend of visitors going to the city only to tour its abandoned factories, much to the chagrin of Detroiters who feel their hometown is shortchanged by being reduced to a ruin playground.[10] Tours of ruins are an example of a broader and more widespread practice called urban exploration, also known as urbex or urban spelunking. Urban explorers venture into off-limits structures ranging from ruins and vacant buildings to sewers and utility systems, in cities across the world. Their excursions often require a good deal of bravery and physical dexterity, and involve very real dangers such as falls or arrests for breaking in.

Urban spelunking and ruin porn attest to the grip of destroyed, mysterious, and menacing environments on a public that *consumes* these spaces by using them for personal exploits, which are recorded in photographs, videos, and verbal testimonies. These spaces are treated as a hybrid of fun house and rock-climbing wall, without the safety net. While these acts may be seen as a form of reappropriation, they are usually motivated by the individual experience of pleasure, thrill, or physical challenge—hence my emphasis on the idea of *consumption*.[11] In counterpreservation,

---

8. See the companion book by Brian Dillon, *Ruin Lust* (London: Tate Publishing, 2014); and *Irresistible Decay: Ruins Reclaimed*, exhibition catalogue, ed. Michael Roth, Claire Lyons, and Charles Merewether (Los Angeles: The Getty Research Institute, 1997).

9. Scholarly studies include Gastón Gordillo, *Rubble: The Afterlife of Destruction* (Durham, NC: Duke University Press, 2014); Bjørnar Olsen and Þóra Pétursdóttir, eds., *Ruin Memories: Materialities, Aesthetics, and the Archaeology of the Recent Past* (New York and Abingdon, UK: Routledge, 2014); Brian Dillon, ed., *Ruins* (Whitechapel: Documents of Contemporary Art; Cambridge, MA: MIT Press, 2011); Dylan Trigg, *The Aesthetics of Decay: Nothingness, Nostalgia, and the Absence of Reason* (New York: Peter Lang, 2006); Tim Edensor, *Industrial Ruins: Space, Aesthetics, and Materiality* (London: Bloomsbury Academic, 2005); Robert Ginsberg, *The Aesthetics of Ruins* (Amsterdam and New York: Rodopi, 2004). A sampling of nonscholarly books: Robert Harbison, *Ruins and Fragments: Tales of Loss and Rediscovery* (London: Reaktion: 2015); Christopher Woodward, *In Ruins: A Journey through History, Art, and Literature* (New York: Pantheon Books, 2001); Sylvain Margaine, *Forbidden Places: Exploring Our Abandoned Heritage* (Versailles: Jonglez, 2009); and several titles by the independent, Darlington, UK–based press Carpet Bombing Culture, such as Andre Govia, *Abandoned Planet* (2014); Rebecca Litchfield, *Soviet Ghosts: The Soviet Union Abandoned; A Communist Empire in Decay* (2014); and Daniel Barter and Daniel Marbaix, eds., *States of Decay* (2013), to name just a few.

10. Interviewed by Thomas Morton in "Something, Something, Something, Detroit: Lazy Journalists Love Pictures of Abandoned Stuff," *Vice*, August 1 2009, http://www.vice.com/read/something-something-something-detroit-994-v16n8. For a discussion of ruin porn and urban exploration in Detroit, see Dora Apel, *Beautiful Terrible Ruins: Detroit and the Anxiety of Decline* (New Brunswick, NJ: Rutgers University Press, 2015).

11. My comment about consumption does not preclude the critical potential of urban exploration. This critical potential has been compellingly discussed by Pablo Arboleda in "Heritage Views through Urban Exploration: The Case of 'Abandoned Berlin,'" *International Journal of Heritage Studies*, vol. 22, no. 5 (2016): 1–14. However, I do not share the unbridled enthusiasm of many scholars and explorers who have published on the topic, which they see as intrinsically subversive and liberating, in books such as *Beauty in Decay: Urbex* (Darlington, UK: Carpet Bombing Culture, 2010), and Bradley Garrett, *Explore Everything: Place-Hacking the City* (New York and London: Verson, 2013). Garrett published

the emphasis is on *production*; decayed buildings are transformed functionally, materially, and symbolically by acts of design: decisive, consequential interventions in architectural and urban space, motivated by activism and an ethical commitment to long-term goals.

Counterpreservation is neither *Ruinenlust* nor ruin porn, but it does have strong affinities with Svetlana Boym's idea of ruinophilia. For Boym, the ruin gaze is one attuned to the temporal and spatial disjunctures of modernity, acknowledging the unavoidable uncertainties and gaps in historical knowledge. Boym's ruinophilia is not the same as the pastime of urban explorers; the ruin gaze she describes is epistemological and ethical, and relates to an emancipatory political and aesthetic project. This is made clear in her distinction between two modes of nostalgia, which she defines with relation to ruins: "Restorative nostalgia manifests itself in total reconstructions of monuments of the past, while reflective nostalgia lingers on ruins, the patina of time and history, in the dreams of another place and another time."[12] Reflective nostalgia not only engages the past critically, but also propels it toward unrealized futures; it is therefore utopian.[13] This utopian impulse is also present in counterpreservation, along with very clear verbal and visual statements that elucidate how and why decay is used. The significance of counterpreservation is not only in the eye of the beholder.

Adaptive Reuse

Defaced or dirty edifices, their masonry and armature exposed through gashes and scratches like innards through a wound, are out of place in the gentrified landscape of central Berlin. The center of the city was beautified by careful historical restoration combined with rigid rules for new construction whereby new buildings blend in almost seamlessly with the old. These rules, known as Critical Reconstruction, were championed by Hans Stimmann (former head of Berlin's Urban Development Department), based on ideas by architectural theorists Vittorio Magnago Lampugnani and Dieter Hoffmann-Axthelm. Critical Reconstruction prescribes materials, colors, heights, and other guidelines, so that new buildings end up as simplified renderings of the nineteenth-century city. As Till puts it, "Planners known as 'critical reconstructionists' . . . argued that their job was to

---

a scholarly ethnography, "Undertaking Recreational Trespass: Urban Exploration and Infiltration," *Transactions of the Institute of British Geographers* 39, no. 1 (January 2014): 1–13. For a critical perspective, see Luke Bennett, "Bunkerology: A Case Study in the Theory and Practice of Urban Exploration," *Environment and Planning D: Society and Space* 29, no. 3 (2011): 421–34.

12. Svetlana Boym, *The Future of Nostalgia* (New York: Basic Books, 2001), 41.

13. Svetlana Boym, *Architecture of the Off-Modern* (New York: Temple Hoyne Buell Center, Princeton Architectural Press, 2008).

bring back the historic texture of the city that was destroyed by poor postwar urban design."[14]

Critical Reconstruction had been in place in West Berlin since the 1980s, but after unification it gained momentum with the city's architectural and urban makeover. New, circumspect buildings with opaque stone façades, uniform windows, and no setbacks from the street filled in the many vacant lots left by the war and its aftermath. They blended in with whatever remained from the old city, and those remains were gradually restored—not necessarily to their original (often less-than-glorious) state, but to a fresher, more sparkling, more upscale version. The apartment buildings (*Mietskasernen*, or "rental barracks") that had once been densely occupied, with dank and dark courtyards and shared bathrooms, were now revamped: side wings torn down to enlarge courtyards, private bathrooms built inside each unit, more light and ventilation, even elevators. They had never been so comfortable and salubrious, despite their ornate façades.

The streets of Berlin began to show a whimsical cohesiveness they had seldom enjoyed before. In this context, the semi-ruined buildings of counterpreservation stand out as dirty and precarious, destabilizing the otherwise clean and controlled cityscape, denying the eye-candy quality of renovated constructions. They do not invite a conventional tourist's snapshot, they do not make for pretty postcards, and they seem downright inhospitable to visitors. And yet, perhaps because of the particularly complicated ways in which Germany and Berlin address memory, these rough buildings are not only effective urban statements; they are also popular destinations for locals and tourists alike. These buildings encapsulate the traumatic histories that have made Berlin attractive for history buffs and memorial scholars: the Holocaust, World War II, the East German dictatorship, and the very intense although less evident traumas of unification. In architecture, these traumatic histories are present as physical traumas: weathering, demolition, neglect, bullet marks, bombings, fires, and alterations.

Preservation and restoration tend for the most part to erase these marks. More recently, less conventional refurbishment projects have taken an approach variously called combined, integrationist-historical, juxtapositional, or archaeological for the respectful incorporation of material remnants and traces of the past.[15] This

---

14. Till, *The New Berlin*, 37. On pp. 45–71 Till provides a detailed explanation of Critical Reconstruction. For documents produced by the proponents of Critical Reconstruction, see Philipp Meuser and Hans Stimmann, eds., *Vom Plan zum Bauwerk: Bauten in der Berliner Innenstadt nach 2000* (Berlin: Braun, 2002); Hans Stimmann and Eric-Jan Ouwerkerk, eds., *Von der Architektur- zur Stadtdebatte: Die Diskussion um das Planwerk Innenstadt* (Berlin: Braun, 2001);, Hans Stimmann, ed., *Berlino–Berlin, 1940–1953–1989–2000–2010: Physiognomie einer Großstadt* (Berlin: Senatsverwaltung für Stadtentwicklung, 2000); Annegret Burg and Hans Stimmann, eds., *Berlin Mitte: Die Entstehung einer urbanen Architektur* (Berlin: Bauwelt; Berlin and Boston: Birkhäuser, 1995); Vittorio Magnago Lampugnani and Michael Mönninger, eds., *Berlin morgen: Ideen für das Herz einer Groszstadt* (Stuttgart: Gerd Hatje, 1991).

15. Harold Kalman, *Heritage Planning: Principles and Process* (Abingdon, UK, and New York: Routledge, 2014), 162; Andreas Kluth, "The Graffiti That Made Germany Better," *The Atlantic*, July 3, 2014, http://www.theatlantic.com/international/archive/2014/07/the-graffiti-that-made-germany-better/373872/; Deborah Ascher Barnstone, *The Transparent State: Architecture and Politics in Postwar Germany* (Abingdon, UK, and New York: Routledge, 2005), 190.

approach is not the same as counterpreservation; however, because at first sight they may appear similar, it is important to explore their differences so as to define not only what counterpreservation is, but what it is not.

In these combined or "integrationist-historical" approaches, the traumas or marks are displayed and spotlighted, much as a fresco, sculpture, or historic relic might be. This is the case with the "Wunden der Erinnerung" in the Villa Parey. As I mentioned in the introduction, these "wounds of remembrance" are deep bullet pockmarks left by the street battles at the end of World War II.[16] The villa has been restored, its stone masonry cleaned to a light gray, creating a chiaroscuro effect that makes the dark pockmarks appear even sharper by contrast. The effect is striking, as the holes are impressively deep and numerous, but the overall composition is finished and controlled—polished, even, if one can apply this word to bullet holes.

David Chipperfield also incorporated fragmented, marred, and pockmarked walls into his redesign of the Neues Museum (1997–2009); and architects Hilmer & Sattler and Albrecht kept blackened and maimed sculptures in front of the restored façades of the Martin-Gropius-Bau (1998). The previous location of the C/O Photo Gallery, in the old Kaiser Postfuhramt building (from 2006 to 2013), juxtaposed crisply framed and expertly lit photo exhibitions and a background of peeling, severely weathered walls. These walls were set off all the more bluntly by the refined graphic design and smooth freestanding surfaces of the photo exhibitions.[17]

This is also the approach in Norman Foster's refurbishment of the Reichstag building (1992–99), which he gutted to make room for a new assembly room famously topped by a glass dome open to the public. Construction work revealed graffiti made by Russian soldiers upon their arrival in Berlin at the end of the war, and some of this graffiti was carefully preserved—but "in such a precious way as to diminish their power in the minds of many observers."[18] Foster preserved other marks of the past, "arguing that these traces comprised the record of the building's history," including "rubble arches . . . a crumbled stone frieze . . . disfigured stonewalls . . . fragments of nineteenth-century moldings and mason's marks."[19] But the overall effect is not one of pervasive, ongoing decay. The clear hierarchy of design elements, and the refined balance of old and new—along with gleaming floors, bright lighting, and digital panels—circumscribe the fragments and graffiti as contained details within an otherwise sleek environment.

---

16. Ulf Schubert, "Einschusslöcher in Berlin: Narben im Stein," *Tagesspiegel.de*, May 5, 2015, http://www.tagesspiegel.de/berlin/einschussloecher-in-berlin-narben-im-stein/11718016.html.

17. Kolja Reichert, "Des Kaisers neue Kuppel," *Tagesspiegel.de*, June 11, 2006, http://www.tagesspiegel.de/kultur/des-kaisers-neue-kuppel/719294.html; Oliver Kranz, "C/O Berlin im Amerika Haus: Aus dem Dornröschenschlaf erwacht," *Deutschlandfunk.de*, October 30 2014, http://www.deutschlandfunk.de/c-o-berlin-im-amerika-haus-aus-dem-dornroeschenschlaf.807.de.html?dram:article_id=301830.

18. Barnstone, *The Transparent State*, 188. See also Frederick Baker, Deborah Lipstadt, and Norman Foster, *The Reichstag Graffiti* (Berlin: Jovis, 2003).

19. Barnstone, *The Transparent State*, 190.

All of the examples above integrate elements traditionally seen as anathema to preservation: dirt, destruction, gaps, spurious interventions, and defacements. But these elements never dominate the design, nor do they set the tone for the form of the building as a whole. These elements may be present, and they may even be important, but they are ultimately ancillary to the architectural parti pris (for example, in the case of the Reichstag, the parti is the cupola and assembly room, not the walls with graffiti).

These examples should be understood, as Rolf J. Goebel proposed, as "architectural citations." Goebel argues that fragments and signs of destruction, when incorporated into new designs, motion toward the past without allowing for its retrieval. By virtue of being mixed with the new, the citations dispel any cognitive or phenomenological illusion of historical totality: "The obvious artificiality of partially historic and partially modern spaces, by virtue of their collagelike incongruity and continual surprise effect, deliberately draws attention to the work of interrogating the past."[20] These citations might have a critical potential, but they are not the whole text. They are supporting elements bracketed by an all-encompassing design that is as conventionally controlling, comprehensive, and final as most other projects of architecture or historic preservation.

Goebel's concept of architectural citations belongs in the more general practice of adaptive reuse—the repurposing of existing buildings to new uses through alterations of form and structure.[21] While adaptive reuse has arguably been practiced since the beginning of architecture (for example, the conversion of ancient Roman basilicas to Christian churches), it was singled out and named as such in the second half of the twentieth century. Adaptive reuse has become more popular with the growing inventory of vacant industrial structures due to deindustrialization, and because of environmental concerns about the conservation of energy and materials. Despite its popularity, and the high profile of many of its examples, adaptive reuse is not always endorsed by official preservation guidelines, internationally or locally.[22] Adaptive reuse takes material and stylistic liberties, departing freely from the principles of the original building, and destroying much of its extant fabric. In some cases, buildings are completely gutted so all that remains is the outer shell, to

---

20. Rolf J. Goebel, "Berlin's Architectural Citations: Reconstruction, Simulation, and the Problem of Historical Authenticity," *PMLA* 118, no 5 (October 2003): 1275.

21. David G. Woodcock et al., eds., *Adaptive Reuse: Issues and Case Studies in Building Preservation* (New York: Van Nostrand Reinhold, 1988); Ernest Burden, *Illustrated Dictionary of Architectural Preservation: Restoration, Renovation, Rehabilitation, Reuse* (New York: McGraw-Hill, 2004); Ismail Serageldin et al., eds., *Historic Cities and Sacred Sites: Cultural Roots for Urban Futures* (Washington, DC: World Bank, 2001).

22. Jukka Jokilehto, *A History of Architectural Conservation* (Oxford: Butterworth-Heinemann, 1999); Gottfried Kiesow, *Denkmalpflege in Deutschland: Eine Einführung* (Darmstadt: Wissenschaftliche Buchgesellschaft, 2000); Miles Glendinning, *The Conservation Movement: A History of Architectural Preservation, Antiquity to Modernity* (Abingdon, UK, and New York: Routledge, 2013); Michael A. Tomlan, *Historic Preservation: Caring for Our Expanding Legacy* (Cham: Springer, 2014).

be filled in by new architecture (this has been called façadism). In other cases, even the façades and outer appearance are changed.

The premise of adaptive reuse is that architecture—however old or unique—should be dynamic and responsive to changes in social demands and expectations. This dynamic perspective approximates adaptive reuse and counterpreservation. Both approaches see transformations as part of a building's history, and not as mistakes or detours. Like adaptive reuse, counterpreservation does not aim to protect buildings from further interventions, even if they are anachronistic. This is different from the faithful restoration of buildings according to their original stylistic principles. Traditional architectural preservation can fall into a taxonomic approach to styles as a basis for preservation and restoration decisions. The taxonomic approach owes much to "Hegelian notions of the dialectical progression of world history" that imply "that each style is singularly connected to the historical period it is supposed to represent."[23]

Some adaptive reuse designs are very conscious of the complexity of their social and historical contexts, while other projects are less judicious, so that it is impossible to make blanket statements about the category. It is, however, possible to assert that in adaptive reuse in general, the *reverence* for the building's original design or stylistic cohesiveness is forgone, even if there is *acknowledgment* of the past. Conventional preservation treats historic buildings as immutable objects that can only be touched in order to clean, preserve, or restore the original condition. When modernization happens, it is as subtle and discreet as possible, and only used when absolutely necessary for safety or functionality. Adaptive reuse is more radical. Instead of gently nudging the building toward modernization through localized and minimal interventions, adaptive reuse appropriates the built substance as raw matter for new designs and forms. The whole building is irrevocably altered.

Adaptive reuse projects sometimes incorporate architectural decay, either by framing eroded surfaces or damaged fragments, or by cutting through parts of a building and exposing masonry, floor slabs, and other elements. Sometimes this is done through architectural citations, in a controlled and localized manner. In other cases, the fabric of the building is transformed more radically. The "original" is used in novel ways; old walls, columns, or ornaments might still be *visible*, but they are not *seen* as they originally were. They become part of a collage, a new composition. If architectural citations are akin to an academic quoting of historic vestiges, then this more radical kind of adaptive reuse is a creative rewriting of buildings.

This is the case, for instance, in the restoration of the Harvey Theater of the Brooklyn Academy of Music, by the architectural firm H3 Hardy Collaboration Architecture in 1987, where the architects "took advantage of what nature had accomplished" by preserving the decayed interior surfaces, which had been

---

23. Goebel, "Berlin's Architectural Citations," 1287.

damaged by rainwater. The resulting "rich tapestry of color and texture . . . became a major element of the design," and "taunts the senses with random juxtapositions brought about through the layering of time."[24] In the Pinacoteca (State Art Collection) building in São Paulo, Brazil (1999), architect Paulo Mendes da Rocha sliced through thick bare brick walls. His design draws attention to their rough and unfinished character through the contrast with smooth white surfaces, black rubber floors, and metal platforms, which completely changed original circulation and use patterns. And in the Documentation Center at the Nazi Party Rally Grounds in Nuremberg (2001), Günter Domenig used the ruins of the unfinished Congress Hall building to set off his new glass-and-steel accretion.

These examples suggest a kinship with counterpreservation through the appropriation and display of decay. But adaptive reuse projects exert a much higher level of control over the redesign and final appearance of the architectural object. They predefine down to the smallest detail the spatial and aesthetic qualities of the building, such as finishes, fixtures, colors, materials, equipment, exteriors, and interiors. This definition includes both the new elements that are added to the existing building, and the original structure. Once construction is finished, these spatial qualities are also fixed, closed to further transformation. Indeed, redesigns such as the examples mentioned above achieve such a fine-tuned balance between new and old that any further changes would be very difficult to make.

Adaptive reuse designs do not accommodate gradual change, adaptation, weathering, or unpredicted transformations. They do not look decrepit; they look artfully remixed. Counterpreservation, in turn, makes room for these changes by incorporating accident, chance, and even more deterioration. The formal result is not as refined or controlled as adaptive reuse projects, because the emphasis of counterpreservation is not on an end result—the emphasis is on process. Adaptive reuse should be understood in terms of what Jorge Otero-Pailos describes as "the stamp of incompleteness"[25]—a contemporary, sophisticated understanding of preservation that allows more freedom to the architect's treatment of old buildings, with an apparent but strategically limited open-endedness. While these projects may be based on a complex view of history that incorporates discontinuities and repressed events, they still operate within the basic premises of preservation and architectural design, whereby the finished product is fully composed and arranged, the result of an architect's creation and not of the passage of time.

Counterpreservation provides a way to incorporate a more dynamic view of history into the treatment of architecture and urban space. It privileges change instead of any single specific moment or style. The layered imprints of time and

---

24. "BAM Harvey Theater," H3 Hardy Collaboration Architecture, http://www.h3hc.com/&flashid=1124.

25. Jorge Otero-Pailos, "The Contemporary Stamp of Incompleteness," *Future Anterior* 2 (Fall 2004): iii–viii.

the ongoing process of weathering result in open-ended, ambiguous, and even somewhat puzzling buildings where different periods are entangled. Those who use and visit these spaces are not offered fully spelled-out historical messages, but rather have to perform the task of historical interpretation themselves by engaging with the architectural object in a variety of ways (from intellectual reflection to phenomenological experience to everyday use).

In counterpreservation, historical narratives are not clearly conveyed by form or program, and instead may only be evoked in an incomplete or opaque way. This is not a failure, but rather a goal. For instance, a visitor to the Haus Schwarzenberg cultural center (which I discuss in more detail in chapter 3) may not be able to understand the history of the building transparently at first sight. But the building offers clues, small provocations, intriguing features. Broken or eroded moldings fuse into each other and dissolve in the play of light and shadow over roughly textured surfaces. These elements form a complex environment, but cannot be completely teased out or isolated as individual components, partly because many of them are fragmented or incomplete. Thus counterpreservation has a cryptic quality. This resistance to complete legibility relates to the romantic sense of mystery. At the same time, it resonates with the idea that history is not immediately accessible in a clear narrative, where all of the elements make sense and connect to each other logically. The visual opacity of counterpreservation parallels the semantic opacity of a history of conflicts, diverging narratives, and controversial events.

This does not mean illegibility. The Haus Schwarzenberg offers enough elements to provoke curiosity and suggest that something significant might lie behind its murky façades. There are two museums devoted to the history of the Holocaust and the Nazi era (the Otto Weidt Blind Workshop Museum and the Anne Frank Center), for example. But it is not immediately clear why the museums are sited there (the first has a connection to the building's history; the latter does not). Visitors to the Otto Weidt Museum will find bits and pieces about this history; even so, they will not be provided with a master narrative on the whole history of the building beyond the spaces and period of the exhibition. And the building houses much more than these two small institutions: a café, nightclub, movie theater, art galleries, studios, and bookstore. Not everyone who visits the Haus Schwarzenberg, whether occasionally or regularly, goes inside the museums.

A building preserved or restored traditionally—abiding by the integrity of a particular moment in time, a well-defined style, or a specific event—is a building that tells a story unequivocally, didactically. The Sanssouci Palace in Potsdam, the Goethe Haus in Weimar, the House of the Wannsee Conference in Berlin, the Bauhaus in Dessau—these sites convey their messages clearly, and not only because of their plaques, pamphlets, and tours. Polished marble floors, unified decorations, and period-appropriate materials form cohesive architectural narratives. They signal the origins of the building, where and when it belongs, and what kind of social values or status it represents. In the Haus Schwarzenberg these questions reverberate unanswered, or only partly answered, by the peeling walls, cracks, and missing fragments. Visitors must extract possible narratives on their own. This task is never complete, not only because buildings continue to change and weather, but also because the meanings are socially produced and as such change as social conditions change. Counterpreservation is dialogical, rather than merely iterative.

The sense of incompleteness is also meant as a prompt for visitors to situate the Haus Schwarzenberg building with relation to a larger context, so that inquiries into history, culture, ethics, architecture, or representation do not end once the visit is over. The artists' association behind the Haus Schwarzenberg makes this goal clear in their mission statements. They organize activities where local groups, especially schoolchildren, can appropriate the building's materials creatively and with a sense of history. The exhibition and publication *Fundstücke*, for instance, which collected objects found in the building—ranging from old cigarette cases to coins, stamps, and shoes—also incorporated texts written by children who had been invited to engage with these objects.[26] As James Young would say of the unconventional Holocaust memorials he calls countermonuments, counterpreservation does not place the "burden of memory" in spaces themselves, but on those who use, transform, observe, and reflect on these spaces.[27]

The reference to Young's concept of countermonument is not casual, as counterpreservation engages memory and represents history in ways that are similar to those of public memorials. A discussion of memorials can illuminate aspects of counterpreservation that are left in the shadows by heritage and conservation theories. For example, the iconoclasm of counterpreservation—its apparent self-destructive proclivity—is not easily explained with reference only to the incorporation of signs of destruction in adaptive reuse. The radical openness to weathering and the embrace of decay are design approaches of a different kind from the dedication of some wall space to graffiti or unrestored broken moldings.

Here, Young's countermonument proves helpful. For Young, the countermonument is a contrived effort at memory-work—in line with the commemorative character of traditional monuments—with the difference that it resorts to provocative, self-extinguishing strategies in order to complicate the very idea of memory. If traditional monuments suffer from an "essential stiffness" that "turns pliant memory to stone," countermonuments are "brazen, painfully self-conscious memorial spaces conceived to challenge the very premises of their being."[28] Some of these countermonuments are designed to disappear completely—such as Jochen and Ester Gerz's Monument against Fascism in Harburg, a black metal pillar gradually

---

26. Frank Eckart et al., *Fundstücke: Die verborgene(n) Geschichte(n) des Hauses Rosenthaler Straße 39* (Berlin: Anne Frank Zentrum, 2004), 25–39.

27. James Young, *The Texture of Memory: Holocaust Memorials and Meaning* (New Haven, CT: Yale University Press, 1993), 30.

28. Ibid., 13, 27.

lowered underground on six separate occasions in the course of five years until it was completely buried and invisible. In Young's discussion of the Monument against Fascism, he notes not only this self-destructive quality, but also its connection to a somewhat belligerent critical attitude:

> The countermonument thus flouts any number of cherished memorial conventions: its aim is not to console but to provoke; not to remain fixed but to change; not to be everlasting but to disappear; not to be ignored by passersby but to demand interaction; not to remain pristine but to invite its own violation and desanctification; not to accept graciously the burden of memory but to throw it back at the town's feet.[29]

The embrace of decay in counterpreservation echoes the countermonument's self-destructiveness: a critical attitude so implacable that it does not spare anything, not even itself. The countermonument is provocative; so are buildings where architectural decay is exposed, encouraged, and displayed. There is something aggressive about these buildings, almost a punk sensibility; grimy walls are affronts to beautified surroundings, and decaying fixtures that look on the verge of cracking appear to threaten passersby with the possibility of injury (a threat that is only visual in most, if not all, cases).

The countermonument is polysemic, and even semantically murky; it is not simply open-ended; it is also intentionally unfinished, incomplete. Similarly, counterpreservation strives to make the solidified, built matter of spaces into a more flexible medium, where *multiple historical narratives* might be read. These multiple narratives may be differing accounts of the same event—for instance, and hypothetically, an evocation of German complicity with Nazism may be present at the same time as the memorialization of German resistance. The physical traces of these narratives would not simply be layered, but might sometimes be inseparable from each other, irrevocably connected. The refusal of a single narrative with univocal meanings also makes room for the history of conflict and embattlement itself: the ambiguous feelings of Germans toward a war in which they were both perpetrators and victims, or the divergent expectations of East and West Germans with relation to unification. Counterpreservation, like the countermonument, conjures up this multiplicity without trying to gloss over contradictions.

Romance of Ruins

So far I have argued that counterpreservation is eminently a socially grounded practice, involving participation, activism, and historical reflection. I have also hinted at the aesthetic component of counterpreservation in my discussion of ruinophilia. This aesthetic component, while not central (as it is, for example, in romanticism

---

29. Ibid., 30.

or in ruin porn), is nonetheless important. The cultivation of grime, rust, and fragmentation betrays a romance of glumness, the eternally returning fascination with ruins, which Walter Benjamin famously called "irresistible decay."[30] Counterpreservation is not immune to the seductions of semi-destroyed structures, of surfaces slowly carved out by time and use—or violently torn by aggression, haunted by the signs of the past even when the memory of events has faded.

This fascination with ruins, as suggested by *Ruinenlust*, is exclusive neither to counterpreservation nor to romanticism. Contemporary cities and rural landscapes feature ruins that, in some way or another, have become landmarks, monuments, or involuntary attractions: the Foro Romano, the Athenian Acropolis, the shells of Catholic mission churches scattered across the Latin American countryside, the remnants of empty structures turned into adventure parks for urban explorers in postindustrial cities, even the site of Ground Zero in New York City as a decade-long pilgrimage destination before its reconstruction. In Berlin, the Kaiser-Wilhelm-Gedächtniskirche cuts a chiseled silhouette against postwar modernist structures, forming one of the most recognized postcard views of the city.

As Elizabeth Spelman notes, "Ruins are not just any state of disrepair"; she adds that "*Ruinenlust* tours don't include sites of urban blight." Spelman implies a distinction between, say, the attractive ruins of classical antiquity, and the repellent sites of inner-city decay. In her words, "There is a difference between a state of disrepair to which one eagerly rushes and a state of disrepair from which one desperately flees."[31] The difference may be aesthetic, but it is not purely so—it might also be temporal and contextual. After all, abandoned factories were not always treated with the same interest they now arouse.

Counterpreservation straddles the line between the disrepair to which one rushes and that from which one flees. All of the examples of counterpreservation presented in this book are much closer to blight than to the picturesque. Some of the buildings were never particularly beautiful to begin with, and none of them aged gracefully: muddy grime on the walls instead of soft patina; scattered fragments on the ground instead of towering façades; nondescript metal beams instead of fluted columns. A first look at the Haus Schwarzenberg or the Køpi *Hausprojekt* might suggest these are derelict tenements, which at some point they were. It is the particularities of Berlin culture and history—from its postwar countercultures to its post-Wall alternative scenes—that have pushed the perception of these sites into a favorable light. And, as Engle suggests with relation to decayed buildings in Prenzlauer Berg during the GDR era, this perception was often ambivalent and contradictory.[32]

---

30. Walter Benjamin, *The Origin of German Tragic Drama* (London: NLB, 1977), 177–78.
31. Elizabeth Spelman, *Repair: The Impulse to Restore in a Fragile World* (Boston: Beacon Press, 2002), 113.
32. Greg Engle, "Ruinous Charm: The Culture and Politics of Redevelopment in Eastern Berlin" (PhD diss., University of Wisconsin, Madison, 2009), 37.

Additionally, in counterpreservation the fascination with ruins is mixed into the functional and utilitarian preoccupations of everyday activities such as inhabiting, working, eating, and recreation; it is applied to apartment buildings, galleries, cafés, offices, print shops, soup kitchens, movie theaters. This is different from the enjoyment and use of most ruins, which are usually removed from everyday or practical concerns, and set in the context of leisure or contemplation. Travelers or painters can appreciate ruins in a landscape, and tourists can stroll freely through the Foro Romano or the city of Pompeii, which are set up as open-air museums. Some ruins are converted into event sites, thus incorporating function without losing their contemplative quality. The ruin of the Franziskaner Klosterkirche in Berlin offers a poignant setting for open-air concerts and everyday wandering, with its roofless brick walls, but the site does not have to accommodate bathrooms or dressing rooms, or provide shelter from rain or sun. Not so in counterpreservation, where people live, work, dine, meet, party, make and display things, launder clothes, and go to the bathroom.

If counterpreservation harbors, to some measure, an aesthetic fascination with decay, it cannot be reduced to this aspect, as it simultaneously encompasses a variety of other impulses that stem from a critical view of history and urban life. The marks of time must be shown not just for their visual seductiveness, but because they are an imprint of history. In this sense, counterpreservation should be compared to John Ruskin's writings on architectural history and preservation, which mediate between a romantic background and social, cultural, and political ideals. Ruskin famously praised the patina left by time as a sign of the character and spirit of a building. Ruskin viewed historical reconstruction, or restoration, as "the most total destruction which a building can suffer" because it erased the signs of weathering and falsified the building's history.[33] For Ruskin, authenticity in architectural preservation did not consist in following an abstracted system of stylistic cohesiveness like that proposed by Eugène Emmanuel Viollet-le-Duc, the other nineteenth-century exponent of preservation.[34]

Rather, for Ruskin authenticity or "truth" resided in the whole incarnation of an edifice. Ruskin saw "truth" as one of the essential virtues of architecture, the qualities that every worthy building should have—in his words, the "seven lamps."[35] Truth and honesty meant among other things expressing the characteristics and nature of building materials, the original values and beliefs that informed the building's conception, the craftsmanship and work of the master builders, and the

33. John Ruskin, "The Lamp of Memory," Aphorism 31, in *The Seven Lamps of Architecture* (New York: Thomas Y. Crowell, 1880), 256.

34. Eugène Emmanuel Viollet-le-Duc, *Dictionnaire raisonné de l'architecture française* (Paris, 1866), 8:24.

35. The seven lamps are Sacrifice, Truth, Power, Memory, Beauty, Obedience, and Life.

meanings of spatial and ornamental elements for designers, builders, and users.[36] A building had to be understood in relation to its place in history and its existence over time, including alterations, decay, and additions. In his careful study of Venice architecture, Ruskin does not strive to isolate stylistic periods for buildings, but describes the different contributions from each century, which he calls "interpolations."[37]

Ruskin rejected the classical canon, and with it the very idea of beauty. A building was interesting not because of its harmonious composition, exquisite materials, or pleasing appearance. For Ruskin, these could be empty qualities if the building did not relate to its immediate and historical environment. He was an early champion of English Gothic not simply because he found the pointed arch more attractive than the round one. His argument was sociocultural: the Gothic expressed the relationship between artisans and the materials naturally available to them, between religious beliefs and sacred buildings, between folk culture and ways of inhabiting and perceiving space.

A consequence of Ruskin's propositions is that, according to his approach, the value and meaning of architecture extend far beyond the physical limits of a building's walls or foundations. The building cannot be seen as a static object whose formal properties can be abstracted in a coherent system, immune to context or change. A relic such as a Carolingian scepter or a Saxon crown may be safeguarded in a museum and congealed within narratives of historical progression and stylistic belonging (although even these narratives can be questioned in their refractoriness to social and symbolic change). The same cannot be said of a building. Architecture is irrevocably rooted in everyday use.

The opposition between Ruskin and Viollet-le-Duc is echoed in the opposition between preservation and restoration. Supporters of preservation advocate limited and ongoing maintenance, and more extensive repairs only when absolutely necessary for a building's integrity. Those in favor of restoration argue for more intrusive work, from scraping and cleansing to the reproduction of missing parts with new materials. In early twentieth-century Germany, this debate converged in the discussion about *restoring* the ruins of the Heidelberg Castle to its former integrity, or just *preserving* the remnants of the castle in their ruinous state.[38]

Is counterpreservation, then, not simply a more radical form of preservation? Indeed, counterpreservation's dynamic view of architecture owes much to Ruskin and those who followed him. But Ruskin would not have advocated letting buildings weather and decay until they disappeared. On the contrary, he advised

---

36. John Ruskin, "The Virtues of Architecture," *The Stones of Venice* (New York: John Wiley and Sons, 1890), esp. 37–39 and 43–44.

37. See, for instance, his remarks on the church of St. Mark in the preface to *The Stones of Venice* (v, vi).

38. Georg Dehio and Alois Riegl, *Konservieren, nicht restaurieren: Streitschriften zur Denkmalpflege um 1900* (Braunschweig: Vieweg, 1988).

ongoing maintenance: "Take good care of your monuments and you will not need to repair them. . . . Watch an old building with anxious care; guard it as best as you may, and at any cost, from every influence of dilapidation."[39] Counterpreservation, in contrast, welcomes and even promotes dilapidation. Counterpreservation is not mainly concerned with prolonging duration indefinitely. Preservation cares for a building's integrity (and safety), while counterpreservation opens the building to the action of time, invites this action, and sometimes immerses the building in self-destructive elements. The building's extinction or death becomes part of its life.

Preservation in the sense devised by Ruskin, and reconstruction according to Viollet-le-Duc, are both caught in the pursuit of the past, in prolonging the duration of buildings in their historical form—either in an idealized original state for Viollet-le-Duc, or as an enduring witness of time for Ruskin. There is indeed room for change in both views. Ruskin's opposition to clearing a building's patina (which spurred the so-called Anti-Scrape movement)[40] incorporates the worn film that covers and softens surfaces over time. Viollet-le-Duc's restoration principles, based on rebuilding a unity of style that may never have existed, and making use of the best possible available techniques, introduce change more assertively. But neither attitude privileges ongoing transformation. They advocate controlled or moderate intervention so as to emphasize and guarantee duration. Ruskin goes so far as to say that even new buildings, that is, the "architecture of the day," should be rendered "historical" so as to bear witness of their time for generations to come.[41]

Utopia or Social Practice?

Counterpreservation is at once a form of preservation that engages social groups and invites a critical stance, and a utopian conception that can never be fully realized. If a building were left completely vulnerable to the action of time, it would be completely destroyed. This would also pose practical difficulties to most quotidian uses; the building would become an aesthetic or poetic object detached from function or utility. Therefore, the examples of counterpreservation presented in this book also resort, at points, to tools and practices of conventional preservation. They attempt to conserve materials, and to foreclose or limit weathering. They also frame history. For any group involved in the reflection over a building's historical meaning, certain periods and events have more importance than others. Therefore, signs of weathering and transformation are presented selectively, according to specific narratives, as I explain for each case study in the chapters that follow.

---

39. Ruskin, *Seven Lamps of Architecture*, 258. See also John Delafons, *Politics and Preservation: A Policy History of the Built Heritage, 1882–1996* (London: E & FN Spon, 1997), 17.

40. John Summerson, "Ruskin, Morris, and the 'Anti-Scrape' Philosophy," in *Historic Preservation Today: Essays Presented to the Seminar on Preservation and Restoration, Williamsburg, Virginia, September 8–11, 1963* (Charlottesville: The University Press of Virginia, 1966).

41. Ruskin, Aphorism 27, in *The Seven Lamps of Architecture,* 235.

The first shortcoming of counterpreservation is the impossibility of incorporating change, time, and open-endedness completely. Practical concerns limit the scope of counterpreservation—that is, how much weathering, transformation, and destruction a building can sustain. Architects or tenants are compelled to prevent deterioration, safeguard current structures or components, and restore broken pieces. And if we are to interpret the concept of counterpreservation as complete and absolute openness of meaning, then it is an impossibility. For even the choice to open up a building to weathering and decay is a particular approach that excludes many other possibilities such as painting, cleaning, restoring, refurbishing, or adapting. Leaving a building completely open to the effects of time might indeed encompass a multiplicity of meanings, but it cannot include them all.

It is easier to incorporate the idea of a dynamic, interactive memory in monuments than it is in buildings. Memorials, installations, and sculptures—even those that attempt to penetrate the prosaic and quotidian aspects of life—are less encumbered by practical or functional concerns than an apartment building, a film theater, or a park. Jochen and Ester Gerz's Monument against Fascism can be sunk underground because its primary function is that of a memorial, and its disappearance will not hamper everyday activities or practical life. While art is never separate from social and political contexts, there is a difference between the Gerzes' memorial installation and a building where people live, work, watch movies, visit exhibitions, and eat and drink at a café. The Haus Schwarzenberg cannot gradually disappear, because its spaces are constantly used for a variety of purposes. Its façade cannot be left to weather indefinitely, unprotected, because it will fall on the heads of passersby.

There is another limitation. To a great extent, counterpreservation derives its force from the contrast with renovated, conventional surroundings. The Haus Schwarzenberg cultural center would lose its effect if all buildings around it kept the same characteristics: gray, eroded façades with fallen pieces and exposed wires. Not only would the aesthetic impression be diluted in the overall homogeneity, but the intentionality behind the dilapidation might also be lost. This would be a problem insofar as the social, economic, cultural, and political causes and consequences of urban blight are quite different from the self-reflective, contrived statement of the Haus Schwarzenberg.

At the same time that counterpreservation is a utopian stance that cannot be fully realized, it is also an actual practice. The cooperative that manages the cultural center Haus Schwarzenberg, in Berlin's central district, or the inhabitants of apartment buildings in the neighborhood of Prenzlauer Berg are identifiable agents actively involved in concrete processes: cultural programming, architectural design, temporary interventions in buildings, street demonstrations, public discussions and events. These are real instances, not purely conceptual ones. I insist on this point because it contains the significance of counterpreservation not only for Berlin, but also for other contested places and disputed histories. Counterpreservation attests to the possibility of alternative spatial practices, however flawed or imperfect.

Although the examples of counterpreservation cannot fully embody its ultimate consequences, they are valuable for carrying out the concept into real social contexts. Moreover, the very opposition between utopia and reality is problematic. Utopia is not simply a non-place: it is a place that exists—not as an actual site, but as a discursive one. The underlying tension between counterpreservation as utopia and as an actual practice allows for meaningful transactions between conceptual speculation and practical experimentation. This tension also points to the impossibility of drawing a clear-cut line between theory and practice. When the artists behind the Haus Schwarzenberg meet to discuss their cultural or architectural projects, and then publish a text on their website or print pamphlets, are they engaging in theoretical debate or concrete action? Is not the very process of critical reflection itself already a form of action? Conversely, is the refusal to restore the façade restricted to the materiality of the building, or does it not make a more far-reaching statement about history and urbanism?

The contribution of counterpreservation is not so much a specific model for the treatment of buildings as it is a critical way of thinking about history and the city. Although each counterpreservation example starts out from a particular building, all share a common preoccupation with the city as a whole—with the spread of corporate culture, the privatization of spaces, the aggravation of economic disparities, and the loss of political participation. The discourses that accompany counterpreservation make it clear that the object of criticism is not necessarily a single building, but the city and beyond; and that their cultural and political project is aimed at a wide and diverse social body. Each intervention hopes to inspire similar actions, to spur engagements elsewhere, to spread over the cityscape. Even if the shapes, uses, and meanings of buildings—as well as the forms of social organization around them—might have to be reformulated, counterpreservation still carries the potential for a different and more open history, for *another* history.

Beyond Berlin

The use of decay and ruination as an expression of alternative cultures, collective residential projects, and antigentrification sentiment is the most salient way in which counterpreservation can be seen across different cities and countries beyond Berlin. These examples usually include squats (or former squats), cultural and art venues, and spaces for leisure and sociability, in cities with thriving squatter cultures: Hamburg, Amsterdam, Copenhagen, New York. There are anonymous examples, and notorious ones: the Blitz House in Oslo and the defunct Ungdomshuset (Danish for "the Youth House") in Copenhagen, both centers for cultural activities, music concerts, and meetings; Freetown Christiania, a whole squatter neighborhood in Copenhagen; Fort Thunder in Providence, Rhode Island, a decrepit warehouse used by an artists' collective for residences, studios, and concerts from 1995 to 2001; and the many squats in the East Village in New York in the 1980s and 1990s, such as Serenity House and the Fifth Street Squat. Of East Village squatters, a *New York Times* journalist notes: "Where some saw blight, the squatters saw new opportunity."[42]

The artful cultivation of decay present in Berlin's Haus Schwarzenberg is comparable to the spaces and façades of the Kunsthaus Raskolnikow in Dresden, an arts center that originated as a squat in 1989, and which now houses galleries, a restaurant, and a small hotel.[43] In Budapest, ruin bars and pubs have become a trend for tourists and locals alike. They are "one example of a radical use of public space that is not designed to satisfy the constant need for urban development. . . . It allows people who do not have a lot of money to make their mark on the city."[44] These are not the words of a Lefebvrian scholar or a radical activist, but rather of a journalist writing for an in-flight magazine (*Scandinavian Traveler*, published by Scandinavian Airlines). As an index of worldly middle-class tastes in a commercial vehicle, this article might herald a bright future for counterpreservation—or else, perhaps more likely, its co-optation by the market.

Many cities boast alternative cultures as lively and vocal as those of Berlin; and many groups cultivate an international network of cooperation and solidarity, such as the website Squat!net (http://planet.squat.net), which congregates information on squats and important events such as demonstrations and evictions. The attitude is similar in all of these places. Dilapidation is worn on the face of buildings as a mark of distinction from mainstream landscapes, expressing affiliations with anarchism, identity politics, radical leftist politics, and the punk scene.

If in some cases the emphasis is on the cultural and aesthetic expression of dissonance, in others the political dimension is more clearly articulated. In New York, members of the squatter movement founded the Museum of Reclaimed Urban Space, in an East Village building known as C-Squat.[45] The museum is a hub for activities and publications that promote squatting as a way of making urban space more democratic and affordable. The sense of social justice means that for the museum, squats are not simply specific solutions to the housing needs of a particular

---

42. Colin Moynihan, "Squatters' Paradise Lost," photographic essay by Ash Thayer, *New York Times,* October 4, 2013, http://www.nytimes.com/interactive/2013/10/06/nyregion/album-squatters. html.

43. Raskolnikoff, http://www.raskolnikoff.de/geschichte.html. Please note that while the Kunsthaus uses the spelling "Raskolnikow," the restaurant, pension, bar, and website use the spelling "Raskolnikoff."

44. Emma Olsson, "Ruinophilia: A New Phenomenon," *Scandinavian Traveler,* December 14, 2014, https://scandinaviantraveler.com/en/food-drink/ruinophilia-a-new-phenomenon. See also the website Ruinpubs, http://ruinpubs.com/, which maps and promotes Budapest's ruin bars.

45. "Experts Lay Out a Comprehensive Primer to Squatting in NYC," *Curbed,* February 28, 2014, http://ny.curbed.com/archives/2014/02/28/experts_lay_out_a_comprehensive_primer_to_squatting_in_nyc.php.

group of people, but rather models that can potentially create a more inclusive city on a large scale. The museum defines its mission in the following terms:

> The Museum of Reclaimed Urban Space promotes and archives the work of community activists and artists in the squatting movement, which successfully reclaimed and repurposed derelict housing stock . . . as an alternative sustainable strategy for social and community development in blighted landscapes.[46]

Squatting is seen as a movement that can teach lessons, and an "alternative sustainable strategy." The choice of words is important. While a squat may evoke negative connotations of crime and illegality, the idea of "reclaiming" implies a restitution of something to people who are rightfully entitled to it. This is not merely the transference of property to different hands, but a questioning of the meaning and ethics of private property (obviously a radical proposition in an age where most alternative models, from the welfare state to Socialism, have given way to financial, speculative capitalism).

But squatting is not the same as counterpreservation (and vice versa). Not every squatter community appropriates decay, and not every example of counterpreservation is a squat or collective residential project. In most cases, squats and residential communities that resort to counterpreservation are located in affluent societies: North America, Europe, Australia. The punk aesthetics works in opposition to the bourgeois mainstream (or what is assumed to be a bourgeois mainstream). The rejection of conventional or trendy groups (be they traditional nuclear families, conservatives, hipsters, young urban professionals, techies, etc.) is a powerful motor for the adoption of decrepitude as a badge of identity.

This does not work in the same way in societies that are poorer or more unequal. In Latin American cities, for instance, where slums house a huge portion of the population, and urban poverty permeates cities in every way (from shantytowns to the homeless), dilapidation has deeply ingrained connotations of destitution, lack of alternatives, despair, and oppression. In poor societies, blight is the mark of poverty. While there are examples of rough-looking squats in these societies, this is a circumstantial contingency rather than a choice. The preoccupation with a layered history, a complex past, or even the romantic fascination with ruins and decay is not present.

For example, the squat on 342 Mauá Street in São Paulo, one of the many active squats organized by the city's homeless community, was refurbished in 2013 by the inhabitants themselves, who cleaned graffiti and moisture stains off the façade, and painted it in fresh white and red, a sober color scheme that emulates the aesthetics

---

46. "What We Do," Museum of Reclaimed Urban Space, http://www.morusnyc.org/reclaiming-space-squats/.

of bourgeois apartment buildings in the city.[47] The question of why this is so can only be sketched here in preliminary hypotheses; it would be necessary to do a focused investigation of specific case studies, through fieldwork and cultural analysis, to untangle the culture-specific meanings of decay and their variances.

It is possible that in poorer or less equal societies, the struggle for basic living conditions such as shelter, nourishment, and health services is so urgent as to take the focus away from more rhetorical reflections. Instead of subscribing to an anti-bourgeois attitude, squatters fight for inclusion in bourgeois standards and modes of living. Perhaps "roughing it up" by choice is a luxury of people who have other options, who were not raised in destitution, or who possess enough cultural (if not economic) capital to move elsewhere, if they wish. Maybe this luxury is also afforded by a prosperous society with a public welfare safety net. Social security benefits and provisions, and public services, are much better and more widely accessible in Europe than in Latin America. Or is it possible that the embrace of decay is also, at the same time, a sign of change—that social disparities are worsening and becoming more permanent and pervasive even in wealthier societies? These questions must remain unanswered here, as the scope of this book is limited to an in-depth study of Berlin, but they suggest possible avenues for further research on the topic. They are stated here as ways to illustrate the sociocultural specificity of counterpreservation and decay.

Back to Berlin

This is a book about Berlin, and that is where the story begins. Berlin is not only the source for the concept of counterpreservation, but also a particularly resonant place for its application. The examples are numerous enough to make their mark on the urban landscape as a whole and not only as exceptions; and their myriad forms and variations allow for a rich and expanded view of counterpreservation. It does not mean that the city is unique in this way—many other cities are shaped by creatively appropriated ruins, from Havana to Detroit; and the factors that make Berlin into such a prolific place for counterpreservation are also present elsewhere. But Berlin presents a condensed and intense example, partly because of the city's longtime association with a bohemian and liberal culture, leftist politics, and a gritty landscape. This grittiness was more evident in the preunification city, but some areas of Berlin still retain this atmosphere. Although the influx of investment and visitors has transformed the city since the Wall was torn down, this transformation has been

---

47. Piero Locatelli, "Sem tetos reformam o próprio prédio no centro de São Paulo," *Carta Capital*, February 5, 2013, http://www.cartacapital.com.br/sociedade/sem-tetos-reformam-o-proprio-predio-no-centro-de-sao-paulo/.

uneven and focused on particular neighborhoods (the unevenness is itself a hall-mark of contemporary urbanism).[48]

The association of Berlin with roughness, grittiness, and ugliness is not lost on cultural observers and mass media, and has become not only a distinctive mark of the city, but also an attraction in its own right. In 2002, a *New York Times* article about the growing trend of living in East German *Plattenbauten* announced: "In Chic New Berlin, Ugly Is Way Cool."[49] A few years later, the same newspaper announced the emergence of an alternative art district in the area of Brunnenstraße, younger and more avant-garde than the established galleries of Auguststraße, by praising the "New Art District's 'Raw' Charm."[50] The writer, Kimberly Bradley, noted the mixture of "new polish" with "decrepit buildings, fast-food kiosks and empty storefronts . . . like a crooked smile with missing teeth." Bradley quoted an American who opened a bar in the area as saying, "It's a bit like the old '90s Berlin scene. There's a certain brutality to the street, but it's the coolest part of Mitte." A more recent article continues to propagate the perception, declaring that "grimy graffiti" is part of "Berlin's cool factor."[51] Even housing listings capitalize on this; an apartment for rent was once advertised as "Classic East-Berlin Anti-Chic."[52] Berlin mayor Klaus Wowereit's assertion that bankrupt, trendy Berlin is "poor, but sexy" might be interpreted in this light: the city makes its roughness attractive.[53] While in more recent years there have been signs of prosperity, this has accordingly brought a conflict of identity; the city is, in the view of some, "torn between wealth and cool."[54]

This predilection for grit and grime—and the appropriation of a rough aesthetics not only for identity, but also for tourism and marketing—might help explain, at least partly, why counterpreservation has flourished in the city. Decay, along with other markers of urban roughness, gains positive connotations: it is trendy, artsy, interesting, unique; the sign of creativity, hipness, of belonging to a desirable alternative scene; it is associated with liveliness, with the potential for thriving activities

48. Neil Smith, "New Globalism, New Urbanism: Gentrification as Global Urban Strategy," *Antipode* 34, no. 2 (2002): 434–57.

49. Alisa Roth, "In Chic New Berlin, Ugly Is Way Cool," *New York Times*, January 24, 2012, http://www.nytimes.com/2002/01/24/garden/in-chic-new-berlin-ugly-is-way-cool.html.

50. Kimberly Bradley, "A New Art District's 'Raw' Charm," *New York Times*, March 25, 2007, http://www.nytimes.com/2007/03/25/travel/25surfacing.1.html?_r=0).

51. Chloë Webster, "Berlin's Cool Factor: Hipster Clubs, Grimy Graffiti, and an Honour Payment Metro," *Daily Mail Online*, November 1, 2013, http://www.dailymail.co.uk/travel/article-2483668/Berlins-Cool-Factor-Hipster-clubs-grimy-graffiti-honour-payment-metro.html.

52. Message number 4807, posted on the Berlin Scholars Yahoo Group, December 3, 2008, Berlin Scholars Group Archives, https://groups.yahoo.com/neo/groups/BerlinScholars/conversations/messages/4807 (access to the group archives is restricted to members).

53. Quoted, among other places, in "Poor but Sexy," *The Economist*, September 23, 2006, 61–62.

54. "Berlin Torn between Wealth and Cool," *BBC News*, March 28, 2012, http://www.bbc.com/news/world-europe-17538025.

such as nightclubs, art galleries, bars, residential projects.[55] The multivalence of ruins and blight is illustrated by this context-dependent interpretation. The context illuminates not only why dilapidation may acquire positive meanings, but also why it is used as a protest against urban renovation and regeneration. Picture-perfect renovated buildings appear to betray Berlin's proverbial ugliness.

This applies not only to the appearance of renovated buildings, but also to their new uses: chic restaurants and art galleries, boutique hotels, touristy shops and cafés, business offices, upscale apartments for sale as opposed to cheap rental flats. The clean and bright façades of these buildings appear foreign in Berlin, associated with the invasion of tourists and hipsters. These renovated buildings look as if they were pasteurized and homogenized for safe consumption rather than produced out of lively everyday life (an association reinforced by the German word for "renovation," *Sanierung*, with its evocation of cleansing, health, and sanitization). The new colors of old buildings in Berlin do not necessarily follow original coats of paint found beneath soot or plaster. The elaborate ornaments and moldings are in many cases completely new, since the original ornamentation was often removed in the postwar period.

As Henri Lefebvre might have put it, renovation and gentrification turn urban space into a commodity of exchange value, while counterpreservation appropriates urban space for its use value to everyday social practices. The idea of counterpreservation may thus figure as a "social space" in what Lefebvre identifies as the

> potentialities—of works and of reappropriation—existing to begin with in the artistic sphere but responding above all to the demands of a body 'transported' outside itself in space, a body which by putting up resistance inaugurates the project of a different space (either the space of a counter-culture, or a counter-space in the sense of an initially utopian alternative to actually existing 'real' space).[56]

Thus understood, counterpreservation's election of dilapidated and dirty spaces is not a celebration of morbidity, destruction, and death. It is the defense of vital and imperfect social contexts. Moreover, there is no direct equation between social diversity and architectural decay. Dilapidation is neither an end result nor the symbol for social or cultural values. Rather, counterpreservation is the condition that makes it possible for certain social groups to use urban spaces within the context of globalization and gentrification. Counterpreservation is instrumental. Seen this way, counterpreservation is the defense of the right to the city. This approach is present in all of the examples in this book, although it is most clearly seen in the

---

55. Anja Schwanhäußer, *Kosmonauten des Underground: Ethnografie einer Berliner Szene* (New York and Frankfurt: Campus, 2010); Ulrich Gutmair, *Die ersten Tage von Berlin: Der Sound der Wende* (Stuttgart: Klett-Cotta, 2013); Engle, "Ruinous Charm."

56. Lefebvre, *Production of Space*, 349.

residential communities discussed in chapter 2 and the alternative art centers in chapter 3.

There is another sense of inclusiveness. The right to the city is not just the right to affordable housing, leisure, and public services, but also the right to a multiple and democratic history and memory, open to debate and dissonant voices. Such a democratic memory is one that allows for the inclusion and representation of conflicting groups and narratives, not only as objects of representation, but also as subjects: those who interpret, ascribe, and build meaning.

This returns us to Young's participatory countermonuments. Young suggests that monuments in and by themselves are mere stones in a landscape.[57] By the same token, stones in a landscape can be animated by active engagement. Memory-work and historical consciousness can revive sites and buildings quite independently from official or conventional ideas of restoration or museum display. As long as there are social groups or individuals who perform the work of remembrance, silent heaps of stone come alive. Counterpreservation cannot be the exclusive province of designers or housing collectives. In order to realize its own goals of memory and social participation, it needs interlocutors. Counterpreservation points the way toward a communicative architecture whose ever-changing quality lies not so much in crumbling walls and rusting mullions, but in the ever-changing nature of the social realm.

---

57. Young, *The Texture of Memory*, 2.

2

LIVING PROJECTS

Collective Housing, Alternative Culture, and Spaces of Resistance

In the trendy Prenzlauer Berg neighborhood circa 2004, amid a profusion of graffiti and tags, a stenciled slogan proclaimed: "Der Prenzlauer Berg sagt: man kann alles kaufen" (fig. 2). The slogan was printed on sidewalks and walls throughout the neighborhood. The sentence can be translated as "The Prenzlauer Berg says: Everything can be bought." Formerly part of East Berlin, and therefore outside of the private real estate market before unification, the district of Prenzlauer Berg has been overhauled by a flurry of investment, development, and commerce since 1989. Apartment buildings that had been property of the East German state were turned over to their legal owners and, more often than not, subsequently purchased by developers and put on the market as condos, office space, or upscale rentals.[1] Hip and fashionable destination areas developed, such as Kollwitzplatz, a leafy square surrounded by stately apartment buildings. Designer shops selling clothes, furniture, stationery, and other consumer goods popped up alongside new restaurants, cafés, bars, grocery stores, and an organic public market. A shopping mall, the Schönhauser Allee Arkaden, was built near one of the area's

---

1. On the privatization of real estate after the end of the GDR, see Elizabeth Strom, *Building the New Berlin: The Politics of Urban Development in Germany's Capital City* (Lanham, MD: Lexington Books, 2001), esp. 64–67, 122–24.

Figure 2. Prenzlauer Berg graffito (2004): "The Prenzlauer Berg says: Everything can be bought."
© Daniela Sandler

main subway stations in 1999.[2] If the initial post-Wall liveliness of Prenzlauer Berg had been due to the festive alternative culture of squats, parties, and nightclubs, the area soon was taken over by a more diverse public—from hipsters to yuppies (to use a term often heard locally), from tourists to families with young children.

The stenciled slogan alludes to this transformation. "Everything can be bought": buildings, common spaces, the merchandise for sale in the new shop windows, and, metonymically, the whole neighborhood. The slogan, as part of an active local graffiti output, can be read as a critical voice representing those who were displaced by the new developments: the squatters and their communities, the students and artists who enjoyed low rents immediately after unification, the East German citizens who had lived in the area for decades before the fall of the Wall (including pensioners, artists, and dissidents). The statement can be understood as bemoaning commercialism and consumerism in general, and the commodification of urban space in particular. The words have a dark ring to them; if "everything" (spaces,

---

2. K. Brüning and J. Tillmanns, "Händler: 'Schönhauser Allee wird keine tote Straße," *Berliner Zeitung*, March 4, 1999, http://www.berliner-zeitung.de/archiv/die--arcade---das-neue-einkaufscenter--zog-gleich-am-eroeffnungstag-30-000-besucher-an-haendler---schoenhauser-allee-wird-keine-tote-strasse-,10810590,9603814.html.

cultural practices, communities, objects) can be bought, something is lost in the process of buying. Buying means not only acquisition, but also loss. At the same time the statement has a hint of sarcasm, pointing at those who believe they may belong in an alternative scene by buying into it: even the hipness of Prenzlauer Berg is for sale.

But the voice behind this deceptively simple stencil is not only the assumed critical voice of displaced social groups. It is also, and explicitly, the voice of the neighborhood: "The Prenzlauer Berg says." This voice inscribes itself as an intrinsic identity, not a transient one (as a person or a group might be), as if the neighborhood were a stolid witness to transformations in time. More than that—Prenzlauer Berg figures in the statement as an oracle. Just as an ancient Greek priestess, this modern-day oracle discloses hidden truths and reveals prophecies: all is for sale, including the vibrancy of an alternative culture that, once reified, can be consumed more or less voyeuristically. Inevitably, as the slogan prophesies, everything—even the whole neighborhood—is sold. The gravitas of the slogan (its curt, serious, almost cryptic delivery; the finality of its declaration) also builds on the myth of the "legendary Prenzlauer Berg," which, before the fall of the Wall, was a site of political activism and bohemia, clandestine art galleries and subversive salons, lively corner *Kneipe* (bars) and reputedly crazy parties.[3] After 1989, this myth was compounded by the effervescent *Wende* years—the period of transition from the end of the GDR to the early phase of unification.[4] At the time, Prenzlauer Berg became a hub for squatting, alternative art projects, and a vibrant nightlife. To this day, the myth is continually evoked in publications and walking tours that take visitors along the sites of the "wild years" of the GDR.[5] It is this legendary, venerable, and elusive Prenzlauer Berg that announces its own defacement through the seemingly ineluctable urban, social, and economic processes that the fall of the Wall and German unification set in motion.

This particular stencil speaks a truth that is by now obvious, not only because the gentrification of Prenzlauer Berg is glaring and extensive, but also because gentrification as an urban process in general has been a hallmark of "contemporary global

3. Greg Engle, "Ruinous Charm: The Culture and Politics of Redevelopment in Eastern Berlin" (PhD diss., University of Wisconsin, Madison, 2009); Daniela Dahn, *Kunst und Kohle: Die "Szene" am Prenzlauer Berg, Berlin, DDR* (Darmstadt: Luchterhand, 1987).

4. The word *Wende* means "turn" and evokes the social, political, cultural, and material transformations that accompanied the end of the Socialist regime and the reknitting of the two Germanys after forty-five years of division. The periodization of the *Wende* is not clear-cut. While some see the fall of the Wall in 1989 as the defining moment of change, others argue that the change had started a few years earlier in East Germany. Some circumscribe the *Wende* to the years 1989 and 1990, and others consider that the period extended into the mid-1990s. See Inge Stephan and Alexandra Tacke, eds., *Nachbilder der Wende* (Cologne, Weimar, and Vienna: Böhlau, 2008); Bill Niven and J. K. A. Thomaneck, eds., *Dividing and Uniting Germany* (London: Routledge, 2001).

5. Peter Richter, "In oder im Prenzlauer Berg?," in *Hier spricht Berlin*, ed. Georg Diez et. al. (Cologne: Kiepenheuer & Witsch, 2003), 208.

urbanism" since at least the 1980s.[6] Gentrification is hardly a surprise anymore, but this does not make it any less fraught with conflict and opposition. The stencil is also interesting for more than its revelation. It suggests a mode of engaging with the city in the public sphere that opens up spaces for communication, even if the dialogue is truncated. The stencil both verbalizes and makes visible a perception otherwise shared and discussed only within the limits of specific, private or semi-private circles (not only the circles of squatters or students or former GDR citizens, but also the circles of academics, urban planners, and activists). Through this opening up, the stencil "makes the city speak"—an idea that Rosalyn Deutsche explores in her essay "Reasonable Urbanism." Deutsche sees the possibility that a city may "speak for those with no voice of their own, even . . . in defense of their rights."[7] In her essay, the city speaks through ekphrasis (the literary description of a work of art) and prosopopoeia (the figure of speech that gives voice to inanimate things):

> Among the silent, immobile objects that can be brought to life and lent a voice through ekphrasis and prosopopoeia are the things of the city—buildings, monuments, streets, parks and the built environment as a whole.[8]

The stencil that gives voice to the neighborhood is a kind of skewed prosopopoeia. It erases "human" authorship by ascribing the statement to Prenzlauer Berg; in doing so, it allows the whole neighborhood to speak as both an imagined place (the idea of Prenzlauer Berg, its identity) and concrete sites (the places where the graffito was stenciled are actual points of inscription and iteration).

This mode of "urban speech" is not exclusive to graffiti; it is also a common strategy of activists, squats, and cultural projects, widely used in Berlin since the postwar era.[9] In this tradition, which continued after the fall of the Wall, the façades of buildings are treated as manifestos. Banners and posters with political and countercultural messages hang from the façades; the large lettering of these messages is visible from a distance, readable from the other side of the street or from inside a passing car or bus, and easily propagated in photographs and videos. The banners blur the boundaries between public and private, between text and architecture, between a building as a place to live and as a support for artistic or political views. They turn otherwise laconic structures into eloquent, loud participants in open-ended dialogues. These dialogues can be potentially carried out by any passerby,

---

6. Neil Smith, "New Globalism, New Urbanism: Gentrification as Global Urban Strategy," *Antipode* 34, no. 2 (2002): 434–57.

7. Rosalyn Deutsche, "Reasonable Urbanism," in *Giving Ground: The Politics of Propinquity,* ed. Joan Copjec and Michael Sorkin (New York: Verso, 1999), 185.

8. Ibid., 188.

9. Belinda Davis offers a broader context for this practice in her analysis of West Berlin as "theater of protest." Davis, "The City as Theater of Protest: West Berlin and West Germany, 1962–1983," in *Spaces of the Modern City: Imaginaries, Politics, and Everyday Life,* ed. Gyan Prakash and Kevin M. Kruse (Princeton, NJ: Princeton University Press, 2008), 247–74.

any fellow city-dweller, or even any reader or viewer who might see the messages in a newspaper, TV broadcast, or online social media. The perspectives and agendas of graffiti artists, activists, and squatters model a powerful form of collective communication—a public sphere in the age of digital reproduction, carved out in the interface between the space of the street and the space of the private building. Such communication points the way to a more participatory and involved polity, inseparable from the urban and architectural spaces it inhabits. Architecture itself, resignified, becomes more than an object of aesthetic enjoyment, connoisseurship, or preservation; more than a utilitarian means to shelter or comfort; and more than a backdrop. It is this socially energized architecture, inseparable from the agents who occupy and transform it, that is the subject of this chapter.

Living Projects

This chapter focuses on *Hausprojekte*, or "living projects." *Hausprojekte* are the most prolific category of counterpreservation, in terms of number of examples. They embrace and deploy architectural decay for sociopolitical goals related to affordable housing, diversity, and personal experimentation. In this chapter, *Hausprojekte* are examined through the focused discussion of two case studies: the KA 86 and Tuntenhaus (considered together, as they are both in the same building), and the Køpi . As with any such selection, the case studies typify the category in general, while also at the same time presenting unique characteristics. So this chapter considers both *Hausprojekte* in the plural—as a broad social movement that illuminates important aspects of counterpreservation—and the singularity of each case study. The KA 86 and Tuntenhaus and the Køpi are important characters in the post-Wall history of Berlin, yet they have figured only fleetingly—if at all—in scholarly studies. This chapter therefore also wishes to contribute by telling their stories, and recognizing their role in shaping urban spaces and debates.

Hausprojekte are residential communities with a political bent, which have had a formative role in many central areas of Berlin since unification. *Hausprojekte* have a long tradition, dating back to 1970s counterculture and the squatter movement on both sides of the Wall (see the introduction). The fall of the Wall in 1989 refreshed the role and vibrancy of *Hausprojekte*, as population and property fluxes opened up room for their proliferation. Related to squats and communes, but not always identical to them, *Hausprojekte* boomed in the early 1990s, and were gradually curbed by police and legal actions, gentrification, and official urban policies. They represent a crucial moment in the construction of the New Berlin, as the revamped capital has been called, and continue to shape the cityscape and urban discussions.

Here, I analyze *Hausprojekte* as sites of socially produced space as defined by Henri Lefebvre and Michel de Certeau. However, the present work is not a social history. I take the architecture of these sites seriously—their materiality, the choices made in the configuration and refurbishment of their spaces, their visual appearance, their relationship to the immediate and not-so-immediate urban context. *Hausprojekte* represent alternative ways of treating historical buildings, in line with the concept of counterpreservation. They are also an example of guerrilla or insurgent urbanism: the creation of meaningful urban spaces outside of official plans, often with improvised means and limited duration.[10] The instability of *Hausprojekte*, which is both social and architectural, is not a shortcoming but rather a crucial condition for their role as counterpoints to an increasingly gentrified, globalized Berlin—a city that is relinquishing precisely the kind of free, noncommercial, experimental urban spaces that made it so unique since the postwar era and well after unification.[11]

The word *Hausprojekt* describes communal living arrangements where the residents are joined not only by the necessity to cohabitate, but also by the desire to create a cooperative way of life outside of mainstream forms of rented apartments, condos, or single-family houses. The word *Projekt* connotes the proactive, constructive, and sometimes utopian character of these communities. A "project" implies an impulse to create, to propose, and to display. *Hausprojekte* attempt to forge and maintain a set of social relations realized in space and time; they are oriented both toward their urban context as dissonant enclaves, and toward the future as new, possible models. They may also be read as utopias insofar as they create spaces of self-determined living conditions that are different from the social norm.[12]

Germany has a strong tradition of such communal and alternative living situations. They are also known by other words, each with a slightly different meaning: *Wohnprojekte* (residential projects), the ubiquitous *Wohngemeinschaften* (residential communities, known by the acronym WG, which are house-sharing and roommate arrangements), and *Kommunen* (communes, which are more overtly political and collective).[13] These living communities encompass a wide range of ages, life stages, family situations, professions, and socioeconomic conditions. Today, *Wohngemeinschaften*—the most common type of collective living—do not necessarily correspond to cooperative political goals, but can be formed simply for financial or social reasons. At the start, however, *Wohngemeinschaften* stemmed from revolutionary and critical positions, and were the forebears of contemporary *Hausprojekte*. As

---

10. See the introduction, note 2.

11. Michael A. LaFond, "eXperimentcity: Cultivating Sustainable Development in Berlin's Freiräume," in *Insurgent Public Space: Guerrilla Urbanism and the Remaking of Contemporary Cities,* ed. Jeffrey Hou (New York: Routledge, 2010), 61–70.

12. Heide Kolling, *Honig aus dem zweiten Stock: Berlin Hausprojekte erzählen* (Berlin: Assoziation A, 2008); Elisabeth Voß, *Wegweiser solidarische Ökonomie: Anders Wirtschaften ist möglich!* (Neu-Ulm: AG Spak Bücher, 2010), 29–31; Kollektiv Orangotango, *Solidarische Räume & cooperative Perspektiven: Praxis und Theorie in Lateinamerika und Europa* (Neu-Ulm: AG Spak Bücher, 2010), 72–89.

13. Hartmut Häußermann and Walter Siebel, *Soziologie des Wohnens: Eine Einführung in Wandel und Ausdifferenzierung des Wohnens* (Weinheim and Munich: Juventa, 1996), 326–29.

Hartmut Häußermann and Walter Siebel put it in their comprehensive study of living arrangements in Germany,

> *Wohngemeinschaften* entered public consciousness as a special revolutionary development of the student revolts in the second half of the 1960s. *Wohngemeinschaften* are the sole new type of household consciously developed from a political perspective against the dominant lifestyles and residential forms of the "repressive" bourgeois nuclear family. They were created, and theoretically grounded, with social-revolutionary intentions: de-individualization of lifestyles, collective economy, and collective political engagement.[14]

Although this description might not fully apply anymore to the majority of *Wohngemeinschaften* in Germany, it does apply almost to the letter to *Hausprojekte*, which can be understood as the heirs of the original residential communities, updated to the context and political issues of the twenty-first century: gentrification, globalization, neoliberalism, and the loss of social welfare.

In Berlin, the countercultural and hippie movements in the 1960s and 1970s created *Wohngemeinschaften* and *Hausprojekte* in particular neighborhoods, forming niches in the city where these communities shaped social relations, street life, and the cityscape. In East Berlin, *Hausprojekte* flourished in the neighborhood of Prenzlauer Berg, inhabited not only by artists, musicians, and students, but also by political dissidents.[15] In West Berlin, these communities were concentrated in the district of Kreuzberg, a self-fashioned haven for people who did not agree with West Germany's sociopolitical and economic regime—from leftist radicals to punks, from army-service objectors to students and artists.[16] There were *Hausprojekte* in other neighborhoods as well, such as the western district of Schöneberg, long associated with gay culture and bohemian lifestyles.[17] Many communities were closely related to the *Autonomen* movement.[18] *Autonomen*, or "autonomists," are political militants not affiliated with a party or government (hence the term "autonomous"), engaged in leftist and Socialist causes. The origins of *Autonomen* date back to workers' movements in Italy in the 1960s, particularly *operaismo*, but the movement changed depending on location and context. It was particularly strong in Germany, and was first associated with the radical leftist politics of the RAF and Baader-Meinhof groups. Over time it developed into more diverse practices and perspectives, concerned with issues such as feminism, environment, war and international politics,

---

14. Ibid., 327.
15. Dahn, *Kunst und Kohle*; Krista Tebbe and Klaus Bzdziach, *Kreuzberg, Prenzlauer Berg. Annähernd alles über Kultur* (Berlin: Kunstamt Kreuzberg, 1990); Engle, "Ruinous Charm."
16. Barbara Lang, *Mythos Kreuzberg. Ethnographie eines Stadtteils, 1961–1995* (New York and Frankfurt: Campus, 1998); Susan Neiman, *Slow Fire: Jewish Notes from Berlin* (New York: Schocken Books, 1992).
17. Paul Knox, *Palimpsests: Biographies of 50 City Districts; International Case Studies of Urban Change* (Basel: Birkhäuser, 2012), 206–8.
18. Thomas Schultze and Almut Gross, *Die Autonomen: Ursprünge, Entwicklung und Profil der autonomen Bewegung* (Hamburg: Konkret Literatur, 1997).

and—significantly for this book—squatting. *Autonomen* have not only practiced squatting as a way of finding housing, but also as a political gesture in defense of affordable urban living; squatting is thus both a practice and a rallying cry.

After 1989, many new *Hausprojekte* were founded in the former eastern neighborhoods of Mitte, Prenzlauer Berg, and Friedrichshain. Initially, these *Hausprojekte* participated in the euphoric climate of the immediate post-Wall period—a time of informal nightclubs, clandestine parties, and occupied buildings.[19] As official development plans and gentrification started to spread over these neighborhoods, the *Hausprojekte* acquired more and more the role of antigentrification enclaves, fighting for their right to exist in an increasingly hostile environment, and hoping to spread their messages to the rest of the city.

Although there are variations among *Hausprojekte*, most of them share certain characteristics. These communities have a strong public dimension, even though there are clear limits between insiders and outsiders. They are aware of their impact on the city, and are concerned with larger urban processes such as gentrification, affordable housing, and cultural diversity, as indicated by the political discussions and actions they support, by banners and posters on their façades, and by texts on their self-maintained websites and publications (fig. 3). Most *Hausprojekte* are connected to each other in some way, and they often join forces or demonstrate reciprocal support. Contemporary *Hausprojekte* take advantage of digital communication and social media by maintaining their own websites, where they publicize current events, display images and texts associated with their communities, and list other *Hausprojekte*, art projects, and organizations connected to their goals.

The public face of *Hausprojekte*, either on their façades and banners or in their online presence, is not their whole story—there is also, of course, a private (and socially meaningful) dimension to the lived everyday experiences and spaces of their inhabitants. But the public face endows the *Hausprojekte* with civic significance; that is, it turns these residential spaces into spaces of public political discussion, struggle, and exchange. It is an inflection of the "personal as political," made powerful through the collective character of each *Hausprojekt*, and through the collaborative network created among them throughout the city. So while in many senses the *Hausprojekte* are a specific phenomenon, restricted to a particular subset of the population (by no means the majority), at the same time they are also bigger than themselves, participating in a broader dialogue about the production and transformation of urban space. They are a vocal and proactive minority whose impact on the city is both symbolic and material. *Hausprojekte* are thus significant for the whole of Berlin, not only as exotic attractions that display the city's famous alternative scene to potential tourists or voyeurs (although this is undoubtedly and

---

19. Anja Schwanhäußer, *Kosmonauten des Underground. Ethnografie einer Berliner Szene* (New York and Frankfurt: Campus, 2010); Ulrich Gutmair, *Die ersten Tage von Berlin. Der Sound der Wende* (Stuttgart: Klett-Cotta, 2013).

Figure 3. KA 86 and Tuntenhaus, street façade on Kastanienallee 86 (2003): "We remain different."
© Daniela Sandler

increasingly a part of the experience), but also as agents of urban change and active participants in Berlin's public sphere and public spaces.

The *Hausprojekte* have other characteristics in common. While their social composition is varied, they often include artists, musicians, students, political activists, punks, anarchists, and *Autonomen*. The population of *Hausprojekte* is usually young, but also includes people of all ages; sometimes families raise children there. They rely on a collective organization structure for managing the community and making decisions about every aspect concerning the use, form, and character of their spaces. Some of the buildings have private apartments, but sometimes the living arrangements are collective (shared kitchens or bathrooms, for example). Courtyards, storefronts, and sidewalks are turned into spaces for formal and informal gatherings. Finally, and crucially, *Hausprojekte* are low-rent spaces. Some of them started as squats, but almost all have been legalized in one way or another. Because of Berlin's rent control policies and the lack of renovations, their rents have been kept low. This does not mean that *Hausprojekte* are safe from eviction. Often, there are legal disputes involving new landlords who purchased the buildings after unification (and after they were already occupied) and want to renovate the buildings and rent them at more profitable rates. These landlords might refuse to renew rent contracts, and threaten or pressure residents in various ways.

Hausprojekte are usually installed in buildings dating from the end of the nineteenth and beginning of the twentieth centuries, which in German are called *Altbauten,* or "old buildings." The inhabitants refashion the external and internal spaces through gradual interventions and accretions. The result is an architectural bricolage, improvised and ephemeral, always changing, reflective of the actions of the inhabitants. On some of these buildings, the paintings and inscriptions resemble urban tattoos. Applied to the surface of street façades, they create a permeable membrane that simultaneously allows for porous communication—drawing attention, alluding to social or cultural meanings—and creates an opaque skin between street and interiors. The eye stops at the colorful paintings and does not go beyond, breaking correlations of form and function; often the windows are obscured by paint, graffiti, and posters. If the façades are sometimes forbidding, the interiors blur relationships of public and private. Common-area walls in entrance halls, doorways, interior corridors, and courtyards become surfaces for communication through posters, banners, images, and notices.

The architectural design of these *Hausprojekte* does not follow conventional principles of conservation or restoration—most of them look weathered, downright dilapidated, and incorporate improvised new installations and fixtures. At the same time, the treatment of space cannot be misunderstood for vandalism or neglect. These are resourceful communities that have the cultural and material means to alter their living spaces, as demonstrated by the interventions they do carry out (from fixing structural problems to installing awnings, sculptures, and murals). They make a deliberate choice to present these buildings in a state that is rough looking, different from conventionally restored structures, and open to further interventions, keeping the signs of the passage of time without freezing buildings into a single historical point or style.

Hausprojekte use counterpreservation as a marker of their alternative character, and as a response to the widespread programs of urban conservation, architectural revamping, and economic development in Berlin since 1989. This response is twofold. First, counterpreservation is a way to stake claims to buildings or urban areas. By keeping buildings dirty and run-down, local inhabitants produce actual spaces of difference and resistance. Using Lefebvre's distinction, which will be examined in more detail later in this chapter, these spaces are enclaves of social and cultural practices (use value) in an urban environment increasingly dominated by commercial and speculative transactions (exchange value).[20] Because the buildings are run-down, rents are much lower than the ever-rising average for Berlin's central-eastern neighborhoods.[21]

Second, counterpreservation is a discursive response to gentrification. Grimy façades and dingy courtyards express dissent from values such as consumerism, globalization, and neoliberalism—values associated with "Disneyfied" areas (con-

---

20. Henri Lefebvre, *The Production of Space* (Malden, MA: Blackwell, 1991), 100.

21. According to a resident of the KA 86 *Hausprojekt*, the inhabitants are conscious of the fact that if their buildings were to be renovated, their rents would skyrocket. Werner Kernebeck, interview, June 2010.

trolled by private entrepreneurs, kept clean and safe through surveillance, with idealized and smoothed-out backdrops of historical architecture). Given the communicative dimension of *Hausprojekte* mentioned above, the symbolic allusions evoked by the physical state of their buildings are part and parcel of the way these communities express their political positions in the city. A glancing look at these buildings from outside, even from afar, will suffice to reveal the dissonant and sometimes aggressive stance of their inhabitants toward their urban milieu.

The current state of *Hausprojekte* is delicate. The last squatting *Hausprojekt* in the neighborhood of Mitte, the Brunnen 183, was evicted in November 2009. One of the most important and visible *Hausprojekte* in the district of Friedrichshain, the Liebig 14, was evicted by police in January 2011.[22] There are fewer *Hausprojekte* than before, and they are being pushed out of the most coveted areas of the city. After the fall of the Wall, there were more than two hundred squats in Berlin, including older squats and newly formed ones.[23] According to the website Berlin Besetzt, which maps Berlin squats geographically and historically, in 2015 there remained about sixty *Hausprojekte* that had been founded in or after 1990.[24] Many of these do not have guaranteed tenure in their buildings even if they have lease contracts; leases have limited terms, and sometimes new landlords come in with different plans for the building—this will be illustrated in the discussion of the KA 86 and Tuntenhaus and the Køpi below. At the same time, the *Hausprojekte* continue to be part of Berlin's unique identity. Berlin's alternative culture has long been a source of attraction and interest for tourists, new residents, new development, and artistic and intellectual practices. The *Hausprojekte* not only lend alternative flavor to the image of Berlin, but have also become sites of tourist visitation.

KA 86 and Tuntenhaus

The Kastanienallee is one of the main thoroughfares in the district of Prenzlauer Berg, and it is accordingly lined with bustling sidewalk cafés, clothing stores, leafy trees, and bright apartment buildings. The renovated façades brim with

---

22. "Polizeieinsatz in der Brunnenstraße 183: Hausprojekt in Berlin-Mitte geräumt," *TAZ.de*, November 24, 2009, http://www.taz.de/!5151995/; "Räumung Liebigstraße 14 in Berlin: Das Ende der Besetzung," *TAZ.de*, February 1, 2011, http://www.taz.de/!5127477/; "Berlin Police Mount Huge Operation to Evict Tenants of Former Squat," *The Guardian,* February 2, 2011, http://www.theguardian.com/world/2011/feb/02/berlin-liebig-14-squat-eviction-police.

23. "Räumung Liebigstraße 14 in Berlin."

24. The Berlin Besetzt website tracks the foundation date and place of each squat, its eviction or end when applicable, in addition to providing a historical overview and chronology of squatting in Berlin since 1970. The website still identifies these communities as squats even when, as is the case with almost all of the surviving ones, they have been legalized. There are many more than sixty surviving squats today, but most of them were founded in the 1980s and therefore belong in a different period and discussion, since they were for the most part well established by the time of unification. I arrived at the number sixty by counting the post-1990 squats marked on the map. I excluded the Tacheles, which was evicted in 2012. See Berlin Besetzt, http://berlin-besetzt.de/#.

architectural details: crisply restored moldings, neatly coursed masonry, polished railings, columns and pediments, bay windows and balconies. In the middle of the picturesque homogeneity of the area—which can be found in many other European cities—one building stands out (fig. 3). It is, like most of its neighbors, a nineteenth-century building. Unlike its neighbors, its whole façade is a sooty, bumpy gray—the same grime that covered most of the neighborhood under the GDR, when coal heating spewed dark fumes, and façades went uncleaned and unpainted for decades.

On this particular building, the outer layer of paint and stucco has disappeared at points, revealing the bricks underneath in irregular, lighter-colored patches. Some sections of the façade have been turned into small bright murals, with splotches of colorful paint. On the ground floor, and along the right side of the building all the way up to the roof, overgrown plants, bushes, and ivy shoot up as thick greenery during the summer, and as wiry tangled branches in winter. A tall archway, highlighted by a brightly painted rainbow, marks the entrance to the building and to the inner courtyard.

The rainbow leads to the Tuntenhaus, or "Queer House"—a residential project created and maintained by and for gay men.[25] The origins of the community go back to West Berlin in 1981. At that time a group of gay squatters occupied a building in the bohemian West Berlin district of Schöneberg, on Bülowstraße. The squat was dismantled a few years later, and revived in 1990 in East Berlin—first, very briefly, on Mainzer Straße, but the community was evicted along with many other squats on that street after riots and violent confrontations with the police.[26] The Tuntenhaus migrated to the Kastanienallee in May of that year. There the squat was eventually legalized, and the Tuntenhaus members acquired the right to remain in the building as tenants.

The Tuntenhaus occupies the back of the building. The building is known, as is common in Berlin, as Kastanienallee 86, after its street address; other tenants, sympathetic to the philosophy of the Tuntenhaus and similarly organized in a communal *Hausprojekt*, inhabit the front of the building as the KA 86 *Hausprojekt*. The Kastanienallee 86 and its neighboring building, the Kastanienallee 85, form

---

25. Urania Urinowa, "Tuntenhaus Kastanienallee: Entwicklungen im Schatten des Hauptstadt-wahns," Etuxx.com (archives), http://www.etuxx.com/diskussionen/archiv2000_th_kastanienallee.html; "Tuntenhaus Bülowstrasse: Berlin in den 80gern," Etuxx.com (archives), http://www.etuxx.com/diskussionen/archiv2000_th_buelowstr.html; "Tuntenhaus Mainzer Straße: Der kurze Sommer der Anarchie," Tuntenhaus Berlin, https://tuntenhaus.org/?Geschichte:Mainzer_Strasse. See also the documentaries *The Battle of Tuntenhaus 1*, directed by Juliet Bashore, 30 min. (1991), and *Battle of Tuntenhaus 2*, directed by Juliet Bashore, 20 min. (1992), which trace the earlier history of the Tuntenhaus. Both are on YouTube (http://www.youtube.com/watch?v=8ozaR26ehu8 and http://www.youtube.com/watch?v=K3ePVeUZa-4).

26. On the Mainzer Straße riots, see Andrej Holm and Armin Kuhn, "Squatting and Urban Renewal: The Interaction of Squatter Movements and Strategies of Urban Restructuring in Berlin," *International Journal of Urban and Regional Research* 35, no. 3 (May 2011): 650–51.

a minicomplex of alternative social and cultural projects besides the Tuntenhaus: the vegetarian Café Morgenrot, the collectively managed Buchladen zur schwankenden Weltkugel (Bookstore by the Floating World Globe), a Volxküche (people's kitchen, a leftist and lay version of a soup kitchen), and a shop that distributes free groceries to low-income citizens.[27] For about a year, in 2009 and 2010, there was also a free-goods store, the Umsonstladen, where all things on offer cost nothing and were donated by customers; previously, that space had housed an alternative art gallery.[28] The Umsonstladen was vacated against the desires of the house inhabitants, in an effort by the landlord to reclaim a portion of the building spaces for more profitable uses (the ground and basement floors of the front of the building are especially coveted because they face the street and could house commerce and services). In addition to the social initiatives described above, the inhabitants of the Kastanienallee 86 (including the Tuntenhaus) periodically organize parties, events, and festive demonstrations in the courtyard.

Architecturally, the building on Kastanienallee 86 is typical of its time: built around 1870,[29] it contains walk-up apartments distributed around a central courtyard, with some facing the street in the front wing (*Vorderhaus*), and some in the side and back wings (*Seitenflügel* and *Hinterhaus*). It has plenty of the kind of architectural detail that, when restored, makes a building look "historical" and "whimsical," qualities that garner attention and higher rents. It is also included in the Berlin Preservation Authority monument list as part of the Kastanienallee historic ensemble of apartment buildings. If the building were to be restored, it would blend into its surroundings more or less seamlessly. It would gain physical and stylistic integrity according to conventional criteria for historic preservation, but at the same time the building would lose what makes it unique. The spatial interest of the Kastanienallee 86 lies in the combination of its old, intricate, and decrepit architecture with the juxtaposed, often chaotic, and improvised additions of its current inhabitants.

This symbiosis begins on the street, where the inhabitants have turned the façade into a dynamic, ever-changing surface: the architecture keeps weathering; signs and posters are added, displaced, twisted; plants grow, shed leaves, are cut, grow again; strokes of colorful paint are added here and there. The façade establishes

---

27. Kristina Pezzei, "Kapitalismus stiftet Verwirrung," *Die Tageszeitung*, November 30, 2010, http://www.taz.de/1/archiv/digitaz/artikel/?ressort=ba&dig=2010%2F11%2F30%2Fa0135&cHash=4b 85fab138ea619fe3dd394bb05507bd.

28. Kastanienallee 86, postcard, http://ka86.de/pic/postkarte.pdf; "Umsonstladen schon wieder von Räumung bedroht," *Wir bleiben alle!* (blog), August 24, 2010, http://wba.blogspot. de/2010/08/24/umsonstladen-schon-wieder-von-raeumung-bedroht/; Caspar Schlenk, "Räumung in der Kastanienallee: Polizisten als Zuschauer," *Die Tageszeitung,* August 31, 2010, http://www.taz.de/ !5136428/.

29. Denkmaldatenbank, Berlin Senatsverwaltung für Stadtentwicklung und Umwelt, OBJ-Dok-Nr.: 09065105, http://www.stadtentwicklung.berlin.de/cgi-bin/hidaweb/getdoc.pl?DOK_TPL=lda_ doc.tpl&KEY=obj%2009065105.

a contradictory, ambivalent relationship with the street. On the one hand, it announces itself loudly because of its difference, exuberance, and posters; verbal messages in particular mark the building as a site of enunciation and dialogue. It thus beckons, screams, and invites attention. On the other hand, it pushes away outsiders—the passersby, mere onlookers, residents of the gentrified surroundings. It marks itself as different and accessible only to those who belong; its surfaces are dirty, rough, and aggressive, in a kind of punk architectural aesthetic. The entrance, despite the rainbow painted on top, is not clearly marked; it is tucked to the side and partially obscured by overgrown plants. The façade is hard to decipher, except for the messages it delivers with intentional glare in posters and banners. The building is a blemish in the renovated streetscape, a kind of unhealed scar, and as such it commands the eye both to look and to look away.

The rainbow painted on the arch over the passageway that leads to the building and to the courtyard signals the sexual sympathies of the community, and also invites one in. Walking under a rainbow is a camp, even trite proposition; but the use of the architectural molding as a basis for the rainbow outline is formally clever, and the connection between the rainbow and the Tuntenhaus alludes to the widespread use of rainbow flags and stickers to signal gay and gay-friendly spaces. The gesture comes off as both candid and self-conscious. Once past the rainbow, the passageway offers a dark, long space, covered in posters and graffiti, in contrast with the wide openness of the street. The darkness, grime, and confinement of the passageway evoke the innards of an organism. The corridor then transitions into a canopy built by the occupants of the house, finally opening up into the expansive courtyard.

This space, although open and apparently arranged at random, is also picturesquely contrived. Overgrown plants fall down in cascades from the corners of the building, evoking a romantic garden. A large blue chandelier hangs overhead in the middle of the courtyard, with wiry arms that curve downward (fig. 4). The space contains not only the usual furnishings and objects of a typical Berlin courtyard (trash bins, bicycles), but also pieces of domestic furniture: a couch, a round table, chairs. A banner hangs on the back wing of the building, where the Tuntenhaus is located: "Berlin ohne Tuntenhaus is wie ein Garten ohne Blumen"— "Berlin without the Tuntenhaus is like a garden without flowers." The walls are painted with colorful images, and a black sign with red lit-up lettering announces: "Tuntenhaus—seit 1990" (Tuntenhaus since 1990). In the middle of it all, there is a metal sculpture that looks like a stylized drag queen, with an upright ponytail and exaggerated, full red lips. This roofless space, enclosed on all sides, is the theatrical setting for everyday life—chance encounters, people walking to and from their apartments or having coffee at the table—and for special events and festivities. The whole arrangement has a rough and provisional quality, as an accretion of elements that can continually be added or removed, or left to weather and decay; it is both overfilled and unfinished. Provisionality is not only a hallmark

Figure 4. KA 86 and Tuntenhaus, chandelier in inner courtyard (2010).
© Daniela Sandler

of the architecture, but also part of the mind-set and lifestyle, at least for some inhabitants.[30]

On the variegated canvas of the street façade of the Kastanienallee 86, a large-scale message is spelled out in vertical and horizontal words made of thick metal lettering; the letters, affixed individually to the wall, jut out a little from the surface. The letters say: "Kapitalismus normiert, zerstört, tötet" (fig. 5), meaning: "Capitalism normalizes, destroys, murders." The lettering was put up in protest in 2004, after the building was bought by the current owner (Kastanienallee 86 GbR, which stands for Gesellschaft bürgerlichen Rechts, a type of business partnership), who wants to renovate the building. The new landlord's plan to renovate the building

---

30. Werner Kernebeck, interview, June 2010.

Figure 5. KA 86 and Tuntenhaus: "Capitalism normalizes, destroys, murders" (2007).
© Daniela Sandler

would inevitably entail the eviction of the current inhabitants and a steep rise in rents—this has been the norm in the restoration and management of historic properties in the area (as opposed to other possible approaches, which have not been prevalent since unification—say, publicly funded restorations for social-interest housing). The members of the Tuntenhaus and the KA 86 are aware of this, and their treatment of the building's architecture—from the lettering to the material conditions of surfaces and spaces—is a conscious response to the threat of disappearance through gentrification. Therefore the fragmented, unfinished, and partly decrepit state of the building can be seen as carefully cultivated; it is a marker of difference from gentrified, bourgeois, yuppie surroundings. Additionally in the case of the Tuntenhaus, the difference extends to sexual identity, so that the dissonant, effusive, strange appearance of the building might also be understood as a self-fashioned queer space (the queerness of the space is not limited to its appearance, but extends also to the communal domestic arrangements inside, which do not follow the conventional partition of private spaces and functions of homes inhabited by typical nuclear families).

Before the current lettering was installed, the façade had supported other banners and messages. In the early 2000s, it featured two large banners that displayed similar statements: "We remain different," and "Against the yuppification of

Prenzlauer Berg and the disappearance of cheap housing." On the ground floor, over the door lintel on the left side of the building, the words "No SpekuLand" were painted directly on the wall. The combination of political messages with dilapidated background highlights the character of the manifesto: the banners reiterate what the architecture of decrepitude signifies. In the middle of freshly painted façades and cute ice-cream stores, decay is appropriated as a material and symbolic stand against gentrification, allowing the city to speak and suggesting the critical possibilities of counterpreservation. "Wir bleiben anders" means to remain different from the majority in terms of urban politics, sexual identities, and sociocultural practices.

Since unification, rental prices have risen steeply in Prenzlauer Berg, even in dwellings originally designated as social-interest housing and partly subsidized by the government.[31] When a landlord renovates a building, he or she is allowed to increase the rental price accordingly.[32] The Kastanienallee 86, having been built before 1918, falls within a highly valued category because of its age and historical details. Because it has not been renovated, the rent is very low for the area. This means that residents have to deal not only with a decrepit façade, but also with communal bathrooms, worn-out materials and fixtures, and coal heating; if something needs maintenance or repairs, the residents have to carry out the work themselves. The housemates do not mind these conditions. Werner Kernebeck, an inhabitant of the Kastanienallee 86, explained to me in an interview that they know their rents would rise if the house were made more comfortable, so they prefer dealing with small discomforts, such as messy coal bricks for winter heating.[33]

The Kastanienallee 86 should not be taken as a paradigm—nor would the people who live there want it to be. It is an exceptional space for particular groups of people, from the gays who live in the Tuntenhaus to the activists who embrace collective lifestyles in the KA 86. According to Kernebeck, most people who live in the house have some sort of connection to a political project and leftist sympathies. New housemates are usually found through word of mouth, so that there is a certain degree of proximity or validation through friends and acquaintances.[34] This is a small-scale model of affordable housing, which is not only inclusive in some

---

31. Ulrich Paul, "Das kann ich nicht bezahlen," *Berliner Zeitung*, November 2, 2011, http://www.berliner-zeitung.de/berlin/mieterhoehungen—das-kann-ich-nicht-bezahlen-,10809148,11093846.html; Christian Unger, "Der Bundestag beschließt die große Mietbremse," *Berliner Morgenpost*, December 13, 2012, http://www.morgenpost.de/wirtschaft/article112008053/Der-Bundestag-beschliesst-die-grosse-Mietbremse.html; Soraya Sarhaddi Nelson, "Germany's Housing Market Is Hot. Is It Overheating?" *NPR*, January 5, 2012, http://www.npr.org/2013/01/05/168617178/germanys-housing-market-is-hot-is-it-overheating; "Ein Recht auf Stadt für alle: Ein Mietenpolitisches Dossier," Berlin, 2011/2012, pamphlet published by the Steigende Mieten Stoppen! Movement, November 8, 2011, http://mietenstopp.blogsport.de/images/Mietendossier2011.pdf.

32. Senatsverwaltung für Stadtentwicklung und Umwelt, "Berliner Mietspiegel 2015," pamphlet, http://www.stadtentwicklung.berlin.de/wohnen/mietspiegel/de/download/Mietspiegel2015.pdf.

33. Werner Kernebeck, interview, June 2010.

34. Ibid.

ways, but also exclusive and restricted to a particular social set. As such, this model is not reproducible, nor could it easily be adapted or co-opted by an institution or a government. But this does not make the project of the Kastanienallee 86 any less valid, or any less important for Berlin. It is precisely because it is a space of exception, social dissonance, and cultural difference that it contributes to the overall diversity of the city. In a neighborhood that is becoming ever more homogenized in its architecture, social and demographic composition, and economic activities, the Kastanienallee 86 offers a critical counterpoint—a physical space for people who dissent from hegemonic views, and a symbolic reminder of the need for diversity.

Køpi

The Køpi, sometimes also known as Køpi 137 (after its street address, Köpenicker Straße, number 137),[35] is one of Berlin's most legendary *Hausprojekte*, a radical and enduring site of alternative life in Berlin, associated with anarchists, punks, and *Autonomen*. It has enjoyed somewhat of a cult status as a center of alternative culture since its foundation, with an international reputation beyond Germany (which sometimes, according to a Køpi resident, makes her feel as if she were "living in a bus station," given the constant stream of guests).[36] It is not only "one of the most important sites where leftist groups and *Autonomen* carry out organized political work," but also "an important meeting point for those who seek alternatives to commercial entertainment: . . . concerts and parties, cheap food, affordable theater plays and cultural events."[37] That is, the Køpi is a site of political activity and sociability, where everyday practices can themselves be read as politically charged counterstatements to mainstream capitalism: for example, a nonhierarchical system for

---

35. The name "Køpi" is often written with different diacritical marks. The Køpi community, in its presentation materials such as posters and web pages, uses the Danish ø. Many publications follow this; however, several other sources, from newspapers to websites, use the German umlaut, which indicates a sound similar to that of the Danish ø. Some sources, especially in languages such as English or Spanish, write Kopi with no diacritics. In my own text, I follow the Køpi community's spelling; however, when citing sources that use "Köpi" or "Kopi," I reproduce these sources' orthography. This explains the variance in spelling found in this text.

The use of the Danish ø may be a reference to the Danish city of Copenhagen (in Danish, København). When the Køpi was founded, there was an important center of alternative culture and leftist politics called Ungdomshuset in Copenhagen. The Ungdomshuset had also started as a squat, and lasted from 1982 until 2006. It was famous among the squatter scene in Germany. See Mary Manjikian, *Securitisation of Property Squatting in Europe* (Abingdon, UK: Routledge, 2013), 131–32.

36. Stefi, resident of the Køpi, in a 2000 documentary about the building. Assi TV, *2000 10 Jahre Koepi*, 50 min. (Berlin, 2000), at 27 min.14 sec. This documentary is on YouTube, http://www.youtube.com/watch?v=KYqSa2jt2pA. See also "Köpi-Wohnprojekt: Aufmarsch gegen Zwangsversteigerung," *Der Tagesspiegel*, May 4, 2007, http://www.tagesspiegel.de/berlin/koepi-wohnprojekt-aufmarsch-gegen-zwangsversteigerung/842702.html.

37. Michael Philips, "Räumung einkalkuliert," *Scheinschlag: Berliner Stadtzeitung*, no. 1 (1999), http://www.scheinschlag.de/archiv/1999/01_1999/texte/news04.html.

decision making, relying on weekly assemblies; shared living quarters and communal meals; and the choice of many residents to live on little to no money.[38]

The Køpi, self-described as a "living and cultural project" (*Wohn- und Kultur-projekt*),[39] is home to about one hundred people—fifty in the building, and fifty in an adjacent *Wagenplatz* (trailer park).[40] In addition to the residences, the building includes an active roster of social and cultural venues, all of which are noncommercial, free or affordable at a small cost, and committed to political and social causes. There is a bar; spaces for concerts, parties, and theater performances; a vegan *Volks-küche*; a free movie theater known as Peliculoso, which in nice weather shows movies in the open air; a printing workshop called Kommandatur, which is open to the public for do-it-yourself projects; a gym; music rehearsal spaces; an information shop (*Infoladen*), which also houses a videoarchive of political movies; and a "self-organized, non-commercial" and "queer-friendly" climbing room (*Kletterraum*) with vertical and inclined walls and climbing equipment.[41]

Despite the waves of gentrification lapping from all sides, the area where the Køpi is located—in the neighborhood of Mitte, in what was formerly East Berlin, very close to the border with the western district of Kreuzberg—is relatively undeveloped: many vacant lots with overgrown vegetation, ruined or dilapidated structures, nondescript apartment buildings. The industrial past of the area still shows in warehouses and industrial buildings, not far from the River Spree—which here has not yet been fashioned into scenic waterfront as elsewhere in the city. The street is wider, grayer, grimier than the ultragentrified centers of Prenzlauer Berg and Mitte. Critic Michael Philips, writing for the *Scheinschlag*—a magazine devoted to the urban and architectural transformation of the center of Berlin since unification—described the area as a "torn landscape" in 1999; ten years later it still remained rough around the edges.[42] Philips went on to say that "the sight includes something monumental": the Køpi building, which looms tall and wide, surrounded by open space and set back from the street.[43] Philips deems the Køpi "an imposing structure," a quality that stems as much from the building's relative isolation—which enhances the perception of its size—as it does from its formal aspects (fig. 6). If this is an "imposing structure," it is not so in the conventional sense of beauty or self-glorification, but because it is aggressive, uncanny, intimidating. The residents might want it to be so, at least to a certain audience—there are signs warding off tourists and picture-takers, and a plaque that states that the Køpi is

38. Jan Pfaff, "Hausprojekt: Die Nische für ein anderes Leben," *TAZ.de*, June 7, 2008, http://www.taz.de/Hausprojekt/!18332/.

39. "History," Koepi137.net, http://www.koepi137.net/history.html.

40. Konrad Litschko, "Köpi-Wagenplatz versteigert—Es bleibt beim Risikokapital," *TAZ.de*, November 7, 2013, http://www.taz.de/Koepi-Wagenplatz-versteigert/!127070/.

41. "Køpi 137: Projekte & Kontakt," Koepi137.net, http://www.koepi137.net/projekte-kontakt.html.

42. My descriptions are based on the state of the street up until my last field visit in 2010.

43. Philips, "Räumung einkalkuliert."

Figure 6. Køpi, exterior view of façade on front yard (2009).
© Marcela Faé—Fotostrasse.com

risky business ("Køpi bleibt Risiko-Kapital"). This is the motto of the community, repeated on its website and in demonstration posters, aimed at potential developers.

The building is massive and dark, and fronted by a tall screen of thick, untamed shrubs and trees. On the left side it adjoins a boarded-up, halted construction of cinder blocks covered in graffiti. To the right, its party wall faces an overgrown garden and trailer park. The *Gründerzeit* façade that runs parallel to the street, separated from the sidewalk by a deep front yard, is symmetrical, with five stories of small rectangular windows and a central internal stairwell.[44] The courtyard is partly enclosed by two short building wings on either side that jut out toward the street, so that the whole structure forms a shallow U footprint. These building wings are really stumps, remnants of a formerly larger structure partly destroyed by bombing

---

44. The *Gründerzeit* is a period of industrial, economic, and cultural flourishing in the third quarter of the nineteenth century. *Gründerzeit* means "Founders' Time" and carries the connotations of a mythical original period for the nation-state. In architecture, it is associated with neoclassicism and historicism; *Gründerzeitstil* sometimes extends up to 1914. Michael S. Cullen, *Bauwerke der Gründerzeit* (Hamburg: HB-Verlags- und Vertriebs-Ges.; Stuttgart: Pegasus-Buch- und Zeitschr.-Vertriebsges., 1984); Tilmann Buddensieg, "Der 'Tumult aller Stile': Nietzsches Kritik der 'Gründerzeit,'" in *Architektur weiterdenken*, ed. Sylvia Claus and Werner Oechslin (Zurich: gta, 2004); Elisabeth Castellani-Stürzel, *Der Historismus und die Gründerzeit: Kult der Vergangenheit?* (Freiburg: Universitätsverlag, 1980); *Gründerzeit, 1848–1871: Industrie & Lebensträume zwischen Vormärz und Kaiserreich*, exhibition catalogue, ed. Ulrike Laufer and Hans Ottomeyer (Dresden: Sandstein, 2008); Christian Jansen, *Gründerzeit und Nationsbildung, 1849–1871* (Paderborn: Ferdinand Schöningh, 2011).

at the end of World War II. On the street side, the walls of these stumps still display the outlines of lost rooms, floor by floor, bookending the central façade surreally.

There used to be a front wing as well, close to the sidewalk, so that the courtyard was enclosed on all sides, and what is currently the main façade was the back wing (*Hinterhaus*). The front wing was completely destroyed by bombs in February 1945.[45] The war destruction resulted in a building that ends abruptly, a common sight in the aftermath of the war, but which is rare today. The bombing also carved out the generous setback from the street, atypical for a *Gründerzeit* building. The surfaces of the building are all severely damaged from the bombing and ensuing decay: most of the molding has fallen, except for a few jagged and isolated remains of pediments, lintels, and corbels; the stucco is also mostly gone, surviving in scattered patches—including a section where the decorative coursing remains (seen on the right side of fig. 6). Most of the exposed surface of this building is now brick, small and gray, of the kind meant to be hidden behind stucco or stone facing. This is the backdrop for an irregular, ever-changing collage of graffiti, banners, and posters with political messages, often related to the Køpi or other *Hausprojekte* and to issues of urban development, public space, and gentrification. At the entrance gateway to the front yard, under a wiry metal canopy, one of these signs reads: "You are leaving the capitalist sector"—a play on the signs from the postwar era that announced the borders between different occupied zones in Berlin.

Carving out a space for alternative living, as much as possible outside of the constraints of capitalism, means that the Køpi is both a welcoming and free space, and a regulated and exclusive one. The Køpi community is open to *Autonomen*, sexual minorities, punks, anarchists, musicians; it offers free culture and entertainment because it is opposed to commercialism and capitalism; and it operates on a democratic and egalitarian structure because of the community's Socialist and anarchist political views.[46] At the same time, and precisely because it is a space of dissonance and dissent, it excludes by necessity a host of social groups: not only potential developers and authorities, or right-wing groups and individuals, but also anyone directly or indirectly associated with gentrification and commercialism. This might mean tourists, yuppies, hipsters, anyone who is middle class, conventional, or *spießig* (bourgeois).

The exclusion of these groups relies on spatial cues—from the obvious messages printed on plaques and signs to the ostensibly displayed dilapidation of the building to the makeshift aesthetics of the street fence, the trailer park, and the courtyard. The Køpi represents a radical version of counterpreservation, worn loudly on the streetscape as a sign of identity comparable to tattoos, piercings, dreadlocks, or a

---

45. Erik Smit, Evthalia Staikos, and Dirk Thormann, *3. Februar 1945: Die Zerstörung Kreuzbergs aus der Luft*, exhibition catalogue, ed. Martin Düspohl, bound ed. (Berlin: Berlin-Kreuzberg, 1995).

46. Blase Rösch, resident of the Køpi, interview by my research assistant Irene Hilden, August 14, 2015.

Figure 7. Køpi, exterior, detail of façade and side-wing entrance (2010).
© Daniela Sandler

Mohawk (fig. 7). The combative architectural and urban stance of the Køpi can be better understood with relation to its history, which from the beginning was marked by transgression (trespassing and occupying property), conflict (protesting and resisting eviction), and struggle (fighting for the right to remain in place in an increasingly gentrified environment).

The *Hausprojekt* began as an occupation or squat (*Hausbesetzung*), when a group of *Autonomen* from West Berlin decided to occupy the vacant, semi-destroyed building at Köpenickerstraße 137, on February 23, 1990, in what was then East Berlin, near the border with the western district of Kreuzberg (a center of *Autonomen* culture and occupations).[47] The squatters were attracted by, among other things, the many large rooms in the building—the double-height ceilings on the ground floor, and the open spaces in the basement.[48] The building was then owned by the GDR government. It had been used as a sports facility during the GDR era, which also took advantage of the large spaces (for a bowling alley in the basement, for example), but by 1990 it had been vacated and was slated for demolition.[49] The building was in precarious shape, dirty, missing windows and other fixtures, with a nonfunctioning infrastructure. It was the squatting and the creation of the Køpi that prevented its demolition. The occupation was peaceful and did not meet with police repression. This was common in the immediate aftermath of the fall of the Wall; it was only after unification in October 1990 that the police began to evict squatters systematically and often by force, as this is when it became clear that those buildings would eventually rejoin the private real estate market and be the object of property restitutions. The most controversial thing about the Køpi at the time, according to members of the Køpi community itself, is that it was the first squat inhabited by West Berliners that was located in what was still East Berlin.[50] This was significant: although at the time the Wall had already fallen down, Germany was not yet officially unified as a political entity; moreover, the cultural and physical differences between East and West Berlin remained strong in the minds of Berliners long after unification. There had been a lively *Hausbesetzer* scene in East Berlin, just as in West Berlin, but they had been separated by the Wall as much as everyone else in the two Germanys.

As was the case with many *Hausprojekte* in the early 1990s, the squat was an illegal occupation that took advantage of the no-man's-land status of buildings caught in between owners in the transition from Socialism to capitalism. While many of these projects were ephemeral, several were granted official status and could survive longer; this was the case of the Køpi. In 1991, through an agreement with the administration of the Mitte district, the squat was legalized, and the occupants were granted some security.[51] This legalization notwithstanding, the tenure of the Køpi would be challenged several times in the ensuing decades. In

---

47. "Köpi-Flugblatt Feb. 97," Squat.net (archives), February 1997, http://old.squat.net/de/berlin/koepi.html. This document is a collectively written pamphlet recounting the history of the Køpi, published by Squat.net. See also "Köpi-Wohnprojekt: Aufmarsch gegen Zwangsversteigerung."

48. As recounted by Blase Rösch in the documentary *2000 10 Jahre Koepi*, at 3 min. 47 sec.

49. P. Schwoch, "Köpenicker Strasse 137/138 in Berlin Mitte," *Die Köpenicker Straße in Berlin Mitte und Kreuzberg*, http://www.köpenicker-strasse.de/Koepenicker137.html.

50. "Köpi-Flugblatt Feb. 97."

51. In 1993 the management of the building passed to the Gesellschaft für Stadtentwicklung (GSE), which became responsible for the rental contracts. "Köpi-Flugblatt Feb. 97."

1995, Volquard Petersen received the property from the government through the property restitution process that marked the liquidation of Socialist holdings, and became the new owner. Petersen founded a company to redevelop the Køpi site, and proposed an ambitious plan under the name Sonnenhöfe (Sun Courtyards). The building would be renovated, the ground floor would be leased as commercial or office space, and the apartments in the upper stories would be sold as condos. The *Wagenplatz* area would be home to a new structure with offices, condos, and an underground parking lot. These plans were approved by the Mitte administration, but the developer was not able to raise enough money.[52] In the meantime, Petersen threatened the Køpi residents and attempted to evict them, with no success.

As the plans languished, the Køpi *Hausprojekt* continued to flourish, by then almost a decade after the initial occupation. The Køpi residents refurbished the building to fit their needs, from guest rooms and apartments to the common areas and cultural spaces. According to the residents, "It cost a lot of money and labor to fix and keep the apartments, garden, event venues . . . in usable condition."[53] The documentary *2000 10 Jahre Koepi* registers some of the work that was carried out by the residents themselves—plumbing, resurfacing, cleaning.[54] This underscores the fact that groups like the Køpi community are able and willing to invest energy and resources in renovating and maintaining their living spaces according to their own designs. Although the argument could be made that they have limited resources and must focus on infrastructure before cosmetics, there are many accretions to the building that are not purely functional, such as murals, sculptures, and reliefs (figs. 7 and 8).

If they leave spaces and surfaces in an unfinished, partly decayed, or rough state, this can be interpreted as an intentional choice. Indeed, an interview with Blase Rösch, a longtime resident of the Køpi who often represents the building in public pronouncements, confirms this, as he states that leaving the façade in its dilapidated state (as they had encountered it) was "intentional" (he used the word *Absicht*). According to Blase, the motivation was "to show that Berlin is a city with a history."[55] Blase mentions the prewar past of the building as a "dance hall . . . where poor people went dancing," then brings up its bombing during World War II, explaining: "We believe that people must live with their own past, and for us this includes even Fascism." The Køpi community engaged this history by organizing an exhibition of Nazi-era objects and fragments found in the building, such as swastika flags, steel helmets, and mail correspondence. The exhibition was temporary, but the counterpreservationist attitude is an enduring way of alluding to this history:

52. Philips, "Räumung einkalkuliert."
53. "Köpi-Flugblatt Feb. 97." The Køpi residents add: "In the past seven years, we haven't received a single Mark from the owner, landlord, the state, or anybody else. AND IT SHOULD REMAIN THIS WAY." This is further indication of the resistance to institutionalization and public support.
54. *2000 10 Jahre Koepi.*
55. Blase Rösch, interview by Irene Hilden, August 14, 2015.

Figure 8. Køpi, interior, stairwell (2009).
© Marcela Faé—Fotostrasse.com

"We wanted to show that . . . World War II had happened, but also that [there were] new people with new aspirations, and that's why there are all these colorful murals there . . . but that we haven't forgotten history." And then he adds: "I believe that the building looks really good."[56]

Further indirect proof of this intentionality is that other groups have provided models of affordable housing in gentrifying neighborhoods with self-financed, self-built architectural renovations carried out by tenants, not by developers or landlords, restoring buildings in a more conventional way. For example, the Mietergenossenschaft SelbstBau e.G. (a registered cooperative of tenants whose name, SelbstBau, is the equivalent of SelfBuild), founded in 1990 in what was still East Berlin, has developed sustainable and low-cost restorations in Prenzlauer Berg and Friedrichshain, with the motto "Comfortable and affordable dwellings in central areas are not myths."[57] The buildings renovated by the SelbstBau e.G. look sparkling clean; while the cooperative is also critical of gentrification and profit-oriented urban policies, it does not share the radical political orientation of the Køpi.

The decade came to a close, and soon the Køpi would face a cycle familiar to many *Hausprojekte* and alternative cultural projects: forced auctions, protests, changes in ownership, unrealized proposals for private development, lack of investors, a period of quiet, more forced auctions . . .[58] A few years after gaining property rights to the site, Petersen fell into debt, owing more than 2 million euros to the Commerzbank; the property was foreclosed, and the Commerzbank became the legal owner. In 1999 the Mitte administration enacted a "compulsory auction" (*Zwangsversteigerung*) to recover the money that was owed to the bank. The Køpi community and numerous supporters organized protests in public spaces; these protests have themselves become part of the identity, iconography, and memory of the Køpi. Every time there is a protest, journalists delight in describing the protesters' dark hoods, their anticapitalist posters and rallying cries, and their tactics.[59] Photographs of the protests are reproduced by the Køpi community itself, displayed on its website as part of a selected gallery of images of the *Hausprojekt*. Side by side with photos of the building and *Wagenplatz*, the photos of protesters holding banners are presented as a significant element in the Køpi's self-definition, even if the protests were held elsewhere in the city.[60] This underscores the political dimension of the *Hausprojekt*—in the self-presentation of the Køpi, it is not enough to live

---

56. Ibid.

57. *Das SelbstBau-Modell: Eine Mietergenossenschaft in Prenzlauer Berg*, published by Energiekontor GmbH; Architekten Kny & Weber; and S.T.E.R.N. GmbH (Berlin: Ch. Links, 1998), 6.

58. Holm and Kuhn, "Squatting and Urban Renewal," 655; Philips, "Räumung einkalkuliert;" "Köpi-Wohnprojekt: Aufmarsch gegen Zwangsversteigerung."

59. See, for instance, Antje Frieling, "Commerz gegen Köpi: Das alternative Kulturzentrum mag mit dem Tempo in Berlin nicht mithalten," *Jungle World,* February 17, 1999, http://jungle-world.com/artikel/1999/07/31799.html; Litschko, "Köpi-Wagenplatz versteigert."

60. The photos were shown in a section of the website called "Gallery," which was visible until early January 2014, when the website was redesigned and the page was taken down.

an alternative lifestyle or inhabit an alternative space if these experiences are not also accompanied by political action. The protests and their imagery (photographs, posters, banners, T-shirts) are another example of the public dialogue with the city I described in connection with the KA 86 and Tuntenhaus. Here, again, the *Hausprojekt* creates an interface with other, broader audiences, through the occupation of public space and communication via both mainstream and alternative media.

This dialogue, in its different iterations, is not a futile exercise. Some commentators speculate that the difficulty of finding investors willing to buy the Køpi site or to back up development projects there is at least partly related to the resistance they expect to find from the Køpi community and supporters.[61] In the words of a *Scheinschlag* writer, "Investors have a choice of many other sites in the Berlin market, and will hardly opt for tying themselves to the rebellious Køpi residents."[62] These statements suggest that, at the very least, the Køpi's many occupations of urban space—from public demonstrations in the city to the actual occupation of the building—have played a role in securing the community's existence over two decades. The *Scheinschlag* writer is sympathetic to the Køpi and other similar projects, but more conservative media outlets sometimes represent the situation with a touch of fearmongering. In the newspaper *Die Welt*, a short article summarizing the history of squatting in Berlin—where the Köpi is one of two examples mentioned by name—describes the "potential for violence" (*Gewaltpotenzial*) of squatters, devoting as much space to these potential dangers as to the history of the scene: "Even if the [squatter] scene is much smaller now, it remains now as ever highly prone to violence. . . . Arson and other forms of property damage are preferred modes of action."[63]

The police also tend to be overly vigilant whenever there is a demonstration or protest; for example, on the occasion of another forced auction of the building in 2007, there were three hundred police officers at the ready to protect the courtroom—and three hundred protesters, among members or supporters of the Köpi.[64] While it is true that squatters and *Autonomen* have been associated with violent demonstrations, violence does not represent the modus operandi of the majority of *Hausprojekte* residents. If the perception of squatters, *Autonomen*, and residents of alternative *Hausprojekte* as violent and radical leftists has helped to stave off investor interest and therefore protected the Køpi—as noted above—this

---

61. According to the newspaper *Tagesspiegel*, "Offenbar fürchteten potenzielle Käufer Racheaktionen der Linken" ("It appears that potential buyers fear vengeful reactions from the left"), "Köpi-Wohnprojekt: Aufmarsch gegen Zwangsversteigerung." See also Sebastian Puschner, "Die Köpi soll für Schuldner bluten," *TAZ.de*, February 26, 2013, http://www.taz.de/FREIRAeUME/!111787/.

62. J. S., "Køpi bleibt volkseigen," *Scheinschlag* 11 (1999), http://www.scheinschlag.de/archiv/1999/11_1999/texte/news1.html.

63. "Historie: Hausbesetzer in Berlin," *Die Welt*, December 9, 2007, http://www.welt.de/regionales/berlin/article1445153/Hausbesetzer-in-Berlin.html.

64. "'Köpi' für 834.000 Euro zwangsversteigert," *Die Welt*, May 8, 2007, http://www.welt.de/regionales/berlin/article858583/Koepi-fuer-834-000-Euro-zwangsversteigert.html.

perception also contributes to the difficulties that *Hausprojekte* face when searching for ways to secure their status.[65] One difficulty is the public and mainstream media conflation of legal, rent-paying *Hausprojekte* (which applies to the Køpi and to most former squats) with illegal squatters.

Another challenge is garnering public sympathy toward their cause, which in such negative representations is seen as illegitimate. But the demands to secure "free spaces for alternative lifestyles," to curb gentrification, and to increase the amount of affordable housing are far from unreasonable, and indeed resonate with the needs of many other social groups. Affordable housing, be it for alternative social groups, ethnic minorities, or other low-income populations, is one of the most important issues for contemporary cities—which, as many sociologists and urban geographers have argued, are increasingly becoming polarized, exclusive, and segregated along extreme social, ethnic, and financial divisions.[66] Not only that, but for the first time in decades Berlin is facing a severe and possibly worsening housing crisis. The crisis of the housing market, under pressure from rising migration into the city, has been met with the typical response of socially engaged Berlin: street protests, such as in the summer of 2015.[67] While the model offered by the Køpi and other *Hausprojekte* would not fit most other circumstances and situations—the collective organization, the unconventional physical spaces—the fight for affordable housing resonates with the needs of a large population (a population so diverse that solutions are bound to be varied).

The two attempts to auction off the Køpi in 1999 were not successful. There were no serious bidders, and the Køpi residents proposed buying the property for the symbolic amount of one mark.[68] This would have meant, of course, not an attempt to compensate the Commerzbank within the rules of the real estate market, but rather to secure public support and sanctioning for special status outside of the private market. The residents wanted the Mitte administration to declare the Køpi building and garden a "special-use site for experimental living" (*Sondernutzungsfläche für experimentelles Wohnen*), and ensure the community's long-term

---

65. A systematic study of mainstream, alternative, and social media representations might yield insights into public depictions and perceptions of the Køpi and other *Hausprojekte*. Such a systematic study is outside the scope of the present work, and therefore my observations are preliminary hypotheses based on a small sample of news stories.

66. See esp. David Harvey, *Social Justice and the City* (Athens: University of Georgia Press, 2009); Harvey, *Spaces of Hope* (Berkeley and Los Angeles: University of California Press, 2000); and Harvey, *Spaces of Global Capitalism* (London: Verso, 2006). See also Mike Davis, *Planet of Slums* (London: Verso, 2006); Saskia Sassen's now classic *The Global City: New York, London, Tokyo* (Princeton, NJ: Princeton University Press, 1991); Neil Smith, *Uneven Development: Nature, Capital, and the Production of Space*, 3rd ed. (Athens: University of Georgia Press, 2008), among others.

67. Norbert Schwaldt, "Warum in Berlin Wohnungsnot herrscht," *Die Welt*, April 9, 2015, http://www.welt.de/finanzen/immobilien/article139345241/Warum-in-Berlin-Wohnungsnot-herrscht.html; Eliot Brown, "Berlin's Housing Problems Boil Over," *Wall Street Journal*, October 6, 2015, http://www.wsj.com/articles/berlins-housing-problems-boil-over-1444123804.

68. J. S., "Køpi bleibt volkseigen."

existence.[69] The bank and the Mitte district did not accept this proposal. After the first failed forced auctions in 1999, another auction was enforced in 2007.[70] This time around, the building and adjacent *Wagenplatz* were bought in the name of a developer called Novum Köpenicker Straße 133–138 GmbH, based in the West German city of Duisburg.[71] This is a common pattern for East Berlin, where many properties were bought by absentee developers based in West Germany; this pattern has helped define the image of investors as foreign, removed from the local realities of the city, and concerned only with profits. Right after buying the property, the Novum company threatened the residents with eviction, but in 2008 the company signed a thirty-year lease with the Køpi community.[72] According to Friedrich Spek, a real state lawyer who represents the Novum company, the developer wanted to start building on the site as early as 2007, right after the purchase, but could not obtain financing from banks to fund the redevelopment because of the many protests by the Køpi residents.[73]

As it turns out, the Novum company too fell into debt, and the Commerzbank again called for a compulsory auction, this time in 2013. There were several auctions, all of them involving portions of the *Wagenplatz* and not the building (the lease status of the *Wagenplatz* was less clear and secure than the thirty-year contract extended to the building). Early in the year, the first auction resulted in a pro forma change of hands, as the winning bid came from a company related to the previous owner.[74] The winning bid was relatively small, as it was the sole offer (another interested party gave up). Later in the year, another parcel of the *Wagenplatz* was sold in a forced auction for 210,000 euros. There were three offers—one from the legal representative of the current owner; one from a man who wanted to convert the area into a social-interest recycling project in conversation with the Køpi; and the highest and winning bid from a man named Rolf Nordström, manager of

69. Sebastian Puschner, "Eigentümer hängt an der Köpi," *Taz.de*, February 28, 2013, http://www.taz.de/FREIRAUM/!111997/.

70. "Kopi Berlin Radical Space to Be Auctioned Off," *UK Indymedia*, April 26, 2007, http://www.indymedia.org.uk/en/2007/04/368853.html. The starting bid was reported as 1.67 million euros for the Køpi building, and 1.81 million euros for the garden. Køpi residents and supporters complained that the forced auction was kept secret until less than a month before its court-appointed date, and that the appraisal of the value of the site was "made up" (*UK Indymedia*) and misrepresented the legal status of the Køpi residents as squatters instead of legal renters.

71. The building had been valued at 1.67 million euros, but the winning bid was only 834,000. See Litschko, "Köpi-Wagenplatz versteigert"; "'Köpi' für 834.000 Euro zwangsversteigert."

72. Puschner, "Die Köpi soll für Schuldner bluten"; "Köpi-Bewohner erhalten Mietverträge," *Die Welt*, October 3, 2008, http://www.welt.de/regionales/berlin/article1784340/Koepi-Bewohner-erhalten-Mietvertraege.html; "Køpi Update," Køpi 137 News, Køpi137.net, March 10, 2008, http://www.koepi137.net/10032008.htm (this page is not available anymore after the website was redesigned).

73. Puschner, "Eigentümer hängt an der Köpi."

74. The new company, Startezia GmbH, is associated with the former landlord (Novum Köpenicker Straße 133–138 GmbH). Andrea Beyerlein, "Köpi-Areal unter Wert verkauft," *Berliner Zeitung*, March 1, 2013, http://www.berliner-zeitung.de/berlin/zwangsversteigerung-koepi-areal-unter-wert-verkauft,10809148,21970374.html; Puschner, "Die Köpi soll für Schuldner bluten."

the I.R.E. Zweite Immobiliengesellschaft in Berlin. The purchase was too recent for any plans to be divulged, and attempts by the Køpi community's lawyer at a conversation with Nordström were not successful. Described as a "pinstripe-suited man," Nordström seems to augur a new phase in private development plans and potential clashes with the Køpi.[75]

The social and political role of the Køpi community is one part of the argument for the significance of the site in its current condition. As one of the last surviving radical projects in the center of the city, the Køpi bears witness to a defining moment in Berlin's history. The proliferation of alternative, utopian living communities and cultural projects was once a key feature of the city's central-eastern neighborhoods, a distinctive phenomenon of the transitional conditions during the early years of unification. Even if these projects did not last, their presence at a particular point in time—for weeks, months, or years—shaped the city, and the subsequent expectations, memories, and claims of certain groups. In the early 1990s, the central-eastern neighborhoods were in many ways a giant playground, a realm of *jouissance* and use value, a free space for artistic and social experimentation, when the city was transformed by the festival and not by the marketplace. This is a unique, irreproducible historical moment. It is not surprising that this moment disappeared given the constraints and rules of capitalism, but its memory is still important in the recent history of Berlin. Although the Køpi itself has changed since 1990, and although it is a living entity and not a museum piece, it is also at the same time a carrier of this history.

But there is more to the building from the perspective of architectural and social history. The complex was built at the beginning of the twentieth century as an apartment building for army officers (in keeping with Berlin's history as a "casern city" since the eighteenth century); it included a large establishment called Fürstenhof, where parties, wedding celebrations, and meetings could be held (and which was the reason for the generous, large spaces on the ground floor).[76] While the building type, architecture, and function were not exceptional for the time, today it is the last prewar building remaining in that portion of Köpenickerstraße. This is one of the oldest streets in the city (originally created to link the then-smaller city of Berlin to the neighboring town of Köpenick), but it would be difficult to glean the street's old age from a walk around the vicinity of the Køpi.

Other areas of Berlin have benefited from more generous preservation listings, but the Køpi is not officially protected as a historical monument and therefore could be demolished.[77] One could perhaps argue that the destruction of other

75. Litschko, "Köpi-Wagenplatz versteigert."
76. The establishment is mentioned as early as 1905 in a newspaper advertisement, and is featured in a postcard from 1900. Schwoch, "Köpenicker Strasse 137/138 in Berlin Mitte."
77. Landesdenkmalamt Berlin, *Denkmalliste Berlin*, as of April 7, 2016, http://www.stadtentwick lung.berlin.de/denkmal/denkmalliste/downloads/denkmalliste.pdf; Philips, "Räumung einkalkuliert."

prewar buildings around the Køpi has disfigured the street landscape to such an extent as to invalidate any attempt at preserving the historical view, especially since the building is not an exceptional architectural monument in itself. This argument assumes that preservation value lies in urban and contextual integrity and cohesiveness. A less cosmetic view of preservation would find value precisely in what the torn landscape reveals: the Køpi, along with the empty lots and nondescript modern buildings around it, is an index of twentieth-century urbanism, from the devastation wrought by the war to the devaluation of historical buildings in the postwar era. This is not to say that the area should remain as it is forever, as a frozen panorama of a particular century, but that the Køpi building—itself already a fragment of a larger complex—has reason to survive as an eloquent structure even amid urban changes around it.

It is not only as an architectural object that the building deserves attention. During the war it was used to house French forced laborers working for the AEG (Allgemeine Elektricitäts-Gesellschaft Aktiengesellschaft), or General Electricity Company.[78] The AEG was one of the largest German industries in the early twentieth century, producing a range of items from electrical power to industrial and domestic electrical equipment. It was a pioneer of technological developments, design, and corporate identity practices. But, like many other industries of the time, the AEG was also a collaborator with the Nazi regime, donating money to the Nazi Party and using slave laborers and concentration camp inmates for some of its production lines.

There have been many efforts in Berlin to mark sites of Nazi persecution and death: train platforms used for the deportation of Jews and other groups; sites of events such as the 1933 book burning ceremony; places of detention, torture, and execution of political prisoners, mentally and physically disabled people, sexual and ethnic minorities; and even the former residences of Jews who died in concentration camps.[79] In comparison, there are not as many markers of sites associated with forced labor, perhaps because the victims are not as recognizable a group as Jews, gays, or the Roma and Sinti, or perhaps because these sites—workshops

---

78. The earliest documented mention of this is from 1941. Laurenz Demps, *Zwangsarbeit und Zwangsarbeiterlager in der faschistischen Reichshauptstadt Berlin 1939–1945* (Berlin: Gesellschaft für Heimatgeschichte und Denkmalpflege Berlin im Kulturbund der DDR, 1986), 104.

79. Holocaust and Nazi-era memorials in Berlin have been profusely analyzed in countless articles and books. See Stefanie Endlich, *Wege zur Erinnerung: Gedenkstätte und -orte für die Opfer des Nationalsozialismus in Berlin und Brandenburg* (Berlin: Metropol, 2007); Johannes Heesch and Ulrike Braun, *Orte erinnern: Spuren des NS-Terrors in Berlin—Ein Wegweiser*, ed. Günter Braun (Berlin: Nicolai, 2006); James Young, *The Texture of Memory: Holocaust Memorials and Meaning* (New Haven, CT: Yale University Press, 1993); Young, *At Memory's Edge: After-Images of the Holocaust in Contemporary Art and Architecture* (New Haven, CT: Yale University Press, 2000); Jennifer Jordan, *Structures of Memory: Understanding Urban Change in Berlin and Beyond* (Stanford, CA: Stanford University Press, 2006); Karen Till, *The New Berlin: Memory, Politics, Place* (Minneapolis: University of Minnesota Press, 2005); and Brian Ladd, *Ghosts of Berlin: Confronting German History in the Urban Landscape* (Chicago: University of Chicago Press, 1997).

and housing—were too embedded in German everyday life. Jennifer Jordan, in her study of memorials in Berlin, recounts a conversation with historian Laurenz Demps, who conducted one of the earliest and most respected surveys of forced-labor sites in Berlin: "Demps has counted 1,000 forced labor camps and factories in Berlin, and 100 Gestapo sites. They cannot all be marked, he says, but they are there."[80] Associated with household brand names such as AEG, and located in otherwise "normal" neighborhoods, these sites belie the claims by postwar Germans that they should not be considered complicit with the Holocaust because they did not know the extent of Nazi terror. The fact that this building housed forced laborers is not an exception in Berlin or other German cities, but it is nonetheless historically meaningful as an indication of the enmeshment of Nazi terror with everyday or "ordinary" life.

Admittedly, Germany has done more than most nations to address its victims and past crimes, but this has been done in a way that isolates both the victims (forever cast as the "other," in the form of minorities whose numbers are even lower than before the Nazi era) and perpetrators (circumscribed as the official members of the Nazi Party, and restricted to a past from which younger generations feel disconnected). Even when more glaring sites of oppression such as concentration camps were located near cities, the current presentation of these sites in memorials and museums tends to section them off and sever their historical and urban connections with the immediate surroundings (see chapter 4). Therefore, the opportunity to indicate this tangled history at the site of the Køpi is important. This history is not yet explicitly marked by the Køpi community, nor would it have been by any of the developers' plans for the site. But according to Blase, some residents, including himself, are interested in this history and have researched at least parts of it.[81] Given the special circumstances of the Køpi building—from the leftist, anti-Fascist political position of the residents to the physical conditions of the building, still bearing marks of the war—this history becomes more significant and adds to the importance of the site as it is.

Although the Køpi has so far benefited from a lack of investors willing to fund development projects, this might change. The whole Köpenickerstraße is part of an area designated by the city government for urban renovation (*Sanierungsgebiet*)— the area known as North Luisenstadt.[82] This means that the public power will seek partnerships with private capital to fund developments aimed at the private

---

80. Jordan, *Structures of Memory*, 242 n. 92.

81. Blase Rösch, interview by Irene Hilden, August 14, 2015.

82. Senatsverwaltung für Stadtentwicklung und Umwelt, Stadterneuerung – Mitte: Sanierungsgebiet Mitte – Nördliche Luisenstadt, http://www.stadtentwicklung.berlin.de/staedtebau/foerderprogramme/stadterneuerung/de/noerdl_luisenstadt/index.shtml; Uwe Aulich, "Der lange Schatten der Mauer: Die nördliche Luisenstadt in Mitte hat ihre Zukunft erst noch vor sich," *Berliner Zeitung*, June 6, 2011, http://www.berliner-zeitung.de/archiv/die-noerdliche-luisenstadt-in-mitte-hat-ihre-zukunft-erst-noch-vor-sich-der-lange-schatten-der-mauer,10810590,10790938.html.

market. In addition, the Køpi is located near the boundaries of the Mediaspree, one of the most ambitious urban renovation projects of unified Berlin. The Mediaspree encompasses a public-private partnership for commercial, business, and entertainment developments on a large scale (some of which have already been built), along with the refurbishment of the river shoreline on both sides so as to create a landscaped, attractive waterfront. This is entirely in line not only with the urban renovation policies for unified Berlin (see my discussion of gentrification below), but also with a global turn to waterfronts, reclaimed in postindustrial societies for leisure and economic regeneration.[83] While the Mediaspree has been slow to start, with the pioneering projects (for instance, shiny corporate high-rises) scattered over an unevenly developed area, there is now more interest and pressure to push ahead. The lawyer who represents the Køpi community stated, on the occasion of the last auction of the *Wagenplatz* in December 2013, that the area has developed significantly, attracting the interest of potential investors who in the past would have stayed away.[84]

Gentrification in Berlin

The struggles of the Tuntenhaus, KA 86, and Køpi need to be understood in the context of the gentrification of their respective districts—Prenzlauer Berg and Mitte. After unification, investment was concentrated initially on the central neighborhood of Mitte; from there, gentrification spread to the central-eastern districts of Prenzlauer Berg and Friedrichshain over the next two decades. The western district of Kreuzberg had already experienced a measure of gentrification before 1989, and this tendency continued into the postunification period. In the late 2000s, a second wave of gentrification moved westward from Prenzlauer Berg and Kreuzberg, reaching the working-class and immigrant enclaves in the western districts of Neukölln and Wedding.[85] The initial path of gentrification was centrally based (the center of the city being a privileged place for symbolic, spatial, infrastructural, and

83. Ingo Bader and Martin Bialluch, "Gentrification and the Creative Class in Berlin-Kreuzberg," in *Whose Urban Renaissance? An International Comparison of Urban Regeneration Strategies*, ed. Libby Porter and Kate Shaw (New York: Routledge, 2013), 96–99; Albert Scharenberg and Ingo Bader, "Berlin's Waterfront Site Struggle," *City* 13, nos. 2–3 (2009): 325–35; Bader and Scharenberg, "The Sound of Berlin: Subculture and the Global Music Industry," *International Journal of Urban and Regional Research* 34, no. 1 (2010): 76–91; Claire Colomb, *Staging the New Berlin: Place Marketing and the Politics of Urban Reinvention Post-1989* (New York: Routledge, 2012), 292–94.

84. Puschner, "Die Köpi soll für Schuldner bluten."

85. See, among others, Andrej Holm, *Die Restrukturierung des Räumes: Stadterneuerung der 90er Jahre in Ostberlin. Interessen und Machtverhältnisse* (Bielefeld: transcript, 2006); Matthias Bernt, Britta Grell, and Andrej Holm, eds., *The Berlin Reader: A Compendium on Urban Change and Activism* (Bielefeld: transcript, 2013); Peter Gerlach and Ingrid Apolinarski, *Identitätsbildung und Stadtentwicklung: Analysen, Befunde, planungstheoretische und -methodische Ansätze für eine aktivierende Stadterneuerung—dargestellt am Beispiel Berlin-Friedrichshain* (Frankfurt am Main: Peter Lang, 1997). See also the introduction, note 21.

social reasons), and east-oriented, markedly focused on former East Berlin. The attention to East Berlin might be explained partly because of the area's glut of vacant, cheap properties liquidated by the Socialist state or returned to the market at the hands of former owners (or their heirs).

East Berlin was also attractive because of its thriving nightlife, art projects, young population, and alternative culture. In the years soon after unification, the East not only held the promise of cultural ebullience, but also had an exotic and mysterious appeal—the area had been inaccessible to most West Germans and foreigners for forty-five years. West Berlin fell out of fashion in the 1990s as public and private eyes turned toward the "newest" part of the city. Of course, East Berlin can be defined as "exotic" and "new" only from the point of view of someone from West Germany or another country. Officially, East Germany ceased to exist and joined West Germany, which, as a political, legal, and national entity, continued to exist in its basic form; this political inclusion of the former East was paralleled by a western-based cultural perspective that marked both the tone of urban transformation (gentrification of the former East, as opposed to, say, socialization of the former West) and the narratives that framed such transformation. As Andrej Holm puts it,

> East Berlin stands for the transformation of the autonomous, socialist German Democratic Republic into the eastern portion of the capitalist Federal Republic of Germany. At the same time it also stands for the collision between two urban bodies that had been separated for decades, and the attempt by Berlin elites to develop the city into an international metropolis, as the new historical capital of Germany.[86]

The starkness of gentrification in the eastern neighborhoods is due at least in some measure to the contrast between their current commodified trappings, and the preceding Socialist landscape of East Berlin. Mitte, Prenzlauer Berg, and Friedrichshain were located in the eastern side of the city, in the GDR. Socialism had kept these areas out of the private real estate market for forty-five years.[87] The GDR government did carry out urban improvements, but it had a limited amount of resources.[88] It invested in showpiece projects such as Karl-Marx-Allee,

---

86. Holm, *Restrukturierung des Raumes*, 12.

87. Peter Williams identifies gentrification in Eastern Europe *before* the collapse of the Soviet Union. He notes that, despite crucial differences between Socialist and capitalist cities, the patterns of residential segregation in Eastern European cities "indicate the persistence of class inequalities under different modes of production" that translate in unequal distribution of wealth, resources, and material conditions. This prevents a naive portrayal of Socialist cities as "virgin territories" in terms of market differentiation and inequality. Williams, "Gentrification in Britain and Europe," in *Gentrification, Displacement, and Neighborhood Revitalization,* ed. J. John Palen and Bruce London (Albany: State University of New York Press, 1984), 224–25.

88. Jörn Düwel describes the GDR's reaction to the economic constraints in terms of priorities: "Throughout East Germany, reconstruction work began with residential buildings on the outskirts of cities. The first phase of development brought lively building activity in Berlin, but did not reach the centre until the mid-1960s." Düwel, "The New Centre: Architecture and Urban Planning in the Capital

Alexanderplatz, housing projects, and the renovation of Husemannstraße in Prenzlauer Berg.[89] But large sections of Mitte, and most of Prenzlauer Berg and Friedrichshain, were neglected and dilapidated.[90] Many of their inhabitants were misfits in East Germany—artists, students, dissidents, retirees.[91] This marginality may be partly explained by the proximity to the Wall, as the area of Mitte was cut off from its surroundings on three sides. The formerly central neighborhoods became peripheral, and the Wall marred their reputation with evocations of immobility, imprisonment, control, and repression. Official policies and social perceptions contributed to turn the city away from these areas. Once the Wall was gone, this changed. After unification, parts of Mitte, such as the Spandauer Vorstadt (see chapter 3), underwent quick and intense upgrading. The area where the Køpi is located, at the southern tip of Mitte, has been much slower to develop, and is only now drawing more attention with the designation of the North Luisenstadt *Sanierungsgebiet* (see above).

Like Mitte, the neighboring district of Prenzlauer Berg—home to the Tuntenhaus and KA 86—also experienced extensive gentrification. The area was particularly attractive to investment because of its proximity to the center of the city and its wealth of historical architecture—block after block of nineteenth-century apartment buildings made "the neighborhood in the 1990s into 'Europe's largest historical renovation area.'"[92] A large portion of Prenzlauer Berg (including 80,000 apartments) was officially designated as a *Sanierungsgebiet*, and as such it was the object of concerted urban policies by the government. Unlike previous instances of urban renovation, however—such as the large-scale modernist urban renewal efforts of the 1960s and '70s (*Kahlschlagsanierung*), and the grassroots-oriented "careful urban renovation" (*behutsame Stadterneuerung*) of the 1980s—this time the government expected to fund most of the renovation through private investment, meaning that the transformation of the district would necessarily be geared toward private profit and steered by developers as much as, if not more than, by other political actors such as the government or local organizations.[93] Apartment rents in

of the German Democratic Republic," in *Urban Visions: Experiencing and Envisioning the City*, ed. Steven Spier (Liverpool: Liverpool University Press, 2002), 167.

89. Greg Castillo, "Building Culture in Divided Berlin: Globalization and the Cold War," in *Hybrid Urbanism: On the Identity Discourse and the Built Environment*, ed. Nezar AlSayyad (Westport, CT: Praeger, 2001), 183–86; Harald Bodenschatz et al., *Berlin: Auf der Suche nach dem verlorenen Zentrum* (Hamburg: Architektenkammer, 1995); *Alexanderplatz: Städtebaulicher Ideenwettbewerb = Urban Planning Ideas Competition*, ed. Kristin Feireiss (Berlin: Ernst & Sohn, 1994); Uwe Kieling and Johannes Althoff, *Das Nikolaiviertel: Spuren der Geschichte im ältesten Berlin* (Berlin: Berlin Edition, 2001), 111–20; Ralf Schmiedecke, *Berlin-Mitte: Herz der Hauptstadt* (Erfurt: Sutton, 2004).

90. Florian Urban, *Neo-Historical East Berlin: Architecture and Urban Design in the German Democratic Republic, 1970–1990* (Farnham, UK, and Burlington, VT: Ashgate, 2009).

91. Bernt Roder and Bettina Tacke, eds., *Prenzlauer Berg im Wandel der Geschichte: Leben rund um den Helmholtzplatz* (Berlin: be.bra, 2004), 98–124, 139–49.

92. Holm, *Restrukturierung des Raumes*, 12. See also Thomas Dörfler, *Gentrification in Prenzlauer Berg? Milieuwandel eines Berliner Sozialraums seit 1989* (Bielefeld: transcript, 2010).

93. Holm, *Restrukturierung des Raumes*, 76, 83–85.

the area averaged 12.28 euros per square meter in 2016, making it the fourth most expensive district in Berlin (the most expensive is Mitte at 14.85, followed by the traditionally posh western district of Grunewald at 13.23).[94]

Next to Prenzlauer Berg and Kreuzberg, another neighborhood—Friedrichshain— also went through similar processes. Friedrichshain is still home to several *Haus-projekte*, including a cluster on Rigaerstraße near Liebigstraße where counter-preservation mixes with the colorful aesthetics of vibrant murals and graffiti. These *Hausprojekte* are not discussed here, but a brief mention of them and of Friedrichs-hain serves to delineate their place in this history. Friedrichshain was once touted as "the next Prenzlauer Berg"—first by students and artists who moved there, turning away from Prenzlauer Berg when the area began to gentrify; then by investors in search of profits. Friedrichshain—like Mitte—is a large district that gentrified ir-regularly. The area around Simon-Dach Straße and Boxhagener Square, with pic-turesque streets and old apartment buildings, was the first to become trendy. The district is bisected by the monumental Karl-Marx-Allee (rebuilt by the GDR ac-cording to principles of Stalinist architecture: imposing and ornamented apartment buildings along grand boulevards and plazas).[95] The *Stalinbauten,* as the edifices have been nicknamed, enjoyed renewed popularity after unification. Tenants value the spacious apartments, comfortably equipped with elevators and central heating, clad with Meissen porcelain tiles, and boasting generous vistas of Berlin through large picture windows. The revalorization of the *Stalinbauten* as desirable living spaces helped spread gentrification from the southern part of the district north-ward. Because this front of gentrification came later, several communities north of Karl-Marx-Allee were able to survive for a relatively long time—for example, the *Hausprojekte* on Rigaerstraße, including the XB Liebig, Rigaer 78, Rigaer 94, Rigaer 105, and the Liebig 14 (the latter evicted in 2011).[96]

Gentrification and the Scene

Gentrification has a particular link to art, culture, and architecture. Governments may use cultural facilities as anchors of gentrification, initiating urban upgrading through museums, concert halls, or public spaces.[97] The role of art and culture in gentrification is not limited to public art projects. The valorization of a neighbor-hood is often associated with a lively artistic or bohemian community—the "scene."

94. "Mietspiegel Berlin 2016," Wohnungsboerse.net, http://www.wohnungsboerse.net/mietspiegel-Berlin/2825.

95. Ladd, *Ghosts of Berlin*, 181–89.

96. "Räumung Liebigstraße 14 in Berlin."

97. See, for instance, Ronan Paddison and Steven Miles, eds., *Culture-Led Urban Regeneration* (Abingdon, UK: Routledge: 2007); Chris Hamnet and Noam Shoval, "Museums as Flagships of Urban Development," in *Cities and Visitors: Regulating People, Markets, and City Space,* ed. Lily M. Hoffman, Susan S. Fainstein, and Dennis R. Judd (Oxford: Blackwell, 2003), 219–35.

In her discussion of alternative cultural projects in Berlin, Melbourne, and Amsterdam, Kate Shaw defines the "scene" with relation to alternative cultures:

> The concept of "scene" thickens that of alternative culture by including not only all the arrangements of proponents, participants, audiences, supports and infrastructures involved in cultural production, but the connections between particular forms (music, film, theatre, literary, art etc.).[98]

Alternative cultures encompass individuals, groups, and activities, while the scene conjoins them in networks and environments that are more than just the sum of their parts. The scene is a spatiotemporal formation that lives off continuous, multiple activities; it transforms districts or neighborhoods, giving them "character"—I use the word consciously to evoke the dramaturgical connotation of an "urban scene." The term is not just a label attached by cultural critics. "Scene" is commonly used in German in reference to an ebullient combination of art practices and spaces, entertainment, and sociability patterns that are both trendy and alternative—"die Szene."[99] The Berlin scene, moving about the central neighborhoods of Spandauer Vorstadt, Prenzlauer Berg, Kreuzberg, Friedrichshain, and more recently Neukölln, Wedding, and Moabit, includes artists, students, architects, academics, performers, DJs, writers, journalists, and media workers; it is located on the sites of the city's famous techno music culture (clubs, parties, record stores), and also in art galleries, independent bars and restaurants, alternative clothing and design stores, and the lively milieu of sidewalk cafés where the scene spills over the street.[100]

To a certain extent the "scene" is a spectacle; it presupposes performers and spectators—and not just because it involves art and artists. The scene, understood as the ongoing social and cultural transactions in a certain place, is itself a performance in display. Elke Grenzer suggests the theatrical dimension of "scene" in her discussion of high-profile architectural projects in Berlin, aptly titled "Setting the Stage for a New Germany: Architecture and the Scene of Berlin."[101] Through analyses of the Reichstag, Postdamer Platz, and the Jewish Museum, Grenzer goes into detail on the theatrical meaning of scene, but does not address the sociocultural connotation described above. Taken together, Shaw's and Grenzer's texts provide

---

98. Kate Shaw, "The Place of Alternative Culture and the Politics of Its Protection in Berlin, Amsterdam, and Melbourne," *Planning Theory & Practice* 6, no. 2 (June 2005): 151.

99. See, for instance, the use of the term in Mechtilde Kißler and Josef Eckerr's discussion of a gentrifying Cologne neighborhood. Kißler and Eckerr, "Vom Arbeiterquartier zum Szenestadtteil: Die Entstehung eines innerstädtischen Kölner Wohnviertels nach Abschluß der Urbanisierung," *Die Alte Stadt* 19, no. 1 (1992): 51–74.

100. The newspaper *Berliner Morgenpost* published a series of articles on "scene areas" in 2003: Friedrichshain, Prenzlauer Berg, Kreuzberg, Spandauer Vorstadt, Schöneberg (which was trendier before 1989), and Charlottenburg (upscale, mainstream). See "Szene-Meilen in Berlin," *Berliner Morgenpost*, August 21–26, 2003, http://morgenpost.berlin1.de/content/themen/1283.html.

101. Elke Grenzer, "Setting the Stage for a New Germany: Architecture and the Scene of Berlin," *Public* 22/23 (2001): 219–42.

a more complex understanding of the scene, which oscillates between the two connotations—the sociocultural and the dramaturgical. The oscillation points to the emancipatory potential of spatial appropriations, in the idea that performance (in the broad sense of the social and cultural transactions alluded to above) may transform urban spaces, change their meanings, and affect the rest of the city.[102] However, it is also the spectacular quality of the scene—how it easily produces images and icons, how it attracts and seduces a wide public—that makes it into a potential tool for gentrification.

The role of the scene is ambiguous. Artists, musicians, students, intellectuals, and activists who make up the "scene" are neither gentry nor proletarians. Although some may have been born and raised in the potentially gentrifying area, they are often outsiders who moved in precisely because rents were low and there were empty or neglected spaces malleable to creative intervention. The "scene" may join the locals in solidarity and fear of displacement, but most artists, students, and intellectuals possess a cultural cachet that gives them more mobility and clout in asserting their right to the city.[103] In addition, the presence of an art scene—studios, galleries, clubs, performances, installations, parties—no matter how "alternative" and outside of the mainstream, increases the potential value of a neighborhood. The art scene makes the neighborhood attractive, entertaining, pleasurable; it gives color, character, and identity. It may be the case that the artists and students also end up displaced if rents become too high or if most apartments are available only for sale and not for rent. There are also distinctions within cultural communities—the difference between commercial, mainstream galleries and alternative exhibition spaces; between glossy nightclubs and improvised parties; between an alternative scene and "the culture industry—art dealers and patrons, gallery owners and artists, designers and critics, writers and performers—which has converted urban dilapidation into ultra chic."[104] But none of this mitigates the fact that an art scene is also a factor of gentrification, and that a local scene, "if not displaced by gentrification, is a candidate for appropriation by the market."[105]

---

102. Jacqueline Groth and Eric Corijn explore the power of "informal actors"—a concept that overlaps with that of the "scene"—in transforming urban spaces and influencing urban planning and politics. Groth and Corijn, "Reclaiming Urbanity: Indeterminate Spaces, Informal Actors, and Urban Agenda Setting," *Urban Studies* 42, no. 3 (March 2005): 503–26.

103. Brian Sullivan, "The Displacement Enigma," *Pratt Planning Papers* 1, no. 1 (October 1981): 16. Sullivan does not deny that gentrification displaces artists or intellectuals as well as low-income groups, but he notes that the latter have more difficulty relocating and reestablishing social and cultural communities: "Displacement means more than not living within walking distance of a Häagen Dazs or quiche boutique. It means the disruption of many important social, economic, religious, and institutional connections that enable them to survive" (16).

104. Neil Smith, *The New Urban Frontier: Gentrification and the Revanchist City* (London and New York: Routledge, 1996), 18.

105. Shaw, "The Place of Alternative Culture," 156. See also Rosalyn Deutsche and Cara Gendel Ryan, "The Fine Art of Gentrification," *October* 31 (Winter 1984): 91–111.

The other "perverse" link of gentrification is architectural preservation. Spaces become affordable to low-income populations for a reason—isolated neighborhoods that lack infrastructure; small houses and plots; neglected public and private spaces. Landlords may be uninterested enough to ignore squatters for long periods. Affordable central neighborhoods such as Mitte, Prenzlauer Berg, or Kreuzberg in the early 1990s had been neglected for decades. Most of these buildings might not have been exceptional monuments, but the concept of heritage has expanded since the postwar era to include vernacular architecture and whole urban ensembles where the fabric of buildings and streets is more important than any single object. These urban ensembles are now prized by architectural historians, architects, and preservationists.[106]

The effort to preserve and restore these sites poses a quandary. The social displacement associated with urban conservation is often described as a side effect. However, some texts suggest that the relationship goes both ways—that is, social displacement may be used as a tool to improve spatial conditions. Writing in 1984, Peter Williams admits that "many planners and architects see social upgrading as a necessary cost of the preservation of the built environment."[107] In Williams's ambiguous formulation, cost can mean a calculated price, a step toward the final goal, an inevitable consequence—or all of the above.

In historical areas architectural heritage adds extra value. Heritage attracts tourism, and it makes the cityscape profitable by creating commercial and entertainment districts and promoting the consumption of urban spaces.[108] Architects, historians, and critics sometimes dissociate spatial improvements from their social context, and celebrate the conservation of architecture in praise like this: "The nineteenth-century fabric of European cities has been renovated. . . . Suddenly, fine old buildings sparkle again, forgotten squares and streets have new life."[109] Similarly to the creation of public cultural institutions, the renovation of historical districts seems justifiable. Indeed there is nothing essentially or intrinsically exclusionary about recuperating historical buildings or improving living spaces. But the repeated correlation between renovation and displacement has forged long-lasting social representations and meanings. It is these meanings that fuel resistance to preservation, and in the case of Berlin the display of decrepitude and decay—counterpreservation.

---

106. Nahum Cohen, *Urban Conservation* (Cambridge, MA: MIT Press, 1999); Gregers Algreen-Ussing et al., eds., *Urban Space and Urban Conservation as an Aesthetic Problem* (Rome: "L'Erma" di Bretschneider, 2000); Anthony M. Tung, *Preserving the World's Greatest Cities: The Destruction and Renewal of the Historic Metropolis* (New York: Clarkson Potter, 2001).

107. Williams ascribes this view to official programs such as the European Campaign for Urban Renaissance. Williams, "Gentrification in Britain and Europe," 224.

108. Janet Stewart, "The Kunsthaus Tacheles: The Berlin Architecture Debate in Micro-Historical Context," in *Recasting German Identity: Culture, Politics, and Literature in the Berlin Republic*, ed. Stuart Taberner and Frank Finlay (Rochester, NY: Camden House, 2002), 52.

109. Peter Davey, "City Shifts," *Architectural Review* 215, no. 1285 (March 2004): 42.

In Friedrichshain, Prenzlauer Berg, and Mitte, inhabitants of buildings not yet renovated try to resist gentrification by adopting a counterpreservationist standpoint, highlighting the association of spatial improvement with social exclusion. As Grenzer suggests, Berlin is a stage—but not only for commercial spectacles such as Potsdamer Platz. The city is also a stage for alternative performances, with an engaged audience that is receptive and used to such demonstrations. The scene of Berlin has a history. Alex Vasudevan identifies a dramaturgical dimension to squatting whereby squatters perform "their counterclaims to the city . . . as architectural 'events.'"[110] Vasudevan focuses on a particular squat, the K77 (founded on 77 Kastanienallee in 1992), whose members "deliberately recast the act of squatting as a form of 'continuous performance' (*unbefristeten Kunstaktion*) or installation art" inspired by the work of, among others, Joseph Beuys.[111] Visitors and Berliners are acclimated to the appropriation of the city for artistic and political demonstrations, from the informal exhibitions and cultural gatherings of Prenzlauer Berg to the riots, demonstrations, and banners of Kreuzberg. The people who put up posters, graffiti, banners, and installations today do so with a consciousness of the public dimension of the city. The fact that these actions are not permanent architectural designs does not make them less worthy of consideration. Although squats may be short-lived, banners put down, and graffiti erased, these manifestations convey a pointed, unmistakable message that resonates with a wider public and may reverberate beyond the actual duration of each demonstration.

This participatory, critical, and performative attitude represents a particular approach to the city, one that views urban space as open for transformation and occupation, regardless of legal property considerations. This attitude may have been favored by the peculiar status of both West and East Berlin, where the postwar landscape had been peppered with vacant buildings. Perhaps the ubiquitous sight of unused, empty buildings, which was a hallmark of divided Berlin and continued into the first years of unification, contributed to the formation of a more flexible view of the city, one predicated on the use value of space as defined by Lefebvre as opposed to its monetary or exchange value. In *The Production of Space*, Lefebvre explains his understanding of use value versus exchange value with relation to Karl Marx's theory of capital, and applies this distinction to space and architecture.[112] Exchange value is associated with the insertion of space as an abstraction in global fluxes of capital, while use value is the hallmark of social practices in particular places:

> Exchange with its circulatory systems and networks may occupy space worldwide, but consumption occurs only in this or that particular place. A specific individual,

110. Alex Vasudevan, "Dramaturgies of Dissent: The Spatial Politics of Squatting in Berlin, 1968–," *Social and Cultural Geography* 12, no. 3 (May 2011): 286.

111. Ibid., 295.

112. Lefebvre, *The Production of Space*, 100.

with a specific daily schedule, seeks a particular satisfaction. Use value constitutes the only real wealth, and this fact helps to restore its ill-appreciated importance.[113]

Lefebvre criticizes disciplinary approaches to space based purely on quantitative measurements, and instead proposes that "a science of space or 'spatio-analysis' would stress the use of space, its qualitative properties."[114] Use value is not always or necessarily emancipatory, but because it is spatially situated, it is a precondition for the democratic, countercultural reappropriation of space Lefebvre called for as a way of asserting a collective right to the city.[115]

The house squatting movement distills this attitude and remains a symbolic force in Berlin, even though the number of squats and *Hausprojekte* has steadily declined since the mid-1990s. In the early 1990s there were approximately 120 new squats in East Berlin, mostly in Mitte, Prenzlauer Berg, and Friedrichshain.[116] In July 1990 the city issued an ordinance against new squats, marking an inflection point from the initial proliferation. Not only did this curb the formation of new squats, but the police also started to carry out evictions, several of them violent. This culminated in protests, confrontations, and a street riot on Mainzer Straße, a street on which a number of politically active squats were concentrated. From then on, squatters increasingly engaged in "negotiated solutions," which legalized their status whenever possible;[117] on the one hand, this afforded them some safety and stability, but on the other hand, it entailed contracts, rents, and a formal and official status that did not always appeal to squatters' ideologies. By the mid-1990s, most squats had been legalized.[118] Even after legalization (which, as seen above, is no guarantee of stability), most squats continued to participate in leftist political actions, to promote alternative and communal lifestyles, and to keep their living spaces in an intentionally rough and dilapidated state. They continued to organize parties and events, and kept on hanging banners and signs on their façades. The vibrancy and potential for urban change of squats survive after legalization.

In her seminal study of Kreuzberg, Barbara Lang proposes the concept of symbolic gentrification to describe the neighborhood in the 1980s, when signs of spatial upgrading appeared, but gentrification (as measured in real estate values and population displacement) had not taken hold.[119] The average rent might not have gone up, and the proportion of renovated apartment buildings or fancy eateries might

---

113. Ibid., 341.
114. Ibid., 404.
115. Henri Lefebvre, *Writings on Cities* (Malden, MA: Blackwell, 1996).
116. Holm and Kuhn, "Squatting and Urban Renewal," 650.
117. Ibid.
118. Mechthild Henneke, "Als ginge es noch um die große Schlacht," *Berliner Zeitung*, October 31, 1997, http://www.berliner-zeitung.de/newsticker/es-gibt-nicht-mehr-viele-besetzte-haeuser-in-berlin-und-doch-werden-sie-als-eine-grundsatzfrage-der-politik-gehandelt-von-mechthild-henneke-als-ginge-es-noch-um-die-grosse-schlacht,10917074,9357238.html.
119. Lang, *Mythos Kreuzberg*.

have still been small, but even small changes were seen as having a potentially significant impact; the ever-widening *perception* of change was real, and it spread among inhabitants with the force of fact. Once the symbolic dimension of gentrification took hold, it fueled further demographic, architectural, and economic changes in both directions—Kreuzberg residents moving out in search of more "authenticity," more mainstream residents moving in and creating both more supply and demand for upscale services.

If Lang speaks of "symbolic gentrification" (and the concrete resistance to it), we may now speak of "symbolic squatting" (in the face of concrete gentrification) to understand the role and potency of legalized squats. The reverberations of the squatter movement go beyond the actual number of surviving squats or *Hausprojekte*.[120] House squatters, or *Hausbesetzer*, tried to build an alternative society. They viewed themselves as social and urban agents not just capable of, but *entitled* to transform the city, to use its existing raw matter and mold it into a new form. Spatial practice was inseparable from social action and from a cultural and political project. As a result, conventional concerns for property or law were not only irrelevant, but intentionally called into question. This dynamic, democratic, anarchic view is reflected in spaces that accommodate all of these qualities in their chaotic appearance and organization. Counterpreservation is not tantamount to squatting. However, both have in common the transformative appropriation of the city, and the opposition to the exchange value of urban space.

The antigentrification movement, which is not exclusive to Berlin, has taken strong hold in the city partly thanks to the presence of alternative cultures, which are not only affected by gentrification, but also prone to mobilization. In 2011, Konrad Litschko, a journalist and active chronicler of social movements in Berlin, announced: "Gentrification is the new combat word." Litschko was covering the notorious May 1 demonstrations in Berlin, which often turn into riots. In 2011, according to Litschko, the demonstrations were both more politicized and more peaceful than in the recent past, and they all focused on the right to the city, fighting "against rising rents, for alternative living spaces, against sleek upgraded façades." Litschko concluded that the "day is finally repoliticized," thanks to the focus on the issue of urban renovation.[121]

The *Hausprojekte* are an important part of this movement, as centers of political activity and criticism. In this sense, the *Hausprojekte* are more than just enclaves, but acquire a larger role as activists and as models of alternative housing. However, there are limitations to the reach and aspirations of *Hausprojekte* and even of the antigentrification movement. Litschko, the journalist, notes that the May

---

120. Holm and Kuhn suggest this in their examination of the potential contribution of squatting to urban policies, in "Squatting and Urban Renewal."

121. Konrad Litschko, "1. Mai in Berlin wieder politisch: Die neue G-Frage," *TAZ*.de, May 2, 2011, http://www.taz.de/1-Mai-in-Berlin-wieder-politisch/!70005/.

1 demonstrations in 2011, for all their concern with the "integration of city residents," lacked the participation of important sectors of the population who are also
affected by rising rents: "the average renter, migrants."[122] Ethnic minorities, which
in addition to economic challenges also face social, cultural, and religious issues, are
by and large not a strong part of *Hausprojekte* (either as residents or as part of their
political fights). Even though *Hausprojekte* cannot be faulted for not taking on all
the different issues of the world, at the same time the absence of ethnic minorities is
glaring in the German context. The complicated status of immigrants is a pressing
problem in Berlin and in Germany; in numbers, more so than the plight of *Hausprojekte*. The deep-seated racial prejudices that have marked German history, and
which in the postwar era were felt more intensely by the Turkish population (and,
in the post-Wall era, by Eastern Europeans), might be more pervasive than leftist
groups would like to admit. One could argue that if *Hausprojekte* are committed
to a democratic city and an inclusive Socialist politics, the question of immigration
and ethnic minorities in the city must be part of the agenda. At the very least, the
limitations of *Hausprojekte* as political actors and models must be recognized alongside their potentialities.

---

122. Ibid.

3

Cultural Centers

History, Architecture, and Public Space

Since the fall of the Wall, alternative cultural projects have flourished in what was formerly East Berlin, for the same reasons as the *Hausprojekte* discussed in the previous chapter: affordable spaces in neighborhoods such as Mitte and Prenzlauer Berg, a lively and young social scene, and a run-down cityscape full of opportunities for creative appropriation. Artists, activists, and intellectuals have set up galleries, performance spaces, studios, cafés, and clubs, and created independent cultural and art centers. These centers are devoted to alternative art and cultural practices, mostly outside of the pressures of the art market and mainstream entertainment and commerce. However, they are not niches for segregated subcultures; rather, they are integrated into the wider social and cultural life of the city, attracting a diverse public. These cultural centers also represent the vibrant alternative culture and bohemian life that have made the city famous since the postwar era and even before. They are entwined with the urban and architectural transformation of Berlin since 1989, expressing debates and embodying conflicts over the development and future of the city.

Alternative cultural and art centers have endured despite social and economic changes. These centers were founded at a time of uncertainty, euphoria, and experimentation. In the limbo after the fall of the Wall, the derelict and vacant buildings in the middle of Berlin appeared to be up for grabs. Over time, some of these centers became so prominent as to attract a more mainstream public, from tourist groups to children doing school projects, while still keeping their unconventional character. As the central areas of Berlin have become more and more gentrified, these cultural centers have struggled to remain in their original buildings, under pressure from landlords and potential developers interested in more profitable uses. The debate over the future of alternative cultural spaces is also a debate over the future of Berlin. Alternative art and cultural projects contribute to a plural urban environment by providing affordable studio and living spaces, diverse cultural programs, and a dissonant voice in an increasingly commercialized cityscape. These projects offer the possibility of a more inclusive and flexible city.

While several projects illuminate the issues discussed above, one in particular serves as a magnifying lens for the possibilities and pitfalls of alternative cultural centers: the Haus Schwarzenberg, which is the main focus of this chapter (see fig. 1). The Haus Schwarzenberg was founded in 1995 in the district of Mitte, at the core of unified Berlin. In the early 1990s, the alternative scene in Mitte peaked with a fresh incoming population, new galleries showing young artists, informal parties and music events, squats and art installations. The Haus Schwarzenberg (which was never a squat) represents this moment of experimentation and spontaneous appropriation of architectural and urban spaces. In the ensuing decade, the Haus Schwarzenberg would go on to face the threat of eviction by a potential private investor, a challenge common to practically all alternative cultural centers. In addition, the Haus Schwarzenberg faced the challenge of institutionalization, as the victory against eviction was achieved through public sponsorship and thus meant being subject to government oversight. This is the story, give or take, of other cultural projects, such as the now-defunct Tacheles, possibly the most famous of them, and the Schokoladen. The themes of resistance, market pressures, and art projects run through the history of all these cultural centers, but the Haus Schwarzenberg adds yet another thread: that of history and memory. The building was the site of a hiding place for Jews during the Nazi era, now turned into a historical museum. The mission statement and self-presentation of the Haus Schwarzenberg incorporate this and other physical markers as signs of a "living history," bringing up that familiar Berlin trope: the ever-present past. The tangle of politics, real estate, alternative culture, and memory makes the Haus Schwarzenberg a particularly rich and complicated example. But before examining it in detail, it is necessary to understand its larger urban context.

Gentrification and Culture in Mitte

The Haus Schwarzenberg is located in the neighborhood of Mitte, the center of reunified Berlin, and formerly a part of East Germany. The immediate surroundings of the building are known as the Spandauer Vorstadt, a tangle of narrow, winding streets that had been "in the shadows of [public] attention" in the GDR.[1] East German planners and politicians turned to the Spandauer Vorstadt only in the mid-1980s, in preparation for the celebrations of Berlin's 750th anniversary in 1987. The area along Sophienstraße, for instance, was renovated as "an historical picture-book street" in the 1980s, but this was an isolated project.[2] Before the GDR government could undertake further historical renovations in the area, the Wall fell down, and the fate of the city changed. Without the Wall and the border, the Spandauer Vorstadt and the whole of Mitte were suddenly reterritorialized as central rather than peripheral, right in the middle of the soon-to-be capital of reunified Germany and boasting some spectacular historical architecture to boot.

The Spandauer Vorstadt, with its vacant buildings and empty lots, was also fertile ground for squatting and informal cultural projects. Soon after unification, it became the headquarters of Berlin's alternative culture:

> Since the political transformations of 1989 the Spandauer Vorstadt has developed itself as an art and culture center—initially "clandestine," and since then the most extensive art and culture neighborhood of Berlin. In the beginning of the nineties many galleries, alternative theaters, and scene-bars were established in mostly ramshackle houses with cheap rents. Countless vacant buildings were occupied by artists and used for residential and cultural projects.[3]

The most famous of these cultural projects was the Tacheles, the cultural center managed by an artists' collective in the ruins of the Friedrichstraßenpassage, which lasted from 1990 to 2012. The artists occupied the Tacheles illegally, and successfully fought the city's plans to demolish it.[4] The cultural center grew in popularity, and functioned as a magnet, attracting alternative artists, mainstream visitors, and commercial enterprises. But the Tacheles was only the most visible of Mitte's many cultural projects. Several small, independent galleries popped up and closed almost as fast because of rising rents and property disputes.[5] Other projects were more long-lasting, such as the KuLe (Kunst und Leben, or "Art and Life"), located at the heart of the gallery scene on Auguststraße; the Schokoladen; and the Haus Schwarzenberg, perched in one of the most successful commercial blocks of the Spandauer Vorstadt.

1. Harald Bodenschatz, *Berlin auf der Suche nach dem verlorenen Zentrum* (Hamburg: Junius, 1995), 180.

2. Ibid., 179, 180.

3. Wolfgang Feyerabend, *Quer durch Mitte: Die Spandauer Vorstadt* (Berlin: Haude & Spenersche, 1999), 119. See also Bodenschatz, *Berlin auf der Suche nach dem verlorenen Zentrum*, 180–81.

4. Bodenschatz, *Berlin auf der Suche nach dem verlorenen Zentrum*, 181.

5. Feyerabend, *Quer durch Mitte*, 120. See also Thomas Krüger, *Die bewegte Stadt: Berlin am ende der Neunziger* (Berlin: FAB, 1998); and Anke Fesel, ed., *Berlin Wonderland: Wild Years Revisited, 1990–1996* (Berlin: Gestalten, 2014).

The "scene" converged toward the Spandauer Vorstadt partly because it was abandoned. The area had not been densely inhabited in the GDR, and it—like much of East Germany—lost a considerable amount of population in the final years of the East German regime, when travel restrictions to bordering Socialist countries were lifted, and many East German citizens left through those borders. An estimated 400,000 people left East Germany for West Germany yearly during this two-year period.[6] After the fall of the Wall, the Spandauer Vorstadt, like much of East Berlin, sat in a vacuum because of lengthy property disputes that kept investors at bay while the legal owners (or heirs) of buildings and lots were defined in court. Vacant, unattended properties were ripe for squatting, exploration, and experimental uses. The ease of occupying buildings whose ownership was still unclear favored a thriving alternative scene of art projects, illegal nightclubs and parties, independent music events, and residential squats. This was the spirit of the Spandauer Vorstadt at the time, nestled between East and West, in a point of convergence and centrality that nonetheless remained liminal because it had been a border, a no-man's-land for such a long time.

Collective art and cultural projects such as the Haus Schwarzenberg, the Tacheles, and the Schokoladen were landmarks in this scene. Formed by groups of artists, designers, musicians, and others, these projects aimed to provide spaces for artistic experimentation and creation outside of the pressures of the mainstream art market. They were managed collectively, and offered not only gallery and studio spaces, but also sites for sociability—from bars and cafés to courtyard parties and meeting rooms. The impulse was not merely to find affordable or free studio space, but also to cultivate the conditions for a collective creative ferment. These cultural projects established an ongoing dialogue with each other and with the city as a whole, opening up their doors through exhibitions, performances, parties, and assemblies.

In the course of the decade, the ownership of buildings and sites in East Berlin was gradually defined. As rightful owners and heirs were identified, private investors were able to purchase buildings and redevelop them.[7] The Mitte was prime real estate in the new German capital: right in the middle of Berlin, close to the new government and business centers, and dense with architectural heritage and historically significant sites. In 1993 the government determined that 70 percent of the Spandauer Vorstadt buildings were in precarious conditions, and designated

6. Steffen Kröhnert and Samuel Skipper, "Demographic Development in Eastern Germany," in *Online Handbook Demography,* Berlin Institut für Bevölkerung und Entwicklung, http://www.berlin-institut.org/en/online-handbookdemography/population-dynamics/east-germany.html. This number focuses on migrations from East to West Germany and so does not include those who moved to other countries. See also "East-West German Immigration Statistics (1961–1990)," German History in Documents and Images, http://germanhistorydocs.ghi-dc.org/sub_document.cfm?document_id=925.

7. Elizabeth Strom, *Building the New Berlin: The Politics of Urban Development in Germany's Capital City* (Lanham, MD: Lexington Books, 2001).

the neighborhood as a "renovation area" (*Sanierungsgebiet*).[8] This designation "heralded the transformation of the area into a yuppie district."[9] The massive restoration of the area, which ended officially in 2008, managed to renovate 87.9 percent of the buildings that had been deemed precarious.[10] Property disputes were resolved, and investors transformed derelict buildings into offices, condos, and fancy rentals. Squares, public gardens, streets, and sidewalks were cleaned up and refurbished with new equipment, fixtures, public artworks, and memorials. Restaurants, hotels, and art galleries popped up. Wolfgang Feyerabend describes how local inhabitants felt toward the new specialty stores and upscale restaurants in the early 1990s:

> The inhabitants of the neighborhood . . . face the tide of gastronomic establishments with mixed feelings. Steeper rents displace local retail; bars move into commercial premises. The distance to [everyday] shopping becomes longer and longer.[11]

The same crooked lanes and alleyways that had appeared undesirable to the modernist eyes of the early and mid-twentieth century were now seen as attractive and unique. Squats were dismantled or, as in the case of the Tacheles, legalized. Harald Bodenschatz points out that in the Spandauer Vorstadt the pressure of private investors found strong resistance from local initiatives and the government. This resulted in more restrictions to private development than in areas such as Potsdamer Platz or Friedrichstadt. Bodenschatz considers that the government seemed intent on preserving the area's cultural and social diversity, at least on paper.[12] Despite such provisions, and isolated examples of public support for alternative spaces, the area became the most expensive district to live in Berlin (the average rent for an apartment in Mitte was 14.86 euros per square meter in 2016; the average in the whole city was 10.05 euros per square meter).[13] Within this context, places like the Haus Schwarzenberg have become sites of exception, embodying not only the memory and history of alternative culture in the *Wende*, but also new forms of resistance against urban commodification.

In some ways, alternative cultural centers are not completely out of place in Mitte today, as the district has a "cultural vocation," expressed in a dense array of institutions, activities, and events devoted to art, performance, education, history, religion, and entertainment. The Mitte houses major institutions such as the

8. Bodenschatz, *Berlin auf der Suche nach dem verlorenen Zentrum*, 181.
9. Jan Bauditz, "Aufbruch gegen Abriβ: Die Bürgerinitiative Spandauer Vorstadt," in Gesellschaft Hackesche Höfe e.V., ed., *Die Spandauer Vorstadt: Utopien und Realitäten zwischen Scheunenviertel und Friedrichstrasse* (Berlin: Argon, 1995), 47.
10. Senatsverwaltung für Stadtentwicklung und Umwelt, "Stadterneuerung–Mitte," http://www.stadtentwicklung.berlin.de/staedtebau/foerderprogramme/stadterneuerung/de/spandauer/index.shtml.
11. Feyerabend, *Quer durch Mitte*, 122.
12. Bodenschatz, *Berlin auf der Suche nach dem verlorenen Zentrum*, 181.
13. Data from the real estate website Wohnungsboerse.net, "Mietspiegel Berlin 2016," http://www.wohnungsboerse.net/mietspiegel-Berlin/2825.

German Historical Museum, the Märkisches Museum, the New Synagogue on Oranienburgerstraße, and the Volksbühne—not to mention the five major museums on Museum Island.[14] The Unter den Linden boulevard, a grand, tree-lined avenue linking Mitte to the western part of the city, is home to the State Opera (*Staatsoper*), Humboldt University, an outpost of the State Library (*Staatsbibliothek*), and several monuments, including the Brandenburg Gate. This cultural constellation forms a polished, well-kept landscape with state-of-the-art resources and facilities. Nothing of this is unusual for a city aspiring to be a global center of mass tourism and investment—the museums and performance halls of the New Berlin measure up to those of London, Paris, or Barcelona (just to name three European cities that underwent large-scale urban revamping since the 1980s). And the Mitte's cultural proclivities are not limited to public or nonprofit organizations. The district, especially the area known as Scheunenviertel along Auguststraße and surroundings, has also become a center of private upscale art galleries.

Alternative cultural centers fit at least programmatically within this context of cultural and art venues; in some cases, they also end up appropriated by capital and commerce as thrilling, exotic attractions. This may be the case—the Tacheles, for example, before its demise in 2012, had crossed into the mainstream both as a tourist attraction and as potential real estate investment, as will be discussed below. At the same time, alternative cultural centers still function as spaces for creation and exchange outside of the private market, harboring independent artists and experimental projects that would find no other room in Mitte, and displaying a rough architectural aesthetics quite different from the restored façades of the neighborhood. If alternative cultural centers indeed participate in the tourist and development economy of Mitte, at the same time they consciously, often fiercely oppose it, carving out spaces for socioeconomic difference and experimental practices. These two states—co-optation and opposition—coexist in an uneasy balance, fraught with internal criticism and external pressure.

The most obvious way in which these cultural centers stand out from their context is their physical state: they are rough and dilapidated, mixing architectural decay with new accretions such as posters and graffiti. In part, this rough appearance stems from a practical reason: run-down buildings are cheaper to rent, or easier to squat. But the dilapidation so proudly displayed in these sites is also a programmatic choice related to the main goals of each cultural center. The refusal to restore becomes a conscious opposition to gentrification and the commercialization of urban space that flooded central areas of East Berlin after unification. The display of material decay also hints at a complex representation of history, which incorporates the passage of time instead of stopping at one particular era.

---

14. The Museum Island (Museumsinsel) is a small island in the Spree River, which contains some of Berlin's most significant museums: the Alte Nationalgalerie (Old National Gallery), the Altes Museum (Old Museum), the Neues Museum (New Museum), the Pergamon Museum, and the Bode Museum.

In contrast, most buildings in Mitte have been modernized inside and out since 1989. The peeling paint and grimy surfaces, dark gray after decades of coal heating in East Berlin, have given way to smooth coats of fresh paint in pastel or vibrant colors. These generically restored buildings mingle with sharply designed contemporary structures that have smoothly filled the gaps in the urban fabric. The result is a district where most buildings blend into cohesive, well-groomed streetscapes. Some critics refer to this seemingly insatiable gentrification of Mitte as *Sanierungswut* (renovation rage), denoting the voracious hunger of developers to clean up and renovate. The term is all the more emphatic because of its history—it had been used in the 1980s and 1990s to refer pejoratively to the modernist urban renewal of historic neighborhoods. In the original context, *Sanierungswut* decried the loss of historical fabric to bulldozing and modernist housing blocks. Now, in what is only an apparent paradox, historical renovation takes the blame for the loss of history.[15]

One of the most successful commercial developments in the area, the Hackeschen Höfe, serves as a case study for the typical pattern of urban transformation in Mitte since unification. The Hackeschen Höfe is a large, early twentieth-century ensemble of courtyard buildings,[16] just across from the lively Hackescher Markt square and urban rail station. It has become a popular destination, with a Starbucks, a movie theater, an art gallery, restaurants, and trendy commerce. The investors who refurbished the building in the early 1990s restored the inner façades of the main courtyard to their *Jugendstil* splendor.[17] The façades had almost been removed in 1950, when, under the Socialist regime, housing and new construction took precedence over historical restoration; they were saved by the protesting efforts of the building's residents. The street façade was modernized in 1961, with no concern for preservation guidelines. It was only in 1977 that the building was placed under preservation protection. The building would not be restored, however, until after unification, thanks to a private developer. After ownership of the building was legally determined (it had been confiscated by the Nazis and then by the East German government), in 1994 the site was bought by two investors, from the West German cities of Heidelberg and Hamburg.[18] The pattern of contested

15. See Barbara Felsmann and Annett Gröschner, eds., *Durchgangszimmer Prenzlauer Berg* (Berlin: Lukas, 1999), 14; Martin Hildebrandt et al., *Kulturverführer Berlin* (Hamburg: Helmut Metz, 2005), 105. For the original use of the term—against modernist urban renewal—see Jochen Boberg, Tilman Fichter, and Eckhart Gillen, eds., *Industriekultur in Berlin* (C. H. Beck, 1986), 2: 373.

16. It was built in 1906. Peter Schubert, *Die Hackeschen Höfe: Geschichte und Geschichten einer Lebenswelt in der Mitte Berlins* (Berlin: Argon, 1993), 49, 61.

17. The façade and other spaces in the complex were designed by August Endell. See Tiziana Romelli, *Eine Spaziergang durch die Hackeschen Höfe: Ethnographische Erkundungen eines neuen urbanen Ortes* (Berlin: Lit, 2002), 30–31.

18. "Hackesche Höfe History," Die Hackeschen Höfe, http://www.hackesche-hoefe.com/?page=24; "Hackesche Höfe, Berlin," Witte Project Management, http://www.witte-projektmanagement.de/projekte/hackesche-hoefe/; Romelli, *Eine Spaziergang*, 23–24.

ownership, followed by purchase by West German investors, and then restoration and commercial redevelopment, is typical for Mitte.

The restoration of the Hackeschen Höfe, and its transformation into a mixed-use, historical-looking shopping and entertainment complex, are but one example of the type of private development that thrived after 1989. Such developments did not happen simply as a result of marketplace forces, but were courted and supported by public policies and *Sanierungsgebiet* designations that had a very concrete impact on architectural forms—an impact that was premeditated and which, according to Florian Urban, stemmed from the fact that the urban planning policies themselves were based on images and "picture postcards of urbanity" rather than socioeconomic or demographic data typical of large-scale urban planning.[19]

These public policies had affected the city since Hans Stimmann's ideas of Critical Reconstruction were first proposed in West Berlin (see chapter 1). In 1999, these policies gained the force of law as the Berlin department for city planning (then called Senatsverwaltung für Stadtentwicklung, Umweltschutz und Technologie) approved the Planwerk Innenstadt, which had first been presented in 1996.[20] As Urban notes, the Planwerk was conceived through a process of "thinking in pictures," based on an antimodernist vision that tried to recover the "prewar street layer of Berlin's inner city" through mixed uses, public transportation, walkability, small-scale public spaces, and streets framed by a look of historical integrity.[21] Urban lists the many criticisms thrown at the Planwerk: it produced an idealized version of history, it served gentrifying commercial interests while paying lip service to social diversity, and it "cast one particular moment in history into perennial authority," among many other problems.[22] This particular moment—the nineteenth century—privileged certain forms, such as the boulevard and the interior courtyard (*Hof*), detaching these forms from their previous lived realities and glossing over their history (such as the history of squalor and inequality in courtyard tenement buildings).

For Urban, "the problematic nature of the Berlin master plan for the inner city can be summarized by the fact that its authors were caught up in a series of powerful images, which they chose to reproduce instead of consciously debating them." Crucially, Urban does not argue that images as such should not factor into contemporary urban thought—he acknowledges them as inevitable, a "condition that [architects and planners] have to face and work with" critically.[23] The visual has become more

---

19. Florian Urban, "Picture Postcards of Urbanity," *Journal of Architectural Education* 57, no. 1 (2003): 68.

20. Senatsverwaltung für Stadtentwicklung und Umwelt, "Archiv: Planwerk Innenstadt—Planungsprozess," http://www.stadtentwicklung.berlin.de/planen/planwerke/de/planwerk_innenstadt/planungsprozess/.

21. Urban, "Picture Postcards," 68–69.

22. Ibid., 68–71.

23. Ibid., 73, 72.

than a way to depict cities or disseminate information about them. Increasingly, the visual *is* the way in which buildings and cities are experienced. Hal Foster suggests that much of contemporary architecture (especially the starchitecture of celebrity architects such as Rem Koolhaas and Frank Gehry) only becomes fully legible in aerial views and perfectly angled photographs, as their figurative allusions or iconic shapes cannot be read "at ground level"; he posits that "media reproduction . . . is a primary site of such architecture."[24] Foster (on architecture) and Urban (on urban planning) are aligned in their view that visual culture is not just a means of representing the built environment, but a means of experiencing and producing it.

The emphasis on the visual privileges surface, staged views, and prescribed viewpoints, as a result pushing aside multiple, contradictory, and possibly conflicting social realities. As Urban argues, the city produced by the Planwerk Innenstadt does not easily accommodate diverse social groups and plural historical narratives. It is not a surprise that such smoothed-out urbanity has proven popular and commercially successful among tourists and Berlin inhabitants, through developments such as the Hackeschen Höfe.[25] Such environments are easily marketed, and just as easily consumed. As Andreas Huyssen notes, the "current discourse of the city as image is one of 'city fathers,' developers, and politicians trying to increase revenue from mass tourism, conventions, and office or commercial space."[26] It is also not a surprise that such spaces have elicited criticism for their pasteurized version of history and commercialism.

Take the Rosenhöfe commercial complex, for example, which sits just a few buildings down from the Hackeschen Höfe on Rosenthaler Straße. The renovation of the Rosenhöfe was done by architect Hinrich Baller, known for whimsical and ornamented designs evocative of art nouveau. His earlier residential complexes in the neighborhoods of Kreuzberg and Schöneberg responded to a context of cultural and visual diversity, and ended up well integrated into the urban landscape and social life of their neighborhoods. The Rosenhöfe complex, however, coated in creamy pink paint and decorated with curlicued railings, substitutes saccharine commercialism for context. Berlin architecture critic Ulrike Steglich, reporting on the newly renovated Rosenhöfe in 2003, called it "shoddily executed, pretentious kitsch" and "a nightmare in dusty pink and turquoise."[27] Steglich, a chronicler of everyday life in Mitte since unification, is clearly sympathetic to the district's pregentrification identity and history. She turns her critique from the Rosenhöfe to its

---

24. Hal Foster, "Image Building," *The Art-Architecture Complex* (London and New York: Verso, 2011), 14.

25. Urban, "Picture Postcards," 71.

26. Andreas Huyssen, *Present Pasts: Urban Palimpsests and the Politics of Memory* (Stanford, CA: Stanford University Press, 2002), 50.

27. Ulrike Steglich, "'Herrlisch!'—Neueste Errungenschaften am Hackeschen Markt," Stadt.plan. mitte, April 10, 2003. The website does not exist anymore, but the page can be seen as a screenshot in the Internet Archive Wayback Machine at https://web.archive.org/web/20030628031031/http://www.stadt-plan-mitte.de/index/587/.

even flashier neighbor, the Hackeschen Höfe, and finally to the alternative Haus Schwarzenberg, which sits dissonantly between the two:

> One walks through the Rosenhöfe as the incarnation of the new millenium's per-verted fantasies of a storybook town, and then one enters the Hackeschen Höfe, ren-ovated in the middle of the 1990s . . . and . . . already a farce with its empty claim to recreate the erstwhile "Berlin mixture." Leaving these stage-sets and going back on Rosenthaler Straße, one swings into the building on number 39, which is jammed be-tween the previous two. There one finds a building complex where actual history—especially from the last century—is still legible: the Haus Schwarzenberg.[28]

Steglich's preferences clearly lie with the mission and aesthetics of the Haus Schwar-zenberg, which she upholds as a last bastion of authenticity thanks to the design and preservation choices made by the building occupants—their use of counterpreserva-tion. If Steglich glimpses the potential for critical dissonance and the experience of "actual history" in the Haus Schwarzenberg's decayed spaces, Urban argues that the adoption of decrepitude, which he discusses through the examples of the Tacheles and the KuLe, is just as much a case of idealized "thinking in pictures" as the Planwerk Innenstadt—only this time, idealized pictures of alternative culture.[29] I will engage Urban's argument later in this chapter, as it has important implications for my discus-sion of counterpreservation; but first, I will examine the Haus Schwarzenberg in de-tail, in order to probe its claims to authentic representation and cultural legitimacy.

The Haus Schwarzenberg

Small, cramped, and minimally restored, the Haus Schwarzenberg announces itself on Rosenthaler Straße by displaying the old lettering of a long-gone com-mercial tenant: Gebr. Majanz (the Majanz brothers). In 2009 the street façade was cleaned of the grime and soot that had covered it for most of the twentieth century, but the cleaning was discreet, and the façade is still muted in light-gray stone—a much dowdier building than its glossy and colorful neighbors. The building dates from the nineteenth century,[30] and occupies a cramped, irregular plot with a

---

28. Ibid. "Berlin mixture" refers to the mixed uses found in traditional neighborhoods, where the nineteenth-century apartment buildings also house commerce, services, and even factories. Sometimes called *bunte Mischung* (colorful mixture), it alludes to a vibrant and diverse street life.

29. Urban, "Postcard Pictures," 71–72.

30. Surviving documents mention a building on the same site as early as 1769, although the struc-ture was much smaller. Successive renovations throughout the nineteenth and early twentieth centuries enlarged the front wing and added side and back wings. In the 1920s the neoclassical ornamentation of the façade (which had been added in an 1864 renovation) was removed, giving the façade its plain appearance—much less decorated than buildings from the same era. Dates for constructions, renova-tions, and additions differ depending on the source. See Frank Eckart, *Fundstücke: Die Verborgene(n) Geschichte(n) des Hauses Rosenthaler Strasse 39* (Berlin: Anne Frank Zentrum, 2004), 12–13, 17; and Landesdenkmalamt Berlin, "Gutachten zur Denkmaleigenschaft: Rosenthaler Straße 39, Fabrikflügel mit ehem. Bürstenfabrik in Berlin-Mitte," printed document number LDA D 22, June 25, 1999.

narrow street front. The five-story façade (counting the attic) has very little ornamentation and molding. On the ground floor, the small Café Cinema takes up the
left side, and to the right a dark passageway leads into the first courtyard, with its
spectacularly decayed façade: exposed wires, crumbling walls, overgrown ivy, graffiti (fig. 9). A long wing of the building extends along this courtyard, at the end of

Figure 9. Haus Schwarzenberg, first courtyard (2009).
© Daniela Sandler

which there is a small, perpendicular wing, and yet another passageway leading onto the second courtyard. There is also a small, third courtyard beyond the second. In the first courtyard, in addition to open-air seating for the café, there are two museums: the Anne Frank Center, and the Otto Weidt Blind Workshop and Silent Heroes Memorial (two interconnected exhibitions), all of which will be explored in more detail below. In the second courtyard, there are the Kino Central (a cinema devoted to independent films), the Club Eschloraque, and the Dead Chickens art project and space. A mechanical metal sculpture, part of the Dead Chickens project, sometimes fills the courtyard with clanging noises when someone sets it in motion. In a corner, a small doorway and narrow staircase lead up to the Neurotitan gallery, a large exhibition space devoted to "painting, illustration, comic-book and urban art," and which often features the work of young or unknown artists.[31] In addition to these venues, the Haus Schwarzenberg also contains artists' studios, fashion and design stores, and a bookstore.

The Haus Schwarzenberg takes its name from its main tenant, the Schwarzenberg association, founded in 1995 by a group of artists.[32] They never squatted the building; from the start, they were there as legal tenants, renting most of the available space. In this respect the Schwarzenberg association is different from most of the other alternative cultural projects in Mitte in the early 1990s, which squatted buildings rather than leasing them. This is the case with the Tacheles, the Schokoladen, and the KuLe, all of which began as squats in 1990—the Schokoladen in a derelict, semi-vacant residential building on Ackerstraße; the Tacheles in the condemned ruins of the former Friedrichstraßenpassage on Oranienburgerstraße (an early twentieth-century shopping arcade); and the KuLe on Auguststraße.[33] Henryk Weiffenbach, one of the founding members of the Schwarzenberg association, explained this partly as a function of their main goal: securing a site for alternative art and creative practices.[34] This concern with stability and security was to allow for long-term projects without the distraction of confrontations. In addition, the other three art centers mentioned here were founded at the height of post-Wall squatting in 1990, before police crackdowns and the allocation of property to legal owners made it almost impossible to squat a building, much less to remain in it for any considerable period of time. However, despite the Schwarzenberg association's desire to create a safe haven for art production and experimentation, it would end up facing the threat of eviction and a lengthy dispute with prospective developers.

The dilapidated appearance of the buildings of all four cultural centers mentioned above is typical of preunification East Berlin. During the whole existence of

---

31. "Das Haus," Haus Schwarzenberg, http://www.haus-schwarzenberg.org/haus-schwarzenberg-und-seine-mieter/das-haus.

32. The cooperative is officially recognized in the legal form of a "registered association"—in German, *eingetragener Verein* or *e.V.* The official name of the association is Schwarzenberg e.V.

33. Schoko-Laden e.V., "Projektvorstellung," unpublished document, 2010, [3]; Heike Stuckert, "Tacheles: 'To Speak Clearly,'" *Drama Review* 36, no. 1 (Spring 1991): 169.

34. Henryk Weiffenbach, interview, June 2010.

Figure 10. Udo Hesse, *Zionskirchstraße, East-Berlin, 1981.*
© Udo Hesse

the GDR, most of East Berlin was coated in grime from coal heating and air pollution; chips, dents, and bullet marks punctuated the landscape of run-down façades. Vacant lots and empty spaces were common. This frozen-in-time landscape lives on in period photographs, films, and texts about the city before 1989, such as Udo Hesse's evocative black-and-white photos of East Berlin (fig. 10). Today it can be difficult to conjure up such a sight, when one stands on "postcard-picture" streets lined by spotless façades. The Haus Schwarzenberg is one of the last structures in Mitte to incarnate this spatial memory. In the words of a 2007 report by the Berlin Preservation Council (*Landesdenkmalrat*): "The building is the only one in its immediate surroundings . . . to have preserved the historic aura of the pre-*Wende* era and the post-*Wende* phase, formed by decades of neglect and spontaneous artistic appropriations."[35]

While in most renovated buildings, interior wings were torn down to make wider, light-filled courtyards, the Haus Schwarzenberg keeps the labyrinthine, cramped feel of these spaces. The courtyards are crisscrossed by open-air electrical wiring, covered in graffiti and growing weeds, old signs and lighting fixtures, dark

---

35. Manfred Kühne, "Protokoll: Beschlüsse des Landesdenkmalrats Berlin," April 20, 2007, 2, http://www.stadtentwicklung.berlin.de/denkmal/landesdenkmalrat/de/beschluesse/download/beschluss_ldr_20070420.pdf.

Figure 11. Haus Schwarzenberg, first courtyard, detail (2004).
© Daniela Sandler

metallic sculptures, and posters (fig. 11). Most renovations in the Haus Schwarzenberg were limited to basic infrastructure, heating, and emergency structural repairs. Overall, the Haus looks obstinately unkempt. Onto the grime and gloom from the preunification years, the Schwarzenberg members added layers of new interventions, from murals and window paintings to sculptures. Public areas such as stairwells and passageways have a kaleidoscopic quality, covered by the sediment of juxtaposed posters, tags, and graffiti built up over two decades. This is also the case with the other cultural centers mentioned here.

As I argued in chapter 1, counterpreservation is a self-reflective form of preservation. Those whose practices I call counterpreservation—architects, planners, artists, squatters, tenant cooperatives—are so concerned with the passage of time and its imprint on the built environment that they reject any single fixed form or moment. The Haus Schwarzenberg cultural center provides an exemplary illustration. The weathering, disintegrating façades display the whole life of the building. The façade's masonry and crumbling plaster hint at the cheap construction materials of most apartment buildings in Berlin from the beginning of the twentieth century. The building's precarious aspect also evokes the lack of embellishment and maintenance during the economic troubles of the Weimar Republic. The grime and missing fragments recall the bombings of World War II, when parts of the building burned or collapsed. The façade also tells of the disinterest in historical architecture during most of the GDR era, when similar buildings were left in disrepair.[36] The marred surfaces have a kinetic quality, as if the building were constantly, slowly, imperceptibly changing—a process not visible to the naked eye, but suggested as a latent promise endlessly whispered by the decomposing walls.

The counterpreservation of the Haus Schwarzenberg resonates with Henri Pierre Jeudy's description of ruined sites as dynamic and open. For Jeudy, ruins and their "aesthetics of abandon" provide a more open-ended relationship with the past, one that engages and captivates visitors through exploration, speculation, and contemplative reflection—as opposed to museums, where historical narratives are neatly spelled out with no gaps to fill. This is also in line with John Ruskin's apologia of the weathered quality of old buildings and their inimitable patina—an "aura" given not by uniqueness or artistic genius, but by time.[37]

But the façade and spaces of the Haus Schwarzenberg do not show only decay. There are also signs of vibrant new life: the movie theater signboard announcing current movies at the Central Cinema, the bright-red neon lettering of the Café Cinema, the plaques marking the entrance to the museums and art galleries, the constant traffic of people, the sediment of posters and announcements on the walls. These signs speak of reunification, the flourishing of alternative cultures, and resistance to real estate speculation. This combination of disparate material signifiers is a rich, if muddled, historical evocation.

The Haus Schwarzenberg retains traces from the past even as it is transformed by new interventions. Two related ideas intertwine here: one, the layering of histories (not always visible); two, the successive inscription of new narratives that only partially obscure earlier ones. The second idea has become its own Berlin trope: the palimpsest. Both concepts are by now ingrained in the scholarship on Berlin, after their use by two influential scholars on the city. Brian Ladd structured his book *Ghosts of Berlin* around the idea of layers, describing Berlin's multiple historic identities: the Wall, "Old Berlin," "Metropolis," "Nazi Berlin," "Divided Berlin," and "Capital of the New Germany."[38] And Huyssen described Berlin as a city of juxtaposed narratives, whose signs (visual, textual, symbolic) speak alongside and over each other, overlapping, jumping to the foreground, obscuring others,

36. Greg Engle, "Ruinous Charm: The Culture and Politics of Redevelopment in Eastern Berlin" (PhD diss., University of Wisconsin, Madison, 2009); Bettina Reiman, "The Transition from People's Property to Private Property," *Applied Geography* 17, no. 4 (1997): 305; Ulrike Steglich, "Die Wohnungen, die Menschen, der Markt: Stadtentwicklung in Prenzlauer Berg," in *Prenzlauer Berg im Wandel der Geschichte: Leben rund um den Helmholtzplatz*, ed. Bernt Roder and Bettina Tacke (Berlin: be.bra, 2004), 198–222.

37. Henri-Pierre Jeudy, *Mémoires du social* (Paris: Presses Universitaires de France, 1986), 149–54; John Ruskin, "The Lamp of Memory," Aphorism 31, in *The Seven Lamps of Architecture* (New York: Thomas Y. Crowell, 1880), 256.

38. Brian Ladd, *Ghosts of Berlin: Confronting German History in the Urban Landscape* (Chicago: University of Chicago Press, 1997).

disappearing.[39] The view of Berlin as a city where traces of the past are deposited over each other as microgeological strata resonates because of the particularly intense, extreme nature of the city's history (many cities in the world, after all, have developed through accretions and layers, but they are not all celebrated for this to the same extent as Berlin—or Rome, for that matter).

The idea of the palimpsest is related but not identical to the concept of multi-layering. The original meaning of palimpsest indicates a material, or substratum, over which text is written and then erased so that new text can be written; in the process, traces of the original remain, as they can never be fully effaced. I restate this well-known meaning here in order to stress that a palimpsest is not simply about layering—a palimpsest is neither a collage nor a sedimentary rock. The palimpsest is defined precisely by the constant process of erasure and rewriting, scraping and reinscription. In the palimpsest, the sense of destruction, of loss and forgetting, is as important as the sense of endurance, of vestigial or spectral memory.[40]

Huyssen underscores this duality as he notes the incessant and destructive transformation of Berlin through war, postwar urban renewal, the building of the Wall, and postunification rebuilding. He decries contemporary policies and designs that elide historical periods (Critical Reconstruction's implicit hatred of Weimar-era modernism; unified Germany's targeted destruction of GDR-era structures)—a condition that he identifies as dominant in the reconstruction of the city since 1989. Huyssen puts up resistance to such erasures in the form of his own labors as a literary critic "attracted to the notion of the city as a text,"[41] from which he plucks and unravels narratives, some still visible (such as Nazi-era buildings), some meaningful precisely because of their absence (the spatial, social, and cultural voids of the city, from the former no-man's-land along the Wall to the extermination of the prewar Jewish community). He also hails a few projects as responsive to both the tangles and the gaps in the palimpsest, notably Daniel Libeskind's Jewish Museum and his unbuilt proposals for Alexanderplatz and Potsdamer Platz. But most of the New Berlin, for him, forecloses such historical prospections while reducing contemporary urban life to consumerism—whether in the restored fabric of Mitte or in the new corporate buildings of Potsdamer Platz and Friedrichstraße.

The Haus Schwarzenberg, along with most examples of counterpreservation in this book, lives up to the idea of historical layering. As such, it does justice to Berlin as a city whose complicated history cannot be reduced to a single, neat narrative, and where the threads are not yet all untangled—a city where there might still be new meanings to discover, as well as room for building new forms alongside the old

---

39. Huyssen, *Present Pasts*, 72–84.

40. For a similar use of the concept of an urban palimpsest, see Benedito Lima de Toledo, *São Paulo: Três cidades em um século* (São Paulo: Duas Cidades, 1980); and Peter Gunn, *Naples: A Palimpsest* (London: Chapman and Hall, 1961).

41. Huyssen, *Present Pasts*, 57.

ones (a key difference from preservation, where old meanings are preserved, and new forms proscribed). However, the Haus Schwarzenberg and most examples of counterpreservation do not fit so easily within the idea of the palimpsest, where erasure and destruction are constitutive; in fact, in most cases counterpreservation stubbornly resists erasure. The counterpreservationist strategy is one of sedimentary accretion and collage without deletion. The gaps in counterpreserved buildings were already there before the squatters and artists arrived; if they embrace such gaps, it does not mean they create new ones. The one exception is Daniel Libeskind's Project Mo✗rning, for a site of former SS barracks in Oranienburg, which is the focus of the next chapter. There, the slow disappearance of ruined barracks is part of the design—a critical appropriation of the palimpsest, turned around in the service of remembrance as opposed to forgetting.

If the Haus Schwarzenberg presents itself as an open-ended, ever-growing layering of history, it does not treat all periods with the same deference. The state of disrepair so prominent in the building's exterior evokes life in the GDR, while the dedication of prime space to the Otto Weidt Blind Workshop Museum and the Anne Frank Center foregrounds the Nazi era (Otto Weidt was the German owner of a brush and broom workshop located in the building who protected blind and deaf Jews during the Third Reich).[42] In a text describing the significance of the building, published on its website for much of the 2000s, the Schwarzenberg association named these periods of interest, stating: "In the Haus Schwarzenberg, the early and recent history of the neighborhood is not simply depicted, but can be experienced in a living context: the expulsion and extermination of European Jews between 1933 and 1945; the division and reunification of Germany."[43]

The Schwarzenberg association wants the building to be a "piece of living history," as it put it in a text in English pasted on the walls of the building in 2004 during a fund-raising campaign to avoid eviction. The implication is that the "historic" does not lie in the idealized candy-colored façades of restored buildings, but in the gritty state of a decayed construction. The sanitized Mitte tells the history of unification, commodification, and globalization; the Haus Schwarzenberg tells instead the history of multiple traumas, as well as multiple possibilities for present and future hope. The association aligns itself with the civil courage of figures like Otto Weidt, but notes that memorializing this history does not preclude novel and experimental uses. "There is no contradiction between a site of memory, and a site of avant-garde art," it asserts, alluding to the contemporary art featured in the

42. *Blindes Vertrauen: Versteckt am Hackeschen Markt 1941–1943,* exhibition catalogue (Berlin: Haus Schwarzenberg, 1998).

43. "Haus Schwarzenberg: Ein Fenster in die Geschichte Berlins," Haus Schwarzenberg, http://www.haus-schwarzenberg.org/republik/haus.html. This text has since been taken down, but can be found in the Internet Archive Wayback Machine at https://web.archive.org/web/20100408030016/http://www.haus-schwarzenberg.org/republik/haus.html. The pamphlet *15 Jahre: Haus Schwarzenberg, Berlin-Mitte,* published in 2010, phrases the same idea in different words, on p. 15.

Neurotitan gallery, and produced in the building's many studios.[44] The Schwarzenberg association reverses the cliché about learning lessons from history before acting in the present. Instead, the association suggests that one first needs to have a project for the future before dwelling in the past: "Without visions for the present and the future, all remembrance is pure pose. . . . The Schwarzenbergers draw hopes for the future from brave men such as Otto Weidt. . . . The utopia lives on!"[45] The last sentence is a reference to the origins of the name Schwarzenberg, which I will now explain, as it elucidates not only the original goals of the association as reflected in the building, but also its present significance.

East Germany

The name of the Haus Schwarzenberg stems from the Republik Schwarzenberg, an independent state created by Stefan Heym in his 1984 novel, *Schwarzenberg*.[46] Heym's fictitious republic was inspired by facts: after the end of the war, the German town of Schwarzenberg and the area around it remained unoccupied by Allied forces for forty-two days—newly free from Nazism, not yet occupied by either the Soviet Union or American troops. In the absence of an external or higher government authority, the inhabitants had to organize themselves.[47] In Heym's novel this becomes the chance to realize a utopian community, autonomous and so not subject to an authoritarian regime, and based on social justice and solidarity. The choice of name for the Haus Schwarzenberg brings up parallels between 1945 and 1989, when the fall of the Wall left East Germany free from the GDR dictatorship, and not yet occupied by capitalism. Like the Schwarzenberg inhabitants at the end of the war, East Germans faced a situation of uncertainty and lack of definition. An authoritarian regime had just ended; people enjoyed a newly discovered freedom; a whole society, turned upside down, needed to be rebuilt. This situation of seeming openness harbored the potential for starting anew, and, for those with hopes of a better society, the potential for "getting it right" this time: for finally realizing the ideals of equality and justice that the East German Socialist state had betrayed, and which were not perceived as present in the West German capitalist democracy. The Schwarzenberg association drew parallels with Heym's utopian republic by claiming for itself a space of exception and self-determination.[48]

---

44. Schwarzenberg e.V., "Gegenwart und Zukunft," Haus Schwarzenberg, http://haus-schwarzenberg.org/schwarzenberg-e-v/gegenwart-und-zukunft.

45. Ibid.

46. Stefan Heym, *Schwarzenberg: Roman* (Munich: Bertelsmann, 1984). On the inspiration for the Schwarzenberg association, see *15 Jahre: Haus Schwarzenberg,* 10, 24; and Jens Uthoff, "Dass wir noch da sind, ist schon ein Statement," *Taz.de*, April 11, 2015, http://www.taz.de/1/archiv/digitaz/artikel/?res sort=bl&dig=2015%2F04%2F11%2Fa0140&cHash=05a0ebe6fe3223e6f649aa9fa68e8b6a.

47. Lenore Lobeck, *Die Schwarzenberg-Utopie* (Leipzig: Evangelische Verlagsanstalt, 2004).

48. Ulrike Steglich, "Zum ersten, zum zweiten, zum dritten," in *15 Jahre: Haus Schwarzenberg,* 10.

The Haus Schwarzenberg political project resonates with the social movements that animated and brought about the *Wende*—the period of transition around the fall of the Berlin Wall and German unification. These social movements started out in the mid-1980s as localized protests of intellectuals, writers, and Protestant preachers.[49] Inspired by Mikhail Gorbachev's political and economic liberalization (*perestroika* and *glasnost*), and by signs of democratization elsewhere in Eastern Europe, the opposition to the East German regime demanded political opening. The members of this movement did not necessarily oppose the idea of economic Socialism. They were strongly against the repressive East German government, which imposed censorship, surveillance, travel restrictions, indoctrination, and punishments. While other governments behind the Iron Curtain gradually eased out similar policies, East Germany's repressive stance persisted. In addition, the country's once model Socialist economy had stagnated throughout the 1980s, in part because of obsolete infrastructure and inefficient management, which helped spread discontent among growing sectors of the population.

Protests, strikes, and demonstrations against the government, which started in Dresden and Leipzig, drew hundreds of thousands of people toward the end of 1989. The movement became known as "Peaceful Revolution" or "Silent Revolution," culminating in the fall of the Wall on November 9, 1989. While many East Germans were eager to visit the West and captivated by its material opulence, those who had initiated the movement did not necessarily want to substitute democratic capitalism for authoritarian Socialism. Rather, many wanted "Socialism with a human face," democratic Socialism, a third way. They talked about freedom and self-determination, not unification with the West.[50] But they were not the majority. One of the first political events of their newly democratic state was a plebiscite, in which most East Germans voted for unification with West Germany and the adoption of West German capitalism.

The project of the Haus Schwarzenberg carries on the initial goals of the Silent Revolution as a claim for independent social reconstruction. In the face of the partial defeat of these goals through unification, the Haus Schwarzenberg acquires a second significance: as a site of resistance. Entrenched in the confines of the narrow, tortuous building, the Haus Schwarzenberg resists the encroaching forces of gentrification and commodification. This insular, anticapitalist, and utopian stance echoes the history of the western district of Kreuzberg and the eastern district of Prenzlauer Berg in the years of division. In this way, the Haus Schwarzenberg also connects with the local histories of Berlin, particularly with the city's entrenched oppositional attitudes.

---

49. Bernd Gehrke and Wolfgang Rüddenklau, *Das war doch nicht unsere Alternative: DDR-Oppositionelle zehn Jahre nach der Wende* (Münster: Westfälisches Dampfboot, 1999).

50. Ibid.

As argued above, the Haus Schwarzenberg must be understood in relation to the Peaceful Revolution and the *Wende*, both of which mark the final stage in the history of the GDR. This history has been the focus of intense interest on the part of academics and the public in general. Conferences, publications, and courses have dealt with all aspects of life under the Socialist regime, from film to consumption. In 2003, the exhibition Art in the GDR drew a steady stream of visitors to the New National Gallery in Berlin. There are several public and private museums devoted to aspects of life in the GDR—from everyday material culture to the workings of the Stasi.[51] Popular interest is manifest in movies dealing with the period (*The Lives of Others*, *Sonnenallee, Goodbye, Lenin!*) and in TV programs, from documentaries to variety shows (e.g., *The GDR Show*, broadcast by the RTL TV network, and the *Ostalgie Show*, by the ZDF network).[52] There was even talk of a planned GDR theme park.[53] Products related to East Germany abound, including food, games, and cosmetics.

This phenomenon has been called *Ostalgie*: "nostalgia for the East (*Ost*)." *Ostalgie* is a multivalent confluence of social currents, often contradictory.[54] East Germans suffer from homesickness for the country where they grew up, where they built their lives and social networks, their modes of being and cultural references. While this land, geographically, has not moved, it has transformed itself drastically in the time since unification. This homesickness is inseparable from disappointment with unification and capitalism. While certain sectors of the East German population have quickly adapted, especially younger ones, others have felt alienated by the social and economic changes; they feel they were given short shrift by the process. The prospect of wealth, abundant consumer goods, and freedom in 1989 was gradually tempered by the perception of insecurity, marginalization, and loss of welfare benefits.

---

51. The exhibition ran in the Neue Nationalgalerie from July 25 to October 26, 2003. Public and private museums include the Dokumentationszentrum Alltagskultur der DDR in the town of Eisenhüttenstadt, the DDR Museum in Berlin, the DDR Museum Zeitreise (Timetravel) in the Dresden suburb of Radebeul, the Zeitgeschichtliches Forum in Leipzig, and the DDR-Museum in Auerstedt. There are also museums devoted to specific aspects, such as the Stasi Museum and the Memorial Foundation at the Hohenschönhausen Political Prison in Berlin.

52. The website of the magazine *Stern* had a section listing GDR shows and related programs under the title "DDR Revival: Ostalgie im Fernsehen," now archived in the Internet Archive Wayback Machine at https://web.archive.org/web/20140106073409/http://www.stern.de/kultur/film/ddr-revival-ostalgie-im-fernsehen-512223.html. A critic spoke of a "wave of GDR shows" in the second decade after unification (see "TV-Moderatoren lassen Kritik nicht auf sich sitzen," *Stern.de*, http://www.stern.de/kultur/film/ddr-shows-tv-moderatoren-lassen-kritik-nicht-auf-sich-sitzen-3517942.html).

53. Paul Smith and Ken Taylor, *German Secrets: Achtung to Zeitgeist* (Munich: PSA International, 2009), 55.

54. On *Ostalgie*, see Paul Cooke, *Representing East Germany since Unification: From Colonization to Nostalgia* (Oxford: Berg, 2005); Daphne Berda, *On the Social Life of Postsocialism: Memory, Consumption, Germany* (Bloomington: Indiana University Press, 2010); Paul Betts, "The Twilight of the Idols: East German Memory and Material Culture," *Journal of Modern History* 72, no. 3 (September 2000): 731–65; Roger Hillman, "Goodbye Lenin (2003): History in the Subjunctive," *Rethinking History* 10, no. 2 (June 2006): 221–37; Mélanie van der Hoorn, "Consuming the 'Platte' in East Berlin: The New Popularity of Former GDR Architecture," *Home Cultures* 1, no. 2 (2004): 89–126.

Ostalgie is not a longing for the dictatorship, ideological indoctrination, censorship, and spying. Neither is it a longing for Socialism per se, although many people report missing the sense of security and camaraderie formed in a system without the competitiveness of the private market. *Ostalgie* is rather a fond memory of everyday life, personal experiences, and material culture. These memories are idealized, minimizing oppressive aspects of the Socialist regime. This idealization is encapsulated in a scene in *Goodbye, Lenin!* (2003), where the main character, Alex, admits that the East Germany he longed for and lovingly recreated had never existed, except as an ideal and perfect state in his and his mother's minds.

Westerners also participate in *Ostalgie*—in this case, it might be explained as the curiosity for the exotic. Despite the contiguity of East and West Germany, transit to the East was a bureaucratic, time-consuming affair (and also costly, as the East German government imposed a mandatory minimum currency exchange that had to be spent during one's visit), and not every West German who tried to cross the border was granted entry. *Ostalgie* puts this previously inaccessible country within reach. The products, programs, and events of *Ostalgie* transform the former experience of visiting the "other" Germany—a multidimensional, often unsettling venture—into decontextualized nuggets of information and sensation. It is alterity, only pasteurized and wrapped for easy consumption.

The Haus Schwarzenberg's self-conscious attempt to display GDR history through the evocation of its cityscape is *not* one more manifestation of *Ostalgie*. While *Ostalgie* is a complex phenomenon, it is often (if not always or exclusively) marked by historical detachment. This detachment stems not simply from the nostalgic idealization of life in East Germany, but perhaps more significantly because *Ostalgie* seems to focus on distractions—elements associated with consumption and entertainment. Florena skin cream, Halloren chocolate truffles, and Spreewald pickles, once produced and consumed in the GDR, are now back in production and marketed as little tastes of East German life. They share shelf space with new creations, such as memory card games, board games, paper models of buildings, and clothing articles displaying the GDR acronym in German: DDR. All of these items are ready-made, store-bought tokens for memory, and they are counterparts to the documentaries and TV shows where current celebrities affectionately reminisce about how much fun they had at Pioneer camp or during *Jugendweihe* (the secular initiation of teenagers into adulthood encouraged in the GDR in lieu of religious confirmation). Like the gift shop in a high-profile museum, this collection of memorabilia—found on websites with names such as Ostprodukte and Osthits, in tourist gift shops, and in trendy or offbeat stores—boils down the complexity of everyday life and material culture in East Germany to trinkets that aestheticize historical experience and banalize it at the same time.[55]

---

55. Ostprodukte, www.ostprodukte.de; Osthits, www.osthits.de (Osthits, which collected information on East Germany, does not exist anymore, but snapshots can be seen in the Internet Archive Wayback Machine at https://web.archive.org/web/20130828130002/http://www.osthits.de/).

The Haus Schwarzenberg's approach to East German history is different. The desire to maintain a trace of the physical landscape of the GDR is not propelled by idealization, but by the recognition of a complicated past that at the same time harbored the promise of a different, better future. The Haus Schwarzenberg displays a dilapidated urban landscape as it was, evoking aspects of life under the GDR that were connected to this urban decay: the difficult place of "history" in official discourse; the precarious living standards of a large part of the population; and the social practices and alternative cultures that developed precisely because older urban areas were neglected by the government. The Haus Schwarzenberg's mixture of utopian idealism and artistic experimentation, as well as the communitarian feel of its cooperative structure, harkens back to the stories of resistance and community associated with "alternative" social groups in the GDR, and points to the unrealized utopia of the Peaceful Revolution. If there is nostalgia in the Haus Schwarzenberg, it is the utopian and productive kind described by Svetlana Boym (see chapter 1).

Mietskasernen

If the first impression of the Haus Schwarzenberg brings up the landscape of East Berlin under the GDR, the building also evokes other threads, which, as Huyssen argues, can be unspooled and read as texts. One of these threads leads to the *Mietskasernen,* the apartment buildings that made up the bulk of Berlin's urban fabric in the nineteenth and early twentieth centuries.[56] The history of *Mietskasernen* is incarnated in the body of the Haus Schwarzenberg building. However, representing the history of *Mietskasernen* is not a simple matter. The perception of *Mietskasernen* in contemporary Berlin is shaped by a romanticized version of life in nineteenth-century European metropolises. Locals and tourists covet the beautifully restored *Altbauwohnungen* (old apartments), which are the dwelling units of Berlin's *Mietskasernen*. Historians and urban planners wax nostalgic about the harmonious beauty of the nineteenth-century cityscape. However, this attitude ignores that the beautiful streets lined with ornate façades, behind which lie spacious apartments with high ceilings and hardwood floors, are a product of contemporary urbanism, preservation, and economics, rather than "purely historic" objects that reach us straight from the past.

The *Mietskasernen* of yore were a jumble of tiny apartments, most of which lacked even minimal ventilation, sanitation, natural light, and private bathrooms. Collective toilets were located in outhouses in the courtyards, or in public hallways. Tenants piled up in cramped single-room apartments where all the different functions of daily life coexisted—cooking, eating, sleeping, making love, rearing

---

56. Harald Bodenschatz, *Platz frei für das neue Berlin: Geschichte der Stadterneuerung in der "grössten Mietskasernenstadt der Welt" seit 1871* (Berlin: Transit, 1987); Ladd, *Ghosts of Berlin,* 96–110; Walter Benjamin, "Die Mietskaserne," *Beroliniana* (Munich: Koehler & Amelang, 2001), 220–31.

children, resting—without privacy, cleanliness, or space. Admittedly, some *Miets-kasernen* boasted splendid bourgeois residences in their prime space (the upper floors of front wings), but the rest of the apartments, located in attics, side and back wings, and inner courtyards, were small and inadequate. Those living in the inner courtyards (some buildings had as many as six or more successive courtyards) often shared space with small factories and workshops. Rather than housing a salutary social diversity, these structures reproduced patterns of economic and material oppression.

The inadequate state of *Mietskasernen* inspired several indictments,[57] and motivated the strong social-interest housing movement in interwar Germany. Despite several landmark attempts at improving them during the Weimar Republic—from urban laws to modernist housing complexes—the dismal conditions persisted until World War II. After the war, many *Mietskasernen* were lost to urban renewal in both East and West Berlin.[58] Of those that remained, only a small number underwent improvements in the postwar era; most were minimally repaired and continued to serve a low-income population. It was only toward the end of the twentieth century that planners, architects, and citizens alike turned their attention to these buildings as potentially valuable. In a reaction to the tabula rasa mentality of urban renewal, a movement to preserve the prized *bunte Mischung* (colorful mixture) of social groups, uses, and architectural forms of *Mietskasernen* grew stronger.[59] Finally, in the 1980s, the rising global trends of preservation, gentrification, and tourism caught up with this new outlook, and more and more *Mietskasernen* were renovated. The process accelerated after unification. The buildings were cleaned up, repainted, retrofitted with private bathrooms, heating, and even elevators in some cases; side and back wings were torn down to make for larger courtyards and allow more light into apartments; walls were demolished to join single-room apartments into larger units. Although sometimes the work was carried out by a variety of cooperative arrangements, more often it was done by private investors who bought the buildings and raised rents or sold them as condos, displacing preunification dwellers.

---

57. Rudolf Eberstadt, *Handbuch des Wohnungswesens und der Wohnungsfrage* (Jena: G. Fischer, 1909); Werner Hegemann, *Das steinerne Berlin: Geschichte der grössten Mietskasernenstadt der Welt* (Berlin: G. Kiepenheuer, 1930).

58. Florian Urban, "Recovering Essence through Demolition: The 'Organic' City in Postwar West Berlin," *Journal of the Society of Architectural Historians* 63, no. 3 (2004): 354–69; Hans Stimmann, *Stadterneuerung in Ost-Berlin: Vom "sozialistischen Neuaufbau" zur "komplexen Rekonstruktion"* (Berlin: S.T.E.R.N., 1988).

59. J. C. Wartenberg, *Kreuzberg K36: Leben in (der) Bewegung; Kreuzberg inside bis zum Fall der Mauer* (Bockenem: Jörg Lühmann, 2005); Christopher Klemek, *The Transatlantic Collapse of Urban Renewal: Postwar Urbanism from New York to Berlin* (Chicago: University of Chicago Press, 2011); Johannes Modersohn and Antje Freiesleben, *Kritische Würdigung der Kritischen Rekonstruktion: 71 Beiträge von Wegbegleitern und Widersachern des Hans Stimmann* (Munich: Deutscher Kunstverlag, 2006).

The renovated *Mietskasernen* of today are evidently a laudable improvement over unsanitary and congested conditions. But in the process of upgrading the spaces of *Mietskasernen*, their historical context has been lost. Materiality has been dissociated from social relationships as the original and longtime incarnation of these buildings as slums or tenement houses has been forgotten. Instead of awareness, restorations have served the commodification of urban space through increased rentals and property values, real estate speculation, and gentrification. Today's restored *Mietskasernen* are best described as condos and upscale rentals that happen to be housed in historical-looking shells. These shells form a convincing backdrop for streets that seem to recreate the feel of nineteenth-century Berlin, but the city was never as genteel and harmonious as it looks today. What is more, the effect of restoring individual *Mietskasernen* spreads out to the whole urban environment, including public or semi-public spaces and thus affecting more than just the value of each renovated property—they gentrify the whole urban landscape, including services and commerce. One way to honor the history of *Mietskasernen* while bringing in much needed architectural improvements could have been to restore them as social-interest housing (through rent controls, subsidies, or other programs). This historical "nod" to the original inhabitants of *Mietskasernen* would have had the added benefit of potentially avoiding social displacement. Such a policy might also have prevented the unsurprising housing crisis (*Wohnungsnot*) that has engulfed the city in the last decade, and which many blame on the lack of subsidized housing for low- and middle-income citizens while the government encouraged upscale private developments.[60]

The idealized view of *Mietskasernen* propagated by so many pastel-tinted façades contrasts with the appearance of the Haus Schwarzenberg. In some ways, the Haus Schwarzenberg does more justice to the history of *Mietskasernen* than its restored counterparts—although this is not to say that *Mietskasernen* should not be restored—in that it effectively conveys the sense of confinement and precariousness that characterized the original buildings. By visiting the narrow inner spaces and dark courtyards of the Haus it is possible to have a tangible, spatially lived understanding of what life in Berlin was like one hundred years ago. Such a phenomenological experience is far more powerful than the retinal impression of a freshly painted façade.

---

60. Berlin's former mayor Klaus Wowereit "sold off around 110,000 apartments that had been government property between 2002 and 2007. He also eliminated a support program for 28,000 state-subsidized apartments." Peter Wensierski, "Gentrification's Victims: Berlin Fears Rise of New Slums," *Spiegel Online International*, March 2, 2011, http://www.spiegel.de/international/germany/gentrification-s-victims-berlin-fears-rise-of-new-slums-a-748532-3.html. See also Norbert Schwaldt, "Warum in Berlin Wohnungsnot herrscht," *Die Welt*, April 9, 2015, http://www.welt.de/finanzen/immobilien/article 139345241/Warum-in-Berlin-Wohnungsnot-herrscht.html. For recent countermeasures, see Joel Dullroy, "How Berlin Is Fending Off Property Developers," *The Guardian*, March 14, 2016, http://www.theguardian.com/housing-network/2016/mar/14/property-developers-berlin-council-social-housing.

This understanding, however, only comes to the fore if the visitor is aware of the history of *Mietskasernen*. The visitor needs to squeeze out the historical reference, so to speak, from the materiality of the Haus Schwarzenberg. Each person must excavate this history anew, and in the process confront not only the *Mietskasernen* but also the critical stance of the Haus Schwarzenberg. This is an opaque semantics that prompts the visitor to engage actively in memory work; as such, it works in a fashion akin to the countermonuments described by James Young, and evokes Karen Till's analysis of "digging" and active historical research in her discussion of the Topography of Terror site in Berlin, following from Walter Benjamin's text "Excavation and Memory."[61]

Such active engagement is also required to pry other historical meanings from the building. The dingy courtyards might evoke the squalor of the interwar period, and the Nazi past is indicated by the museums. But none of these semantic threads is explicitly presented. On the contrary, the decaying façade has a tangled quality that blurs meanings, preserving symbolic openness at the expense of semantic clarity. It is somewhat of a gamble to let visitors do the work instead of providing full-circle narratives; there are risks of misunderstandings, false assumptions, or lost meanings. The risks might not be too big, however, in the context of contemporary Berlin, where residents are surrounded by references to the past (plaques, memorials, educational initiatives, even TV programs), and many tourists arrive seeking precisely the experience of history and memory. The Haus Schwarzenberg is also an established, famous destination for locals and tourists; public attention and visitation have helped publicize the goals of the association and the subjacent narratives of the building.[62]

Nothing can reasonably function with complete openness and dynamism, however. The deteriorating façade was a threat to the integrity of the building, and to the safety of users and passersby. Because the Schwarzenberg association refuses so adamantly to renew and repaint the building, they searched for ways not to erase the traces of the building's history, so that the façade could "be 'conserved,' the traces [of history] . . . maintained."[63] In a "gentle renovation" from 2009 to 2011, the façades were sealed beneath a layer of transparent veneer, which maintains the current visual and textural aspect of the surface while protecting it, insulating the building from humidity, and preventing stucco pieces from falling off (a real threat, not only to the integrity of the building but also to the safety of those using the

---

61. James Young, *The Texture of Memory: Holocaust Memorials and Meaning* (New Haven, CT: Yale University Press, 1993); Karen Till, *The New Berlin: Memory, Politics, Place* (Minneapolis: University of Minnesota Press, 2005), esp. 92–97; Walter Benjamin, "Excavation and Memory," published posthumously in *Selected Writings*, vol. 2, pt. 2 (1931–1934), ed. Marcus Paul Bullock, Michael William Jennings, Howard Eiland, and Gary Smith (Cambridge, MA: Belknap Press of Harvard University Press, 2005), 576.

62. Uthoff, "Dass wir noch da sind, ist schon ein Statement."

63. Meike Danz, press coordinator for the Schwarzenberg association, pers. comm. via e-mail, April 20, 2006.

courtyard).[64] The veneer is undetectable visually. I visited the Haus during the application in 2010, and I could not tell which parts had already been treated and which parts were still in their original, unvarnished state just by looking up close. The same treatment had been applied earlier in the KuLe art center, also housed in a decrepit-looking building, in the mid-1990s.[65]

The veneer complicates the idea of counterpreservation in the Haus Schwarzenberg. At first sight, it contradicts a "dynamic view of history" completely: the veneer congeals the façade in its current state. It is not just the worn-out bricks and cement pieces and grime particles that seem to have been captured alive, as it were, beneath the surface. It is the process of change itself that the veneer captures, displays, and encapsulates. The veneer turns the multilayered façade into a frozen waterfall, suspended in time but not yet extinguished; always on the verge of, but not quite, becoming. I argue, however, that the veneer itself does not *introduce* a contradiction. Rather, it *evinces* a subjacent contradiction. The attempt to "preserve a living history" by not interfering in any way, by keeping the façade untouched with no veneer, is already a *preservationist* stance, and an oxymoron—if something is "living," it does not need to be preserved as history. The only way to open a building radically and completely to transformation is to remove all discursive framings, and to allow any and all material interferences. The Haus Schwarzenberg would be totally open to becoming only if it could be razed, rebuilt, refurbished, modernized, cleaned, left to decay, littered, altered, painted over, hit by lightning, rebuilt again, revamped, replaced, in a potentially endless cycle. This complete openness to transformation becomes meaningless and destructive—the pile of rubble that Benjamin's Angel of History sees in the progression of time.[66]

In addition, and in contrast to other sites of preserved ruins, the veneer does not rearrange the building's elements. There is no cutting and pasting, no trimming of rough borders, no picturesque enhancement or dramatic composition. The veneer is a simple, minimal addition over the building as it is. It operates as a snapshot, capturing a moment created by chance with little framing. Usually, preserved ruins follow a studied design conception that commands spatial organization, changing the arrangement carved out by random damage or weathering. Such studied rearrangement is akin to a conventional pictorial composition. The difference between the Haus Schwarzenberg and a preserved ruin such as the Kaiser-Wilhelm-Gedächtniskirche is the difference between a snapshot and a landscape painting. Unlike the chiseled dents of the Kaiser-Wilhelm-Gedächtniskirche, the Haus Schwarzenberg preserves a certain ugliness more than lyrical poignancy. The

64. Meike Danz and Henryk Weiffenbach, interview, June 2010; Anne Lena Mösken, "Das letzte Haus am Platz," *Berliner Zeitung*, April 8, 2015, http://www.berliner-zeitung.de/berlin/haus-schwarzen berg-am-hackeschen-markt-das-letzte-haus-am-platz,10809148,30379062.html.

65. "Façade," KuLe, http://kunsthauskule.de/Facade. See also Urban, "Picture Postcards," 71.

66. Walter Benjamin, "Theses on the Philosophy of History," *Illuminations*, ed. Hannah Arendt (New York: Schocken Books, 1968), 257.

veneer does indeed prevent the Haus Schwarzenberg from forever accommodating every change and every mark of time, but beneath its still surface it harbors not only the traces of diachronic experience, but the very idea of transformation.

Not all scholars see it this way. Several pages ago I brought up Urban's critique of the Planwerk Innenstadt as image-based urban planning, which for him was at fault not because it thought in pictures but because it reproduced them uncritically. Urban extends his argument to the counterculture, which, he maintains, aestheticizes itself through fixed images of precariousness. Urban notes that Berlin in the 1990s was distinguished by "the ubiquity of marginal space"—ruins, vacant lots, sites of undefined use and indeterminate form; in sum, the *terrain vague* defined by Ignasi de Solà-Morales (see chapter 6). Urban argues that the Tacheles and the KuLe seized the image of the *terrain vague* and, in their formal choices, projected this image back to the city as a fixed and idealized version of alternative culture. The Tacheles did so by glazing its back façade with "glass that communicates the impression of the ruin"; the KuLe, by covering the façade "with transparent varnish, as to conserve the image of the decayed condition."[67] Urban's language is suggestive: in the Tacheles, all that remains is an impression; in the KuLe, an image. Urban criticizes these examples because they freeze and tame a condition that is ephemeral and recalcitrant by nature; and because of their promotion of counterculture qua image.

Implicit in his criticism is the assumption that the creative or democratic potential of such countercultures, their promise of an alternative and inclusive urbanity, are irretrievably lost in the process. This assumption might be logical if countercultures, especially those that thrive in makeshift and liminal spaces, were defined only by their provisionality. But the argument holds only to a certain degree. The problem is that it makes too much and too little of images at the same time. It makes too much of them in reducing the critical ferocity of countercultures to the look of their buildings. The preservation of a dilapidated façade cannot be understood on its own as an aesthetic gesture dissociated from a sociopolitical program. It has to be probed against other practices. In the case of the Tacheles, the façade glazing did accompany a turn to the mainstream through commercial decisions that would have been anathema to the rebelliousness of the original occupation. Urban's argument there makes sense: the Tacheles occupants exploited the image of their "in-between condition" just as they began to capitalize financially on an increase in public. But in the case of the Haus Schwarzenberg, the mission and actions of the association have remained the same, as committed to independent thinking and marginal artistic practices as before the veneer. The subjacent contradiction of "preserving living history" does not invalidate this mission, even if it adds a tension or complication.

---

67. Urban, "Postcard Pictures," 71.

At the same time, Urban downplays the potential of images to be subverted and transformed despite their apparent fixity. Visual culture is dynamic and dialogical; images may be reappropriated and resignified by a variety of social actors, in defiance of their intended original uses—whether they are postcard pictures of urbanity, or visual stereotypes of counterculture. Ultimately, though, Urban is correct in considering that images of decay in themselves are not synonymous with a counterculture, just as a nose piercing alone a punk does not make. Urban's suggestion that countercultural decay runs the risk of being aestheticized and idealized as any other "postcard image" is hard to ignore, especially considering a related complication: the problem of institutionalization.

The Institutionalization Threat

The utopian project of the Haus Schwarzenberg is represented not only in the "alternative" character of the building and its establishments, but also in the program and mission of its museums. Both the Otto Weidt Blind Workshop Museum and the Anne Frank Center tell stories of resistance and parallel worlds "outside" of the ruling state. In the first decades of the twentieth century, Otto Weidt had a workshop for manufacturing brooms and brushes in the side wing of the Haus Schwarzenberg (these rooms are now part of the museum). Weidt came from a working-class family and had a job as a wallpaper hanger, but had to stop working as he started to lose his eyesight. In 1936 he set up the broom workshop, which from 1940 was located in the building of the Haus Schwarzenberg.

In a kind of affirmative action avant la lettre, he hired employees who were mostly blind and deaf. They were also mostly Jewish. Weidt, who himself was not Jewish, increasingly sought to hire, hide, and protect Jews during the Nazi era. He succeeded in protecting a number of Jews for some time, securing false Aryan identities and extra food rations, and even hiding a whole family in a nook in his workshop. Although many of Weidt's protégés were caught by the Nazis, some managed to escape, including Inge Deutschkron, who emigrated to Israel and published her memoirs as *Ich trug den gelben Stern.*[68] Weidt survived the war in freedom, even though he was quite daring—he sent food parcels to Theresienstadt, and even traveled to Auschwitz to try to rescue an employee, Alice Licht, who also survived (he endured severe hardships, though). After the end of the war, he ran the workshop until his death in 1947, passing it on to his wife; in 1952, the East German government closed it down.[69] Weidt's courage earned him popular comparisons

---

68. In English, the title means "I wore the yellow star." The work was published in English as *Outcast: A Jewish Girl in Wartime Berlin* (New York: Fromm, 1989).

69. "Otto Weidt's Workshop for the Blind," Museum Blindenwerkstatt Otto Weidt (website), http://www.museum-blindenwerkstatt.de/en/ausstellung/themen/otto-weidts-workshop-for-the-blind/.

with Oskar Schindler.[70] In 1971 Yad Vashem recognized him as Righteous Among the Nations, an honor bestowed by Yad Vashem on behalf of the State of Israel on non-Jews who risked their lives to help Jews during the Holocaust.[71]

Anne Frank's story is a similar tale of self-determination in the face of oppression, as she and her family spent over two years hiding in Nazi-occupied Amsterdam before being found and deported to concentration camps. The Anne Frank Center in Berlin is one of five "Anne Frank organizations" in Europe and North America connected to the Anne Frank Museum in Amsterdam. The Amsterdam museum is located in the house where Anne and her family hid. While the Anne Frank Center in Berlin lacks this spatial connection, its main goal is not to be a traditional museum with original artifacts, but an educational institution where the exhibition, movies, cultural events, and special programs have a pedagogic function.

In comparison with most museums and exhibition spaces in the Mitte, the Anne Frank Center and the Otto Weidt Museum are small and discreet. They are tucked away in the narrow, awkward side wings of the building, accessible through small, run-down staircases. The Otto Weidt Museum, however, is a complicated case, and illustrates the issue of institutionalization that threatens the Schwarzenberg association. Since 2005, the Otto Weidt Museum has been under the jurisdiction of the German Resistance Memorial Centre—a larger, older institution headquartered elsewhere in Berlin. This is a significant departure from its origins.

Initially, the Otto Weidt Museum was independent. It began as a school project of museology students at the Berlin Hochschule für Technik und Wirtschaft. The students discovered, by chance, the site of Otto Weidt's workshop, which was then empty. In March 1999 they organized an exhibition in the former spaces of the workshop; the exhibition was a popular success and was made permanent, and in 2001 it fell under the management of the Jewish Museum (located in the neighborhood of Kreuzberg and famous for its Daniel Libeskind–designed main building).[72] At the time, the Otto Weidt Museum was still a very small-scale and modest operation, even under the tutelage of the Jewish Museum.

---

70. Klaus Harpprecht, "Der kleine Schindler aus Berlin," *Zeit Online*, September 6, 2001, http://www.zeit.de/2001/37/Der_kleine_Schindler_aus_Berlin; Tony Paterson, "The Blind Hero: New Film Tells of 'Unsung Schindler' Otto Weidt Who Saved Jews from Nazi Death Camps," *The Independent*, February 17, 2014, http://www.independent.co.uk/news/world/europe/the-blind-hero-new-film-tells-of-unsung-schindler-otto-weidt-who-saved-jews-from-nazi-death-camps-9042395.html; "Berlin Exhibition Honors Little-Known Nazi Opponent," *Deutsche Welle,* May 8, 2007, http://www.dw.com/en/berlin-exhibition-honors-little-known-nazi-opponent/a-2482023; and Andrea Schulte-Peevers, *Lonely Planet Berlin* (London: Lonely Planet, 2013), 106.

71. "Featured Stories: Otto Weidt," The Righteous Among the Nations, Yad Vashem, http://www.yadvashem.org/yv/en/righteous/stories/weidt.asp.

72. Otto Weidt Blindenwerkstatt Museum, "Geschichte des Museums," http://www.museum-blindenwerkstatt.de/de/ausstellung/geschichte/; Ariane Kwasigroch and Kai Gruzdz, "'Blindes Vertrauen'—Versteckt am Hackeschen Markt 1941–1943," *Gedenkstätterundbrief* 95, http://www.gedenkstaettenforum.de/nc/gedenkstaetten-rundbrief/rundbrief/news/blindes_vertrauen_versteckt_am_hackeschen_markt_1941_1943/.

In 2004, the whole building of the Haus Schwarzenberg gained financial sup-port and protection from the government, through the Culture Ministry and funds from the Public Lottery, as will be discussed below. The government's attention to the site was motivated not only by the other cultural activities in the building, but also—and very prominently—by the presence of the Otto Weidt workshop. At the time, Berlin was in the throes of a "memorial explosion" of small and large sites, monuments, artworks, and institutions commemorating aspects of German history, often related to the Nazi era. The Otto Weidt workshop appealed to this larger mind-set and became a prime motivation for public sponsorship, with a mandate to create a memorial center (*Gedenkstätte*) to "Silent Heroes" such as Weidt and to ensure the museum's continued existence. The history of Otto Weidt is also given as the main rationale for the preservation of the building by the Berlin Preservation Authority.[73] This spotlighting meant funding and attention to the museum, which are positive. However, it also meant its institutionalization and incorporation into the official German discourse on memory.

In its first version, which changed in only minor ways over the years, the spaces of the Otto Weidt Museum were a concrete evocation of duress during the Third Reich. The exhibition rooms corresponded to the original site of Weidt's work-shop. Equally important were the display strategies and equipment. The walls, floor, door, and window fixtures were unvarnished or crudely painted; there were exposed bricks and peeling coats of paint. The rooms were small, with an unfin-ished aspect (fig. 12). Display props and equipment such as lighting, text placards, and glass encasings were simple and kept to a minimum. The reception desk and all the displays and other furnishings looked somewhat improvised. All of these properties did not detract from, but added to, the goals and spirit of the museum in particular and the Haus Schwarzenberg in general.

The Otto Weidt Museum's simplicity appeared amateurish, which—considering the museum's origins—in some ways it was. But it was also subversive. The mu-seum required a more active engagement from visitors, starting with their physical engagement. Instead of sailing through well-marked entrances and ample recep-tion halls, the visitor first had to find the semi-hidden external door on one side of the Haus Schwarzenberg's first courtyard. The door was always closed, and a small sign told visitors to ring a bell. The door was buzzed open, and visitors let them-selves in, with no guides or docents to greet them.

In the same way that people had to find their own way to the museum, they also had to make their own route through the small exhibition. There was no predefined order for viewing the objects and texts. The contents of the exhibition spilled over from their framings, as artifacts were placed on aging furniture instead

---

73. Landesdenkmalamt Berlin, "Denkmaldatenbank," Obj.-Dok.-Nr: 09050142: Mietshaus & Gewerbebau Rosenthaler Straße 39, http://www.stadtentwicklung.berlin.de/denkmal/liste_karte_datenbank/de/denkmaldatenbank/detailansicht.php?id=6925.

Figure 12. Otto Weidt Museum, exhibition room interior (2004).
© Daniela Sandler

of in professional display cases. One's whole body was engaged by the spatial effect of the rooms, an impression most strongly conveyed by entering the hiding nook at the end of the former workshop where Weidt hid a family of Jews. The unfinished quality of the space retained marks of the past and conjured up impressions of the original workshop (without claiming to reproduce the original experience). The cramped feel of the nook and workshop rooms was compounded by the stories of persecution, resistance, and loss told by the documents and texts on the walls: photographs, personal letters, poems, testimonies. The museum's messages were conveyed both intellectually and phenomenologically, at the same time.

The museum opened up to the rest of the building through windows that looked onto the courtyard. From inside the museum, one could peer freely down the space of the courtyard, onto the cement ground where people walked on their way to other parts of the building, hung out, or parked their bicycles. Looking to the left or right, one could see the crumbling courtyard façades, and catch a glimpse of interior spaces behind other windows. This quotidian, external, non-museal life entered the museum visually and aurally. The Otto Weidt Museum was so small that it was almost inevitable for this permeation to happen. In this way the museum was always already connected to its context—to the whole building, to other activities, and to the cultural program of the Haus Schwarzenberg. The sights of the courtyard, the snippet of sky above the roofline, or the noises floating in from the street nearby were not distractions from the museum's content. Rather, the museum was an integral part of the city around it—a powerful metaphor for the possibility of integrating historical consciousness into present life instead of compartmentalizing it.

In April 2005, the German Resistance Memorial Centre, in the Tiergarten neighborhood (now part of the district of Mitte, but formerly part of West Berlin), "assumed both organizational and specialist responsibility for the museum Otto Weidt's Workshop for the Blind at 39, Rosenthaler Straße in Berlin-Mitte."[74] The Otto Weidt Museum underwent refurbishments, and in 2008, the new Silent Heroes Memorial Centre and the revised Otto Weidt Museum reopened. The German Resistance Memorial Centre, located in the quarter known as Bendlerblock, is an imposing combination of public memorial and exhibition praising German resistance against the Nazi regime. It focuses on the attempted assassination of Hitler by high-ranking Nazi officers in 1944, planned on the same site; it was there that the officers were executed when the plan failed. It includes, as backdrop, other examples of resistance—such as Munich's Weisse Rose group. The exhibition has so many instances of opposition, and such varied examples (students, workers, Nazi officers), that it is easy to get caught up in the courage and valor of the individual stories and forget that they never added up to a significant counterforce to Nazism. Historical accounts suggest that resistance was limited, scattered, and disconnected—and, for the most part, unsuccessful.[75] Unlike the German Resistance Memorial Centre, the Otto Weidt Museum in its original incarnation made it clear that acts of resistance were exceptional, and did not excuse the complicity of German society with Nazism. The two museums represented such divergent perspectives that, in the earliest version of my research in 2004 (that is, before the two museums became associated), I used the German Resistance Memorial Centre as a contrasting case study to illustrate what the Otto Weidt Workshop Museum was *not*.

The new version of the Otto Weidt Museum, conceived and realized by the German Resistance Memorial Centre, enlarged it by connecting it to additional rooms devoted to the new Silent Heroes memorial, which honors other acts of heroism and resistance among Germans. These additional rooms include the storefront on the second floor (a prized space, as it faces the street). The new spaces are designed in the smooth, slightly impersonal style of most mainstream museums (fig. 13). Windows are covered with translucent blinds, which block direct sunlight and street views; the new displays use professional cases, interactive and multimedia

---

74. The announcement was made on the home page of the German Resistance Memorial Center in 2006 (http://www.gdw-berlin.de/index-e.php). Here I reproduce the English version literally. The announcement is not on the home page anymore, but it can be found in the Internet Archive Wayback Machine in a web snapshot taken on February 9, 2006, at https://web.archive.org/web/20060209012328/http://www.gdw-berlin.de/index-e.php.

75. Hans Mommsen offers a balanced account in *Alternatives to Hitler: German Resistance under the Third Reich* (Princeton, NJ: Princeton University Press, 2003).

Figure 13. Silent Heroes Memorial, exhibition room interior (2010).
© Daniela Sandler

features, and sleek graphic design. These new spaces transition into the original site of the workshop, where period objects, photographs, and the hiding nook remain, although in a more streamlined and professional format.

The new rooms function as much more than a simple extension. For one, they are now the main entrance to the museum, and make the first impression on visitors. They encompass and frame the workshop rooms, setting the overall tone. While this overall tone is not so outwardly problematic as the exhibition in the German Resistance Memorial Centre, the Silent Heroes memorial follows similar narratives of redemption and glorification. If these narratives do not undo the critical potential of the workshop rooms, they superimpose a fundamental tension and even contradiction of principles and motivations.

For the average visitor, this tension might not be apparent, and all that is lost might simply be the quirky and unconventional experience of the earlier, "improvised," grassroots exhibition. But for the Haus Schwarzenberg as a whole, and the Schwarzenberg association in particular, the new spaces and new management are an uncomfortable neighbor—and not only because the new sleek spaces contrast with the rough and unfinished rest of the building. The museum is not part of the Schwarzenberg association; it is a cotenant, leasing space and coexisting in the same building. But the Schwarzenberg association not only encompasses most of the other tenants, it also is responsible for the very existence and survival of the building in the first place, as I will explain below. Without the association, it is not likely that Otto Weidt's workshop spaces would have been discovered, nor an exhibition mounted and a museum established.

Weiffenbach (the founding member of the Schwarzenberg association cited above) seemed wary of the new trajectory of the museum with its public oversight, fearing that the association might increasingly lose space, sponsorship, and authority to the museum[76]—now not only a tourist attraction in the ever-popular constellation of memory-places in Berlin, but also a place of pride for the official German discourse on history. It is of course laudable that the government takes interest in the building and in this particular history, which, before the "memory boom" of the 1980s, might not have come to the fore at all. In East Germany, where the building was located, the official attitude toward the Nazi era was to privilege the role of political resistance while underplaying the plight of Jews and other groups.[77] But there could have been other ways for the government to support the museum, keeping its independence and preserving the conceptual, physical, and administrative connections to the Schwarzenberg association.

The Private Market Threat

Like so many buildings in former East Berlin, where issues of ownership dating back to the confiscations of the Nazi era were compounded by the policies of the Socialist state (when buildings were either appropriated by the state, or abandoned by their owners because the maintenance costs were not offset by the state-controlled low rents), the Haus Schwarzenberg was the object of a lengthy dispute over its ownership and use since German reunification. In 1997, the government returned the building to descendants of the former Jewish owner, who had lost the building and his life to the Nazis. The building's heirs, scattered over the world, could not agree on what to do with the structure, and whether the Schwarzenberg association could continue there.

In 2003, a compulsory auction in the name of the heirs was enforced, but ended with no outcome, for lack of interest. Later that year a second compulsory auction took place, and even though the result was favorable to the Schwarzenberg association (the bid was won by the Wohnungsbaugesellschaft Berlin-Mitte, or WBM, a public real estate company that would have supported the association's tenancy), lawyers for a Hamburg-based private investor managed to enforce a third compulsory auction in July 2004. The development firm, Projektwerke Hamburg AG, had

76. Henryk Weiffenbach, interview, June 2010.
77. Jeffrey Herf, *Divided Memory: The Nazi Past in the Two Germanys* (Cambridge, MA: Harvard University Press, 1997).

already bought and renovated many buildings in the area, and wanted to purchase the Haus Schwarzenberg and transform it into a similar enterprise—completely refurbished and upgraded for profitable uses such as upscale office and apartment rentals.[78] The Schwarzenberg association organized a fund-raising campaign, and managed to secure the support of the German Public Lottery Foundation and of Germany's minister of culture, Christina Weiss, who contributed a decisive sum of money to the final auction. Their winning bid was 2.695 million euros. The exceptional victory of the Schwarzenberg association thus provides not only an illustration of typical processes of urban transformation, but also an unusual example of successful and effective resistance (not unlimited, though, as the association now has to answer to the government, under whose jurisdiction the house ultimately falls).

The Haus Schwarzenberg is an exemplary case of the contested property issues in Berlin, and its convoluted recent history conveys the tangle of interests and forces at play in contemporary urbanism. The dispute highlights the role of investors in the transformation of Berlin since unification. It also illustrates the complexity of mechanisms through which this transformation takes place, involving not only private developers and local inhabitants, but also the government. Given the huge amount of abandoned or state-owned property in East Germany, the unified government faced a dilemma: either appropriate all of it, thus making it public property; or return it to its original owners, who had lost their buildings to the Socialist or Nazi regimes. The latter option was a political decision in line with the economic dictates of a global, postindustrial, "competitive" metropolis.[79] The entanglement between public and private is not exclusive to Berlin; however, despite its ubiquity, the role of the government is sometimes overlooked, as the focus remains on the "inimical investors" ("feindliche Investoren").[80] Tellingly, the outcome of the Haus Schwarzenberg dispute, which resulted in the association's victory over the private investor, was achieved through a partnership with public officers.[81]

It has been a decade since the Haus Schwarzenberg became officially protected as a cultural and historic landmark, ensuring that the Schwarzenberg association

---

78. Nancy Krahlisch, "Aller guten Dinge sind drei," *Berliner Zeitung,* July 30, 2004, http://www.berliner-zeitung.de/haus-schwarzenberg-am-hackeschen-markt-konnte-bei-einer-zwangsversteigerung-gerettet-werden-aller-guten-dinge-sind-drei-15604104; Rainer L. Hein, "Haus Schwarzenberg gerettet—Die Künstler dürfen bleiben," *Berliner Morgenpost,* July 30, 2004, http://www.morgenpost.de/printarchiv/bezirke/article103583329/Haus-Schwarzenberg-gerettet-Die-Kuenstler-duerfen-bleiben.html; "Kampagne und Versteigerung," Haus Schwarzenberg, http://haus-schwarzenberg.org/schwarzenberg-e-v/kampagne-und-versteigerung/.

79. Reiman, "The Transition from People's Property to Private Property."

80. Heinrich Dubel, spokesman for the Haus Schwarzenberg, quoted in Marin Majica, "Ein Unentschieden im Hinspiel," *Berliner Zeitung,* April 25, 2003, http://www.berlinonline.de/berliner-zeitung/archiv/.bin/dump.fcgi/2003/0425/lokales/0276/index.html.

81. The partnership concerns only the purchase of the building, which is now public property. The Schwarzenberg association is financially independent and has never received external subsidies or funding. See "Häufig gestellten Fragen," Haus Schwarzenberg, http://haus-schwarzenberg.org/das-haus/haeugig-gestellten-fragen/.

could remain in the building through a ten-year lease. On October 15, 2015, the Schwarzenberg association announced the renewal of the lease for another ten years, until 2026.[82] The period of instability, eviction threats, and potential flux that marked the first decade of the Schwarzenberg association has ended, allowing for its members to settle in and develop their activities and spaces. The galleries and studios have continued to offer active alternative cultural programming, and the association has even put together events commemorating its history.[83] The refurbishment of the building with the protective veneer was made possible by this era of stability and consolidation.

But along with these possibilities, there are challenges created by the very mechanisms that protect the building. Public oversight of the management of the house means that the building's tenants are not as free to experiment as they were originally; and the special attention to the Otto Weidt Museum, described in the previous section, has created tension with the Schwarzenberg association. The association fears that the museum, and other related official uses, might gradually encroach on its current spaces and establishments[84]—the independent Kino Central, the quirky Club Eschloraque, and the Café Cinema with its eclectic customers and affordable menu. For the moment, the arrangement has worked, despite underlying tensions. The counterpreservation of the building continues to resist both institutionalization and appropriation by the market.

Tacheles and Schokoladen

Kate Shaw, in her study of alternative cultural spaces discussed in the previous chapter, cautioned against the risks of institutionalization as potentially robbing such projects of spontaneity (the very quality that made them unique and attractive in the first place), but she was also optimistic about certain politics of protection when applied to radically "strange" spaces.[85] Her Berlin case study was the Tacheles, which employed the same counterpreservation tactics as the Haus Schwarzenberg: the appropriation of decay; the highlighting of rough features such as fragments, rust, missing parts, and multilayered surfaces; and the juxtaposition of posters, graffiti, sculptures, murals, and installations. Shaw considered that the structure was "too dark and cold and strange to be used as much other than a venue for alternative culture, no matter how valorized." She admitted that,

82. The contract is handled by the landlord, the public company WBM Wohnungsbaugesellschaft Berlin-Mitte mbH, which acquired the building in 2004 after the final forced auction with financial support from the Public Lottery and the Culture Ministry.

83. Christine Eichelmann, "Künstler feiern Jubiläum im Haus Schwarzenberg," *Berliner Morgenpost*, October 14, 2010, http://www.morgenpost.de/berlin/article104736254/Kuenstler-feiern-Jubilaeum-im-Haus-Schwarzenberg.html.

84. Henryk Weiffenbach, interview, June 2010.

85. Kate Shaw, "The Place of Alternative Culture and the Politics of Its Protection in Berlin, Amsterdam, and Melbourne," *Planning Theory & Practice* 6, no. 2 (June 2005): 149–69.

after it became more popular, "the impression of the place being 'not what it was' is strong," but she interpreted this as "a case of culture's appropriation of capital, at least for the artists and the locals who use the place."[86]

Her study seemed to provide a feasible model for the coexistence of alternative cultures and private capital in a gentrifying area through the mediation of the public power as a protective agent. The victory of the Schwarzenberg association in 2004 offered further confirmation of this optimistic outlook. However, if the story of the Tacheles was to offer a model of any kind, it would be that of a cautionary tale. As it turns out, not even Berlin's "premier location for off-Kultur" was spared from commodification and eviction. Although the Tacheles has been widely studied, the end of its story was not told (or foretold) by the scholars who dealt with it in the first decade or so after unification.[87] For this reason, I will recount its history here, but now complete with its melancholy coda.

The Tacheles (the official name was Kunsthaus Tacheles, or Tacheles Art House) has possibly been the most notorious alternative cultural and art project in Berlin since unification. The Tacheles occupied the semi-ruined spaces of a former department store, the Friedrichstraßenpassage, which belonged to a Jewish owner and was confiscated by the Nazis. It remained ruined and unoccupied during the years of division, and after the fall of the Wall artists and young East and West Berliners used it for concerts, parties, and studio space:

> In the early 1990s land close to the Wall's path was unserviced and virtually "law-free." . . . Much of the city centre was still in ruins, there were no street lights and Tacheles was occupied by East and West German neo-punks, artists and activists.[88]

Over the years, it attracted a scene of young people, artists, students, and tourists; it made appearances in film, scholarship, and postcards; and it catalyzed debates about urban development, art, and cultural life. For Janet Stewart, the Tacheles could be seen as shorthand for the "Berlin architectural debates" of the 1990s, when the city was the subject of intense discussions and proposals by architects, planners, investors, and citizen groups. Stewart's account is telling of the different urban visions represented by these discussions:

> While at the opposite end of the Oranienburgerstrasse, the Hackesche Höfe (also housing a cinema, theatre, cafes, and shops) were being painstakingly restored to their

---

86. Ibid., 159.
87. Janet Stewart, "The Kunsthaus Tacheles: The Berlin Architecture Debate in Micro-Historical Context," in *Recasting German Identity: Culture, Politics, and Literature in the Berlin Republic*, ed. Stuart Taberner and Frank Finlay (Rochester, NY: Camden House, 2002), 51–66;" Boym, *The Future of Nostalgia*, 204–8; Jeffrey Peck, "Cultural Studies and Foreign Policy in a Strategic Alliance, or Why Presidents of the United States Should Learn German," *A User's Guide to German Cultural Studies* (Ann Arbor: University of Michigan Press, 1997), 84–85, among others.
88. Shaw, "The Place of Alternative Culture": 157.

former glory, the group that had saved the Tacheles from total destruction sought to remodel the available space in order to create something new which thrived on an atmosphere of provisionality. Among the squatters who took possession of the building in the early 1990s, the credo was: "Die Ideale sind ruiniert—retten wir die Ruine!"[89]

The last sentence can be translated as "The ideals are ruined—let us save the ruin!" In this context, "save the ruin" did not mean restoration to former integrity, but preservation of the ruinous state, and an emphasis on "the provisionality of the present."[90]

After initial threats of eviction and demolition, the Tacheles was designated as a protected monument in 1990, and the artists continued using the space. As early as 1993, private investors started to show interest and make plans for the centrally located site; in 1998, the Fundus Group, a real estate development firm in Cologne, bought it from the federal government for 80 million marks. The terms of the sale required the preservation of the Tacheles—in Shaw's words, the "politics of its protection." The Fundus Group sponsored refurbishments that made the building safer—for instance, missing walls were replaced with glass—and the Tacheles artists signed a ten-year lease, which stipulated a nominal rent (at the time, one mark per month).[91]

The legalization and refurbishment contributed to the transformation of the Tacheles into a more mainstream attraction. It drew tourists and a tamer public than before; in 2005, a Berlin nightlife commentator even disparaged the Tacheles as "domesticated."[92] The Tacheles was officially classified as an art institution (*Kunsthaus*), allowing for some protection of the art uses of the building. If, as Shaw argued, the odd spatial character of the Tacheles limited its uses, it did not make it impervious to commercialization. The Fundus Group purchased the site in order to redevelop it as a New Urbanist concoction designed by Andrés Duany, with high-end condos, hotels, commerce, offices, and the manicured open spaces that characterize projects such as Celebration in Florida.

New Urbanism, with its championing of public spaces, urban life, and mixed uses, made an ironic turn with the Tacheles redevelopment project. The New Urbanist design movement and philosophy originated in the United States, led by Duany and Elizabeth Plater-Zyberk; they were inspired by the lively, dense urban contexts of traditional European cities. They transplanted an idealized version of European urban life into new neighborhoods and cities designed in the United States, under the banner of diversity and community (the contradictions between

89. Stewart, "The Kunsthaus Tacheles," 56.
90. Ibid.
91. Harald Bodenschatz, "Fundus am Tacheles," *Bauwelt* 94 (2003): 20. Shaw gives 2000 as the sale date in "The Place of Alternative Culture," 158.
92. Christine Lang, "Falckensteinstraße," *Tagesspiegel*, February 23, 2005, http://www.tagesspiegel.de/berlin/falckensteinstrasse/587500.html.

theory and practice, and the social exclusivity of their designs, have been widely explored).[93] With the Tacheles site, the North American, idealized version of a European city was grafted back onto a real European city. The development was to be speculative and commercial, geared toward the tourists, consumers, and upper-class residents who have been the target of so much redevelopment in the area. In the New Urbanist design, which relied on neotraditional architecture and landscaping, the Tacheles would have added the right amount of "community" and "local flavor"—another case of the conversion of "urban dilapidation into ultra-chic," which Neil Smith observed in New York.[94] The Fundus Group's plans for the area never materialized for lack of investors, but they still deserve consideration for what they reveal about the slippery uses and meanings of art, culture, and history in contemporary urban design.

It appeared that the fate of the Tacheles, like its gaping façade, had been secured, even if it had cost the artists some of their independence and alternative character. But as the years passed and the Fundus Group's plans failed to come to fruition, the whole site changed hands again, and was taken over by the HSH Nordbank, a commercial bank headquartered in the West German cities of Kiel and Hamburg, which lists real estate as one of its main activities. The HSH Nordbank requested authorization to vacate the Tacheles building in order to sell the site. The public power abided, and in September 2012 the police enforced the (peaceful) eviction of the building's occupants—artists whose studios were located there, and establishments such as the Café Zapata (a café and club), the High-End 54 movie theater, a biotope (a "life reserve" of freely growing flora and fauna) called Maggie's Farm, a sculpture park, and a restaurant. The Tacheles was such a recognized landmark of Berlin that the eviction was widely reported not only by major German news media such as *Der Spiegel*, but also by English-language vehicles such as the BBC and the *Guardian*.[95]

The eviction of the Tacheles marks a transitional moment for alternative cultural projects in the heart of Berlin. Because the Tacheles was so visible, and because it had ostensibly been protected by an initial agreement between the government

93. See, for instance, Paul Walker Clarke, "The Ideal of Community and Its Counterfeit Construction," *Journal of Architectural Education* 58, no. 3 (February 2005): 43–52; Neil Smith, "Which New Urbanism? The Revanchist '90s," *Perspecta* 30 (1999): 98–105, esp. 103–5; Eric Detweiler, "Hyperurbanity: Idealism, New Urbanism, and the Politics of Hyperreality in the Town of Celebration, Florida," in *Disneyland and Culture: Essays on the Parks and Their Influence,* ed. Kathy Merlock Jackson and Mark I. West (Jefferson, NC: McFarland, 2010), 150–70.

94. Neil Smith, *The New Urban Frontier: Gentrification and the Revanchist City* (London and New York: Routledge, 1996), 18.

95. "Berliner Institution: Kunsthaus Tacheles geräumt," *Der Spiegel*, September 4, 2012, http://www.spiegel.de/kultur/gesellschaft/tacheles-kunsthaus-in-berlin-mitte-friedlich-geraeumt-a-853743.html; "Authorities Shut Berlin's Iconic Tacheles Arts Squat," *BBC News*, September 4, 2012, http://www.bbc.co.uk/news/world-europe-19473806; Jonathan Jones, "The Closure of Berlin's Tacheles Squat Is a Sad Day for Alternative Art," *The Guardian*, September 5, 2012, http://www.guardian.co.uk/artanddesign/jonathanjonesblog/2012/sep/05/closure-tacheles-berlin-sad-alternative-art.

and the Fundus Group investors, it had appeared to signal a limit to gentrification in Mitte, and the possibility for different urban uses besides commerce and tourism. With the Tacheles eviction, this has changed. The center of the city seems more irrevocably uniform, as the hegemony of real estate development advances over the last remaining empty lots and derelict buildings. In this new context, the Haus Schwarzenberg is the outlier, a rare example of continued existence, and for this reason all the more powerful and significant—although of course its future is no more guaranteed for that. In Weiffenbach's words, "The fact that we are still standing is already a statement."[96]

If the fate of the Tacheles rings a pessimistic tone, a third and final example offers a happy ending. Not far from the Tacheles and the Haus Schwarzenberg, the Schokoladen is another alternative art and living project that began in the *Wende*. Founded in 1990, it is one of the earliest cultural projects in post-Wall East Berlin. Although not as famous as the Tacheles and the Haus Schwarzenberg, it is well known and established among a steady public that frequents its exhibitions, lectures, performances, music events, and courtyard parties (fig. 14). It is located on a quiet block on Ackerstraße, in a less high-profile location at the margins of Mitte (an area initially ignored by real estate developers, who focused on the core of the neighborhood, but which eventually also gentrified).

The building was a *Mietskaserne* with a typically ornate façade; the façade and interior spaces have the same weathered texture of the Haus Schwarzenberg, with similar interventions—graffiti, posters, artwork, and so on. In addition, its street façade is strikingly decorated with murals and shopwindow displays. Originally a squat, the Schokoladen eventually became a legal tenant to a private landlord, a man named Markus Friedrich. Perhaps because it is located in a more peripheral area of Mitte, away from the fanciest and busiest streets, the Schokoladen has survived for a long time. However, as the trendiest art scene eventually moved to what was previously a fringe of Mitte, around Brunnenstraße, the neighborhood margins came into the center field of vision for developers. The Schokoladen fought a long battle against eviction by the landlord, who wanted to rent the spaces to profitable businesses.[97] When it seemed that it, too, would be another casualty, the association was saved by the combined action of the public government and a Swiss foundation called Edith Maryon, which supports art, cultural, and residential projects. The government facilitated the purchase of the building by the Edith Maryon Foundation, which then gave control of the building to the Schokoladen association through a lease in perpetuity.[98] The Schokoladen association was granted not

96. Uthoff, "Dass wir noch da sind, ist schon ein Statement."

97. Ralf Schönball, "Schokoladen-Mitte muss raus—erst einmal," *Tagesspiegel*, September 24, 2011, http://www.tagesspiegel.de/berlin/auszugstermin-schokoladen-mitte-muss-raus-erst-einmal/4654842.html.

98. "Kulturprojekt in Mitte gerettet: Süße Nachricht für den Schokoladen," *Die Tageszeitung*, March 29, 2012, http://www.taz.de/!5097213/; Christoph Spangenberg, "Räumung abgesagt: Der Schokoladen is gerettet," *Tagesspiegel*, February 17, 2012, http://www.tagesspiegel.de/berlin/raeumung-abgesagt-der-schokoladen-ist-gerettet/6223008.html.

Figure 14. Schokoladen, street façade on Ackerstraße (2010).
© Daniela Sandler

only the right to remain in the building, but the responsibility to do necessary maintenance and renovation works.

The Haus Schwarzenberg and the Schokoladen point to ways in which alternative cultural projects can survive even when gentrification, supported both by private investors and by the government, is dominant. In both cases, public intervention was decisive; and in both cases, external financial support (the Public Lottery for the Haus Schwarzenberg, and the Edith Maryon Foundation for the Schokoladen) enabled the compensation of private owners. While public and nonprofit support for the arts is nothing new, in these examples the funds are distributed to small, independent, grassroots organizations instead of being funneled into fewer, larger, public projects. Given the imperatives of contemporary urban economies, this might not be a realistic model for most cultural projects, however desirable it may sound. But at least in these two examples the sponsorship has worked to ensure the continuity of alternative forms of artistic production and enjoyment outside of the mainstream market. The program and mission of the Haus Schwarzenberg and the Schokoladen point the way to a more diverse, inclusive, and experimental city—a city made tangible through unconventional preservation and architectural choices.

4

DECREPITUDE AND MEMORY IN
THE LANDSCAPE

In 1992 the city of Oranienburg—a municipality that sits just outside of Berlin, along its northern border—organized a design competition to develop a dormant plot of land on its outskirts. Like most East German cities, it had suffered through the industrial, economic, and political crises of the GDR. This legacy was apparent in the aftermath of unification, as the eastern provinces of reunified Germany remained economically depressed, with high unemployment, a shrinking population, a dearth of leisure and cultural facilities, and a general sense of stagnation—felt all the more intensely because of the expectations of prosperity following unification with wealthy West Germany. As discussed in the previous chapter, the fall of the Wall in 1989 started as a political movement for democratization within East Germany, but it turned into a call for unification with the West in 1990 in great part thanks to the possibility of material improvements to the East.[1] Expectations might

---

1. Peter H. Merkl, "Reinventing German National Identity," in *The Federal Republic of Germany at Forty-Five: Union without Unity,* ed. Peter H. Merkl (New York: New York University Press, 1995), 1. Recent reports suggest that, despite many gains for East Germans (from income bonuses to social mobility), the net balance of unification is mixed. See Hilary Silver, "The Social Integration of Germany since Unification," in *From the Bonn to the Berlin Republic: Germany at the Twentieth Anniversary of Unification,* ed. Jeffrey Anderson and Eric Langenbacher (New York: Berghahn Books, 2010), 183–206; Nicola Fuchs-Schündel, Dirk Krüger, and Mathias Sommer, "Inequality Trends for Germany in the Last Two Decades: A Tale of Two Countries" paper, University of Minnesota Department of Economics, June 1,

have been particularly intense in a place like Oranienburg, in the immediate vicinity of Berlin. Berlin was poised to be Germany's flagship global city. It was going to be the national capital (a decision made in 1991); it became Germany's largest city after unification; and even before unification West Berlin had already showed signs of economic, cultural, and social revival. After 1990, marketers touted the joys of investing in and visiting the New Berlin; big international corporations bought land and started building; public funds poured into reconnecting the city and renewing its infrastructure; and tourism boomed.[2]

Oranienburg took the opportunity to promote its own revival, expecting perhaps a spillover from Berlin's transformations. As late as 2006, the official website for the city promoted Oranienburg as a "day-trip destination for Berlin tourists."[3] Oranienburg is officially a separate municipal entity from Berlin; it is also located in a different state—while Berlin is one of the three German city-states (the other two being Bremen and Hamburg), Oranienburg belongs to the neighboring state of Brandenburg. However, in several ways Oranienburg functions as a de facto suburb of Berlin. Not only does it border the northern part of Berlin, but it is also seamlessly integrated into municipal networks of transportation (suburban rail and regional train lines). What is more, since the fall of the Wall, urban occupation has tended toward integrating Berlin and its surroundings. This is manifest in residential suburbanization (a process virtually absent from both Berlins until then) and in economic initiatives such as the foundation of business centers in Brandenburg to provide for the expected office demand in the "New Berlin." The integration of Berlin and its surroundings has also been the object of political decisions and discussions, such as the (failed) vote for merging the states of Berlin and Brandenburg.[4] Those who supported the merger argued that it would allow for complementary cooperation in economic and spatial development instead of unfocused competition, which results in redundant developments and oversupply of space and infrastructure.[5] The population of Brandenburg voted against the merger, fearing that Berlin would dominate state politics and polarize resources.

2009, http://www.econ.umn.edu/~fperri/papers/germany2.pdf; and Miriam Beblo, Irwin L. Collier, and Thomas Knaus, "The Unification Bonus (Malus) of East Germans after the Fall of the Wall," *Journal of Economic Integration* 27, no. 2 (June 2012): 222–44.

2. Claire Colomb, *Staging the New Berlin: Place Marketing and the Politics of Urban Reinvention Post-1989* (New York: Routledge, 2012).

3. Oranienburg official website, http://www.oranienburg.de. The Oranienburg city website has since changed, and this text cannot be found there anymore. It can be seen in the Internet Archive Wayback Machine under "Oranienburg im Überblick" at https://web.archive.org/web/20050305163703/http://www.oranienburg.de/.

4. Peter Newman and Andy Thornley, *Planning World Cities: Globalization and Urban Politics* (New York: Palgrave Macmillan, 2005), 172, 176–78.

5. Newman and Thornley (*Planning World Cities*, 177) write that during the 1990s several municipalities "bordering Berlin laid out business parks to attract both economic development and tax income. Few attracted tenants but the building continued even when it was evident that demand was weak. Neighbouring local governments only saw rivals on their borders."

Regardless of the result, the merger vote demonstrates that even though Berlin is formally separate from its surrounding townships and cities, it is in fact integrated with them through the economy, transportation, space, infrastructure, and social and cultural transactions.[6]

This was the climate in 1992, when the city council organized a competition calling for design proposals to turn an underused, large plot of land into a new residential development with houses, parks, schools, and sports facilities.[7] The city council's idea seemed sound enough: developing an underused site with a mixed-use subdivision of low-rise buildings that would provide housing, social infrastructure, and green space to Oranienburg citizens and potential newcomers, and would pay special attention to connections with the rest of the city and transportation networks. Nothing out of the ordinary; in fact, attuned to western notions of business and real estate investment. The development may have had an eye on the suburbanization of Berlin. Without the Wall, Berlin could flow out into the landscape with new housing stock for federal government or private sector employees. It was not unreasonable to expect this suburbanization, given that by the early 1990s suburban sprawl was a phenomenon common to many cities in Western Europe.[8] In addition, the city of Oranienburg also consulted an expert panel that recommended that the unused plot of land mentioned above, next to developed city sections, should be reconnected to the surrounding urban fabric.[9]

The city council's program was also in line with contemporary precepts of mixed urban uses and neighborhood integration. The idea resembled much more Celebration, the New Urbanist town in Florida, than it did the East German residential districts built in the Socialist era, almost completely made up of modernist prefabricated high-rises. The Oranienburg development would avoid the dreary landscape of large-scale apartment buildings severed from their surroundings. Oranienburg would build smaller dwelling units, provide amenities and greenery, and integrate the houses into the city in a seamless continuation of the bucolic, tree-lined, single-family-home streets that fan out of the city center. That was the program of Oranienburg's design competition, and it sounded reasonable enough to five of the six architectural offices invited to enter the competition.[10]

---

6. On the relationship between Berlin and Brandenburg, see also Hartmut Häußermann, "Berlin," in *Metropolitan Governance and Spatial Planning,* ed. W. Salet, Andy Thornley, and A. Kreukels (London and New York: Spon, 2003), 113–24.

7. Stadt Oranienburg, *Gutachterverfahren: Urbanisierung des ehemaligen Geländes der SS-Kaserne Orenienburg* [*sic*]—*Ausschreibung,* (1992?), 68–73.

8. Wolfgang Glatzer, Karl Otto Hondrich, Heinz-Herbert Noll, Karin Stiehr, and Barbara Wörndl, *Recent Social Trends in West Germany, 1960–1990* (Frankfurt am Main: Campus; Montreal: McGill-Queen's University Press, 1992), 78–80.

9. Stadt Oranienburg, *Gutachterverfahren,* 8.

10. Layla Dawson, "Libeskind in Oranienburg," *Architectural Review* 209, no. 1251 (May 2001): 27. For a summary and images of the competition entries, see Stadt Oranienburg in Zusammenarbeit mit der Landesentwicklungsgesellschaft für Städtebau, Wohnen und Verkehr des Landes Brandenburg mbH, *Gutachtverfahren: Urbanisierung des Geländes der ehemaligen SS-Kaserne Oranienburg: Dokumentation* (March 1993), 50–77.

The dormant plot, however, had a charged history. It had been used by Adolf Hitler's SS—the Schutzstaffel, or "protection squad," which had been created in 1925 in the Weimar Republic, and gained new strength under Heinrich Himmler in 1929, who defined the task of the SS as the elimination of the enemies of the Third Reich. The SS used the Oranienburg site to build barracks for Nazi guards, a commandant's villa (the Villa Eicke), single-family houses for high-ranking SS officers, administration offices, a medical clinic, a large kitchen and canteen, and exercise fields. Many of these structures are still extant, and have continued to be used since the war, throughout the GDR era and all the way to the present. The canteen, for example, was used in the postwar era by the Nationale Volksarmee (NVA), or People's Army, whose soldiers nicknamed it "the green monster" ("das grüne Ungeheuer"). The structure ended up empty and fell into disrepair, lingering as a ruin until it was restored in 2013.[11]

The reason why there were so many SS officers stationed there was their next-door neighbor—not the bucolic tree-lined streets of Oranienburg, but the Sachsenhausen concentration camp, where these SS officers worked. Sachsenhausen was inextricably linked to the history of concentration camps, Nazism, and the Holocaust from the camp's inception in 1936. In 1938, it was made into the headquarters of the entire Nazi system of concentration and death camps, and in the years following the war, it served as a Soviet camp for German POWs.[12] The area containing the SS barracks, administration, houses, and infrastructure, covering thirty-eight hectares next to the former camp, continued to be used in the postwar era—first by the Soviets, then the GDR army, and then by several tenants: a police station and academy, a tax office, even a discount store. The single-family homes built for, and occupied by, SS officers were turned over to GDR citizens (mostly NVA officers); today they are unmarked and still used as private homes.[13]

Other parts of the site were not in use; vegetation took over the exercise fields and grew tall around large structures such as the canteen and the Villa Eicke, both of which were left to crumble, half-forgotten (the Villa Eicke was restored in 2006).[14] The canteen, in particular, tottered ominously, its wooden walls turned into a gossamer shell, tinged with the faded green that had once earned it its nickname

11. Stadt Oranienburg, *Gutachterverfahren* (1992?), 23–36, 40–67; Claus-D. Steyer, "Besucherführung unter Polizeiaufsicht: Vom 'Grünen Ungeheuer' zur herrschaftlichen Eicke-Villa: Tour über riesiges SS-Gelände Oranienburg," *Der Tagesspiegel*, December 12, 1995, 11; "KZ-Gedenkstätte Sachsenhausen: 'Grünes Ungeheuer' saniert," *Nordkurier*, June 18, 2013, http://www.nordkurier.de/brandenburg/gruenes-ungeheuer-aus-holz-saniert-18191106.html.

12. Günter Morsch and Astrid Ley, *Sachsenhausen Concentration Camp, 1936–1945: Events and Developments*, exhibition catalogue (Berlin: Metropol, 2008).

13. Jürgen Dittberner, *Schwierigkeiten mit dem Gedenken: Auseinandersetzungen mit der Nationalsozialistischen Vergangenheit* (Opladen: Westdeutscher, 1999), 45–46; Stadt Oranienburg, *Gutachterverfahren* (1992?), 1–3, 8–9, 17–18; Christian Caryl, "Do Not Disturb: Nazis Slept Here," *Wall Street Journal*, November 7, 1996, A20.

14. Konrad Litschko, "Ein Lachen im Haus des Täters," *Taz.de*, October 21, 2006, http://www.taz.de/1/archiv/?dig=2006/10/21/a0247.

"green monster." The whole plot of land—with its mixture of repurposed SS structures and crumbling ones, partly manicured and partly covered by overgrown vegetation—was a persistent connection between Oranienburg and Sachsenhausen. It was a physical link between the camp and the city, but it was also a symbolic link between past and present—and, if the city council's program had its way, it would also become a site of historical forgetting and repression, as the eagerness to build the town's future would bury its involvement in German history.

The Significance of Sachsenhausen

Sachsenhausen was one of the first concentration camps in Nazi Germany, established well before the 1942 Wannsee Conference provided the final solution to the Jewish question by "resettling" European Jews in the East (the Nazi euphemism for deporting Jews to concentration and extermination camps in Eastern Europe).[15] Sachsenhausen started out as a camp for political prisoners. In the mid-1930s Hitler had been interning people considered oppositional in camps and prisons. These were places of imprisonment and torture, although not yet systematic mass murder. At the same time the Nazi state was developing industrial technologies for eliminating undesirable social groups, notably the mass sterilization and murder of people who were handicapped or mentally ill. The most promising technology was the use of Zyklon-B gas, first in trucks (mobile gas chambers) and then in hospitals. The murder of the handicapped and mentally ill was known as the T-4 Operation, named after its headquarters on Tiergartenstraße 4, in the center of Berlin. The parallel development of concentration camps for political prisoners (such as Sachsenhausen in its early days) and of the T-4 Operation would converge later in the creation of extermination sites equipped with large gas chambers, such as Birkenau, Treblinka, and Sobibor.[16] The Eastern European camps would never have been possible without these earlier developments, from the mobile gas chambers to the internment camps, which had taken place *within* Germany. Sachsenhausen's first incarnation as a prison for political opponents puts the camp and the city of Oranienburg right at the start of the history of the Holocaust. And even before Sachsenhausen, Oranienburg had been the site of the first concentration camp in Prussia. The first camp, in operation between 1933 and 1934, was located in an old factory in the center of the city, underscoring the intermingling of "normal" everyday life and Nazi oppression. Sachsenhausen became not only the biggest camp

---

15. Götz Aly, *"Final Solution": Nazi Population Policy and the Murder of the European Jews* (New York: Oxford University Press, 1999); Mark Roseman, *The Wannsee Conference and the Final Solution: A Reconsideration* (New York: Metropolitan Books, 2002).

16. Eugen Kogon, Hermann Langbein, and Adalbert Rückerl, eds., *Nazi Mass Murder: A Documentary History of the Use of Poison Gas* (New Haven, CT: Yale University Press, 1993).

in the Berlin region, but also the center for managing the expanding system of Nazi concentration and extermination camps in 1938.[17]

The Holocaust machinery depended on the interconnection of several elements: collection houses in the middle of German cities, where Jews evicted from their homes waited for deportation; efficient railroad networks; "desktop murderers" such as Adolf Eichmann and their attending office bureaucracies. The memorial magnetism of places like Auschwitz and Theresienstadt often draws all public attention, and obscures the myriad ways in which these far-removed sites were part of a much vaster set of relationships. These relationships involved direct participation of large portions of German society. Essential to carrying out the Holocaust was a complex system of bureaucrats, technical workers, laws, law-enforcing officers, and collaborators, although most of these people may never have set foot in a concentration camp. These connections were not always visible, disguised by the physical distance between camps and administrative centers. There were exceptions, though—camps too close to German cities, in plain sight, such as Buchenwald, just over six miles from the center of Weimar, or Sachsenhausen, within the city of Oranienburg and about twenty miles from the center of Berlin. Local inhabitants not only knew about the camps, but also would establish relationships with them by providing services or products to the camp officers, socializing with them, and occasionally even helping inmates. Conversely, camp officers did not remain exclusively inside the camps, but would also visit neighboring towns. The exceptional value of a site like the area of the former SS barracks in Oranienburg is that it embodies these connections concretely. It is a physical demonstration of the capillary penetration of the Holocaust into everyday German life. This enmeshment was not casual. In Jürgen Dittberner's words, "The SS build its own city in Sachsenhausen, at the center of which was the concentration camp."[18] Around the camp there were workshops, industrial facilities, administrative buildings, the SS officers' homes, and the barracks, all of which made up an integral whole—the "SS-city," which transitioned into the surrounding "civil" city of Oranienburg.

The relevance of Sachsenhausen is not limited to the SS-barracks site. Although relatively small, Sachsenhausen was not just one among the hundreds of camps and murder sites. It was the headquarters of the whole concentration camp system, the central site for the exchange of information, the propagation of decisions, and the convergence of bureaucrats, officers, technical workers, and collaborators. Besides, Sachsenhausen was a model camp. While many camps used previously

---

17. Sachsenhausen was not an extermination camp, unlike places like Treblinka and Sobibor. On the different types of camps, see Wolfgang Sofsky, *Die Ordnung des Terrors: Das Konzentrationslager* (Frankfurt am Main: S. Fischer, 1993); Karin Orth, *Das System der nationalsozialistischen Konzentrationslager: Eine politische Organisationsgeschichte* (Hamburg: Hamburger Edition, 1999); Eugène Aroneanu, *Inside the Concentration Camps: Eyewitness Accounts of Life in Hitler's Death Camps* (Westport, CT: Praeger, 1996).

18. Dittberner, *Schwierigkeiten mit dem Gedenken*, 45.

existing sites (the Germans established Auschwitz in 1940 in Polish army barracks built in 1917), and others were hurriedly built with only basic planning (Treblinka, Sobibor), Sachsenhausen was carefully planned and built as an "ideal concentration camp" in 1936.[19] The triangular plot and the radiating layout of the barracks provided a complete view of the site to the camp guards in watchtowers along the outer periphery, and in the entrance tower over the main gate.[20] The barracks all looked onto the roll-call square, diminishing possibilities for hiding. The camp dimensions allowed for efficient physical and visual control at all times: the camp was big enough for an orderly, widespread distribution of people and buildings always in full view, but not so big as to diminish visibility at its far ends. The design of the camp is comparable to the visual surveillance and confinement principles of Jeremy Bentham's panoptical prison (famously discussed by Michel Foucault).[21] These principles were a common concern of architects tackling the design not only of prisons, but of any environment where activity should be monitored, from radio-axial Renaissance ideal cities to Claude-Nicolas Ledoux's saltworks at Arc-et-Senans (which were also, like Sachsenhausen, arranged in a semicircle with a large and fully surrounded central open space, and which perhaps unsurprisingly were used by the Nazis as an internment camp during the German occupation of France).[22]

Sachsenhausen is both exemplary and unique. It illustrates aspects common to most camps, such as imprisonment systems and installations (crematoria, gas chambers, barracks, and a medical experiment unit).[23] But it also has unique features, such as its ideal design, administrative centrality in the hierarchy of camps, and proximity to Berlin. After the war, Sachsenhausen's history was further complicated by its use as a Soviet internment and prisoner-of-war camp.[24] This adds another layer to Sachsenhausen as a site of murder and memory. The first

19. Perhaps the expression "ideal concentration camp" will strike some as an oxymoron. However, ideal city plans involved authoritarian and controlling spatial measures such as ordered geometry, full visibility, and rigid borders. See Ruth Eaton, *Ideal Cities: Utopianism and the (Un)built Environment* (London: Thames & Hudson, 2007).

20. On the history, design concept, and development of Sachsenhausen, see Günter Morsch and Corinna Cossmann, *Konzentrationslager Oranienburg* (Berlin: Hentrich, 1994); Morsch, "Oranienburg-Sachsenhausen," in *Die nationalsozialistischen Konzentrationslager: Entwicklung und Struktur*, ed. Ulrich Herbert, Karin Orth, and Christoph Dieckmann (Göttingen: Waldstein, 1998), 1:111–34.

21. Michel Foucault, *Discipline and Punish: The Birth of the Prison* (Pantheon Books, 1978); see also Janet Semple, *Bentham's Prison: A Study of the Panopticon Penitentiary* (Oxford: Oxford University Press, 1993).

22. On the principle of surveillance in Ledoux's saltworks and its similarity to Bentham's panoptical prison, see Anthony Vidler, *Claude Nicolas Ledoux* (Basel: Birkhäuser, 2006), 51. On the use of the site as an internment camp, see *The Royal Saltworks of Arc-et-Senans* (Paris: Éditions Scala, [1988?]), 7.

23. Morsch and Ley, *Sachsenhausen Concentration Camp*; L'Amicale d'Oranienburg-Sachsenhausen, *Sachso: Au coeur du système concentrationnaire nazi* ([Alençon:] Minuit, Plon, 1982); Manuela R. Hrdlicka, *Alltag im KZ: Das Lager Sachsenhausen bei Berlin* (Augsburg: Leske + Budrich, Opladen, 1991).

24. Günter Morsch, ed., *Von der Erinnerung zum Monument: Die Entstehungsgeschichte der Nationalen Mahn- und Gedenkstätte Sachsenhausen* ([Oranienburg]: Stiftung Brandenburgische Gedenkstätten; Berlin: Edition Hentrich, 1996).

Sachsenhausen inmates were victims of Nazism. After the war, the inmate population was composed of Nazis and soldiers of the German army. There were also victims of Soviet oppression who were neither soldiers nor Nazis. The camp was first ruled by the Nazis, then by the Soviet occupying force, until it passed on to East German control. However, because East Germany was controlled by the Soviet Union until unification in 1990, the Soviets continued to have a say in the management of the site. This juxtaposition of victims and oppressors turns Sachsenhausen and other East German camps into embattled sites of remembrance. There are many different groups to be memorialized, and each group of victims demands a different form of memorialization.

This is further complicated by the question of *who* remembers. Jews who survived, or their families, mostly emigrated from Germany. The survivors and families who remained in Germany were, for the most part, Germans—including political prisoners, Nazis, German soldiers, and victims of Soviet oppression. German relatives of a Wehrmacht soldier who died in the camp under the Soviets have remembrance patterns and motivations very different from those of emigrant descendants of a Jewish inmate. And who should have a greater say in deciding the fate of the camp and its surroundings—those who were the main target of the Holocaust, those who represent the largest group of victims in each camp (Jews were not the majority of Sachsenhausen inmates), or those who have built their lives around the camp and for whom any memorial decision will have a direct impact?

But Sachsenhausen's history is not only the history of a prison camp. It is also the history of a memorial, and the different political views and social beliefs that have informed the changes in this memorial. The Soviet POW camp was dismantled in 1950, and in 1961 Sachsenhausen became a state memorial. Like other GDR concentration camps, Sachsenhausen told a particular version of the story.[25] Nazism was portrayed as a foreign capitalist aggression. Official ideology represented East Germans as victims of Nazis, and the Soviets as their liberators. East German and Soviet discourse reduced Nazism to a class struggle problem, explained anti-Semitism as a superstructural effect, and portrayed Communism as the only legitimate alternative. The logic was aided by the fact that Hitler had persecuted German Communists until they were all imprisoned, dead, exiled, or in hiding. The East German state founded itself on the myth of a direct succession from the German

---

25. James Young, *The Texture of Memory: Holocaust Memorials and Meaning* (New Haven, CT: Yale University Press, 1993), 49–80; Jeffrey Herf, *Divided Memory: The Nazi Past in the Two Germanys* (Cambridge, MA: Harvard University Press, 1997), 175–80. For a primary source on East German Holocaust memorialization, see the commemorative book by the Komitee der Antifaschistischen Widerstandkämpfer der Deutschen Demokratischen Republik, *Sachsenhausen* (East Berlin: Kongress, [1962]). This book reveals the East German emphasis on Communist resistance and victimhood. In this case, the book's ideological commitment can be judged by its cover: the blue fabric cover bears only the name Sachsenhausen printed in black, and a red inverted triangle—the Nazi symbol for political prisoners, who had to wear it on their lapels just as Jews had to wear yellow stars.

political resistance.[26] This ideological maneuver allowed the GDR to condemn Nazism vehemently while at the same time exonerating itself from any complicity or participation in it. In addition, ethnic or cultural identities were secondary or absent in GDR memorials. The Sachsenhausen memorial lumped all of the Holocaust's victims under the rubric of "victims of Fascism," focusing on Communists and political opponents to Nazism while downplaying Jews, Gypsies, homosexuals, Jehovah's Witnesses, and other groups.[27]

The Sachsenhausen memorial and other East German sites such as Buchenwald and Ravensbrück have been revised and reformed since unification. Now the history of these sites includes not only their use as concentration camps, but also their history as memorials, along with the changing uses, forms, and meanings of each political context. The monument and museum in Sachsenhausen are eloquent witnesses to Soviet occupation, Socialist ideology, and the politics of the GDR. The subsequent revision of the site, which includes a new mission statement, new exhibits, and educational programs, is also telling evidence of historical change—this time, the history of unification and contemporary memorial culture in Germany.[28]

No one involved in the competition program to redevelop the "former site of the SS barracks in Oranienburg" suggested demolishing or building over Sachsenhausen. Sachsenhausen is a state memorial site whose director and professionals are particularly sensitive regarding its prominent location—among the major concentration camps, it is the closest one to the German capital—and promote educational programs for school students, conferences and events for scholars, and information resources for visitors. The city council's competition land did not include the Sachsenhausen memorial site, but it abutted it along the entire length of one the camp's sides, to the southeast. The question is whether the boundaries of the memorial site are sufficient to commemorate and do justice to the history of the concentration camp. Should the large area of SS housing and administrative structures be considered an integral part of Sachsenhausen (and therefore be subject to the same concerns of memorialization and documentary value)? Or does it fall outside of the charged realm of death, torture, and murder associated with the camp and therefore can be normalized under new quotidian uses and without historical markers?

The competition site encompassed an area that included ruins of SS barracks, extant SS structures such as office buildings, and open land (it did not include all Nazi-era buildings in the area—the single-family homes, for example, were outside of the competition site, and so were industrial facilities formerly associated

---

26. Herf, *Divided Memory*, 13.
27. Young, *The Texture of Memory*, 49–80.
28. This includes an exhibition building telling the history of the Soviet special internment camp (1945–50). The building, finished in 2001, sits just outside of the camp, making the connection clear but keeping its history separate from that of the Holocaust and the Third Reich. See "Asymmetrische Balance: Museum sowjetisches Speziallager," *Baumeister* 99, no. 2 (February 2002): 15.

with the camp). The argument could be made that the horrors of a concentration camp were concentrated in certain spaces and structures within the bounded perimeters of the camp: the prisoner barracks, the roll-call square, the gas chamber and crematorium, the watchtowers. But the camp would not have functioned without its supporting, expanding infrastructure where Nazi officers slept, ate, went to the doctor, socialized, exercised, and so on. Put simply, where did the camp end and the non-camp realm begin? The question, I hope, will sound ludicrous, for no concentration camp or other place of imprisonment and death would have functioned without the external support of organizational systems, military power, civilian complicity, and legal and political structures—a point made clear by Theodor Adorno, Hannah Arendt, and the denouncement and prosecution of "desktop murderers."[29] In the case of Sachsenhausen, one is not dealing only with remote sites of logistical management, but also with spatial tentacles that extended the camp's personnel and activities into the fabric and everyday life of Oranienburg.

The area of the SS barracks had been a concrete node between the camp and the city, proof that the life of the camp was intertwined with life in the town. SS officers traveled between the two realms. Their barracks were not in a limbo, but in a transition area; they were the spatial manifestation of the social, cultural, and personal links between "ordinary" Germans and the world of the concentration camps. Perhaps the explicit wish to raze the barracks area masked an implicit wish to move on and sever the ties to the Nazi past, safely encapsulated within the memorial site. Or perhaps the ambiguity of the site, and the ubiquity of such places of "SS domesticity" (if one can put it that way), made it seem that the area and its remnants were not particularly exceptional, eloquent, or archaeologically valuable. Whatever the motivation (and there might have been many different motivations, depending on the person involved), by replacing the remnants of the SS-barracks area with middle-class housing the city would have erased the evidence of connections between town and camp, and the evidence of the implication of the German population in Nazi crimes. Participation in the Holocaust would have been represented in a self-contained way, limited to the gated space of the memorial grounds. Stepping outside of them, one would encounter a normal city, with normal bourgeois homes and normal tree-lined streets.

Boundaries of Memory

It is the liminality of the SS-barracks land that makes it so fraught. This liminality makes the memorial status of the land much more ambiguous than Sachsenhausen. The contemporary cult of memory and museums, associated with but

---

29. Hannah Arendt, *Eichmann in Jerusalem: A Report on the Banality of Evil* (New York: Viking Press, 1963); Theodor Adorno, "Education after Auschwitz," originally published in 1966, in *Critical Models: Interventions and Catchwords* (New York: Columbia University Press, 2005), 191–204.

not limited to the Holocaust, threatens to turn every historic site into a museum removed from everyday life and forever frozen in the representation of one particular moment. Where do the borders of memory stop? If the Holocaust depended on a widespread network of individuals and social groups that pervaded the whole of German society, it may be argued that every plot of land in Germany and its occupied territories is a site of memory. Demarcating a whole continent as a memorial site is an obvious impossibility. Besides, saying that everywhere is a site of memory renders memorialization meaningless. After all, remembrance, memory-work, and reflection on history are situated processes that depend on context and social engagement. They are triggered by the connection of specific sites, events, periods, and persons that anchor historical consciousness in a dynamic relationship, a point made by Pierre Nora in his notorious exploration of "lieux de mémoire."[30] Nora distinguishes between sites "in which a residual sense of continuity remains"—the *lieux de mémoire*—and "settings in which memory is a real part of everyday experience"—the *milieux de mémoire*. For Nora, "*lieux de mémoire* exist because there are no longer any *milieux de mémoire*." If the collective setting for memories of the Nazi experience does not exist in contemporary Germany, there certainly survive residual sites where the "continuity" of memory (to use Nora's word) is anchored by physical structures. The SS area next to the Sachsenhausen concentration camp is one such site. Memory-work is incarnated in the particularities of place and social imaginaries, and this is one reason why vague, general, all-encompassing memorials such as Peter Eisenman's Memorial to the Murdered Jews of Europe in Berlin are so controversial—in the attempt to address everyone, they gloss over so many nuances that they fail to conjure up any vivid sense of historical awareness.

Memorial sites are specific places, but this does not preclude the boundlessness of memory. The history of Sachsenhausen, Oranienburg, and German complicity in the Holocaust could spill out and take over the whole town, the train station where prisoners arrived, the train tracks leading back to their homes. Moreover, the influence of a memorial spreads outside of its confines. The Polish town of Oswiecim extends far beyond the limits of the memorial site of Auschwitz-Birkenau, but the camp is still the city's main claim to fame. Residents may not be too happy about the association with a German-imposed concentration camp, but at the same time local inhabitants benefit from the influx of visitors. Popular memorial sites present local inhabitants and politicians with contradictory associations: an obligation or desire to remember, the incentive to exploit the camp's tourist potential, the wish to move on and build a new history (and a new economic life) based on different or "positive" references. These conflicting forces, which pull social representations and political decisions in opposing directions, are also at play in Oranienburg.

---

30. Pierre Nora, *Realms of Memory: Rethinking the French Past* (New York: Columbia University Press, 1996–98), 1:1.

Memorializing is a function of present uses and views of the past—a point argued in detail by Jennifer Jordan in her study of the social production of memorials in Berlin.[31]

It is impossible to isolate every single site of crime and complicity with the Holocaust—every windowsill where Germans watched passively as their Jewish neighbors were evicted, every store or school where Jews could not enter, every bus or subway stop where a yellow-star-bearing Jew was forbidden to board. At the same time, these places evoke a kind of historical meaning absent from extraordinary sites such as camps or government buildings. The everyday settings of the discrimination and persecution of Jews indicate the myriad ways in which Nazism permeated all aspects of life. A conventional memorial set off from prosaic urban functions, or an exhibition inside a museum, does not fully conjure up this permeation. Countermonuments as defined by James Young (see chapter 1), in turn, are intentionally set up to penetrate the everyday, both by evoking the quotidian face of Nazism, and by engaging contemporary publics in their present realities.

One such example is the *Stolpersteine* installation, by artist Gunter Demnig. The *Stolpersteine*—in German, "stumbling stones"—are small, square cubes of concrete topped by a brass plate set in the pavement of sidewalks in central Berlin neighborhoods and other German cities.[32] Each metal piece is inscribed with the name of a victim of Nazism, the name of the camp where the person died, and the year of death. Each piece is placed in front of the building where the person last lived before deportation. The *Stolpersteine* project makes use of a conventional form— the memorial plaque, with inscriptions of names and dates—in an unconventional way. Instead of placing a reasonably sized plaque on a wall or post, each *Stolperstein* is a miniature memorial plaque on the ground, encrusted in preexisting paving materials such as stone or cement. Unlike conventional memorial signs, the *Stolpersteine* do not occupy a place of honor and high visibility. On the contrary, they are embedded in the floor, small, and hardly perceptible. They are routinely stepped on, sullied by heels and dirt—in a way, desacralized. But they are also pervasive. They insert the ceremonial act of remembering into the banal succession of everyday actions. They collide the oblivious gestures of "normal" life—walking to work, doing groceries, going to a café, waiting for the tram, meeting a friend—with the contrived moment of reflection.

The *Stolpersteine* transform city spaces into porous realms of memory, where past and present mingle irregularly, unexpectedly. The little golden squares imbue

---

31. Jennifer Jordan, *Structures of Memory: Understanding Urban Change in Berlin and Beyond* (Stanford, CA: Stanford University Press, 2006).

32. Gunter Demnig started the *Stolpersteine* project in Cologne in 1992. The first *Stolpersteine* in Berlin were set in 1996. Johannes Heesch and Ulrike Braun, *Orte erinnern: Spuren des NS-Terrors in Berlin— Ein Wegweiser*, ed. Günter Braun (Berlin: Nicolai, 2006), 205. See also the *Stolpersteine* website, http:// www.stolpersteine.eu/.

the city with the obscure force of subconscious mental processes, which propel memories to the surface or submerge them in oblivion. The invisibility of the *Stolpersteine* marks not only remembrance, but also forgetfulness—the inevitable multitude of small forgettings necessary for carrying on everyday life, the forgetting of details or individual names such as those engraved on the metal pieces. The *Stolpersteine* expand their effect beyond their location, changing the perception and experience of city spaces. Someone who does not know about the *Stolpersteine* may easily miss them. However, once the first *Stolperstein* is spotted, others seem to pop up with unavoidable clarity. This prompts the search for even more *Stolpersteine*, so that one now wanders the city attentively looking for them. Regardless of whether there will be *Stolpersteine* at every corner, the ways of looking at the city change and incorporate an awareness of historical significance even in the absence of obvious markers. The *Stolpersteine* coexist with current, diverse uses, and allow for the development and transformation of their sites without losing their poignancy. Is a similar kind of memorialization possible for a large, delimited plot of land such as the SS-barracks terrain in Oranienburg?

Development and Victimization

It is easy to decry the Oranienburg city council's plan for the SS-barracks land as an act of effacement and repression, historically oblivious, even immoral. It is also easy to voice these criticisms from a distance. In the context of Oranienburg's socioeconomic circumstances, it might have been equally easy to understand the idea of an economically sensible development. The mixed-use program of houses and commerce appeared forward looking and up-to-date, at least at the time; it was oriented toward the future. It promised a chance of renovation and rebirth to a town that, in the eyes of some, had fallen—like the whole of East Germany—on the wrong side of the Wall. While West Germany's economy flourished in the 1950s and 1960s thanks to the Marshall Plan (the boom was called *Wirtschaftswunder,* or Economic Miracle), East Germany had to pay heavy reparations to the Soviet Union. East Germany's economic growth was initially stunted by these compensations, which included money, resources, and whole pieces of industrial machinery taken away from the country and reassembled in the Soviet Union. East Germany was a country in ruins, devastated by Allied bombings—two of the most severely hit cities were located there, Dresden and Berlin—and further handicapped by the Soviet removal of resources. Besides the divergence in postwar treatment by the Soviets and the western Allies, East Germany was controlled by prolonged Soviet rule. The nation did enjoy economic development from the 1960s, and eventually became a showcase of the Second World. But this development was restricted by economic planning, local mismanagement, technological shortcomings, and the eventual overall failure of Communism that resulted in the collapse of the Iron

Curtain. By the mid-1980s East Germany was already full of obsolete factories, superfluous workers, and financial difficulties.

A place like Oranienburg was doubly injured, tainted by the association with Nazism embodied by Sachsenhausen. Not only was the town economically depressed, drained by the collapse of the GDR, and pervaded by the anxieties of cultural and political upheaval—it also had the burden of the Third Reich. This is a symbolic burden on the city's image and identity, and a concrete burden that congeals a major piece of land as a memorial removed from profitable uses. The burden of Nazism is associated with a more widespread phenomenon that cuts across boundaries in Germany. It is the representation of Germany as a victim of historical circumstances, which may invoke civil and military victims of the war; the ravaging "Bomber War,"[33] which arguably used far more destructive power than was necessary for victory; and the hardship of the immediate postwar, with the *Trümmerfrauen* (the "rubble women," who cleared up Germany's bombed cities), occupation, division, the Berlin airlift crisis (*Luftbrücke*), and the Wall. But the representation of "victim Germany"[34] can be slippery. It can suggest that Germany was a victim of Hitler and Nazism, that the Third Reich was an alien regime imposed on the German people.

Following this logic, the legacy of the Third Reich, the continuous obligation to atone before the rest of the world, can also be read as an imposition, a renewed form of victimization. Even those who accept historical responsibility for the Nazis may feel unjustly charged with the crimes of their ancestors. This view was expressed publicly by Michael Sturmer, Helmut Kohl's conservative adviser, who decried the prolonged self-imposed modesty of West Germany as a sort of ascetic humility, and used unification as the chance to reassert a proud national identity: "The time has come, in matters of symbols, style, and architecture, to make up for what for forty years seemed superfluous because of the German past and the European future."[35] The idea of a "victim Germany" may be a cynical role reversal, or else a case of projective identification. Regardless, national victimization can be felt as a real phenomenon by inhabitants of places like Oranienburg, in the shadows of a concentration camp and of the Berlin Wall. It was as if Oranienburg itself had been, for all these years, the last remaining inmate of Sachsenhausen.

---

33. Robin Neillands, *The Bomber War: The Allied Air Offensive against Nazi Germany* (New York: The Overlook Press, 2001).

34. Jane Kramer, *The Politics of Memory* (New York: Random House, 1998), 263; Bill Niven, ed., *Germans as Victims: Remembering the Past in Contemporary Germany* (New York: Palgrave Macmillan, 2006). I address the issue of German victimization in memorials in "A Memorial Laissez-Passer? Church Exhibitions and National Victimhood in Germany," in *Memorialisation in Germany since 1945*, ed. Bill Niven and Chloe Paver (New York: Palgrave Macmillan, 2010), 58–68.

35. Quoted in Michael Wise, *Capital Dilemma: Germany's Search for a New Architecture of Democracy* (New York: Princeton Architectural Press, 1998), 17.

MoƐrning

This discussion should by now have provided a context for understanding the problematic status of the design competition for the SS-barracks land in Oranienburg: the complications of memory in a liminal space such as the competition design plot; and Oranienburg's particular socioeconomic circumstances right after unification. The pull of conflicting forces such as the wish for development and the weight of memory explains why all of the architects who entered the competition except for one complied with the city council's program, and why the city council awarded first prize to one of these designs. But it also explains why one of the architects decided to veer away from the stipulated requirements, proposing instead not just a striking design, but a striking new program.

In 1992, Daniel Libeskind's architecture practice was located in Berlin. Three years earlier, he had won the competition for redesigning the Jewish Museum in Berlin and moved to the city for the construction work (the museum would take more than ten years to finish; shortly after it was completed Libeskind moved his office to New York City). Immersed in the architectural scene of Berlin, he engaged fully in the intense debates about design, history, and urbanism that took over the capital as Berlin underwent its massive makeover. Libeskind took part in several of the most important design competitions for Berlin and Germany—and there were many of them, as the public and private sponsors of Berlin's new architecture often preferred to organize competitions rather than commission architects directly.[36] Libeskind submitted an entry to the high-profile Potsdamer Platz master plan contest, won second place in the Alexanderplatz competition, and sent out proposals for contexts as varied as a city planning concept for the area of Lichterfelde South in Berlin, an office complex in Wiesbaden, the Felix Nussbaum museum in Osnabrück (built in 1998), the music hall in Bremen, and the Holocaust Memorial in Berlin. His hermetic blueprints and models did not deter juries, and even when he did not take first place he drew enough attention to influence the debate.

This was the case in Sachsenhausen. Libeskind's proposal was a critical revision of the program, rejecting the "trivializing" uses of housing and leisure, and proposing instead a series of institutions for social and professional development in a setting that maintained the vestiges of the past and the awareness of the SS barracks, as I will explain in more detail below.[37] The focus of these institutions actually overlapped with some of the program requirements of the original competition, which called for social-interest and public facilities.[38] Because Libeskind did not follow the competition brief, he was disqualified, but his proposal elicited

---

36. On the culture of architectural competitions, see Carola Hein, "La culture des concours en Allemagne et au Japon," *A+* 6 (December/January 2000): 96–102.

37. Daniel Libeskind, "MoUrning: Arrangement of the Sachsenhausen Concentration Camp," *L'architettura: Cronache e Storia* 40 (1994): 549; "MoUrning," text submitted with the competition entry.

38. Stadt Oranienburg, *Gutachterverfahren* (1992?), 70–73.

such a strong reaction that he earned an honorary mention.[39] Confronted with the competition's winning entry, and with Libeskind's critical proposal, members of the Oranienburg municipal government called for a change of plans. The chief of Oranienburg's planning department, Christian Kielczynski, stated that "Libeskind's provocation spurred a thought process among us."[40] In addition, the private developer who was going to invest in the mixed-use residential project—and who did not know about the site's history—pulled out upon being informed of the area's use by the Nazis.[41] The city of Oranienburg finally rejected the housing complex project, and asked for the adoption of Libeskind's program and design, which was revised in consultation with the city council.

A few pages above I described the *Stolpersteine* installation and asked whether Oranienburg could have a similar memorial—a critical marker of the city's complicity with Nazism that at the same time did not prevent current and future development. This is what Libeskind managed to do, although in a very different manner and scale. His entry cleverly addressed the need for development—perhaps even more effectively than the housing and commerce proposals. In 1992 there was a flood of real estate investment in Berlin, which may have given Oranienburg the hope to promote the same kind of spatial and economic upgrading. But by the end of the decade Berlin was in a financial crisis. The fiscal deficit was related to a struggling local economy where private investment had been lower than expected. Office and housing vacancies kept real estate prices in the 1990s and 2000s far below those in other large German cities, such as Munich, Frankfurt, and Hamburg. This might not have been the most favorable context for a mixed-used housing development in Oranienburg. Libeskind proposed a different program, which responded to the needs of the local population (instead of catering to an expected influx of new suburbanites) without playing into the logic of private capital enterprises.

Libeskind divided the competition site into three zones (fig. 15). One of the sections would be a newly planted forest, which is both a sign of rebirth and a response to East Germany's pollution.[42] In the middle of the forest Libeskind placed the second zone, which is the centerpiece of the project: a linear area cutting through the topography of the land, and containing a series of small buildings and open spaces, called "Hope Incision." The buildings would house public institutions or private foundations devoted to education, therapy, and personal development: a chapel, a rehabilitation center, studios for local artisans, a memorial foundation, among others. While private developments such as real estate enterprises or corporate

---

39. Daniel Libeskind, interview, October 10, 2014.

40. Quoted in Susanne Lenz, "Libeskind will die Geometrie des Terrors durchbrechen," *Berliner Zeitung*, May 26, 1998, http://www.berliner-zeitung.de/archiv/auch-oranienburg-ist-nun-fuer-den-plan-des-architekten-auf-dem-einstigen-ss-gelaende---einwaende-hat-nur-der-denkmalschutz-libeskind-will-die-geometrie-des-terrors-durchbrechen,10810590,9435026.html.

41. Lenz, "Libeskind will die Geometrie des Terrors durchbrechen."

42. Merkl, "Reinventing German National Identity," 1.

Figure 15. Daniel Libeskind, Project Mo⊠rning, Oranienburg, overview of model. The triangle at the top right of the image is the site of the Sachsenhausen concentration camp. The white irregular pentagon at the top left is the area of SS ruins. The adjacent dark, four-sided polygon is an area of proposed reforestation. The long, narrow white rectangle that cuts across this reforestation area is the Hope Incision. © Studio Libeskind

offices generate revenue but do not necessarily benefit local inhabitants, the Hope Incision would offer the possibility for the social and economic integration of East Germans. This may be a slower development strategy than Berlin's private investment boom, but it is also a more solid and enduring approach grounded on local relations, not on fickle foreign capital. The workshops for handcrafts are one example. In the GDR, artisans were subsidized by the government and could devote themselves almost completely to their production without worrying about having to sell it for a living.[43] After unification—and 1992, the time of the competition, was only two years after the event—these artisans suddenly had to deal with high, free-market rents, and with having to market their production and compete with each other and with seasoned West German artists. The workshops in the Hope Incision would have offered a smoother transition. They would have provided working space, taking the pressure away from finding affordable studios. They would also have offered a sense of community and collaboration without removing artisans from the marketplace. The Hope Incision was explicitly aimed at marginalized social groups. It also carried on the mission of historical awareness and education in the memorial and education foundations.

The Hope Incision cuts through the forest zone. Its slanted orientation leads west to the Sachsenhausen memorial site and to the third section of the competition terrain. This zone was conceived as a place for contemplation, where ruins of the SS barracks would be submerged under water (fig. 16). The lake would be crisscrossed by platforms—a combination of landscape art and memorial where visitors would contemplate the decaying ruins through their embodied experience of this unusual arrangement. The Hope Incision pointed both to this "waterland" and to the Sachsenhausen memorial site. It was a line of force leading to the symbolic gravity center of the whole area—the point of intersection between Sachsenhausen and the competition terrain, the point of convergence between camp and town. In addition, the angle of the Hope Incision aligns with the angle of the death march in 1945, when SS officers forced prisoners to evacuate the camp as they retreated from the advancing Red Army.

By positioning the Hope Incision in this way—an odd angle within the competition plot, which seems to waste space rather than make the most efficient use of it—Libeskind symbolically expanded the terrain to include the Sachsenhausen concentration camp. Instead of turning its back on it, as the housing development would have done, the Hope Incision rejoined the whole area. The competition terrain appeared as the lower part of the extended triangle of Sachsenhausen, instead of remaining a self-contained trapezoid. The crisscrossing bridges over the waterland reinforced this connection as they penetrated the site of the concentration camp, stitching it back to the SS-barracks ruins.

43. Kramer, *The Politics of Memory*, 177–86.

Figure 16. Daniel Libeskind, Project Mo⊠rning, detail. In the foreground, the lighter-colored area is the "waterland" of submerged SS ruins. The black lines on top of it are elevated walkways. In the background, the dark reforestation area is cut by the white volumes of the Hope Incision.
© Studio Libeskind

Libeskind called his design Mo⊠rning, a play on the words "mourning" and "morning" that signals the duality between mourning Sachsenhausen and a new morning (future) for Oranienburg. By crossing the letter *U*, Libeskind resorts to the philosophical gesture of placing concepts *sous rature* (under erasure), a gesture associated with Jacques Derrida, who in turn borrowed the device from Martin Heidegger.[44] *Sous rature* suspends the usual meaning of a word without canceling it out completely; it indicates both an attempt to delete the word (or idea) and the impossibility of doing so. A crossed-out concept remains as an indelible vestige or trace, an imprint of the former integral word. It calls attention to the act of erasure itself, and to the tension between the intended disappearance and the lingering presence. In Libeskind's Mo⊠rning, mourning and morning coexist in a state of permanent and constitutive tension. The development in the Hope Incision provides opportunities for moving on, but it cannot exist apart from the memories of

---

44. Heidegger had crossed the word *Sein* in a 1955 letter to Ernst Junger. For Derrida's use of *sous rature*, see Jacques Derrida, *Of Grammatology* (Baltimore: Johns Hopkins University Press, 1976), 44.

Sachsenhausen or the history of the SS barracks. The tension extends to his design. The waterland places the vestigial remnants of the SS barracks *sous rature*; that is, it erases these remnants while making their lingering presence evident. The word under erasure is, like the buildings, a ruin—a defaced, incomplete sign of multiple and conflicting historical meanings.

Libeskind's design for Oranienburg evokes his project for the Jewish Museum in Berlin, which is also built around an irresolvable tension. The Jewish Museum had originally been commissioned as an extension of the Berlin Museum, housed in a baroque building called Kollegienhaus (later, the Berlin Museum was moved elsewhere, and the Kollegienhaus was repurposed as an ancillary structure to the Jewish Museum, housing a bookstore, café, coat check, and the entrance). When explaining his project, Libeskind speaks of an irreconcilable contradiction, encapsulated by the very program: how can one build a Jewish Museum right next to a Berlin Museum, in the city where the Holocaust was planned, a city whose Jewish community was extinguished by extermination or deportation? And how can one *not* build such a museum, when this Jewish community had been such an integral part of the history of this same city? The quandary, for Libeskind, is precisely what made the commission productive; he sought not to eliminate conflict but rather to expose it.[45]

He gave this quandary material form in the visible disconnection between the new building of the Jewish Museum and the old building of the Berlin Museum. The two structures are connected by a subterranean corridor, the only public access to the Jewish Museum. In order to enter the Jewish Museum, one has to go through the Berlin Museum; however, this connection cannot be seen from the outside, where the two buildings remain separated by an empty space. The invisible connection refers to the relationship between Jewish history and Berlin history—once inextricably linked, then irreversibly fractured by Nazism, and now brought together again. Libeskind wanted to avoid any semblance of reconciliation, compensation, or overcoming—the idea that a Jewish Museum in Berlin could redeem the disappearance of Berlin Jews. In Oranienburg, he does the same, as his project provides for redevelopment without entailing the full overcoming of the past—in German, *Vergangenheitsbewältigung*.

The submersion of the SS-barrack ruins under water is a radical instance of counterpreservation. Libeskind does not treat these ruins as pieces of historic evidence that should be preserved or restored. Instead, he accelerates their decomposition by flooding them in a slowly corroding medium. The ruins would gradually dissolve in the water, as it were. Visitors could gaze at the process from the platforms that would cut the waterland in all directions, a bizarre maze of narrow passageways. The water and the passageways frame the past, draw attention to it,

---

45. Daniel Libeskind, *The Space of the Encounter* (New York: Universe, 2000), 23–28.

and make it into the object of reflection—the sole "function" of the walkways is to lead visitors to this self-immersed contemplation. At the same time, the water underscores that the past is inaccessible. The visual mediation of the water suggests the mediation of time and changing social contexts that separate present reflection from the past. No matter how much thinking, learning, writing, atoning, discussing, and self-reflecting we do about Nazism and the Holocaust, we can never fully know them, nor can we fully comprehend the trauma of a camp survivor or the perplexing complicity of "common" Germans. This may sound obvious, but the curatorial practices of the current "Holocaust industry" put such an emphasis on reconstructed settings, authentic objects, and comprehensive information that they effectively convey the idea that full knowledge is possible and that a museum visitor can put herself in the shoes of a concentration camp inmate.[46]

Libeskind's waterland violates the historical object—an effect not unlike that of the *Stolpersteine* installation, which places victims' names under trampling feet. The water would not be a neutral frame over the SS-barrack ruins—it would promote their decomposition. In the introduction to this book I defined counterpreservation as the incorporation of the passage of time. The waterland in Libeskind's design does more than that—it *becomes* the passage of time, interfering with the process of decay. The water not only frames memory; it is itself part of a memorial process that as such enacts inevitable intervention on the memorialized object. Memory-work is not a simple recollection of facts, an impassive replaying of events in the mind's eye. Remembrance is an active process that changes what is remembered, and engages present affects and emotions. Libeskind's waterland may be a gesture of overcoming, of triumphing over a former site of terror with the renewing, cleansing force of water. The water slowly destroying the SS barracks is a belated revenge, although the proximity to the Sachsenhausen memorial site would prevent any impression that this revenge or overcoming could ever be fully carried out as compensation.

The waterland also recalls the dimming of a historical event's meaning in collective memory. At the beginning of the twenty-first century, the Holocaust is still part of contemporary history, even for younger generations. Some camp survivors, German and Allied soldiers, and even Nazi officers are still alive or have died in the recent past. Their experiences have directly shaped their descendants' relationship to the past. But will the Holocaust, and Nazism, and Adolf Hitler's biography maintain the same sense of urgency in one or two hundred years, regardless of what historians might say about the exceptionality of the event? Certainly the more general questions such as the dangers of authoritarianism, racism, fundamentalism, and belligerence resonate far beyond the Third Reich. But the vivid gruesomeness, the horror of the events in which these concepts were incarnated, inevitably recede

---

46. See Tim Cole's critique of the United States Holocaust Memorial Museum in Washington in Cole, *Selling the Holocaust* (New York: Routledge, 1999), 171.

into the background. The Thirty Years' War, for instance, was one of the most traumatic, prolonged experiences of destruction in Germany, but today it carries none of the terror it probably evoked as a collective memory in the seventeenth and eighteenth centuries.[47]

Quite aside from scholarly debates on the historical uniqueness of the Holocaust or Germany's *Sonderweg,* the piling up of new events and social currents will likely cloud the relevance of Nazism for future generations. The gradual erosion wrought by the water on the SS barracks and the increasing invisibility of the ruins mirror this gradual fading of events in social memory. The project would not do this uncritically, as if to endorse social amnesia, but rather to draw attention to it—because if the ruins disintegrated, the water would remain as a monumental mnemonic sign. In addition, it is important to picture the pace of the process that Libeskind had in mind. His office consulted with experts from different fields to understand how decay would happen, where, and how fast, and to modulate the design accordingly. Libeskind notes that this decay would have been "a very long process, a generational process, it would not happen overnight"; it would have been phased, "gradual and visible"—unlike the weathering that can go unnoticed when one is not paying attention.[48]

Even though the waterland would eventually destroy the SS barracks, it would at the same time perpetuate a bottomless search for the past. The opaque body of water would tease the gaze of visitors, inviting them to solve its mystery but always denying the full disclosure of its contents. Young notes that several of Germany's countermonuments are "vanishing monuments"—objects conceived to disappear, with a programmed limited duration.[49] Although the waterland itself would remain, it would slowly erase the signs of the past. The waterland would be an active memorial, underscoring its own destructiveness. This subtle incorporation of violence and annihilating power refuses the idea of peaceful reconciliation and forgiveness. Rather, it hints at a way of overpowering the perpetrators—a posthumous revenge, maybe, or a belated (and therefore impossible) self-liberation.

The incorporation of destructiveness avoids the univocal reading of water as a symbol of life and rebirth. The symbolism is undeniably present—it is hard not to think of such commonplace images as the bag of water in a mother's womb, the baptismal water (although for Jewish victims this would hardly be an appropriate evocation), or the primordial oceans that were the source of earthly life. So the waterland might be read as a source of new life, or as a cleansing substance purifying Oranienburg's ground from its undesirable past. The association is not completely

---

47. The Thirty Years' War lasted from 1618 to 1648. During the war, the population of Berlin dropped from 12,000 to 6,000. The impact of physical destruction and human losses, as well as the prolonged trauma of the war, reverberated into the next century.

48. Libeskind, interview, October 10, 2014.

49. Young, *The Texture of Memory,* 27–48.

denied by Libeskind's pun on Mo**u**rning and his social and cultural program in the Hope Incision, which would bring new life to the terrain. Libeskind himself has alluded to baptism when speaking about the project.[50] He speaks of the water as "very important. There is an element of reflecting physically, there is an element of water as a piece of nature. . . . Water is a good thing, so many connotations, it would allow you to see something different about it."[51]

Along these positive lines, and in the same vein of sustaining an irresolvable tension, I argue that the waterland emphasizes the destructive potency of water. The waterland would be a murky, slightly threatening body—not a crystalline, cleansing bath. It would be irreversibly contaminated by the Nazi-barracks ruins, and its purpose would be not to fertilize or reconsecrate the land, but to seal it and prevent any further uses, as a kind of perpetual dumping ground of history. This is indirectly demonstrated by the fact that Libeskind explicitly designates another section of the land for life and regrowth: the reforestation around the Hope Incision. There is no duplication of functions in his carefully zoned plot. The waterland is the contemplative area set off from everyday functions, while the forest is fully integrated in the current productive uses of the Hope Incision. It is a complex connection between the impossibility of overcoming the past and the need for new life.

The language of life and death is not new in memorials conceived for Nazi sites. The winning proposal for the competition for the former site of the Gestapo headquarters in Berlin (a competition that took place in 1982 but was never built) called for a rigid grid of trees rising out of the terrain. Jürgen Wenzel and Nikolaus Lang "envisioned a flat plane of cast-iron plates, set off by chestnut trees, imprinted with reproductions of original [Nazi] documents . . . and the footprints of the original buildings, including the Gestapo headquarters."[52] The trees would be planted on living ground, but the ground would be covered with metal plates inscribed with text and images. This dense forest would carry life and rebirth from the invisible fertile land up to the treetops. At the same time, the metal plates and the uncannily regimental ordering of the trees would deny any notion of organic growth or nature. Karen Till notes that the proposal would submit the terrain to "a modern rational perspective to space and time, smoothing a horizon and fixing a moment of time."[53] This could be said to be a double moment: the moment of memorial action, of the iron plates and chestnut trees; and the moment to which the memorial turned in reaffirming the former use of the land as headquarters of Hitler's secret police. The metal plates would prevent future uses that could possibly reinsert the land in normal, everyday life. The combination of trees and

---

50. Mary Williams Walsh, "A Grand Design for a Nazi Camp," *Los Angeles Times*, January 17, 1998, http://articles.latimes.com/1998/jan/17/news/mn-9128.

51. Libeskind, interview, October 10, 2014.

52. Karen Till, *The New Berlin: Memory, Politics, Place* (Minneapolis: University of Minnesota Press, 2005), 91.

53. Ibid.

metal plates would function in a manner similar to Libeskind's complementary conception of the forest and the waterland—two simple, highly evocative devices associated with the opposing forces of life and death. The interest of Libeskind's design, and of Wenzel and Lang's Gestapo terrain memorial, lies precisely in this combination—not in any single one of its components, but in the ongoing tension of their dual coexistence. These two memorial conceptions would have sealed historically charged land against normalizing uses, and they would have also sealed them against forgetting.

Libeskind's use of water also recalls Horst Hoheisel's Aschrottbrunnen memorial in Kassel.[54] The Aschrottbrunnen memorial commemorates a fountain destroyed by the Nazis in 1939.[55] The Nazis called it "the Jew's fountain,"[56] because the structure had been commissioned by a wealthy member of the city's Jewish community, Sigmund Aschrott, in 1908. In 1943 the site of the vacant fountain was turned into a flowerbed and nicknamed "Aschrott's Grave" by local inhabitants.[57] In the postwar era a new fountain was built, "but by then, only a few of the city's oldtimers could recall that its name had ever been Aschrott's anything."[58] The missing fountain in the town's central square attested to forgetting and repression. Hoheisel's memorial design, built in 1987, addresses not only the fountain's destruction during the Third Reich, but the repressed memory during the postwar period. The installation reproduces the original fountain in concrete. Hoheisel displayed the concrete cast for a few weeks before sinking it upside down. Now the concrete mirror-image of the original fountain is inaccessible, placed underground as a "funnel into whose darkness water runs down," in Hoheisel's words.[59] The fountain's site is an empty space in the square, marked by lines and water channels along the fountain's former footprint. The murmur of the water draws attention, inviting the visitor to follow its course from the surface to the submerged memorial. The Aschrottbrunnen memorial anchors the city's central space in the memory of the absent fountain, which stands for the extinct Jewish community of which the original monument was a sign. The memorial makes the absence tangible, calling attention to the shortcomings of Germany's relationship to its past—the fact that the town officially forgot its disappeared Jews for half a century. This contradictory goal—to incarnate an absence concretely—engenders what Young calls the

---

54. Libeskind would rework this water-ruin idea in his design for the slurry wall of the World Trade Center site, but reversing the meaning. The exposed damp ruin would attest to its resilience and not be deteriorated over time.

55. The city's official website (http://www.kassel.de/cms02/stadt/geschichte/gedenktafeln/00105/) gives 1939 as the destruction date.

56. James Young, "Germany's Memorial Question: Memory, Counter-memory, and the End of the Monument," *South Atlantic Quarterly* 96, no.4 (Fall 1997): 865.

57. Young, *The Texture of Memory*, 43.

58. Ibid.

59. Cited in Young, *The Texture of Memory,* 45.

"vanishing" monument. Vanishing monuments construct loud absences and resort to the imagery of voids, wounds, and disappearances.[60]

Hoheisel's buried fountain is a new artifact produced at the end of the century, while the SS barracks in Oranienburg are remains of original buildings. The fountain memorial is an iconic sign of the past, while the barracks ruins are the continued material presence of the past itself. However, it would be unproductive—and perhaps simplistic—to oppose these two examples as the "authentic" versus the "reproduction." The barracks certainly have value as historic evidence, but they only have meaning within social and cultural contexts—otherwise they are just, as Young says, "mere stones in a landscape."[61] To endow these ruins with an intrinsic historical essence is to fetishize them. The danger with fetishization is regarding objects as self-sufficient repositories of meaning, independent of social context—letting the objects do the memory-work for us. The evocative power of the SS-barracks ruins is thus comparable to that of the new Aschrott fountain memorial—as material signs that are able to trigger consciousness within a situated context of cultural and social meanings.

Young defines a countermonument as a memorial irrevocably grounded in the present, which calls attention to its own process of production and reception even as it refers to a past event. Both the Aschrottbrunnen and Libeskind's waterland use water to join the image of the past to reflection in the present. This joining is both symbolic and concrete. The murmur of the subterranean Aschrottbrunnen and the occasional sparkles of running water beneath the metal grilles on the pavement act as triggers for historical meditation. Without spelling out historical facts, they suggest that historical awareness can only be retrieved if the visitor actively engages her imagination in a process of critical thinking—not necessarily, or not only a private "interior" process, but also a social process through dialogue and exchange; a process performed in public, in the open space of a central town square. Similarly, the waterland thrusts the visitor into the middle of an unfamiliar space that reveals just enough to prompt more inquiry and reflection in the threshold between interiority and the vastness of an open space.

But the joining of past and present is not only symbolic. The Aschrottbrunnen links the missing fountain to the town's present on the surface of the square's pavement. The delineation of the fountain's former footprint indicates the points where today's visitors can step onto the original fountain site and thus onto historic ground. Libeskind's waterland joins the image of the past (the submerged ruins) to that of the present (the reflected sky, the mirrored image of visitors peering over the

---

60. Young, "Germany's Memorial Question," 865; Young, *The Texture of Memory*, 43–46. The language and imagery of the void work effectively in the Aschrottbrunnen and in other Holocaust memorials and buildings—including Libeskind's own Jewish Museum—but they have also become somewhat of a cliché in references to Holocaust memorialization.

61. Young, *The Texture of Memory*, 2.

walkways). I have made the distinction between "symbolic" and "concrete" self-consciously because I believe it to be fallacious. The physical presence of the two memorials—their visual and material existence—is inseparable from the meanings they may evoke. The division is as artificial as that between form and content, which is not to say that they are one and the same thing. Rather, I want to suggest an imbrication between meaning and materiality that stresses their interconnection without reducing one to the other.

Libeskind's waterland, however, was too costly and complicated to build. When the city council overturned the competition's decision and demanded Libeskind's plan instead, they asked the architect to revise his plan.[62] One of the revisions was to replace the waterland with crisscrossing water-filled channels. These channels follow the same intersecting, crosscutting pathways of the former suspended walkways over the lake, but the figure-ground relationship is now reversed: the water is contained in these narrow lines, and the surface is dry. In Libeskind's description,

> The canals and the water around the ruins of the SS were implemented in order to separate these houses from the day-to-day routine of the normal. That was the reason we had the canals and the water, to make a distinction between so-called normal and where you are, what you are confronted with.
>
> The canals were two to three meters wide, they were partly not flooded, but only trenches, to help expose the archaeology of the site. . . . You still had a fracturing experience of the site, but not through the completely covered area, but I would say through very precarious walks across the site to your destination. . . . One might see it also as a reflection, a physical reflection and a reflection on the site.[63]

Visitors would be able to meander freely around the barracks ruins, while the water canals would keep the sense of framing and intentional demarcation of the original proposal. The water canals are a different way of penetrating the site, as disruptive as the lake—perhaps even more, because while the walkways over the lake would have provided a sense of continuity for pedestrians, elevating them above the liquid surface, the water canals would have interrupted their hikes across the site and forced them to take different directions through "very precarious walks." This precariousness, both of the walking experience and of the unfinished trench-like appearance of the canals, would have added to the perception of pervasive ruination, incorporating the aesthetics of counterpreservation even further. Still filled with water, the canals would indicate the contemplative and memorial quality of the area, and would interpose a mediation between present and past.

---

62. Libeskind, "MoUrning," 549.
63. Libeskind, interview, October 10, 2014.

Defamiliarization

The water-filled channels do not have the same sweeping effect of the waterland, but they create a unique environment in their own way. The channels would be glistening lines cutting through the ground and interrupting or redirecting the ways to walk. Water channels have been used for infrastructure in several cities, as open canalization, for cleaning or gray water disposal, and to provide drinking water for animals. Open canalization can be improvised or even temporary, as some alleys or streets may be periodically flooded; and in other places it is permanent, built into the street bed—for example, in Freiburg's *Bächle*, which are narrow waterways that line the streets in the medieval core of the city. Originally the *Bächle* served as sewage disposal, as water source for firefighting, and as drinking fountains for cows. With modernization the *Bächle* perform none of these functions anymore, but the city has maintained the crisply cut canals as a distinctive feature of its medieval landscape. Libeskind's canals, taken by themselves, recall such infrastructural drainage or irrigation, which may be a familiar sight in both rural and urban settings. This makes Libeskind's canals at once familiar and strange. Their oddness comes not from sheer foreignness, but from the subjacent familiarity within the apparent strangeness. This sustained friction between the habitual and the uncanny underlies not only the Oranienburg design, but also most of Libeskind's earlier works.

The sense of displacement, defamiliarization, and instability is not merely a final formal result. The emphasis is on the *process* of composition. Take, for instance, Libeskind's installation *Line of Fire*. The *Line of Fire* is the collision between two lines: one, continuous but tortuous; the other, straight but interrupted. The shape of the tortuous line does not appear as a finished, sculpted object, but as the result of conflicting and dynamic forces; it is not so much an intentional zigzag as it is a deformed straight slab. Conversely, the interrupted straight line that cuts across the *Line of Fire* cannot be reduced to a sequence of separate fragments. Rather, it is first and foremost a previously cohesive line that has been dismantled. It evokes the process of splintering and separation by hinting at its lost wholeness. The *Line of Fire* is the encounter between different, conflicting lines of force that transform an ordinary object—a linear, rectangular slab—into a distorted shape.

The Oranienburg design resorts to the same devices of displacement. The whole terrain is reconfigured through crisscrossing and colliding lines: the line between the forest and the SS-barracks area; the bold inclined line of the Hope Incision; the cutting narrow lines of the water canals (or walkways over the waterland in the first iteration). Even the buildings within the Hope Incision are linear—their geometric shapes complement one another as broken fragments of an original whole, like the interrupted straight line of the *Line of Fire*. The repetition of lines is a recurring, self-conscious leitmotif announced in the surface of the *Micromegas* drawing series; in the title of the Jewish Museum project (called *Between the Lines*); and in the guiding compositional principles of projects as varied as the Potsdamer Platz urban redesign and the Felix Nussbaum museum. The lines appear in the narrow, gash-like windows of the Jewish Museum, and in the long, prismatic volume of the Tower of Freedom (part of Libeskind's winning entry in the World Trade Center competition).

Libeskind's drawings and blueprints are textured surfaces without a single vanishing point or line of flight. The eye wanders back and forth over his compositions, along paths that end abruptly or intersect with each other unexpectedly. This is, as suggested above, an aesthetics of irresolvable conflict. But this aesthetics is also an architectural suggestion of Gilles Deleuze's conception of lines of force and assemblages. The Deleuzian assemblage is an epistemological perspective that accounts for the myriad forces that define and reconfigure individuals, groups, contexts, and historical meanings. The assemblage is *not* an all-encompassing explanation that tries to account for every single aspect of history according to an overall principle. The assemblage is also nonteleological. At every point, any given social context is defined by multiple and conflicting impulses, not all of them equal, and not all of them permanent. The interaction of these forces can develop in different ways, not necessarily following a predetermined outcome or telos.

Deleuze's language is quite abstract. He describes the assemblage as "a multiplicity of dimensions, of lines and directions."[64] Any assemblage is constituted and "cut up" by multiple and varied lines. These lines determine identities, trajectories, states, and inclinations. They also remove the notion of intentionality or agency, "as if something carried us away, across our segments, but also across our thresholds, toward a destination which is unknown, not foreseeable, not preexistent."[65] Deleuze's formulation is indebted to Friedrich Nietzsche. Instead of the line, however, the German philosopher uses the concept of force, as in the following passage: "We as conscious, purposive creatures, are only the smallest part of us. Of the numerous influences operating at every moment, e.g., air, electricity, we sense almost nothing: there could well be forces that, although we never sense them, continually influence us."[66] Both Nietzsche and Deleuze suggest the multiplicity and unpredictability of contexts and events. They refuse cohesive, coherent narratives and point instead to the gaps in self-knowledge and self-control, to the obscure and indeterminate influences that shape social and individual life.

This concept has many implications, some of which are especially relevant when discussing Libeskind's architecture. The rejection of an omnipotent, omniscient subject questions basic premises of the architectural profession. Modern architectural design, born out of the philosophical values of the Enlightenment and the rationalism of the Industrial Revolution, assumes a subject that is fully conscious and

---

64. Gilles Deleuze and Claire Parnet, *Dialogues II* (New York: Columbia University Press, 2007), 133.
65. Ibid., 125.
66. Friedrich Nietzsche, *The Will to Power* (New York: Random House, 1968), 357.

fully in control of all the processes of creation. The modern architect orchestrates art, construction, engineering, social ideals, economic considerations, and cultural values in a synthetic expression. This activity, marked by the precision of science and technology, is given creative unity in and by the demiurgic figure of the architect. The myth of individual artistic genius common to other modernist arts is expressed in the modernist architect's charge over all aspects and scales of design, from objects and furniture to individual buildings to whole cities and landscapes. Libeskind's architecture rejects this heroic view and incorporates extraneous elements in the process of design: irrational or unconscious influences, context, history, and even randomness and chance. Libeskind's attention to context, and his attempt to create open designs that can change over time and accommodate multiple meanings, indicate this embrace of unknown or foreign forces, and even—as Nietzsche might have put it—a "love of fate." The intricate patterns of his *Micromegas,* the interwoven texture of his design for the Alexanderplatz area, and the unwieldy complexity of his Potsdamer Platz master plan seem spatial incarnations of the Deleuzian assemblage, complete with differentiated lines of force. But this relationship is also apparent in more straightforward elements. The waterland in Oranienburg integrates a potentially uncontrollable force—water—whose effects on the terrain are not completely predictable.

Libeskind's conception is especially suited to Germany's complicated relationship to history. Any attempt to make sense of Nazism or the Holocaust inevitably stumbles on irreconcilable conflicts. Whether one argues that Nazism and concentration camps were the ultimate outcome of modern rationality (for instance, the characterization of concentration camps as industries of death), or rather that the Third Reich is evidence of a persistent barbarianism that subsisted in spite of modernity and the Enlightenment, the conclusion is always an irresolvable contradiction. It is either the contradiction within a system of thought (modern reason), or the clash between two systems (progress versus destructiveness, modernity versus irrationality, etc.). There is a sense of perplexity in the shortcomings of modern reason, whether because of a fatal flaw or because of a failure to live up to its potential. The concept of assemblage provides a different way of thinking through these contradictions—a way that neither glosses over conflict nor becomes paralyzed in perplexity. The assemblage is always already fraught. Conflicting impulses coexist and are mutually constitutive. They do not exclude each other as they would under a Cartesian logic. This approach avoids the sense of overdetermination (a kind of pessimistic teleology) that accompanies descriptions of Nazism as the inevitable, doomed fate of modern rationality. It also prevents the frustration and sense of failure of those who decry the modern impotence against phenomena such as fundamentalism, racism, and destructiveness. The assemblage admits inner contradictions, and at the same time denies that the product of these contradictions can be determined a priori, according to some hidden logic.

Libeskind's design for Oranienburg plays out these ideas by refusing to solve the town's dilemma between present and past, and instead laying the conflict bare. Perhaps even more clearly than the pathways suspended on the waterland, the water-filled channels express this complexity—a necessarily open-ended view of history that does not redeem a calamity like the Holocaust, but that might help understand how it could come about in an ostensibly civilized society. The water channels, therefore, present the possibility of an incredibly rich web of meaning and historical reflection. They also pose the risk, of course, that all of this—the semantic complexity, the complicated view of history, the sustained tension, the Deleuzian assemblage—be lost in hermeticism. Unlike the evident intervention of the waterland—evident also in its "aggression" toward the site—the effect of the water channels might in the end be simply confusing. Someone walking along their path might lose sight of the bird's-eye view of intricate intersections; the confinement of water in the channels might not be enough to suggest its relationship to neighboring ruins. This is a risk in an open-ended, abstract design that refuses figurative representations or external narrative supports. It is a more general risk in counterpreservation, which, if seen without an understanding of its social context and motivations, might be mistaken for neglect. But it is not an exclusive risk of the appropriation of ruins. The abstract language of many modernist or minimalist buildings and memorials can also leave room for misinterpretations and misuses.[67]

Police Academy

More than ten years after Libeskind's design was chosen for the SS-barracks area, construction work finally began in the "dormant," semi-vacant site. The construction work, however, did not include a Hope Incision or a waterland. Nor did it follow the recommendation of the local preservation authorities (Untere Denkmalschutzbehörde), who wanted to keep the "legibility" of the "witness value of the site."[68] In a bizarre twist that seems to mock such historically conscious alternatives, in 2003 the city government started renovating a large part of the competition site for new facilities for the campus of the Police Academy of Brandenburg (fig. 17).[69] There was historical precedent for this use, as the site had been used in the postwar era by the NVA, and after 1990 by the Oranienburg police administration. The NVA had added three new structures to the extant ones, altering the original Nazi-era ensemble. One of these new structures was a barracks building aligned on the same axis as the two Nazi-era ones; architecturally the three are very

67. See Charles Jencks's critique of modern architecture in Jencks, *The New Paradigm in Architecture* (New Haven, CT: Yale University Press, 2002).

68. Quoted in Lenz, "Libeskind will die Geometrie des Terrors durchbrechen."

69. Rainer Speer, "Grußwort," in *Fachhochschule der Polizei des Landes Brandenburg: Umbau und Sanierung, Neubau in Oranienburg* (Oranienburg: Fachhochschule der Polizei des Landes Brandenburg, 2006), 5.

Figure 17. Police Academy of Brandenburg, entrance gate on Bernauer Straße 146, Oranienburg (2010).
© Daniela Sandler

similar, with minor differences such as roofing and mansards. It is hardly surprising that a site conceived to house SS officers would work well for a different military corps, as the functional and circulation requirements are similar. It is perhaps a little more disturbing that the architectural style was made to match—the barracks employed the simplified vernacular used by Nazi architects for domestic and community buildings. Although the Nazis did not invent the high-pitched, red-tiled roof vernacular, the way they used it—especially in large-scale, repetitive buildings that housed soldiers or forced laborers (as in the Arbeiterstadt Große Halle in Berlin)[70]—should have been enough to establish the authoritarian and ideological associations of these architectural forms in their context. Their normalization under the NVA was part of the particular biases of the GDR in addressing the memory and history of the Nazi era, as I explained above—whereby the Socialist government distanced itself from the deeds of the Nazis and therefore found license to employ similar architectural, iconic, and cultural tropes, justifying them as signs of German identity that preceded the Nazis.

---

70. Helmut Bräutigam, *Arbeiterstadt "Große Halle": Zur unbekannten Geschichte auf dem Gelände des Evangelischen Waldkrankenhauses Spandau*, exhibition catalogue (Berlin: Evangelisches Waldkrankenhaus Spandau, 1997).

After 1990, this established "vocation" of the site continued in civilian form, as many of its buildings were used by the Oranienburg police administration. There was, therefore, a historical continuity throughout the entire postwar era that established this area as a place for governmental safeguarding bodies, whether under the GDR or after unification. I do not mean that this historical continuity justifies using the site for the police or the military, but rather that it *explains* the decision to keep doing so, both in terms of political and social expectations, and in terms of practical considerations. After 1990 no new buildings were added, and one of the Nazi-era buildings was refurbished, but many buildings and open areas were left in various states of disrepair. When ground was broken to rebuild the site as the campus of the Police Academy, a comprehensive architectural plan was applied, encompassing the renovation or adaptive reuse of the extant buildings from the Nazi and GDR eras, and the construction of one new building (a modern gym and sports hall).[71] It is hardly surprising that practical concerns superseded discussions about history and architecture. Many citizens and politicians in Oranienburg felt that the expansion of the Police Academy was necessary.[72]

As I suggested above, the meaning of memory is defined by ongoing social practices. The reported popular support for the Police Academy suggests that safety is a more current concern than memory for the Oranienburg population. The outcome of the 1992 competition had indicated a different climate—memory was a more prominent concern than real estate development. The shift in priorities may be read in terms of the recent history of Germany. At the beginning of the 1990s, the end of the GDR and German unification were catalysts for a memory boom that had started in the previous decade. The events of 1989 marked not only a historical turning point, but a collective and widespread move to engage the past critically. At the same time, Berlin's attractiveness as a site for tourism, investment, the arts, social life, and immigration was enhanced by its memorial charge. The success of Libeskind's proposal in 1992 can be understood as part of this general turn to history (regardless of whether one sees this turn as critical reflection or as mythologization and commodification).

Today the atmosphere is different. The prolific production or revamping of memorials and museums, which swept the city with such flagship works as Libeskind's own Jewish Museum, has culminated in the controversial Memorial to the Murdered Jews of Europe by Peter Eisenman. Eisenman's memorial is in many ways a testament to an overextended, weary memorial culture. The memorial took ten years to be built, cost approximately 25 million euros, involved several controversies (including the choice of design, the location, the size of the plot, the design compromises Eisenman had to make, and the companies involved in the

---

71. "Oranienburg wird noch sicherer: Ney beim Richtfest der Polizeischule," *Märkische Allgemeine*, May 26, 2005, http://www.maerkischeallgemeine.de/cms/beitrag/10496337/61129/.
72. Ibid.

construction), and has arguably failed in many respects (passersby sometimes mistake the memorial for public benches; visitors use the concrete slabs as jumping platforms; guards have to "police" the memorial for "correct" uses).[73] The lukewarm or critical reactions to Eisenman's memorial, whose disappointed tone stands out when compared to the effusive reception of Libeskind's Jewish Museum, are a sign of the weariness to which I alluded above.

At the time of the inauguration of the Police Academy, city and provincial officials publicly stated that this did not preclude the construction of Libeskind's Hope Incision.[74] This would imply only a partial realization of the project, which would effectively invalidate its most critical elements—the incorporation of the barracks ruins, the waterland or water canals, and the joining of two apparently irreconcilable programs (development and memorial). Libeskind's office had worked continuously on this project throughout the 1990s, in constant contact with the city of Oranienburg, the Sachsenhausen Memorial Foundation, and several other offices and organizations. But they stopped working on the project in 1999, "after the Land [of Brandenburg] decided that the police was there."[75] In 2005 Günter Morsch, the director of the Brandenburg Memorials Foundation and responsible for overseeing the Sachsenhausen Memorial and Museum, declared Libeskind's project "definitively aborted,"[76] and in 2006, Kielczynski confirmed that there was little chance for the project to be implemented.[77]

For Libeskind, in addition to the fact that the campus of the Police Academy would eat up crucial portions of his plan for the area, the most egregious offense was the function of the site:

> It was very deliberate to put the police there. It was naïve in a sense, but it is a knowing naïveté. It is a kind of continuity. . . . The city and the Memorial Foundation still thought we could help to integrate the police program into the area. We refused to do so because it was obvious. A resident police squad needs to be protected by fences and guards. We thought that this is a no-go for this area. The police started to use the former SS houses and entrance as well, so it was kind of a return, you know, the fences . . . it is just exactly back to the same use . . . and with the fences, the guards, and so on, it becomes again an inaccessible area of military type.
>
> They made it inaccessible. They made the story inaccessible. It is as if the death camp is some sort of an abstraction. But it doesn't allow the viewer, the person, or

---

73. For a discussion of unexpected uses and reactions to the memorial, see Quentin Stevens, "Visitor Responses at Berlin's Holocaust Memorial: Contrary to Conventions, Expectations, and Rules," *Public Art Dialogue* 2, no. 1 (2012): 34–59.

74. "Oranienburg wird noch sicherer." See also "Polizeischule stört nicht," *Märkische Allgemeine,* May 7, 2006, http://www.maerkischeallgemeine.de/cms/beitrag/10485403/61129/.

75. Libeskind, interview, October 10, 2014.

76. "Oranienburg wird noch sicherer."

77. Christian Kielczynski, pers. comm via phone with my research assistant Anne Doose, April 2006.

the citizen to understand: how did it work? How many people were involved, how much of the town, these surrounding quarters of the town. . . . You really disallowed the public to understand the implicit implication of this whole site in the center of the city, with all this infrastructure. Regular houses, except they are houses for killers.[78]

Libeskind's emphasis on accessibility highlights that collective memory is bound up with the public realm. Curtailing physical access to this site of memory curbs opportunities for learning and reflection, and further plunges the site into social oblivion. Of course, visiting the site in person might not automatically guarantee thoughtful engagement or debate. But such debate is more challenging in the absence of a concrete springboard. It would be different if the site were physically inaccessible but symbolically central. Ground Zero in New York City was fenced off for visitation, but it occupied a highly visible place in local and national debates in various venues and media (not to mention that it was also directly visible from the surrounding streets of lower Manhattan; people could not walk on it, but they could see it). Such centrality is not the case in Oranienburg. Although the site is adjacent to residential neighborhoods, it is also hidden in plain sight from them. The site is located along a wide avenue with scarce foot traffic (see fig. 17); the block is also very long, and most buildings are institutions or private homes, further discouraging street life. Perhaps a discursive centrality could have been enacted, through debates in newspapers or public forums such as the city council, but this was difficult after the decision to locate the Police Academy there. The decision itself made news, reigniting brief interest in Libeskind's proposal, but its seeming finality foreclosed any further public discussions.

The Police Academy campus is well established now. There are some gestures on the part of the Police Academy administration to indicate the historical significance of the site. The pamphlet published on the occasion of the opening of the new campus in 2006 includes, in addition to an overview of the history of the site and its buildings, several statements by politicians that in fact it is a good thing that the police is using this site, because in contemporary Germany the police protects a democratic state. Jörg Schönbohm, who at the time was interior minister for the Land of Brandenburg, wrote that "the spatial proximity of the Sachsenhausen Memorial Site highlights the necessity and importance of a strong police corps for our democratic constitutional state."[79] (Schönbohm was not only part of the conservative CDU party, but also a retired lieutenant general who made his career in the West German military and was responsible for the integration of the NVA into the military forces of unified Germany after 1990.)[80] Rainer Speer, at the time minister of finance for the Land of Brandenburg, notes that the refurbishment of the

---

78. Libeskind, interview, October 10, 2014.
79. Jörg Schönbohm, "Grußwort," in *Fachhochschule der Polizei des Landes*, 3.
80. "Zur Person: Jörg Schönbohm," CDU website, http://www.brandenburg-cdu.de/index.php?ka=1&ska=profil&pid=27.

area was complex because of the connection with the Nazi past and the proximity
to Sachsenhausen, and that some modifications were introduced into the original
plans after consultations with Morsch. Speer recognizes that the Police Academy
"sits on a special, historically sensitive site," which for him means an "obligation"
on the part of the police (especially through the education of its new members on
this very site) to uphold principles of democracy and constitutional rights.[81]

In addition to this pamphlet, the current website of the Police Academy contains some information on the history of the site, in the form of a three-page PDF
document in German, English, and Polish that maps all of the buildings from the
Nazi era (and from the GDR era), along with photos of their state before and after
refurbishment, and brief descriptions.[82] The brief but informative document is a
helpful gesture, but it is somewhat buried in the website. Nowhere on the website's
home page is there a link that points to the history of the site. This document can
be reached only if one first clicks on a pull-down menu called *Polizeiwissenschaft*
(Police Studies or Police Science); then an option for *Polizeigeschichte* (Police History) appears. After clicking on it, one is taken to a web page where the history of
the site and its relevance for a contemporary Police Academy are acknowledged,
somewhat ambiguously—the title of the page and its first sentence hint at a general
history of German police as an institution, but all of the text that follows deals with
the history of the SS and NVA use of the area. The PDF document can be found at
the bottom of the page. Given that most of the space of the page is devoted to this
site-specific history—in the text and linked resources—it is a bit puzzling that the
page title and the link that leads there are so vague and generic. It is one thing to say
"History of the Police," which hints at a chronology and institution much broader
than the Nazi period; it would have been quite another thing to entitle the page
"History of the Site" (or even "Nazi-Era History of the Site") and include this title
on the Police Academy's home page. Given the self-conscious tone of this particular
web page within the site, the ambiguity and elision are surprising and appear to be
more deliberate than simple oversight.

As for the site itself, there are markers of history on location, but they are minor.
Small plaques combining text and photographs are posted inside select buildings;
each plaque explains the history of its respective building in the Nazi era (fig. 18).
The people who work at the Police Academy today are polite and forthcoming
about the history of the site—not only did they take me on a tour, but they also
volunteered materials about the site and about the Police Academy, and stated that
cadets receive lessons in the history of the Nazi era.[83] It was also not difficult to

---

81. Speer, "Grußwort," 5.
82. FH Polizei Land Brandenburg, "Zur Geschichte des Ortes," https://www.fhpolbb.de/sites/
default/files/field/dokumente/150_zur_geschichte_des_ortes_deutsch.pdf.
83. Personal visit, June 2010.

Figure 18. Police Academy of Brandenburg, plaque inside current administrative building (2010). The structure was built in 1938–39 by the SS and used for medical clinics and as a medical training center.
© Daniela Sandler

arrange for a research visit. Still, the site is not open to public visitation, as Libeskind's project would have been.

Moreover, the informational plaques, however well intentioned, are small and inconspicuous. In the administration building, formerly used by the Nazis as a health clinic, the plaque hangs on a wall next to a fire-exit plan, and it can easily be mistaken for a purely pragmatic item—not only because of its size, but also because its graphic design language is unremarkable. There is nothing in the treatment of images, choice of typeface, or frame that could draw attention to the plaque and distinguish it as a unique and intentional memorial gesture. And while the current Police Academy administration can be commended for its open attitude, it is impossible to know what kinds of policies and administrators will be in place in the future. For someone less concerned with historical awareness, it would be quite easy to remove these little plaques—they are lightweight metal-and-glass frames hanging on walls—and erase any marker of historical information. Such a removal would be much more difficult with Libeskind's design, of course—whether the canals or the waterland. Libeskind's destructive waters would do more to preserve the site's historical potency than the Police Academy's informational plaques and restored buildings.

More than twenty-five years after unification, other issues have become more prominent in the collective imaginaries (and anxieties) of Germany: unemployment, cuts in welfare benefits such as pensions and health care, cuts in public spending, privatization, and the lingering disparities between the eastern and western portions of Germany. Germans might be more concerned with economic or practical problems than with memorialization. Moreover, in the early 1990s there was a sense of hope and optimism fueled by the democratization of East Germany, the promise of economic development through unification, and the reconciliation and freedom represented by the united country. This sense of hope and optimism might have allowed for a more daring and creative approach such as the social program of Libeskind's Hope Incision. Now, however, social and economic tensions might prevent such visionary, quasi-utopian gestures.

The appeal to safety and order represented by the Police Academy (one Oranienburg official was quoted as boasting, "Oranienburg will soon become the safest city in the whole [province of] Brandenburg") is telling of a current desire for security, heightened in the age of terrorism, mass immigrations, and refugees.[84] Libeskind's Hope Incision sketched a dream-like vision of social-minded, equitable progress; the Police Academy, in turn, beckons with the promise of order. This might help explain the change in plans for the area. It does not diminish, however, the disturbing overtones of the decision to build a police academy on the site of former SS barracks. The SS and other Nazi organizations were obviously quite different from the police in contemporary, democratic Germany. But both represent their respective government's official institutions for surveillance and punishment. Part of the appeal of Hitler's brownshirts was their promise to restore order and safety in the chaotic Weimar Republic, at a time when many Germans were willing to surrender personal liberties and social tolerance in exchange for security. One can only hope that the current conservative backlash represented by Oranienburg's Police Academy (and by the right-wing inclinations of Germans and Europeans in national elections since at least the mid-2000s) is but a very faint, circumstantial echo of earlier historical tragedies.

---

84. "Oranienburg wird noch sicherer."

5

Counterpreservation in Reverse

The Nazi barracks area in Oranienburg described in the preceding chapter was one among many sites of Nazi power that survived the war. While some high-profile structures, like Hitler's Chancellery, were demolished in the immediate postwar era,[1] many other sites were abandoned or converted to other uses that eventually normalized them and displaced them from collective memory and awareness—from the transformation of the Aviation Ministry in central Berlin into the GDR House of Ministries, to the conversion of a slave-labor camp facility (the Arbeiterstadt Große Halle) into a hospital, and even the continued use of Albert Speer's lampposts along the 17th of June Street.[2] If places explicitly evocative

---

1. The war-damaged Chancellery was destroyed following an official Soviet decree, after the Soviets mined the ruins for materials for the Soviet Memorial in Treptow and a nearby subway station, today the Mohrenstraße station. See Senat von Berlin, ed., *Berlin: Behauptung von Freiheit und Selbstverwaltung 1946–1948* (Berlin: Heinz Spitzing, 1959), 669.
2. On the Aviation Ministry, see Brian Ladd, *Ghosts of Berlin: Confronting German History in the Urban Landscape* (Chicago: University of Chicago Press, 1997), 146. On Nazi structures in Berlin, see Wolfgang Schäche, *Architektur und Städtebau in Berlin zwischen 1933 und 1945: Planen und Bauen unter der Ägide der Stadtverwaltung* (Berlin: Mann, 1991). On the Arbeiterstadt Große Halle, see Helmut Bräutigam, *Arbeiterstadt Große Halle: Zur unbekannten Geschichte auf dem Gelände des Evangelischen Waldkrankenhauses Spandau,* exhibition catalogue (Berlin: Evangelisches Waldkrankenhaus Spandau, 1997). On Germania and the lampposts, see Ladd, *Ghosts of Berlin*, 134–41.

of the Holocaust, such as concentration camps, were eventually turned into memorial sites, most of the myriad and more prosaic buildings commissioned or used by Nazi officers and bureaucrats gradually disappeared into the cityscape, destroyed or forgotten.[3]

In the late 1970s and 1980s, a self-searching attitude on the part of historians and the general public led to the rediscovery of Nazi threads enmeshed in the local histories of neighborhoods and specific places.[4] Since then, the German "memory boom"—a phenomenon discussed by Andreas Huyssen, among many other scholars—has been accompanied by the rediscovery and marking of significant sites, such as deportation platforms in train stations, destroyed synagogues, collection centers for deportees, and administrative buildings.[5] One of these sites is the Topography of Terror—a block in central Berlin that was home to so many official and unofficial Nazi offices and meeting points that it became the de facto Nazi headquarters in the city. I mentioned this site in the previous chapter in relation to an unbuilt proposal for a memorial made of trees and metal grilles on its grounds. It is the new, and seemingly definitive, configuration of the site—inaugurated in 2010—that interests me here. Both the Topography of Terror and Project Mo𝔘rning deal with sites of perpetrators, both operate in gray zones where Nazi terror intermingled with everyday German life, and both deal with places marked by decades-long forgetting before rediscovery. Both also incorporate ruins and fragments of buildings formerly used by Nazi officers for the oppressive and murderous activities of the Third Reich.

But these two projects respond to the respective challenges of their sites very differently. Libeskind's flooded ruinscape is an example of counterpreservation; the Topography of Terror, in turn, frames its ruins much more stably. But if I present the Topography of Terror in contrast to Project Mo𝔘rning, it is not as an implicit judgment of the former, but rather as a comparative and nuanced example. Counterpreservation is not a panacea for all memorial dilemmas, and by no means should it be considered as the default solution, or as a standard against which all other projects should be measured. In addition, the Topography of Terror offers another dimension to this discussion: that of public reactions to the built project. While there are reports of public responses to Libeskind's design, these were responses to the proposal. Project Mo𝔘rning did not have a chance to be tested in the

---

3. For examples, see Karen Till, *The New Berlin: Memory, Politics, Place* (Minneapolis: University of Minnesota Press, 2005), 76–77.

4. Ibid., 79–82.

5. Andreas Huyssen, *Present Pasts: Urban Palimpsests and the Politics of Memory* (Stanford, CA: Stanford University Press, 2002); and Huyssen, *Twilight Memories: Marking Time in a Culture of Amnesia* (New York: Routledge, 1995). See also Eric Langenbacher and Frederike Eigler, "Introduction: Memory Boom or Memory Fatigue in 21st Century Germany?," *German Politics and Society* 23, no. 3 (2005): 1–15; Klaus Neumann, *Shifting Memories: The Nazi Past in the New Germany* (Ann Arbor: University of Michigan Press, 2000); and Till, *New Berlin*, 63.

same way as the built and finished Topography of Terror, and in this way the latter may offer speculative insights" into how the former might have worked.

The Open Wound Metaphor

The Topography of Terror has been extensively dissected in many publications, notably by Karen Till in her study of memory and urban culture in Berlin after unification, and also by James Young, Brian Ladd, and Jennifer Jordan, all of whom published foundational books on memory, memorials, and Berlin.[6] Till's work, in particular, is a landmark reference both for her critical and theoretical understanding of the area, and for her extensive research and documentation, including detailed field notes on the site's changing stages, and interviews with key players in the creation of the Topography of Terror. The site, however, has changed significantly since these works were published; the most recent of these books, Jordan's *Structures of Memory*, came out in 2006, just one year after a competition was held to redefine the layout of the site, and well before the winning proposal was built. The transformation has been so radical as to demand new critical reflection, especially with relation to the arguments raised by these authors. Here, I will recount the prior history of the site, relying on the work of these four authors, so as to set up my discussion of the later transformation and contemporary configuration of the area.

The Topography of Terror is a documentation center and historic site in central Berlin, at the corner of Wilhelmstraße and Niederkirchnerstraße. In the Nazi era, the latter was called Prinz-Albrecht-Straße, and it was the location of many organizations associated with Nazi power and Nazi terror. Hitler's secret police, the Gestapo (*Geheime Staatspolizei*), had been housed there since 1933, occupying a building originally created as a school of applied arts.[7] The Gestapo was central in managing and carrying out the Holocaust. It was responsible for tracking down and capturing people who were deemed to pose a threat to the Nazi regime (Communists, active members of the political resistance, racial and sexual minorities),

---

6. Till, *New Berlin*, 63–152; James Young, *The Texture of Memory: Holocaust Memorials and Meaning* (New Haven, CT: Yale University Press, 1993), 81–90; Ladd, *Ghosts of Berlin*, 154–67; Jennifer Jordan, *Structures of Memory: Understanding Urban Change in Berlin and Beyond* (Stanford, CA: Stanford University Press, 2006), 48–52. See also Stefanie Endlich, *Wege zur Erinnerung: Gedenkstätten und -orte für die Opfer des Nationalsozialismus in Berlin und Brandenburg* (Berlin: Metropol, 2007); Stefanie Endlich et al., *Zum Umgang mit dem Gestapo-Gelände: Gutachten im Auftrag der Akademie der Künste Berlin* (Berlin: Akademie der Künste, 1988); Wolfgang Schivelbusch and Tom Levin, "Berlin-Mitte Below and Above," *Assemblage* 20 (April 1993): 72–73; John Czaplicka, "History, Aesthetics, and Contemporary Commemorative Practice in Berlin," *New German Critique* 65 (Spring 1995): 155–87; Michael Naumann, "Remembrance and Political Reality: Historical Consciousness in Germany after the Genocide," *New German Critique* 80 (Spring 2000): 17–28; and Peter Reichel, *Politik mit der Erinnerung: Gedächtnisorte im Streit um die nationalsozialistische Vergangenheit* (Munich: Carl Hanser, 1995). For a collection of original documents and analyses on the Gestapo terrain, see Reinhard Rürup, ed., *Topography of Terror: Gestapo, SS and Reichssicherheitshauptamt on the "Prinz-Albrecht-Terrain"; A Documentation* (Berlin: Stiftung Topographie des Terrors, Verlag Willmuth Arenhövel, 2001).

7. Young, *The Texture of Memory*, 82; Ladd, *Ghosts of Berlin*, 155–56; Till, *New Berlin*, 63–64.

with free rein to do so independently of the judicial system. The Gestapo headquarters also had cells where prisoners (mostly political) were incarcerated, tor-
tured, and murdered. Other buildings in the Prinz-Albrecht block sheltered
desktop criminals and Nazi officers, such as Reinhard Heydrich, head of the Security Service (SD, or *Sicherheitsdienst*) of the SS.[8] Heydrich's office was located in the
Prinz-Albrecht Palais, an urban palace redesigned by Karl Friedrich Schinkel in
1830 as a residence for Prince Albrecht. Next door, the Prinz-Albrecht Hotel, used
as an informal meeting point for the Nazi elite, became the seat of the SS in 1934.
Across the street was the new Aviation Ministry, a showpiece of Nazi architecture
designed by Ernst Sagebiel and built in 1936, and next to it the former Prussian Assembly, which in 1934 was turned into the People's Court (the Volksgerichtshof, a
court where the laws of the Nazi state were enacted).[9] Josef Goebbels's propaganda
newspaper, *Der Angriff*, had its office there too.[10] Most of the buildings in that block
had a direct connection with the Nazi terror state.

Today, this is a densely used tourist area, served by the Potsdamer Platz subway
station—one of the busiest in the city. Just west of the Topography of Terror, the
pristinely refurbished Martin-Gropius-Bau now functions as a museum for popular temporary exhibitions featuring high-profile artists and themes. In 2014, for
example, there were shows on David Bowie and on the Chinese artist Ai Weiwei;
other past blockbuster themes included photographers Robert Capa and Henri-
Cartier Bresson, filmmaker Stanley Kubrick, ancient Egyptian treasures, and artists Christo and Jeanne-Claude. A couple of blocks farther is Potsdamer Platz, the
postunification mixed-use development of commerce, corporate offices, hotels, and
entertainment.[11] Still within walking distance one can reach the Berlin Philhar-
monic, the New National Gallery, the State Library, the Memorial to the Murdered
Jews of Europe, the Reichstag building, the Brandenburg Gate, the German Chancellery, embassies, state offices, hotels, and the Tiergarten (one of Berlin's largest
urban parks), among many other attractions. This context of heavy tourist traffic
combined with political, commercial, and cultural functions is important for understanding how the Topography of Terror was ultimately shaped into a defined,
controlled, sleekly finished memorial site where the incorporation of ruins is the
opposite of Libeskind's open-ended, iconoclastic approach.

In between the intimidating history of the area under the Nazis, and its glossy
incarnation in contemporary Berlin, there lies a messy stretch of destruction,

8. Rürup, *Topography of Terror*, 61, 63.

9. Once the People's Court moved out in 1935 the building was renamed "House of the Fliers"
(Haus der Flieger) by Hermann Göring. Rürup, *Topography of Terror*, 14.

10. Ladd, *Ghosts of Berlin*, 155.

11. On the construction of Potsdamer Platz as a central commercial enterprise for marketing Berlin after unification, see Claire Colomb, *Staging the New Berlin: Place Marketing and the Politics of Urban
Reinvention Post-1989* (New York: Routledge, 2012), esp. chap. 6; and also Elizabeth Strom, *Building
the New Berlin: The Politics of Urban Development in Germany's Capital City* (Lanham, MD: Lexington
Books, 2001).

forgetting, and conflicting claims to the city and to representations of history.[12] Right after the war, the Prinz-Albrecht block was quickly cleared out as the Gestapo headquarters, the Prinz-Albrecht-Hotel, and the Prinz-Albrecht Palais—all of which had been severely damaged by Allied air raids, but none of which was beyond reasonable repair—were demolished by the North American occupation forces, under whose jurisdiction the area fell. The area was on the border between the Soviet and the American sectors of Berlin. In 1951 the East German government renamed Prinz-Albrecht-Straße as Niederkirchnerstraße in honor of Käthe Niederkirchner, a Communist militant murdered in 1944 in the Ravensbrück concentration camp.[13] In 1961, the Wall was built around West Berlin; on this particular location it sliced the street lengthwise, cleaving the street from the block, so that Niederkirchnerstraße ran on the eastern side of the Wall—more precisely, in the no-man's-land space in between the two parallel walls that formed the border fortifications. The block of the former Gestapo headquarters fell on the western side.

As in neighboring Postdamer Platz, the area adjacent to the Wall was deserted. On their side, East Berliners could not approach it. On the other side, West Berliners only did so to paint graffiti or peek at the other side from observation platforms. The western side of the Wall was otherwise at the margins of Berlin. The Wall marked the end of the city, the point where streets stopped abruptly. In the case of the Prinz-Albrecht block, the Wall was not even lined by sidewalks or streets, as in many other areas. There, the Wall was abutted by a large block of debris and ruins: the site of the demolished buildings on the Prinz-Albrecht block was turned into a recycling facility, and the damaged but extant Museum of Applied Arts was abandoned and occupied by homeless people and drug addicts. This liminal and hard-to-reach site was cut off from the flow of people, from everyday uses and itineraries, and from significant functions and events. The space was excluded from the quotidian experience of the city just as it was from its social imaginary and collective memory. It was so marginal to the city that at some point an expressway was planned to overrun it.[14]

In this way it is not hard to picture how the history of the Prinz-Albrecht block was forgotten—as early as the immediate postwar era. Günther Weisenborn, who had been imprisoned at the Gestapo headquarters, recalls visiting the site in 1950 with Bertolt Brecht, who had also been an inmate there. Weisenborn's report reveals the perplexity of their encounter with the decaying remains of their former prison, overtaken by debris and plants.[15] The report was reprinted in a book by

---

12. Till, *New Berlin*, 64–67; and 117–18 for a pointed discussion of postwar forgetting.

13. Rürup, *Topography of Terror*, 200; Ladd, *Ghosts of Berlin*, 213–14; 208–15 for a discussion of the "politics of street names" with relation to Nazism and East Germany.

14. Till, *New Berlin*, 71–72, 117; Ladd, *Ghosts of Berlin*, 158.

15. Rürup, *Topography of Terror*, 196; see also 190, 197–98. Other sources on the postwar forgetting of the area include Young, *The Texture of Memory*, 85; Ladd, *Ghosts of Berlin*, 157–58; Till, *New Berlin*, 76–79.

the Topography of Terror foundation, where it appears below a photograph taken by Brecht on the occasion of this visit. The photograph shows the ruins of the prison courtyard—the dismantling skeleton of the building forming a backdrop for debris, vegetation, and the standing figures of Weisenborn and journalist Max Schröder. Weisenborn's text and Brecht's photograph capture the site on the verge of its collective oblivion, suggesting that even at that early point in the postwar era it held meaning only for those who were intent on remembering. Given the site's history, it is on some level understandable that many people willingly pushed it aside from attention and from memory—and not just because of its geographical marginality. By the late 1970s, its history had been largely forgotten. There was no public memory or public mention of the Prinz-Albrecht block, even though it had been quite visibly and unmistakably identified as the center of Nazi horror during the 1930s and 1940s.[16]

The symbolic mapping of the city during the Third Reich, which allowed for this site to be the "most feared address in the city," had been erased from the symbolic mappings of postwar Berlin. Part of this erasure lay in the stringent denazification efforts through which the Allies sought to eliminate all vestiges of Nazism.[17] For the Allies, every place associated with Nazism was a potential honor tomb and pilgrimage site; every physical remnant a potentially virulent seed of Nazi ideology. Denazification did not consist only in the prohibition of the swastika, of Hitler's *Mein Kampf*, or of certain words and songs; it also justified razing Hitler's Chancellery, burying his bunker, and destroying buildings associated with his government even if these buildings had a previous, non-Nazi history. The elimination of these material signs and spaces assumed that Germans could be safe from the dangers of Nazism if they were kept away from Nazi objects and ideas. Nazi sites such as the Chancellery or bunkers were perceived by the Allies as potential shrines for recalcitrant or neo-Nazis. As Young puts it, "Many feared that if the ruins of the Gestapo-Gelände were left, they might even be readopted by former SS soldiers as a memorial not to what they had perpetrated, but to what they had lost."[18]

In the 1980s, a young generation of students, scholars, architects, and historians (as well as many "lay" citizens) engaged in a collective rediscovery of history

---

16. "The most feared address in Berlin" is a favorite phrase to describe the site. It appears in English-language news stories, guidebooks, websites, and several scholarly works. See, for instance, Young, *The Texture of Memory,* 82; Till, *New Berlin,* 69; and Ladd, *Ghosts of Berlin,* 156. *Gefürchtete adresse* appears in German, mostly in news stories and websites, but not as frequently as the English version; in any case, German sources concur that the site inspired fear during the Nazi era, as the name of the exhibition indicates.

17. Rand C. Lewis, *A Nazi Legacy: Right-Wing Extremism in Postwar Germany* (New York: Praeger, 1991), 28. Jean-Paul Bier discusses the shortcomings of denazification in "The Holocaust, West Germany, and Strategies of Oblivion, 1947–1979," in *Germans and Jews since the Holocaust: The Changing Situation in West Germany,* ed. Anson Rabinbach and Jack Zipes (New York and London: Holmes and Meier, 1986), 185–207.

18. Young, *The Texture of Memory,* 84.

in West Berlin, as recounted by Till in *The New Berlin*.[19] This rediscovery was multifaceted. It was a reaction to the historical silences resulting from postwar dogmas and taboos (denazification, Nazi denial, the repression of the Holocaust). The members of this new generation desired to confront national history on their own terms. This attitude was expressed in unconventional, dynamic, and participatory approaches, such as "history workshops" (*Geschichtewerkstätten*), educational programs in schools and museums, independent research, informal or unofficial city tours, historical-awareness activism, and so on.[20] As Susan Neiman so vividly recalls in her Berlin memoirs, West Berlin in the 1980s was a citywide arena for the collective engagement with *Vergangenheitsverarbeitung*.[21]

But the historical turn was not exclusive to contesting students, artists, or alternative cultural groups. The interest in the Holocaust and the Nazi era went mainstream with the television series *Holocaust,* broadcast in West Germany in 1979, and with contemporary publications and news stories on the Nazi period (most famously the story of the supposed discovery of Hitler's diaries, which turned out to be a forgery, in 1983).[22] Conservatives also started approaching the past publicly, less concerned with working on the past than with overcoming it once and for all. The engagement with the burden of the Third Reich and the possibility of reinscribing Germany as a "normal" nation culminated in the *Historikerstreit* (historians' debate).[23] Many institutions, exhibitions, heritage programs, and discussions were devoted to rediscovering other periods of German history besides and beyond the Third Reich, and thus finding sources of national pride and cultural value uncontaminated by Nazism. This attention to "prouder" moments of history played a role in the creation of the Topography of Terror, as I will explain below.

The site now called the Topography of Terror had not yet been named as such— it had not yet even been publicly remembered as a site of Nazi power. Attention

---

19. Till, *New Berlin*, 72–73, 79–80, 90, 92–97. See also Ladd, *Ghosts of Berlin*, 158.

20. Till, *New Berlin,* 79–81.

21. If Adorno worried about Germany moving on too fast from its past, a few years later Neiman tells a different story: the young Germans she meets, many of whom are students or artists, focus on the Nazi past almost obsessively, with no intention of putting it behind. Susan Neiman, *Slow Fire: Jewish Notes from Berlin* (New York: Schocken Books, 1992), 14–18.

22. On the impact of the *Holocaust* miniseries on West Germany's engagement with the Nazi era, see the following essays in the book *Germans and Jews since the Holocaust:* Jeffrey Herf, "The 'Holocaust' Reception in West Germany: Right, Center, and Left," 208–33; Andrei S. Markovits and Rebecca S. Hayden, "'Holocaust' before and after the Event: Reactions in West Germany and Austria," 234–57; and Siegfried Zielinski, "History as Entertainment and Provocation: The TV Series 'Holocaust' in West Germany," 258–83. On the Hitler diaries, see Charles Hamilton, *The Hitler Diaries: Fakes That Fooled the World* (Lexington: University Press of Kentucky, 1991); and Peter-Ferdinand Koch, *Der Fund: Die Skandale des Stern, Gerd Heidemann und die Hitler-Tagebücher* (Hamburg: Facta Oblita, 1990).

23. Mazal Holocaust Collection (corp. author), *Forever in the Shadow of Hitler? The Dispute about the Germans' Understanding of History, Original Documents of the* Historikerstreit, *the Controversy Concerning the Singularity of the Holocaust,* trans. James Knowlton and Truett Cates (Atlantic Highlands, NJ: Humanities Press, 1993); Zygmunt Bauman, *Modernity and the Holocaust* (Cambridge: Polity Press, 1989).

first turned to the aforementioned Martin-Gropius-Bau, then still known as the former building of the Museum of Applied Arts. The Martin-Gropius-Bau had originally been designed by Martin Gropius and Heino Schmieden in 1877–81 to house the Museum of Applied Arts; after 1918 it was converted for use as the Museum for Pre- and Early History and the East Asian collection.[24] It was damaged by bombing during the war (unsurprisingly, considering its location next to the Gestapo headquarters) and almost demolished; after two decades as a ruin, it was listed as a protected monument in 1966 and restored in 1978 (it then underwent a second renovation with an adaptive reuse design by Hilmer & Sattler in 1998).

The 1978 refurbishment of the Museum of Applied Arts building was a government initiative that made room for both conservative and contestatory currents. The architectural renovation and the museological approach were conservative. The façade of museum was restored to its formal splendor without any mention of its larger sociourban context during the Third Reich, when it was part of the infamous Prinz-Albrecht block. Architects and preservation officials were concerned with the physical condition of the building, and given its precarious state it is not hard to imagine that constructive and aesthetic aspects alone might have demanded enough attention to obscure symbolic or historical elements. The building was renamed Martin-Gropius-Bau, in honor of one of its architects. This decision suggests a move away from the building's institutional and contextual history before the war and instead a focus on its material presence, drawing attention to the designer's name. Evidently the building could not be renamed after its previous institutions, given that West Berlin already had an Applied Arts Museum and a Museum for Pre- and Early History, installed elsewhere. But as a result the building's institutional history (including the history of its surroundings) was pushed to the background, while the structure's architectural presence came to the fore. In the 1980s, as Germans rediscovered buried histories all around the city,[25] the silence on the larger contextual and urban history of the building stood out by contrast.

The Martin-Gropius-Bau inaugural exhibition was on the history of Prussia, a foundational reference for German identity and more particularly for Berlin, which had been the Prussian capital. This foundational reference was (at least at first glance) protected from Nazi contamination by chronology. Even though many traits of Nazism were common to Prussian society—militarism, regimentalism, centralized power—and arguably explain at least in part the appeal of Hitler to Germans, it does not follow that every supporter of Prussia (or of Prussia-led

---

24. Rosmarie Beier and Leonore Koschnick, *Der Martin-Gropius Bau: Geschichte und Gegenwart des ehemaligen Kunstgewerbemusems* (Berlin: Nicolai, 1986), 75–85.

25. The movement to uncover hidden histories was associated with two factors: scholarly attention to social and everyday histories; and engagement of "ordinary citizens" in historical research and reflection. The movement rested on mottoes such as "Dig where you stand" and "the search for traces" (*Spurensuchen*). See Till, *New Berlin*, 90; and Rudy Koshar, *From Monuments to Traces: Artifacts of German Memory, 1870–1990* (Berkeley: University of California Press, 2000), 226–28.

unified Germany) was a Nazi-in-training. Many Social-Democrats and many German Jews supported the Second Reich, were patriotic, and enlisted in Emperor Wilhelm II's army to fight in World War I.[26] For those looking for a less controversial historical ancestry, Prussian history offered a way out of the Nazi burden (even though, of course, there are many connections between the history of Prussia and that of Nazism).

But several historians working to prepare this exhibition were also in some way associated with the alternative history movements of the time. As they worked on the originally planned exhibition on Prussia, the history of the Prinz-Albrecht block was being slowly uncovered by citizens' initiatives.[27] Groups of historians organized informal tours of the empty land next to the Martin-Gropius-Bau. As a response, the government abandoned plans for an avenue on the site and organized a competition to transform it into a park and memorial (this is the competition I mentioned in the previous chapter). The organizers of the Prussia exhibition incorporated the unearthing of the history of the Prinz-Albrecht block by including informative material on this history inside the exhibition. This material was placed near a window of the Martin-Gropius-Bau overlooking the empty, rubble-covered site, so that a visitor to the exhibition gazing through this window would also be looking at the former site of the Gestapo. In this way, the Nazi history—which had appeared physically and institutionally extraneous to the program of the Martin-Gropius-Bau—was now incorporated with a visual demonstration of the complicated historical and memorial entanglements of the whole block.

Soon after the competition result for a memorial park on the former Gestapo site was divulged, the excavation of the area revealed that, in contrast to what had been previously thought, there still existed physical remains of the site's former buildings. Sections of the cellar, foundation, and prison cells of the Gestapo headquarters had endured, and their discovery transformed the empty lot. The Prinz-Albrecht history could not be dismissed anymore as an immaterial past invoked by a smattering of contesting historians; it was now anchored by the evidential presence of the subterranean Gestapo structure. The area became informally known as the "Gestapo terrain"—*Gestapo Gelände*. A temporary exhibition called Topography of Terror was set up in 1987. The first incarnation of this exhibition bespoke its grassroots, subversive origins: the installations were modest, provisional, and less concerned with an aesthetic or curatorial statement than with displaying and revealing the history of the site, opening up this information to the public, and preventing destructive developments such as the new avenue or even the memorial

26. On the complex position of Jews with relation to politics and nationalism in Germany in the nineteenth and twentieth centuries, see Peter Pulzer, *Jews and the German State: The Political History of a Minority, 1848–1933* (Detroit, MI: Wayne State University Press, 2003).

27. Rürup, *Topography of Terror*, 208–17; Koshar, *From Monuments to Traces*, 226; Till, *New Berlin*, 63–199, esp. 67–75, 82–83, and 94–97; Young, *The Texture of Memory*, 85–86, 88–89; Ladd, *Ghosts of Berlin*, 158.

park (which assumed an empty site and made no provision for displaying or preserving the ruins).

The exhibition underwent many changes over the years, with somewhat more
permanent structures replacing the earlier ones. In 1993 a competition was held for
a permanent structure to house a documentation center, which began to be built according to a design by Peter Zumthor. That structure was then abandoned halfway,
ostensibly because of budget concerns.[28] Some have suggested that Zumthor's design was deemed inappropriate for the site, as it would have been too "spectacular"
and thus would have competed for attention with the mission of the memorial. The
building would have been too "powerful, a symbol in itself," according to Thomas
Lutz, head of the memorial-museums department of the Topography of Terror,
in an interview with scholar Randy Malamud.[29] The change of heart delayed and
eventually halted the construction of Zumthor's building. This added yet another
element of provisionality and fragmentation to the site, as the unfinished walls of
Zumthor's half-built design loomed over the site as a premature ruin, surrounded
by fences and weeds. A new competition was held again in 2005; Zumthor's unfinished structure was demolished, and the whole site gave way, for the first time,
to a cohesive and all-encompassing plan. This was finished in 2010 and is now the
permanent version of the Topography of Terror, which I will discuss below.

Before the 2005 competition, the Topography of Terror had gone from a temporary, provisional, in many ways makeshift exhibition to later incarnations that
adapted it to unexpected and steady public interest, prolonging the duration of
what had been conceived as a finite, ephemeral installation into an established but
still open-ended memorial site. Even a decade into its creation, it retained the improvised and piecemeal quality of the earlier exhibition. Instead of an overarching plan, the site was shaped by partial and localized interventions, many of them
pragmatic, addressing the unpredicted challenges that flared up because the site
had never been cohesively planned for long-term public visitation—for example,
at some point, portions of the site had to be covered with sand to protect some of
the ruins from acid rain, removing these ruins from public view.[30] The site was a
haphazard landscape. On the northern side, along Niederkirchnerstraße and next
to the Wall, the ground sank into an open-air trench, which formed the main path
of the open-air exhibition. On one side, the trench was lined by the ruined walls of
the Gestapo building, punctuated by exhibition plaques containing text and images, and covered by a simple wooden structure. On the other side, the trench was

28. Jordan, *Structures of Memory*, 51; Richard Bernstein, "Finally Filling a Vacant Lot Ravaged by
Tides of Terror," *New York Times*, February 8, 2006, http://www.nytimes.com/2006/02/08/international/
europe/08berlin.html?_r=1&.

29. Randy Malamud, "Meticulously Evil," The Chronicle Review, *The Chronicle of Higher Education*, April 17, 2011, http://chronicle.com/article/Meticulously-Evil/127100/.

30. Till, *New Berlin*, 116.

bordered by a grassy slope that rose toward the middle of the block, above which was perched a metal container housing the documentation center.

Instead of a finished memorial, the Topography of Terror was a dug-out landscape. The layout was not defined, and the wooden structure that protected the ruins along Niederkirchnerstraße looked like a tent over an archaeological exploration in progress. In the early 2000s, this structure evoked the sense of adventure and hands-on history that had suffused the creation of the exhibition more than ten years before. Visitors partook in the impression that they, too, were part of this adventure, of this ongoing discovery housed somewhat precariously under a shabby and worn wooden roof. Different time periods intermingled: the Gestapo ruins below grade, remains of the Wall on the street level, the pile of rubble left over by a former recycling facility in the middle of the site, the interrupted construction of the future documentation center, and the newly restored façade of the Martin-Gropius-Bau. The core of the site was fenced off, the whole area taken over by plants and debris, forming an uninhabited and disordered space. The impression was such that many commentators called the site "an open wound."[31] At the same time, many social forces disputed the site with competing claims for its use and historical narrative—from local residents who wanted a park and not a memorial to conservative politicians interested in more glorious aspects of the German past to the activist historians behind the exhibition.

As Ladd argues, the provisionality and chaotic aspect of the site not only illustrated conflicting tendencies in German society, but also performed the task of memory-work in a profound and meaningful way: "The combination of modest exhibition and lingering debate confronted the Nazi past more effectively than any 'active museum' or any definitive plan for an 'open wound.'"[32] Ladd's interpretation is concurrent with the way other scholars have read the site. The Topography of Terror exemplifies Young's countermonument in its relentless effort at historical exposure.[33] And Till pushes the wound metaphor further:

> The excavated foundations and "forgotten" fields . . . were represented as a gash in the body politic. The open wound was a metaphor for the extreme pain, grief, and anguish caused by the actions of Germans working at this historical national administrative center before, during, and after the war. It also referred to the postwar neglect of this national history. . . . The layers of denial had to be lanced so that the nation could see the exact nature of the injury. . . . The Topography of Terror, as open wound, exposes the scars of history, as well as the contemporary consequences of destruction to the ideal of the nation, and asks visitors to confront this past (and this pain), to keep the wound open in the present, to continue the work of memory.[34]

---

31. Till, *New Berlin,* 97; Ladd, *Ghosts of Berlin,* 165.
32. Ladd, *Ghosts of Berlin*, 165.
33. Young, *The Texture of Memory*, 81–90.
34. Till, *New Berlin*, 98–99.

Had it remained that way—open-ended, potentially always changing in small or large ways, responding to practical needs or social desires—the Topography of Terror could hypothetically have been another example of counterpreservation, not only because of its literal incorporation of ruins, but also because of its embrace of change, the lack of an overriding design, and the attending freedoms that such a site could afford a visitor: meandering in different directions, partial strolls, incomplete vistas taken in unpredictable order, multiple interpretations and questions.[35]

However, as I described earlier, the centrality of the site was too strong. Symbolically, it called for a resolution that would connect the site to official narratives about the place of the Nazi past in contemporary Germany. All around it in central Berlin, other sites were being shaped in definitive terms—the Bendlerblock exhibition center telling the history of German resistance against Hitler; the Memorial to the Murdered Jews of Europe bowing to the need to recognize (some) Holocaust victims; the former Aviation Ministry turned into a bastion of German economic might as the Federal Ministry of Finance, with minimal public acknowledgment of the Nazi past of the structure. The Topography of Terror was another puzzle piece to be fitted into this larger discursive and urban matrix—a matrix that seems to turn the page of the "memory boom," moving away from the probing debates of the 1970s and 1980s, and coming closer to a more reconciling (if contrite) position. Or, if one takes a more cynical view, a matrix that turns the "memory boom" into a tourist attraction, another station to be enjoyed amid other disparate experiences: shopping, movies, art exhibitions, the Reichstag dome, the Brandenburg Gate, *Bratwürste*, beer gardens.

As I noted above, the Topography of Terror is located in a central tourist area of Berlin. Not just any area: within walking distance one can reach the headquarters of the national government, and also Potsdamer Platz, one of the largest commercial developments in the city. After unification Potsdamer Platz was dubbed "the largest construction site in Europe"; it would have been naive to imagine that just a few blocks from it a large site such as the Topography of Terror would have been left to the whims and actions of social activists and local historians. As Till, Strom, and Colomb have argued, the center of Berlin has been claimed by private capital, the government, or a combination of both in the construction of the "New Berlin"—the bustling world city, the gleaming new capital.[36] The Topography of Terror became another exhibition site among Berlin's many "world-class" museums, memorials, and archives. On a more pragmatic level, the needs of the documentation center as a growing institution were also a factor. A metal container was not the most propitious space for the many research, educational, archival, and symbolic activities carried out by the documentation center; neither did it offer the

---

35. For a vivid evocation of the Topography of Terror in the 1990s and early 2000s, see Till's field notes from her visits to the site and interviews with other visitors, in *New Berlin*, 107–19.

36. Till, *New Berlin*; Strom, *Building the New Berlin*; and Colomb, *Staging the New Berlin*.

most adequate facilities to support an increasing volume of visitors (including issues of physical accessibility and safety).

The New Design

The 2005 competition awarded first place to a design by architect Ursula Wilms
and landscape architect Heinz W. Hallmann; the new version was inaugurated in
2010. The proposal won over the jury in part because, according to Lutz, "Wilms's
idea was not to have a building that is itself a symbol."[37] The design was chosen precisely for its removed neutrality—meaning that critiques of the built design should
consider not only the architects' intentions but also the requirements and expectations set by the Topography of Terror foundation. In other words, the design ex-
presses an institutional and curatorial mission as much as the ideas of the architects.
Wilms and Hallmann's design consists of a low-slung gray prism with a square
footprint and a central courtyard, placed in the middle of an open area covered
with gravel and crisscrossed by cement pathways (fig. 19).

On the southeast corner of the site, on the corner of Wilhelmstraße and Anhalterstraße, a large, square plot is covered with locust trees. The dense, organic, free-
growing tree grove contrasts with the rigidly ordered, gravel-covered northern end
of the site. The tree area, a "little forest," still contains the traces of a driving track
used by West Germans in the postwar era, and it has been left as is to offer "an
impression of how the grounds were used during the postwar period."[38] Wilms
notes that it is a nature preserve, and as such "must be kept as it is," but that it holds
another meaning: "For us, the forest also represents the forgetting and suppression
of the postwar era: first the carefree use of the land for pleasure and enjoyment;
then the beautiful green and wild 'nature.'"[39] Wilms's wording referring to the
minimal interventions around this area is telling: "We . . . set it free through the
scraggy stone surface around Wilhelm and Anhalterstraße." Wilms and Hallmann
not only set the space free through ground-covering choices; they also set it free
symbolically, leaving its interpretation open.

Some visitors might understand the forest as a representation of postwar forgetting; others might not (see my discussion of Ana Souto's critique, below). This is
the same risk of misinterpretation I discussed with relation to Libeskind's Project
Mourning and other memorials in the previous chapter. The alternative would
be to include literal or symbolic signposting spelling out the meaning of architectural decisions and formal choices—a "how-to-read" manual. This would, however, not only dumb down the visual and phenomenological experience of the

37. Cited in Malamud, "Meticulously Evil."

38. "The Terrain of the Topography of Terror," Topography of Terror, http://www.topographie.
de/en/the-historic-site/the-terrain-of-the-topography-of-terror/. On the driving tracks, see Ladd, *Ghosts
of Berlin*, 158.

39. Ursula Wilms, interview via e-mail, September 23, 2014.

Figure 19. Topography of Terror, exterior, general view (2010). © Daniela Sandler

design (underestimating both the design and the visitors), but it would also narrow meanings down to a predetermined interpretation. The value of open-ended architectural or memorial designs—be they examples of counterpreservation, countermonuments, or abstraction—is both the possibility for multiple interpretations (and thus for dynamic reflection and public debate), and the necessity for viewers or visitors to engage the memory process actively. This involves risk, including the risk of failure and miscommunication.

Such signposting is present not far away from the site: in 2007, the Topography of Terror Foundation installed thirty plaques telling the history of significant buildings and points on Wilhelmstraße.[40] These plaques are freestanding glass rectangles with text and photographs; the glass allows the contents of each plaque to be overlaid with the sights behind it. Depending on the plaque, these sights are extant original buildings; or else trees or new structures, attesting to the loss of historic

---

40. The Geschichtsmeile was first proposed in 1997. Helmut Engel and Wolfgang Ribbe, *Geschichtsmeile Wilhelmstraße* (Berlin: Akademie, 1997); Claudia Steur, *Geschichtsmeile Wilhelmstraße: Begleitbroschüre zur gleichnamigen Ausstellung* (Berlin: Stiftung Topographie des Terrors, 2006); Volker Hobrack, "Geschichtsmeile Wilhelmstraße," in *Spuren der Geschichte: Neue Gedenktafeln in Berlins Mitte*, ed. Constanze Döhrer, Volker Hobrack, and Angelika Keune (Berlin: Berlin Story, 2012), 165–66; "Strassenausstellung: Geschichtsmeile Wilhelmstraße," Stiftung Topographie des Terrors, http://www.topographie.de/topographie-des-terrors/ausstellungen/geschichtsmeile-wilhelmstrasse/.

spaces, now to be glimpsed only in the photographs. The plaques are collectively called the Geschichtsmeile (History Mile), and attempt to capture the historical significance of a broad stretch of the city that could not have been contained in a memorial or museum (the buildings along the street are used today for government offices, residences, and commerce). Although at points the Geschichtsmeile betrays a certain anxiety—its profuse texts compensating both for the silence of buildings whose history is not apparent, and for the presumed ignorance of passersby—at the same time it is an ingenious way to activate historical awareness in an otherwise opaque public space. The Geschichtsmeile works because it is juxtaposed to an environment not designed for memory; the Topography of Terror site, in turn, already has precisely the kind of forethought and conscious shaping that the Geschichtsmeile tries to make up for, making a similar effort redundant.

The new landscape design of the Topography of Terror site has leveled most of the ground onto a flat surface, except for the trench that abuts Niederkirchner-straße, and for a cluster of sunken ruins. The trench is now protected by a metal-and-glass canopy—a brighter, sleeker, more official-looking structure than the previous wooden cover (fig. 20). The muted color palette and emphasis on stark

Figure 20. Topography of Terror, exterior, detail (2010). On the upper part of the image, in the background, are the windows of the Nazi-built Aviation Ministry (now Finance Ministry). Immediately below, remains of the Berlin Wall. And below them, remains of the Gestapo building. In the foreground, the new glass-and-metal canopy.

© Daniela Sandler

geometries give the site an abstract quality. The whole space reads as a mostly flat, gray expanse cut by geometric planes in different shades of gray and white: the right-angled sides of the building, the squares and diagonals of the landscape grounds. The site was planned with this idea of emptiness in mind. The building is a single flat volume, so as "to leave as much empty space as possible, and to allow for this emptiness to be experienced."[41]

The approach to the site, which Wilms defines as an "urban idea" (and not just as an architectural idea focused on the building as a single object), recalls the trope of the void, which was forged in discussions of how to represent the destruction and absence of Holocaust victims in memorials and buildings.[42] This trope has become somewhat of a cliché, overused by architects and critics without necessarily advancing the original concept; as with all clichés, its original potency ends up somewhat devoid (pun intended). But also, as with all clichés, it maintains a measure of truth. The Topography of Terror site is indeed a site of voids: most of the buildings used by the Nazis were destroyed; the history and memory of the site were blank for almost half a century; and the whole site was a big hole in the urban fabric. Wilms and Hallmann's design does not so much defer to this emptiness, but enhances it—the site looks much emptier today than it did when it housed the dumpster, the driving track, and even the temporary Topography of Terror exhibition. Crucially, Wilms does not describe this emptiness as merely spatial, but also as the symbolic condition that would allow for learning about the site's history and reflecting on its social and individual implications:

> Here it was the history of the site, and with it the responsibility for the legacy of our Nazi past—that was for me, for us, as Germans, the biggest challenge. . . . The core question for us was how to engage the highest number of people as possible, to get them involved. . . . Our formal answer was: openness, no barriers, light, and transparency (to bring history into the light of day, illuminate it, make it knowable).[43]

The reference to light differentiates Wilms's design from the usual rhetoric about architectural and memorial voids as negative spaces. The voids in Libeskind's Jewish Museum or Eisenman's Memorial to the Murdered Jews of Europe are in a sense black holes, referring to an absence that cannot be filled, sucking the visitor into anguished reflection. In Wilms's case, the void is out in the open, bright, almost blindingly so (especially on a sunny day, when the metal, glass, and light gray stones are quite reflective of light). This is a void that exposes not only an absence but the

---

41. Ursula Wilms, interview via e-mail, September 23, 2014.

42. Huyssen, *Present Pasts*, 49–71; Eran Neumann, *Shoah Presence: Architectural Representations of the Holocaust* (Farnham, UK: Ashgate, 2014); Jennifer Hansen-Glucklich, *Holocaust Memory Reframed: Museums and the Challenges of Representation* (New Brunswick, NJ: Rutgers University Press, 2014), and many others.

43. Ursula Wilms, interview via e-mail, September 23, 2014.

material traces of a history still present, in fragments, in ruins, in documents. Everything is out in the open, and the empty space makes room for reflection. This distinguishes Wilms's use of emptiness from the clichéd void metaphor—this, and the intellectual (as opposed to emotional) tone of her design, which I will discuss below.

At the center of the site, removed from the street, is the single building of the documentation center, which houses a library, exhibition galleries, research and archive spaces, offices, and visitor facilities such as restrooms and a café. The building is a strict and minimal composition. The outer walls are metal screens, made of slim metal tubes placed horizontally, creating a carapace that protects a second, inner layer—this time, made of glass. In between the glass and the outer metal, there is a narrow space forming a screened peristyle with a floor of metal grilles. The building is a metal-and-glass cage elevated slightly above grade, clearly separate from the ground on which it stands. The outer carapace of the building appears as either transparent or opaque depending on one's distance and angle of vision. When opaque, it looks like a gray envelope, neutral and forbidding, forming an almost blank backdrop to the open grounds—this enhances its alien quality, as if the building did not belong in there. From other angles, the building walls look diaphanous, semi-transparent, like very taut stretches of tulle fabric, hovering in front of the dark outlines of the interior spaces. The walls look like screens that slid into place, artificial separations that engage neither the inside nor the outside, but float in between them, immaterially. Whether perceived as opaque or transparent, the building's outer envelope is pointedly removed and disconnected from its immediate surroundings.

This disconnection from the site was intentional, as the official presentation of the project suggests: "The cubical mass of the building 'floats' freely above the terrain, intentionally unaligned with any former structures or street axes on the site."[44] Wilms was criticized for this disconnection, which is further enhanced by the building's minimalist aesthetics—a strict geometry of right angles and unadorned surfaces that has been compared to the high modernist New National Gallery by Ludwig Mies van der Rohe nearby.[45] Ana Souto, in her analysis of the site, argues that "the documentation centre could have been located anywhere in Berlin: there is no anchor with the site; the circulation is not encouraging the visitor to look outside and reflect on the fact that some of the events narrated in the exhibition did actually take place there."[46] And Layla Dawson, a critic for *Architectural Review*

---

44. "Topography of Terror, Berlin: Documentation and Visitor Centre and Presentation of the Historic Property," Heinle, Wischer und Partner (English version), http://www.heinlewischerpartner.de/Topography_of_Terror,_Berlin,_Documentation_and_Visitor_Centre_and_Presentation_of_the_Historic_Property.33.1.html.

45. Malamud, "Meticulously Evil."

46. Ana Souto, "Architecture and Memory: Berlin, a Phenomenological Approach," in *The Territories of Identity: Architecture in the Age of Evolving Globalization*, ed. Soumyen Bandyopadhyay and Guillermo Garma Montiel (London and New York: Routledge, 2013), 84.

magazine, bemoans the architecture for cleaning up a "'dirty' history."[47] These critics' reactions reveal a contemporary sensibility primed by the activist approach to history, by site-specific conceptions of memory that owe much to Nora's definition of *lieux de mémoire*,[48] and by notions of authenticity. The Topography of Terror, in its earlier incarnation, set up expectations of what kind of configuration should define the site: rough, unstable, open-ended, and provisional. The public had accustomed its gaze to the overgrown site, and the sight of the organized and sleek new design has been all the more shocking for going against habit.

Against these expectations, and critiques, I argue that the new design offers a productive approach in the ways it engages, or refuses to engage, the "sense of place" of the site—and that it is precisely by subverting expectations, and frustrating the accustomed gaze of the public, that it might jolt visitors into a critical engagement with history. In the new Topography of Terror, the sense of history and authenticity is not provided ready-made for an immediate, sensuous experience; rather, the aloof and abstract quality of the building and landscape design require a stronger effort of reflection and imagination, of recalling historical connections in the mind's eye instead of receiving them on one's retina. This calling forth of participation is a tactic common to countermonuments, and it is worth remembering that many countermonuments resort precisely to abstraction in order to elicit engagement: from Maya Lin's Vietnam Veterans Memorial in Washington, D.C., to Jochen and Esther Gerz's Monument against Fascism in Harburg, to Eisenman's Memorial to the Murdered Jews of Europe.

The architect herself sees the building's disconnection as a means to foreground the site and its history, not only in the present but also potentially in the future, if and when social needs and conditions change—a thought process very much aligned with the premise of the socially produced character of memory and memorials discussed in the previous chapter:

> The building is almost a subordinate . . . addition to the land. The part of the building that sticks above ground is slightly elevated over the surface of the site, and it is purposefully not made of stone. This should underline that the building is an addition, and has no claims to eternal permanence. The building can be removed (if it doesn't work anymore as a site for learning and memory), but the land and its history will remain, always. And with them, our responsibility.[49]

It takes courage for a designer to envision a building in this potentially transitory, and somewhat self-effacing, way. Temporary, adaptable, and replaceable

---

47. Layla Dawson, "Topography of Terror Washed Away Too Much Dirt in Presenting Its Nazi History," *Architectural Review* 227, no. 1361 (July 2010): 29.

48. Pierre Nora, *Realms of Memory: Rethinking the French Past* (New York: Columbia University Press, 1996–98).

49. Ursula Wilms, interview via e-mail, September 23, 2014.

structures have been conceived before—notably by avant-gardes and visionaries, such as the Futurists in the early twentieth century, and the Metabolists, Archigram, Superstudio, and others in the 1960s. But in contemporary mainstream architecture—whether under the aegis of commercialism, the starchitecture economy, or sustainability—this attitude is rare. The lightness and flatness of Wilms's design, its refusal to lay down deep foundations on the ground, remove any pretense that the architect's reading should be a final or overriding voice in the public understandings of the site. At the same time, her design is no wallflower—it changed the configuration and overall form of the site radically and assertively, which is partly why it has irked critics such as Dawson and Souto.

Working closely with Wilms, landscape designer Heinz Hallmann composed an open space completely covered in sterile materials. The landscape of cement and gravel is one in which no further life can grow, in contrast to the previous exhibition, when the site offered grass-covered slopes and overgrown plants. Hallmann covers the terrain under an unforgiving gray seal, comparable in some ways to Libeskind's waterland in the way it focuses attention on the historical charge of the site, preventing other uses that might normalize or obscure the memorial function of the land. It is in a way a cemetery, a gravel yard that alludes to death and circumspection. Unlike Libeskind's waterland, though, Hallmann's design carefully frames the extant remnants of Nazi structures. Swaths of gravel, patches of cement, and panes of glass surround tiled walls, metal beams, exposed staircases, and concrete columns. If Libeskind's water would have been a dynamic and eroding medium, Hallmann's sterile landscaping functions more like a solidifying resin, fixating and preserving the ruins as if they were insects caught in amber. This is not a precise metaphor, for most of the ruins are in fact uncovered (except for a few that had deteriorated in the first Topography of Terror exhibition and were covered to prevent their destruction). Not only are they accessible to touch; they are also exposed to the elements, and therefore to a slow but continuous process of degradation.

In a way, these are the paradoxical preserved ruins I discussed earlier in this book, the carefully cleaned and exposed shells of structures like the Kaiser-Wilhelm-Gedächtniskirche and the Franziskaner Klosterkirche. Indeed, the ruins of the Gestapo terrain are now scrubbed up and framed, rough-looking but otherwise contained and controlled fragments within an overarching design. But they are more than that, and cannot be considered as pretty, picturesque icons like the two church ruins mentioned above. The ruins in the Topography of Terror are carved out by chance, not by artful design; the landscaping follows their outlines, and not the other way around. Along Niederkirchnerstraße, the exhibition plaques make the context and background of these ruins clear. The glass canopy functions as a giant specimen glass, isolating the objects of scientific interest under a bright light (unlike the previous wooden cover, the glass canopy does not offer shade on sunny days). To the southwest of the building, another cluster of ruins disrupts the ground, with underground columns and a descending staircase opening up a hole on the site. These ruins are surrounded by railings, keeping them from public access. This is a compromise necessary for public safety and preservation, but it is frustrating for the visitor, as these ruins beckon for direct exploration.

Near these ruins, a discreet monument marks the site of the former Gestapo House Prison cells. The ruins of these cells are buried underground, not exposed to the public, for preservation reasons; the only way to save these remnants was to hide them from view. On top of them, the gravel is interrupted by low slivers of concrete, which delineate a square outline and section off a portion of the ground. On the side of these low concrete bars, one can read, in German and in English: "On this site were cells of the House Prison at Gestapo Headquarters." Historical representation is indirect, acknowledging the chasm between past and present— and dealing with the literal inaccessibility (and invisibility) of the original remains. One must get close to these concrete outlines to read the text, stepping over the gravel, away from the cement paving. It is an uncomfortable and difficult material on which to walk, serving as a metaphor for the process of engaging with this history, both on the location of this memorial and on the site as a whole. Most visitors keep to the cement paths instead, but there are no physical barriers, and in theory one could wander freely around the site in all directions over the gravel. Wilms envisioned this area as a place for lingering (there are benches nearby). In her words, "As a site of bodily and spiritual mishandling, this spot is almost the memorial place for the victims in the middle of the perpetrator site." She added that "occasionally, people leave flowers there spontaneously" to commemorate these victims.[50]

The ruins left on the site also evoke the memorial lexicon of concentration camp memorial sites, which often resort to displaying the distorted and partial remains of crematoria, gas chambers, barracks, and medical experiment halls. This is a reference that might belong in the visual subconscious of a considerable part of the public of this site—Germans who, as part of their school education, might be taken on concentration camp field trips, and tourists who might have visited other sites of Nazi terror besides the Topography. The visual similarity might not have been a conscious curatorial strategy, but it works as an easily understandable code for the tone of the site—and possibly for establishing a mental connection between Berlin and beyond, between the Gestapo ruins and the concentration camp ruins, just as there had been a connection between the Gestapo officers in Berlin and the concentration camp system as a whole.

When discussing the "rhetoric of ruins" in concentration camp memorial sites, focusing on Majdanek and Auschwitz-Birkenau, Young recalls Nora's concept of "places of memory" to assert that these sites are only meaningful as memorials because they have been socially constructed and framed as such—by governments,

---

50. Ibid.

institutions, visitors, and survivors. After considering the gulf of time that separates these sites from the horrors that once took place there, Young points out that "only a deliberate act of memory could reconnect them, reinfuse the sites with a sense of their historical past."[51] Without such deliberate acts, these ruins are meaningless, both as material remnants and as visual forms. However, Young goes on to note that, despite the constructedness of memorials and of memory itself, there remains a widely held social belief that these ruins are somehow animated by essential meanings that reside in them independently of human action or perception:

> Nevertheless, the magic of ruins persists, a near mystical fascination with sites seemingly charged with the aura of past events, as if the molecules of the sites still vibrated with the memory of their history. . . . As houses come to be "haunted" by the ghosts (memory, really) of their former occupants, the sites of destruction are haunted by phantoms of past events, no longer visible, but only remembered.[52]

This is a belief in authenticity, in a genius loci—or maybe, more appropriately, in a phantasma loci. Young chooses his words carefully: "magic," "mystical," and "aura" all suggest that to see ruins as internally animated by intrinsic meaning, or memory, or ghosts, is to hold a supernatural belief, a matter of faith and not of reason or observation. Critics of the current Topography of Terror reveal such a belief by invoking the concept of authenticity, holding that the previous exhibition was true to the intrinsic powers and meanings of the site, its spirit, and that the current version is not. Take, for example, Souto's observations, based on her phenomenological immersion in the site:

> The Topography of Terror has been transformed into a topography of control, of tidiness that does not connect with the site, with the authenticity of the location, with the weight that the past and collective memory should have in that particular place. . . . There is no sense of "terror" any more.[53]

Souto focuses on the southwest corner of the site, where "the vegetation grows freely, out of control; signposts are non-existent even though there are remains of buildings. The authenticity of this corner is very strong, but not properly acknowledged."[54]

The concept of authenticity merits further discussion here. The idea of authenticity is grounded on notions of material presence, objectivity, archaeological value, and forensic verifiability. I do not dispute the validity of these methods and of their premises. But archaeology, material presence, and forensics belong in particular

---

51. Young, *The Texture of Memory*, 119.
52. Ibid.
53. Souto, "Architecture and Memory," 84.
54. Ibid.

epistemologies—which they not only serve, but also express. What is more, authenticity connotes different meanings, and it is the conflation of these meanings that can blur the lines between the faith in a "magic aura" and the archaeological or documentarian perspective. In the case of the Topography of Terror, there are several competing epistemological approaches expressed by visitors, critics, members of the foundation, curators, and others. Like crossed phone lines, these competing approaches sometimes blend different discourses, and one connotation of authenticity slips into the other. It is thus important to untangle them. For historians in search of material evidence and documentation, the site is a source for authentic artifacts and vestiges. For architectural preservationists concerned with urban history, the site represents an authentic location. For cultural critics such as Souto and Dawson, visitors, or someone approaching the site as a symbolic place, it is the source of a different type of authenticity: the mystical, magical aura described by Young, which goes beyond materiality or a geographical notation—beyond the topography— and evokes the assumed true essence, the sense of the place. Hence Souto's disappointment that the "sense of 'terror'" is gone. This is a complicated connotation of authenticity based on personal and introspective experience—a subjective, multivalent, and constructed authenticity that paradoxically lays claim to a certain version of facts by invoking an unquestionable truth (the very mention of the word "authentic" suggests an authority of knowledge). One feels it, or doesn't feel it, and that becomes the yardstick. I do not mean that such a constructed authenticity has no value or place, because it does perform an important role in social and individual rituals of memorialization. But it is also a narrative, socially and historically contingent. A site that purports to enact such authenticity might be effective emotionally, but it also might obscure other ways of engagement with history—say, research, reflection, critique, discussion—creating an experiential sense of accuracy without furthering historical knowledge or insight.

I do not want to dismiss Souto's point entirely, but rather only nuance it. If her argument about authenticity is problematic, she also at the same time offers a valuable analytical model through her phenomenological approach. As Souto suggests in her exploration of the site, the embodied, spatial perception of places is an important component in the social and individual construction of memories and, ultimately, also in the process of memory-work. On this count, the new Topography of Terror indeed falls short compared to the immersive environment of the previous exhibition. The design of the landscape, open and easily readable, with clear paths and signage, leaves little room for mystery or for the imagination, but rather lays out its elements as a clear, brightly lit "spatial text": it is a site for the intellect. The building repeats the motif of objective presentation combined with a call for critical reflection: first, it presents visitors with a rationally organized space, easy to navigate, with ample room for circulation along exhibition displays. The building and its contents, down to the furniture, are placed on an implicit grid—the modernist matrix of rationality. At the same time, the harsh ground covering, grayness, and flat expanse of the site create a landscape that is quietly disturbing. The site is so strange, so different from its surroundings, so relentless, that it appears slightly out of human scale, oddly unpopulated by people, plants, or buildings. The gray expanse echoes the terrifying sublimity of a desert. In doing so, the site does evoke an emotional response—alienating, a bit sinister, and desolate. It is not the passionate anguish evoked by uncanny voids or mysterious ruins, but it is also a way to jar visitors into a heightened state of attention.

The space of clarity, of scientific exposition embodied in the building, converges in the interior courtyard—an open square in the middle of the building, lined by glass walls and surrounded by benches, with a shallow pool of water at the center (fig. 21). This is a space for meditation, which recalls Zen gardens with its abstract and artful combination of materials (stone, cement, glass, water), and the simplicity of design that heightens the always-changing effects of natural elements: the wind causing ripples on the water, the sun casting bright lights and dense shadows. It is a jewel box of a courtyard, and as it interrupts the interior space it seems to offer a respite, a punctuation mark, a point where one can rest from the exhibition texts and images—perhaps simply to take a break, perhaps to reflect and meditate (it is also functional, as it allows natural daylight and ventilation into the exhibition spaces of the building). This is a building for scientific exposition, for the rational

Figure 21. Topography of Terror, interior courtyard (2010).
© Daniela Sandler

communication of knowledge, and (in the courtyard) for the thoughtful reflection on the knowledge that was imparted. It is not a building for synesthetic experiences, for tactile opportunities, for an engagement of the body and the senses in space and time. The building materials are cool and weightless, without thickness, without mass; the glass and metal are like membranes, immaterial, disembodied; they are not solid and enveloping like thick walls or foundations.

The abandoned design by Zumthor would have offered the opposite type of space, following the kind of phenomenological experience that Souto defends. Zumthor's architecture and writings have become known precisely for his attention to phenomenology, the body, the senses beyond intellectual cognition and detached vision.[55] Models of his unbuilt proposal represent a building with poignant, engulfing plays of light and shadow. The building would have consisted of a monumental rectangular block, its walls made of repeated supporting columns, slim and tall, creating a screen on the outside perimeter. In between these columns, there would have been glass, forming very tall and narrow windows that would have let in light dramatically, almost like a blown-up prison cell. This simple exterior shell would have housed discrete, enclosed volumes and rooms inside, providing an "enveloping space" or "buffer zone" (in Zumthor's own words) that would have gathered exhibition spaces, visitor facilities, and the Gestapo ruins.[56] This "enveloping space" would have formed a cavernous, awe-inspiring interior, flanked by the rhythmic patterns of the lanky pillars and windows of the exterior shell.

Although Zumthor highlighted that "one of the basic concepts of the project was to have an outside view available from every part of the building,"[57] which the tall windows would have allowed for, the structural screen would always have framed these views within its inevitable vertical lines, slicing off the outside panorama and drawing one's eyes upward. Materials would have been left bare ("nothing is covered, plastered or concealed"),[58] enhancing the tactile dimension of the space. The linear and narrow building, with its sculptural unfolding of enclosed rooms and circulation spaces inside a monumental envelope, would probably have afforded visitors a more subjective, emotional, and immersive experience.[59] Its dramatic height and weighty material presence would have had a temple-like quality. It is easy to see how it might have competed with the contents of the exhibition and the site itself, as the foundation directors feared; and it is easy to understand why they adopted Wilms's lightweight, antimonumental design.

---

55. See, for instance, Peter Zumthor, *Atmospheres* (Basel: Birkhäuser, 2006).
56. Peter Zumthor, "'Topography of Terror' Berlin: International Exhibition and Documentation Centre," in Peter Zumthor, *Three Concepts: Thermal Bath Vals, Art Museum Bregenz, "Topography of Terror" Berlin,* exhibition catalogue (Lucerne: Edition Architekturgalerie; Basel: Birkhäuser, 1997), 52.
57. Zumthor, "'Topography of Terror' Berlin," 53.
58. Ibid.
59. Till, *New Berlin,* 104–5; Zumthor, *Three Concepts* and *Atmospheres.*

Aloof Architecture

While in some cases a disconnection from context could be faulted for historical ig-norance and a generic approach, in the case of the new Topography of Terror, the refusal to engage the context—sight lines, angles, and footprints of previous or ex-isting buildings—is a conscious statement about the function of a documentation and exhibition center as a place of reflection on historical narratives that are always already mediated, separated from the present by time and representational tech-nologies. One can have expansive views of the outside from within the building, although these views are always veiled by the metal screens around the building; depending on the angle and proximity, the veiling is more perceptible or else less obtrusive. These views are meant to "establish the connection to the 'here and now,' to the self." Wilms sought to convey that the history of the site is inseparable from the lives that go on outside of it: "The history, which one can discover in the per-manent exhibition inside the building, is not detached from us, but bound up with us. For this reason the building is transparent from the inside out."[60] At the same time, these views are filtered through the metal screens, interrupted by shadows or reflections on the glass. The visitor needs to work to discern the visual information beyond the screens—as opposed to a crystal-clear panoramic view that a picture window would have offered. In other words, there is always a sense of mediation.

This distance between the building and the site is also suggested by the curato-rial orientation of the exhibition, which has eschewed artifacts in favor of narra-tive texts and images based on historical documentation.[61] The detachment of the building avoids any possible impression that one can be immersed into a seem-ingly historical experience, engulfed in an authentic or original environment, as if breathing the air of the past along with its sights. Such an experience would be unavoidably a simulation, with an emphasis on the senses and an illusion of im-mediacy with the past and its historical vestiges. These immersive experiences offer the much-maligned "Disneyfied" version of history that some have condemned in reconstructed historical environments and newly built places such as the United States Holocaust Memorial Museum.[62]

I do not mean to say that an immersion in historical environments or remnants is always or essentially a problem—there is indeed something very powerful about walking into the musty barracks of Auschwitz-Birkenau, even if some of them have actually been reconstructed. But at the Topography of Terror, immersion in the open wound site would belie the fact not only that there are very few and frag-mented remnants of the original Prinz-Albrecht block, but also that the site en-dured a suffocating collective forgetting over almost forty years in the postwar era.

---

60. Ursula Wilms, interview via e-mail, September 23, 2014.
61. Thomas Lutz, head of the memorial-museums department of the Topography of Terror, quoted by Malamud, "Meticulously Evil."
62. Tim Cole, *Selling the Holocaust* (New York: Routledge, 1999).

The cool remove of Wilms and Hallmann's design does justice to this prolonged social erasure—this forgetting, more than the war destruction, is embodied by the new design. The danger of the collective effacement of histories and memories by a whole society is an equally pressing warning as the danger of oppression and war. While the open wound might have soothed a collective conscience with reassuring proof of historical engagement, offering a kind of redemption, the flat gray field denies this moral gratification.

How can one define the "authenticity of the site"? Is it the evocation of the time when the Gestapo and other Nazi institutions were still standing there in full operation? Or of the moment of their postwar destruction, and later oblivion? Or of the recovery of their memory, and the moment of historical activism? Malamud is one of the few critics who hinted at the slipperiness of notions of an "original" historical referent by recognizing the critical potential of Wilms's detached architecture:

> It's hard to imagine, walking through the ultramodern space, what the "topography" must have looked like back in the 1930s, and I think that's exactly the architect Ursula Wilms's intention as she superimposes our contemporary style, our presence, on top of the historical specter.[63]

The aloofness of Wilms's building and Hallmann's landscaping deny facile impressions of historical awareness or immediacy, and instead require more from visitors—that we work hard to conjure up a vision of the past based on the informational texts and images from the exhibition, that we piece together the contents of the exhibition next to the context of the urban surroundings, and that we turn our attention to our thoughts as a response to the site instead of melding our bodies and senses there. By refusing to provide the sense of authenticity and contextual immersion that the public has come to expect, the new site offers a precious chance at disrupting mainstream expectations and providing a less scripted historical experience.

The different incarnations of the Topography of Terror—the previous exhibition, Zumthor's unbuilt design, and the current configuration—pit two memorial approaches against each other: on the one hand, a sensorial and even figurative experience of history, subjective, emotional, immersive; on the other hand, the intellectual and reflective stance, objective, cool, detached. If we probe this to an extreme, we might ask whether the immersive experience distracts from intellectual reflection by providing a cathartic sense of "living history," which exhausts itself as a self-contained moment of awareness instead of prompting long-lasting reflections or further research. Henri-Pierre Jeudy asked the same question of French "eco-museums," immersive reconstructions of historical environments complete with tools, everyday artifacts, and even actors in period dress, which for him were a

---

63. Malamud, "Meticulously Evil."

reductive and prescriptive way of representing history to contemporary audiences. Jeudy instead favored sites where visitors could roam free among untouched, decaying ruins (for example, industrial ruins), and where the engagement with the past would be as open to free associations and individual initiative as the physical exploration of these places. This is a position similar to that of Tim Edensor, in his analyses of abandoned industrial ruins in England.[64]

At first sight one might use Jeudy and Edensor to make a case for the former incarnation of the Topography of Terror—and indeed, in its origins, the grassroots exhibition exemplified the free exploration and possibilities for discovery and new meaning that these two authors see in abandoned ruins. This was the case in the late 1970s, when the site was first rediscovered; it was the case in the 1980s, when it was the object of further excavations and activism; and it was even still the case in 1987, when the first temporary exhibition was set up. But ten or fifteen years later, was the exhibition as free for the roaming—the meanings as free for the taking—as they had been initially? There was already something codified and fixed through the continued existence of the exhibition, through its repeated visitation, through its recurring appearance in news stories, tours and guidebooks, and scholarly works.

When I first visited the site in 2002, although it was thrilling in some ways—not least because popular reports and critical literature had prepped me to encounter the exhibition as participatory, dynamic, and subversive—it already did not appear to be as open-ended and in-progress anymore. The exhibition facilities were slightly less makeshift, the public spotlight had lifted the place into the mainstream, and many portions of the site, including some of the ruins, were not accessible anymore. The inaugural exhibition, which had been housed inside a temporary building, had long been dismantled. But most of all, much as I wished to partake in the "dig-where-you-stand," collective history-making of the 1980s, that moment and that experience were inevitably gone. The Topography of Terror was also, and already, a simulacrum of a previous experience, and a witness not only to the Nazi past of the site, but also to the unique moment of its rediscovery—which itself has become a myth. The new Topography of Terror does not pay homage to this myth (perhaps a different design could have, or perhaps the very requirement of a permanent layout for the site precluded this), and an unacknowledged nostalgia for that mythical moment is possibly behind the critics' laments that the new design is too neat and tidy.

The Topography of Terror is no longer an example of counterpreservation as I have defined it. Even if it had been kept in its "open wound" state, it might still not have fulfilled the dynamic and open-ended promises of counterpreservation because of the ways in which the experience of the site had been scripted and codified

---

64. Henri-Pierre Jeudy, *Mémoires du social* (Paris: Presses Universitaires de France, 1986); Tim Edensor, *Industrial Ruins: Space, Aesthetics, and Materiality* (London: Bloomsbury Academic, 2005).

through public reception and critical literature, as I argued above. The presence of decay, decrepitude, and free ruins is not in itself synonymous with counterpreservation. In the introduction to this book, I defined the concept as necessarily grounded on social practices—community initiatives, activist movements, symbolic discussions. These practices might be concerned with socioeconomic inclusion, as in the case of the *Hausprojekte* in chapter 1; or with creative freedom and a critical representation of history, as in the case of the cultural and art centers of chapter 2; or with the possibility for a dynamic engagement with memory, as in Libeskind's Project Mourning. Without these social practices and social meanings, decaying sites are just that—heaps of stone in a landscape, as Young would say. Conversely, radical decay is not necessary for a complex and participatory approach to history, as demonstrated by the new Topography of Terror.

6

DESTRUCTION AND DISAPPEARANCE

East German Ruins

The most recent spate of ruins in Berlin has occurred in the wake of the fall of the Wall in 1989—the remnants of the Wall being, perhaps, the most prominent among them. Structures from the Socialist era have been at points defaced, both concretely and symbolically, and at points effaced—from discourse, attention, and urban plans—revealing the imbalances that have marked the process of unification of the two Germanys. If East Germany voted for, and benefited from, political and economic union with West Germany, it also was, in many ways, the weaker party in terms of power, giving up its constitution, its political and economic system, its educational and professional frameworks, and many of the trappings of its every-day life. This imbalance has been called, by some, "annexation" or colonization;[1] but one does not need to go that far to recognize that the end of East Germany

---

1. Günter Grass's novel *Too Far Afield* (New York: Harcourt, 2000) is perhaps the most famous example. The protagonists work for the Treuhand, the agency in charge of liquidating East German state property. Grass's novel portrayed "German unification in 1990 as West Germany's de facto occupation of East Germany," in the words of Alan Riding. Grass's statements reinforce this reading: "People in the East were happy in 1989 when the wall came down, but then the West Germans arrived like colonizers. They didn't accept that the East Germans had a different biography, that they had gone from Hitler to Stalin, that they had never had a democratic experience." Alan Riding, "From Gunter Grass, a Tale of Two Germanys," *New York Times*, December 14, 2000, B1.

stood symbolically for greater historical changes: the collapse of Socialism in Europe, the demise of the Iron Curtain, the seemingly ultimate victory of capitalism.

Against this background, the removal, dismantlement, or neglect of structures from the Socialist era has represented a very public "acting out" of the underlying tensions of unification. Destroying statues and buildings became a dramatic reenactment of the initial catharsis of the fall of the Wall, each implosion or demolition replaying a kind of symbolic exorcism. Beyond the drama of the moment of destruction, the disappearance of signs of the GDR from the city was a way of rewriting history, as if to say that the preceding forty-five years had been a glitch in a longer historical continuum, a mistake in need of amendment. This chapter will not retell these stories of destruction and erasure in detail; they have already been told, extensively, by scholars and the popular media alike.[2] I take these stories as background, because the case studies here are the same: the Palace of the Republic and the remnants of the Berlin Wall. I address a particular slice of their afterlife: their long duration as slowly eroding structures in a sort of limbo stage on their road to disappearance. Ambiguous, undefined, deteriorating, some of these buildings of enduring ruination have served as in-between spaces for alternative forms of occupation, from art installations to insurgent urbanism, and as such they have configured what Ignasi de Solà-Morales called a *terrain vague* or "uncertain terrain," vague both in the sense of being vacant and in the sense of being open-ended.[3] For Solà-Morales, and those who have used his work to analyze urban space, a *terrain vague* is often characterized by physical decay, neglect, and marginality, but this is precisely what makes it potentially rich: its meanings are in transition, its uses not defined, and so a *terrain vague* is labile, allowing for interventions that can be novel, experimental, countercultural, critical.

Many East German structures can be seen as such physical and symbolic *terrains vagues*—which is not to say that all of them can be seen this way, or that all of them were suddenly depopulated or bereft of meaning. But some, including very central and symbolic structures, were indeed vacated, closed down, devoid of people, uses, furnishings, and building materials. As these structures sat empty, they were also fecund with possibilities for new occupations. Buildings like the Palace of the Republic or large housing projects gained a different life through new uses and

---

2. See David Clarke and Ute Wölfel, eds., *Remembering the German Democratic Republic: Divided Memory in a United Germany* (New York and Basingstoke, UK: Palgrave Macmillan, 2011); Anna Saunders, "The Ghosts of Lenin, Thälmann, and Marx in the Post-Socialist Cityscape," *German Life and Letters* 63, no. 4 (October 2010): 441–57; Robert Halsall, "GDR Architecture and Town Planning in Post-Unification Germany: 'Geschichtsaufarbeitung' or Aesthetic Autonomy?," in *The GDR and Its History*, ed. Peter Barker (Amsterdam: Rodopi, 2000), 185–214; Jason James, *Preservation and National Belonging in Eastern Germany: Heritage Fetishism and Redeeming Germanness* (New York: Palgrave Macmillan, 2012); and the section on "Socialist Memory and Memory of Socialism" in *Memorialisation in Germany since 1945*, ed. Bill Niven and Chloe Paver (New York: Palgrave Macmillan, 2010), 267–338.

3. "Terrain Vague," reprinted in *Terrain Vague: Interstices at the Edge of the Pale,* ed. Patrick Barron and Manuela Mariani (New York: Routledge, 2013), 24–29.

also, as importantly, through the ways in which they were resignified in the public consciousness in debates and cultural representations. The latter, in the form of historical documentation projects, mapping, and photographic essays, are as central in shaping the city as the more obviously concrete urban and architectural plans of city offices and private practices.

Debates on the preservation or replacement of GDR structures, especially when polarized between Wessi and Ossi allegiances, often consider the city a static field where buildings and decisions should be permanent. Whether this means preserving East German buildings as relics or life-size museums of the GDR era, or demolishing them to rebuild historical reproductions of long-lost buildings that preceded the GDR, both positions in the debate want to fixate visual and architectural signs on the surface of the city, as you would fixate the imprint of light on the surface of photographic paper. But just as the photographic image is an index of a source not present anymore—a spectrum of sorts, as described by Roland Barthes and Susan Sontag—so are these disputed structures also gone, in one way or another, even as their memory or their physical remains linger.[4] Such longing for permanence and continuity is understandable, as temporal endurance is, of course, vital to urban life, not only because of sentimental preferences or for a sense of identity, but also for practical reasons of economy, functionality, and logistics. However, as in the rest of this book, I am not concerned with the "firmitas" in architecture, but rather with the change architecture also harbors and undergoes. I am interested in the in-between state of GDR structures and ruins, the temporal interstices when some of these buildings were allowed to inhabit and constitute a *terrain vague* in the chronology of the city: a transient stage, a finite era, which nonetheless had meaning in and of itself, and which projected visions for the future.

These disappearing sites—the Palace of the Republic, the Wall, *Plattenbauten* housing projects, among others—have endured in a different way. Walter Benjamin's Angel of History experiences progress in reverse, and so progress appears as ruin;[5] it is easy to read the destruction of GDR structures as a literal application of this image, as if they had fallen prey to the "progress" of unification, globalization, gentrification, and other late-capitalist urban processes. But because some of these ruins were occupied and transformed by counterpreservation—by conscious appropriations, new meanings, new forms and uses—I propose that we look at them the other way around. They are not the ruin-victims of progress, but rather they reverse destruction, they turn the Angel on its back and "unstick" his wings from the winds of progress, if only for a moment. Ruins of the GDR, occupied literally or

---

4. Roland Barthes, *Camera Lucida: Reflections on Photography* (New York: Hill and Wang, 1982), 80–81; Susan Sontag, *On Photography* (New York: Farrar, Straus and Giroux, 1977), 15–16.
5. Walter Benjamin, "Theses on the Philosophy of History," *Illuminations*, ed. Hannah Arendt (New York: Schocken Books, 1968), 257.

figuratively, are nodules in time, urban cysts, interrupting the logic and the fabric of the city in alternative, poetic, and sometimes visionary ways.

The Palace of the Republic

The Palace of the Republic (Palast der Republik), a civic structure built by the East German government in the 1970s, was at the center of a prolonged debate for almost two decades over whether to preserve it, demolish it, replace it with something new, or with a reproduction of the old Berlin Palace (Berliner Schloss), which had stood on its site before. I will not recount this debate in detail here, because it has been exhaustively reproduced and dissected in scholarly literature and popular media alike, and because the intricacies are not central to my discussion.[6] It is enough to note a few basic points. The Palace of the Republic had been built on the site where the Berlin Palace had once stood, a site also known as Palace Square (Schlossplatz), and as such the Socialist building always sat on the slow-burning embers of nostalgia, memory, and resentment for the loss of the old structure. The old Palace dated back to around 1442, when Berlin was a small medieval outpost, and it was enlarged and transformed through several construction phases as the power of Berlin and its region grew. The growth of the Palace was bound up with the growth and planning of the city itself, and this is an important point for understanding not only the nostalgic attachments to the building, but also the structural centrality of the site at the urban level, even many centuries later.[7] As the Palace expanded, so did its "political and symbolic meaning . . . according to the rise of Prussia and the German Empire."[8] By the end of the nineteenth century, it anchored Berlin's identity as the capital of Prussia. The building was the stately seat of the ruling Hohenzollern family, and their power was displayed for all to see, since the Palace was located at a traffic and visual nexus on the processional boulevard Unter den Linden, across from the Berlin Cathedral and Museum Island, and not far from the Brandenburg Gate. This was the heart of the city, the focus of triumphal marches and of everyday life in the Second Reich.

The Palace was damaged in World War II. As so many pointed out at the time and later, it was not beyond repair, though the damage was severe. In his plea to

6. Titles on all sides of the debate include Philipp Misselwitz, Hans-Ulrich Obrist, and Philipp Oswalt, eds., *Fun Palace 200X: Der Berliner Schlossplatz; Abriss, Neubau oder grüne Wiese?* (Berlin: Martin Schmitz, 2005); Wilhelm von Boddien, ed., *Die Berliner Schlossdebatte: Pro und Contra* (Berlin: Spitz, 2000); Hans Joachim Arndt and Martin Sperlich, eds., *Das Berliner Schloss auf der Spreeinsel: Wiederaufbau oder Neuplanung* (Berlin: Boldt, 1994); Förderverein Berliner Stadtschloss, *Das Schloss? Eine Ausstellung über die Mitte Berlins,* exhibition catalogue, ed. Kristin Feireiss and Wilhelm Boddien (Berlin: Ernst & Sohn, 1993); Moritz Holfelder, *Palast der Republik: Aufstieg und Fall eines symbolischen Gebäudes* (Berlin: Christoph Links, 2008).

7. Goerd Peschken, "Schloss und Stadt," in *Das Schloss?* 23–32.

8. Adrian von Buttlar, "Berlin's Castle versus Palace: A Proper Past for Germany's Future?," *Future Anterior* 4, no. 1 (Summer 2007): 19.

refurbish the damaged Palace, art historian Ernst Gall argued that its "main fabric remained intact" and "it would have been easy to utilize the remaining structure and to convert it into a fitting administration building."[9] In 1950, the East German president, Walter Ulbricht, ordered its demolition despite protests from East and West Germany. The arguments for the demolition ranged from the ideological (the Palace represented anti-Socialist values of a fallen, belligerent monarchy) to the practical (postwar priorities lay in rebuilding the city and its ligaments, providing housing and other infrastructure). The official Scientific Group commissioned by the Socialist government to assess the prospects for the site concluded that not only would the reconstruction be very costly, but also, because of resources, only possible "in ten years time."[10] Ulbricht did not want to leave the large site as a ruin in the middle of the city for so long, as he feared this would be demoralizing.[11]

Postwar Berlin was so marked by destruction—blocks after blocks of structures damaged to varying degrees, from pockmarks and dents to piles of rubble—that architectural ruination could not acquire a positive meaning, as it did forty years later with counterpreservation. And it was not just that the cityscape was a field of desolation, a difficult terrain to live in, and a reminder of the war losses. There was also a collective drive to restore the body of the city, a drive bound up with the wish to restore many other things: the body politic of the (divided, occupied) nation, the wounded bodies of war survivors, the families missing not only young, army-aged men but also the children and elderly recruited at the end of the war.[12] With such heavy practical implications and symbolic connotations, ruins had a limited place in the official plans for the recovering city on both sides, reserved for select moral gestures, as in the case of the Kaiser-Wilhelm-Gedächtniskirche in West Berlin.

---

9. Ernst Gall, "Will the Palace Be Destroyed?," in *The Palace of Berlin and Its Downfall*, ed. Karl Rodemann (Berlin: Tauber, 1951), 5.

10. Kaiser Strauss, "What Is the Palace of Berlin?," in *The Palace of Berlin and Its Downfall*, 11. Strauss was the director of the GDR-appointed Scientific Group, and his report was published in this volume as an example of "communist ideology," against which the rest of the book pits itself. But even if it was biased by its charge, Strauss's assessment offers a critical position on historical restoration, when he considers that "as the extent of the destruction in the palace is so large, . . . even with reconstruction on its old site the substance would have to be rebuilt" and this "would mean that the inspired creation of Schlüter's [one of the old Palace's architects] would be preserved in its main lines only as a re-creation." This is a more sophisticated take than that of current proposals for the site, which foresee the reconstruction of part of the original exterior—that is, a replica of part of the façade, an unabashed simulation that neither respects the original architectural object nor acknowledges the many events that took place there, including its destruction, creating the impression of a historical environment that cannot speak about its own history. For a discussion of architectural replicas and authenticity, where the reconstruction of the Berlin Palace figures prominently, see Adrian von Buttlar et al., *Denkmalpflege statt Attrappenkultur: Gegen die Rekonstruktion von Baudenkmälern—eine Anthologie* (Basel: Birkhäuser; Berlin and Gütersloh: Bauverlag, 2013).

11. Cited in Brian Ladd, *Ghosts of Berlin: Confronting German History in the Urban Landscape* (Chicago: University of Chicago Press, 1997), 57.

12. On postwar reconstruction, see Jeffry M. Diefendorf, *In the Wake of War: Reconstruction of German Cities after World War II* (Oxford: Oxford University Press, 1993); see also *Stunde Null: The End and the Beginning Fifty Years Ago,* ed. Geoffrey J. Giles (Washington, DC: German Historical Institute, 1997).

Most architectural damage that remained (and a lot of damage did remain) survived out of a lack of alternatives or investment, not because of intentional framing or monumentalization.

The decision to raze the Berlin Palace raised protests in East and West, creating a sore spot that lingered through the postwar era and would resurface as a revived wound after unification. Architects and preservationists decried the loss of the building as an important monument and historic object, and also as a central piece of the urban fabric of Berlin. In between, the interregnum of the GDR produced its own version of this central site: after using the monumental open space for almost three decades as an imposing plaza for parades (with a special tribune and stands built for those occasions),[13] East German planners reshaped it by building the Palace of the Republic in 1976 (fig. 22). With a much smaller footprint than the old Palace, and the cubic, bronze-glass-clad modernism adopted in other Socialist buildings of the time, it looked modest by comparison with memories of the previous building. It left open a wide plaza to allow for the parades and demonstrations that had regularly taken place there in the previous decades. The new Palace—named after the Republic—was approachable not only in its architectural design and scale, but also in its functions. Scholars like to describe how it offered an unusual combination of government functions (assembly halls, one of them for the GDR parliament, or Volkskammer) and social spaces for leisure and informal meetings, creating an everyday civic realm where political consciousness would happen side by side, and perhaps even be fused, with entertainment such as bowling, dancing, and concerts. As Emily Pugh puts it in her detailed study of architecture and politics in divided Berlin,

> By bringing together, in one building, both official governmental functions and leisure and entertainment facilities, such as cafes, restaurants, theaters, and nightclubs, the palace appeared to prove Honecker's commitment to individuals' comfort over pomp and hollow ceremony. . . . Unlike many other structures, the palace was tied closely to the party, materially and symbolically, yet at the same time popularly embraced.[14]

The Palace was by most accounts beloved, even though some "argued that its political role was insignificant, since there were no free elections."[15] On March 18, 1990, free elections for the East German parliament were finally held for the first time, vesting the Palace with the kind of popular and democratic mandate that had been missing from the previous authoritarian regime. It was this first freely elected parliament that voted, on August 23 of the same year, to join West Germany—and

13. Ines Weizman, "Palast der Republik," *Journal of Architectural Education* 67, no. 1 (2013): 135.

14. Emily Pugh, *Architecture, Politics, and Identity in Divided Berlin* (Pittsburgh: University of Pittsburgh Press, 2014), 156.

15. Von Buttlar, "Berlin's Castle versus Palace," 14.

Figure 22. Palace of the Republic, exterior view (2005).
© Christian von Steffelin

the vote was taken inside the Volkskammer in the Palace of the Republic. Soon after, on September 19, the Palace was closed to public access on the grounds that it was contaminated with asbestos and needed to be remediated.[16] In Adrian von Buttlar's words,

> Like Snow White, the Palace fell asleep for seven years and was silently robbed of its political emblems, furnishings and artistic outfit. In 1997, it became clear that decontamination would mean stripping the building down to its skeleton. Thus, by the time the cleanup was finished in 2002, the Palace had already become a mysterious steel-and-glass ruin that could never regain its original character.[17]

By this point, the Palace had existed for twenty-six years—fourteen in full use, twelve as a closed and slowly disappearing building. Taking advantage of the closure, a private initiative called for demolishing the structure and replacing it with a replica of the old Berlin Palace. The initiative, associated with conservative groups

16. See Holfelder, *Palast der Republik*, 78–82, for an account of the decision-making process.
17. Von Buttlar, "Berlin's Castle versus Palace," 13.

and individuals mostly from West Germany,[18] gained political momentum (even if popular support was never unanimous), and after years of public debates and attempts to save the Palace, in 2005 the German government made final its decision to demolish it. In January 2006, the demolition began—not a spectacular implosion as in the case of other objects of architectural destruction such as Pruitt-Igoe, but as a gradual and anticlimactic dismantlement, or, as Ines Weizman put it, as a slow death that lasted two decades.[19] Von Buttlar notes that the dismantlement became both a "public spectacle" and an object of mockery, "ridiculed in a tear-off notepad in the form of the shrinking Palace."[20] But others saw a peculiar kind of beauty in the slow dissolution of the building; in the words of architect Markus Miessen, "There was something totally beautiful about the fact that the building wasn't knocked down, but almost taken apart, like you would disassemble a tent."[21]

Disassembling the new Palace of the Republic was as much a concrete act as it was a symbolic gesture. The gesture echoed the implosion of the old Hohenzollern Palace in its ideological overtones—but now the ideology was reversed. Berlin was the capital of unified, capitalist Germany, and the Socialist symbol had to go, just as the imperialist old Palace had made way for the Socialist GDR half a century earlier. It was a kind of belated historical revenge. Khadija Carroll La noted the spectacularization of the event, and called the dismantlement a "demolition theatre."[22] Indeed, a viewing platform (a *Palastschaustelle*) was erected so people could climb up stairs and watch the demolition.[23] La suggested that we read the process as a second trauma reenacted on the site of the first traumatic experience: the demolition of the Berlin Palace. As such, the second demolition is understood as an attempt to overcome the first trauma (following psychoanalytical theory, especially Sigmund Freud's writings on the post-traumatic drive to deal with painful memories by mastering an initial situation of pain or loss through its reenactment or repetition).[24] La's reading highlights the violence inherent in the slow taking-apart of the Palace, which, she argues, was "theatrically stretched and thereby politically leveraged for all to see."[25] This inherent violence hints at the ideological and political struggles

18. Wolfgang Kil, "Chronik eines angekündigten Todes . . . : Berlin: Palast der Republik," *Werk, Bauen + Wohnen* 92, no. 4 (2005): 31; Anna-Inés Hennet, *Die Berliner Schlossplatzdebatte im Spiegel der Presse* (Berlin: Verlagshaus Braun, 2005), 39–44. See also the book *Das Schloss? Eine Ausstellung über die Mitte Berlins* cited above, which is a catalogue of an exhibition organized by the Förderverein Berliner Schloss e.V. The foundation and its leader, businessman Wilhelm von Boddien, were the main promoters of the reconstruction of the old Palace.

19. Weizman, "Palast der Republik," 135.

20. Von Buttlar, "Berlin's Castle versus Palace," 26.

21. Markus Miessen, interview, *Derzeit: Mercedes-Benz Fashion Week Berlin Daily*, July 2, 2009, 6.

22. Khadija Carroll La, "The Very Mark of Repression: The Demolition Theatre of the Palast der Republik and the New Schloss Berlin," *Architectural Design* 207 (2010): 119.

23. Holfelder, *Palast der Republik*, 95.

24. La, "The Very Mark of Repression," 119–20. See also Sigmund Freud, *Beyond the Pleasure Principle* (London and Vienna: The International Psycho-Analytical Press, 1922), especially the passages on repetition-compulsion on pp. 19–25.

25. La, "The Very Mark of Repression," 119.

between East and West Germans behind the Palace polemics. But even a process originally aimed at effacing and oppressing a particular history might be turned around and imbued with new, opposite meanings by creative spatial occupation. While this process of demolition could not be staved off, it was appropriated and resignified through acts of cultural resistance.

The beauty of the disappearing structure was revealed and transformed through several art and cultural projects. Some of these projects were individual initiatives, such as Moritz Holfelder's book *Palast der Republik: Aufstieg und Fall eines symbolischen Gebäudes* and Christian von Steffelin's *Palast der Republik 1994–2010.*[26] Holfelder's book is a historic and photographic documentation that pays loving homage to the social meanings of the Palace in the GDR, its creative transformation by artists in the mid-2000s, and its final disassembly, which Holfelder captured in zoomed-out shots that record the gradual vanishing of the structure while evoking the scale and grandeur of classical ruins.

Von Steffelin's book is a photographic essay that follows the dissolution of the Palace, beginning shortly after it was closed down for asbestos removal and ending with its disappearance. Steffelin gained access to the Palace when its doors had been closed to the public, and before the asbestos removal, so the first photographs in his book are haunting portraits of abandoned rooms, still decked out in original furnishings and materials, but already dusty, disorderly, and depredated. The photos accompany the progressive breakdown of the Palace, registering the interiors as they were stripped of furniture, rugs, lighting fixtures, marble floors, wood paneling, porcelain tiles, paint, walls—as the skin and flesh were taken away, and all that remained was steel, bronze glass, and concrete. Steffelin's photographs, which illustrate this chapter, are generous in both size and details; the distant shots capture the vastness of the empty structure while yielding a sharp sense of its minutiae: the texture, markings, and rivets on the beams; the pockmarks on the concrete; the milky film of dust on the glass, with someone's finger scribbles on it. The eye simultaneously lingers on the fine-grained foreground and is sucked into the deep focus of long perspectives (figs. 23, 24). This double pull of his photos is compounded by their sublime quality, as Steffelin's wide frames and skillful lighting evoke the overpowering size and strangeness of the vacant structure. The effect is that the photos ceaselessly pull the viewer in, working against both the flatness of the image and the finiteness of the ruin, creating not only their own visual space but also their own extended temporality. The photos resist the destruction of the Palace by reconstructing an almost haptic sense of the building, transcending the visual emphasis

---

26. Christian von Steffelin, Knut Ebeling, and Manfred Schmalriede, *Palast der Republik 1994–2010* (Ostfildern: Hatje Cantz, 2011). See Holfelder, *Palast der Republik*. See also Thorsten Klapsch, *Palast der Republik* (Mannheim: Edition Panorama, 2008), which documented the Palace in 1993, when the interiors were still untouched since the closure three years earlier. Klapsch's documentation is the last before the Palace began to be taken apart; Steffelin's work picks up one year later, when the building had begun to be emptied.

of photography. Although uninhabited, Steffelin's crisply detailed and engulfing images conjure up the experiential dimension of space, cognitively if not concretely. Steffelin speaks of ruined spaces as both historical sites and "reservoirs of human traces, stories, feelings"; as places of both remembrance and fantasy (including fantasies about the future).[27] His photographs evoke this density of meanings even as they frame, appropriate, and display the ruin—and suggest that counterpreservation might also reside in visual or textual representations.

But the gutted, corroding Palace was also appropriated and occupied concretely, during the limbo time that separated the asbestos removal from the demolition, by a series of projects organized under the banner of the Initiative Zwischenpalastnutzung (Initiative Temporary Palace Use). And while the aesthetics of the structure played a major role in the way that artists occupied and visitors experienced the space, form was only a part of the project. The initiative also had political and urban aspirations, as its goal was to spur critical discussion of the future of the site and to provide alternative models for the city. Some of the groups leading the interventions limited their stated goals to the temporary occupation of the structure without questioning its demolition; other groups and individuals also involved in the project were explicitly engaged in the fight to save the Palace of the Republic, and to evince the undemocratic character of the decision to close it down. For although the decision was made through governmental channels such as the German parliament, many have argued that the process was not democratic and did not account for the considerable dissent voiced not only by specialists but also by the general public. Von Buttlar points out that during the debate to save the Palace, the building supporters gathered 80,000 signatures against its demolition, while 1,000 people expressed support for replacing the Palace of the Republic with a reconstructed Berlin Palace (care must be taken in interpreting these numbers though—there might have been people who would have supported the demolition of the Socialist structure without rebuilding the old Palace, and they would not have been counted among those 1,000). In any case, Von Buttlar continues, even the official assessment of the need to demolish the Palace was fraught and could have been swayed the other way, as the recommendation to destroy the Palace by an official commission came out of a one-vote majority and not a unanimous or supermajority decision.[28]

The Initiative Zwischenpalastnutzung was a collective of professionals from several fields—architects, planners, artists, designers, lawyers—formed in early 2003 with the goal of realizing "a temporary (2004–2006) public-interest and cultural occupation of the Palace of the Republic until its demolition."[29] This was explained as the "unique chance to install a limited-time lab for temporary uses."[30] The initiative, first proposed around 2001 and 2002, was initially rejected by the

27. Christian von Steffelin, interview via e-mail, November 12, 2015.
28. Von Buttlar, "Berlin's Castle versus Palace," 23; see also his n. 31.
29. "Verein," Zwischenpalastnutzung, http://www.zwischenpalastnutzung.de/.
30. "Idee," Zwischenpalastnutzung, http://www.zwischenpalastnutzung.de/.

German government, which, as owner of the Palace, had ultimate decision-making power over it. After two years of difficult deliberations, the German government finally relented and allowed the temporary uses to take place.[31] The initial activity was a series of tours conducted in July 2003, which marked the first time the building was open to the public since its closure for asbestos removal in 1990. By this time, of course, the structure visitors toured was much different from the original. The Palace of the Republic had been a polished, carpeted, even garish environment—combining sleek modernist surfaces with festive lighting, furniture, and finishes. The profusion of lamps in the building's main spaces, which went far beyond lighting needs and provided an ebullient background of transparent glass and yellowish light, earned the building the nickname Erichs Lampenladen (Erich Honecker's Lamp Shop).[32]

In 2003, the gutted building was a different entity (fig. 23). Raw concrete slabs and exposed metal beams and columns laid bare the structural skeleton. Without walls or other room divisions, the floors extended visually on all sides, on a tri-dimensional grid, offering a long-distance horizon one usually does not have inside a building unless it is an industrial structure or exhibition pavilion. The bronze-glass outer envelope remained, letting light seep into the cavernous interior spaces; the exposed stairwells, floor slabs, and stadium-seating steps gave the space a processional quality (fig. 24). The 2003 tours explored the space in its unique, striking rawness. Subsequent interventions, some of which I will describe below, took advantage not only of the unusual and somewhat uncanny atmosphere, but also of the vast empty spaces that afforded large-scale installations, in which tall structures were erected and the floor was even flooded with water. Holfelder admiringly describes the many interventions and events of the Zwischenpalastnutzung as "the craziest projects."[33]

The initiative saw the temporary use as an opportunity to achieve certain symbolic, cultural, and spatial goals, which are worth revisiting in detail. In their own words, these goals were the following:

- to take conscious leave of a building whose meaning was central to the GDR like no other, and whose inevitable asbestos removal was perceived by many as a symbolic act of cold demolition;
- to conduct a critical and innovative experimental engagement with the history, present, and future of the site;
- to revive the building and make it accessible for new projects;

---

31. Philipp Oswalt, *Zwischennutzung des Palast der Republik: Bilanz einer Transformation, 2003ff,* pamphlet (Berlin: Zwischenpalastnutzung e.V., Bündnis für den Palast, Urban Catalyst, [2005]), 2.

32. See Holfelder, *Palast der Republik*, 45–48, 54–59, for descriptions and images of materials and furnishings.

33. Holfelder, *Palast der Republik*, 98.

Figure 23. Palace of the Republic, interior, main entrance stairs, west side (2003).
© Christian von Steffelin

- to influence ideas for the future of the site in a positive way, and to extend the limits of previous debates;
- to use the symbolism of the site so as to bring innovative and new ways of city life into the public consciousness.[34]

Although in official statements the Initiative Zwischenpalastnutzung denies that it wanted to save the Palace from demolition, suggesting instead that it was content with (or resigned to) treating it as an experimental space of limited duration, the unstated motivations were more complex. There were several individuals and associations behind the initiative, not all of whom agreed on every point, and for at least some of them demolition was not necessarily the best option for the site.

Philipp Oswalt, a Berlin-based architect and author who was part of the initiative and is also one of the leaders of an investigative architectural nucleus called Urban Catalyst (along with Philipp Misselwitz and Klaus Overmeyer), notes that

---

34. "Chance," Zwischenpalastnutzung, http://www.zwischenpalastnutzung.de/.

Figure 24. Palace of the Republic, interior, main assembly hall (2004).
© Christian von Steffelin

although those involved in the initiative were unanimously opposed to the reconstruction of the old Berlin Palace, they were not all moved by the nostalgic desire
to preserve the Palace in its GDR incarnation—a building that "was gone anyhow"
after the asbestos removal. In this way, the initiative avoided the polarization of the
discourse between Wessis and Ossis, between the conquerors carrying the victory
flag of capitalism and those moved by *Ostalgie* or by a renitent support for Socialist
ideology. But Oswalt adds, "I assume all of us could imagine an unknown solution
which might have included parts of the given structure," be this an architectural
transformation and refurbishment of the structure, or its appropriation for a different use with minimal intervention.[35]

Another organization that supported the initiative, the Palastbündnis, was more
vocal in opposing the demolition and in celebrating the social and architectural history of the building, but it too represented itself as a "new generation" that wanted
to steer clear of the polarization between "old and new Palace," instead being open

35. Philipp Oswalt, interview via e-mail, September 5, 2014.

to a third, future-oriented, novel solution.[36] Such a third way would have reckoned with the historical and spatial conditions of the site. The first of these conditions was the presence of the gutted Palace, whose adaptive reuse would not only have been environmentally sounder than a demolition, but might also have yielded the opportunity for design experimentation and innovation (one of the stated goals of the initiative as a "lab" for urban interventions). The second condition corresponded to the symbolic embattlements that charged the site with the memory of lost buildings (by then, both the old and the new Palaces had been lost in one way or another), with resentment over such losses, and with the desire to repair or make up for what was lost. These symbolic embattlements, which were fought as disputes over the memory, history, and meanings of each building, represented larger social and cultural challenges to the integration between Wessis and Ossis in unified Germany.

After the tours in 2003, a multifarious series of events reanimated the structure: concerts that took advantage of the still-standing stadium seats, roundtables and conversations, plays, performances, lectures, and exhibitions. Some of these events were directly aimed at reflecting on the building, such as roundtables and public discussions with architects—in particular Fun Palace Berlin 200X, a conference organized by Oswalt, Misselwitz, Hans Ulrich Obrist, and Stefan Rethfeld. Fun Palace took as a springboard Cedric Price's project of the same name. Price's Fun Palace, designed between 1961 and 1964 but never built, was a visionary and quirky project for a multivalent, multifunctional community and performance center that would merge leisure and civic life in a dynamic environment. The architectural design was based on a structural framework, which would have been visible, and which could have been transformed by users according to their needs, desires, and whims.[37] The same threads, of course, ran through the discussions about the Palace, this unusual structure in a state of transition and provisionality, which had combined fun and civic life in its previous incarnation and also, in a new way, with the Zwischennutzung.[38] Other events that took place inside the building were not directly related to the debate about the Palace—for example, in 2003 the Chinese Terracotta Army, a traveling exhibition that has toured the world with two hundred full-size replicas of the original terracotta army (which remains in China), was displayed in the building, which offered not only ample room but also weather protection and access control to the large exhibit. In the course of the Zwischennutzung

36. "Über das Bündnis für den Palast," Palastbündnis, http://www.palastbuendnis.de/pages/info/info_dasbuendnis.html.

37. *Fun Palace 200X;* on Price's design, see Stanley Mathews, "The Fun Palace: Cedric Price's Experiment in Architecture and Technology," *Technoetic Arts: A Journal of Speculative Research* 3, no. 2 (2005): 73–91; and Hans-Ulrich Obrist, ed., *Re: CP* (Basel: Birkhäuser, 2003).

38. For a complete list of events and installations under the Zwischenpalastnutzung, see Oswalt, *Zwischennutzung des Palast*, 6–12, 21–24.

activities, the Palace was rechristened Volkspalast, as a reclaiming of the structure for the people.

Some of the projects combined a disciplinary reflection on urbanism and architecture with a playful approach that appealed to the senses as much as the intellect, blurring the lines between pleasure and "seriousness." This was the case with *Fassadenrepublik*, or *Façade Republic*, which in Holfelder's words was "wonderfully bizarre," as "the Palace was flooded with water and set up with a labyrinthic fake metropolis. Visitors moved through the space in groups in small boats, accompanied by tour guides" who talked about urban issues.[39] The project was carried out under the auspices of the Volkspalast by the creative collective raumlabor, which deals with design, urbanism, art, and architecture through innovative projects, often experimental and temporary; and by the like-minded duo Peanutz-Architekten. *Fassadenrepublik* thrust visitors into the guts of the building, highlighting its uncanny, inhospitable condition through the use of water—something one might associate with a broken pipe, a malfunction, a flood, a disaster. The ruined character of the building was hard to miss—the fact that it did not function or look anymore as it once should have. Through the water, *Fassadenrepublik* appropriated, displayed, and encouraged the building's ruination; and it went further. With the exhibition setting and performances by the tour guides, the installation also provided a series of possibilities and forward-minded urban projects, which the visitors could experience as multiple voices in a dialogue and not as a single prescription for city life. *Fassadenrepublik* offered a transformative and constructive path, a view—or many views—into the future, while leaving the public free to draw conclusions.

A similarly immersive installation was *Der Berg*, or *The Mountain*, organized by raumlabor in collaboration with the Sophiensaele, a Berlin-based theater group that was also a member of the Initiative Zwischenpalastnutzung (many of the participants and authors of the other projects were not formally part of the initiative, but simply guest artists or curators). The installation's centerpiece was a translucent, jagged, multifaceted mound made of metal and white plastic foil (fig. 25). The multiple "faces" of the mountain were triangles of varying sizes, so that the whole had an appearance that was at once geometric and organic, the stark angles of the metal rods counterbalanced by the irregular way in which the structure grew, climbed, and turned this or that way. The mountain was perched on one of the former auditoriums, or what remained of its stadium seating, and looked like a kind of geometric force taking over the space. This was an object of architectural dimensions, which alone caused a strong impression. It was engulfing and monumental, and allowed visitors to understand the massive scale of the building in its gutted state by drawing attention to its height and open spaces. (The *Berg* installation can

39. Holfelder, *Palast der Republik*, 98.

Figure 25. raumlaborberlin, *Der Berg* (*The Mountain*), installation and performance in
the Palace of the Republic (2005).
© raumlaborberlin

also be seen in figure 22 on the outside of the building, as white prismatic volumes
in the central portion of the façade.)

But this was not only an installation; coorganized by a theater group, it was also
a combination of performance and interactive experience, as visitors were invited
to choose one of three possible routes along which they encountered different people, objects, and scenes—from screen projections to Polish artists peeling potatoes
(visitors were invited to join) to drag queens.[40] Each of the three possible routes
had a name: the Philosopher's Way, the Pilgrim's Route, and the Climber's Way.
Although in one sense they created an individual, introspective, and even meta-
physical experience—where each visitor would be free to discover the meaning of
the journey—the three routes were also conceived as a commentary on the site and
the fate of the Palace. One of the creators of the installation, Benjamin Foerster-
Baldenius, pondered that after the Palace's demolition, there would be an open,
empty space, a "desert" (*Wüste*). This desert is what he sets the *Mountain* against:

> The old Prussian Palace—that cannot be. Now the situation is defined: There is the
> symbolically loaded Palace [of the Republic], and the symbolically loaded decision to

40. Sebastian Harcombe, "The Magic Mountain," *New Statesman*, August 29, 2005, 28–29; Anto-
nia Götsch, "Palast der Republik: Gipfel der Kreativität," *Spiegel Online*, August 25, 2005, http://www.
spiegel.de/kultur/gesellschaft/palast-der-republik-gipfel-der-kreativitaet-a-371158.html.

demolish it, and the Mountain struggles against that. Societies are always looking for places like mountains, for symbolic power. Myths or kings sit on top of mountains. Mountains are in every sense more potent than a desert.[41]

For him, neither rebuilding the old Palace nor restoring the new Palace was a desirable outcome, as either option would be a falsification of history mired in the past; and simply razing the Palace and opening an empty field, the "desert," could not be the only alternative. A different option would have looked to the future of the city by combining the search for something new with the mining and discovery of the rich, hidden potentials already present on the site—in the gutted structure. This, of course, is what the *Fassadenrepublik* and the *Mountain* did. They took full advantage of the structure, of its atmosphere and its spatial possibilities, and in doing so they not only created ingenious experiences for visitors, but also opened these visitors' eyes to as-yet-unseen possibilities, ways of using space, and of connecting the building to the city.

One of the most publicized and influential projects of the whole initiative was Lars Ramberg's 2005 installation of oversized lettering on top of the building spelling "Palast des Zweifels" (Palace of Doubt). Perhaps it owed some of its publicity to the fact that it was clearly visible from the outside, and so could be experienced even by those unwilling to enter the structure or unaware of the other actions. The lettering draws from the logic of billboards and commercial signage, by placing loud, simple, clearly legible text on top of the building. The installation was made out of "three-story-tall letters sculpted in aluminum and filled with white neon-tube lighting," and it remained on the Palace from January 26 to May 15. It took Ramberg six years and many bureaucratic and political hurdles to realize the installation, a sign that he might have touched a chord with his allusion to doubt. As Buttlar observes, "Doubts, of course, in the mental uncertainty and economic depression of modern Germany, are a subversive and officially unwelcome state of mind."[42] Jennifer Allen, in a review for *Artforum*, reads the sign "as a temporary monument to the history of hesitations that have surrounded the building's fate since 1990," over whether it should be preserved or demolished, whether it meant something as a historical artifact or had "use value for the present."[43] The doubt, just as the building, extended to more than its physical incarnation. It was also doubt about the past and future roles of East and West Germans in the unified country, and about how to read (and write) the history of division, negotiating the different experiences and expectations of both sides.

---

41. Katja Bigalke, "Bergsteigen in 'Erichs Lampenladen': Rauminstallation im Palast der Republik," *Deutschlandradio Kultur*, August 4, 2005, http://www.deutschlandradiokultur.de/bergsteigen-in-erichs-lampenladen.999.de.html?dram:article_id=155742.

42. Von Buttlar, "Berlin's Castle versus Palace," 14.

43. Jennifer Allen, "Lars Ramberg: Palast der Republik," *Artforum* 43, no. 9 (May 2005): 258.

The Initiative Zwischenpalastnutzung is a concentrated example of counter-preservation. The artists and urbanists involved were highly conscious of the architectural and spatial implications of their plans. The *Hausprojekte* of the first chapter of this book were much more spontaneous and pragmatic in their use and transformation of decayed buildings; their interventions more piecemeal and often more turned toward the private and domestic realms of the community and its everyday living needs. In comparison, the Initiative Zwischenpalastnutzung was always already public-minded, appropriating the Palace as a statement in one of the most visible and central sites of Berlin. Their projects reveal a great degree of knowledge about the history of the site, and of reflection about its architectural and urban aspects. The counterpreservation of the Palace as a lively, multivalent ruin in the 2000s is a particularly significant case study, even if it is also one of the most short-lived examples in this book. It illustrates counterpreservation in all of its dimensions: political, social, cultural, urban, aesthetic. The tangle of these threads cannot be tidied up. Some of the interventions in the Palace, such as concerts, were more focused on the powerful sensorial experience of the space as a gutted building, but they cannot be faulted for being formalist—as they were bound up with a larger, diachronic, and multivocal project where social engagement and political visions were also present. This consideration applies to counterpreservation more generally. It is not possible to make sense of it as only one thing or the other (just romantic or just political), and if there are irreducible moments of purely aesthetic fascination, these coexist in productive tension or symbiosis with moments of social action.

After the Zwischenpalastnutzung animated the structure for two years, in 2006 the slow dismantlement began, continuing until the end of 2008. The steel structure was melted and sold; part of it was used in Volkswagen car engines,[44] and part was used as construction material in the world's tallest man-made structure, the Burj Khalifa skyscraper in Dubai, designed by Skidmore, Owings & Merrill and completed in 2010.[45] The irony of the afterlife of the ruin should be obvious—from the Palace of a Socialist republic, where politics, arts, leisure, and civic life coexisted, to a monument of capitalism, which houses private apartments, offices, and an upscale hotel. In 2012, work on the now-vacant site of the Palace of the Republic began, to erect the Berlin Palace–Humboldt Forum. This is a partial reconstruction of the Hohenzollern Palace, which will be devoted to cultural uses such as archives, exhibitions, and events, and will be split among the Stiftung Preußischer Kulturbesitz (Prussian Cultural Heritage Foundation), Humboldt University, and

44. "Memories of East Germany's Showcase: New Book Reveals Last Photographs of Berlin's Palast der Republik," *Spiegel Online*, September 21, 2010, http://www.spiegel.de/international/germany/memories-of-east-germany-s-showcase-new-book-reveals-last-photographs-of-berlin-s-palast-der-republik-a-717697.html.

45. "Berlin's Demolished Socialist Palace Is Revived in Dubai," *Deutsche Welle*, August 11, 2008, http://www.dw.com/en/berlins-demolished-socialist-palace-is-revived-in-dubai/a-3554502.

the Land (federal state) of Berlin. On June 2015, the topping out ceremony marked the completion of the structural elements of the building; the Humboldt Forum is expected to be finished and ready for the public in 2019.[46]

The revanchist drive against the Palace of the Republic succeeded; the Palace and its remains are gone. But the Zwischennutzung lives on, not as a concrete site, because it was never proposed as such: temporary and provisional by definition, it was not a place, not even a program. It was a heterogeneous grouping of collective actions, debates, and visions for the city; these visions persist, in other forms, in the work of those who were a part of the Zwischennutzung. Although the memory of those festive, experimental installations and performances might potentially fade, the impulses that set them in motion can survive on their own, in forms yet to be determined.

The Berlin Wall Memorial

Like the Palace of the Republic, the Berlin Wall also underwent a protracted dismantlement, in fits and spurts rather than gradually, with some portions disappearing quickly after the night of November 9, 1989, when the East German government lifted travel restrictions to East Germans, making the structure obsolete. The sections of the Wall to go first were those interrupting the flows of the freshly reunited city—blocking off streets, sectioning neighborhoods, cutting through central open spaces. But the Wall was a very long structure that encircled West Berlin completely for 96 miles (155 km). The part of the Wall that separated West Berlin from East Berlin (the "intraurban" Wall) measured 26.8 miles (43.1 km), a little less than a third of this length; the rest separated West Berlin from neighboring towns and the countryside, running through suburbs, sparsely populated areas, and empty land.[47] These sections, more remote from the center and in some cases less encumbering to the rejoining of the city, survived for a longer time than central ones.

The disappearance of the Wall also had different overtones depending on location and timing. Prominent spots at the heart of the city, such as the sections that ran across and near Potsdamer Platz and the Brandenburg Gate, were famously hacked away soon after November 9 (reports say that "some were beginning to

---

46. "Palast der Republik: Untergegangen in Ruinen," *Berlin.de*, https://www.berlin.de/tourismus/insidertipps/1727324–2339440-palast-der-republik-untergegangen-in-rui.html; Stiftung Berliner Schloss—Humboldt Forum, http://www.sbs-humboldtforum.de/de/Startseite/. This website contains an updated timeline of construction (complete with webcam), and information on the design and program of the building, including a PDF brochure with details on the construction plans and process. The brochure, written by Manfred Rettig, is entitled *Das Berliner Schloss wird zum Humboldtforum: Rekonstruktion und Transformation der Berliner Mitte* and can be downloaded at the bottom of the section "Das Berliner Schloss" at http://www.sbs-humboldtforum.de/de/Berliner-Schloss/.

47. Gordon L. Rottman, *The Berlin Wall and the Intra-German Border, 1961–89* (New York: Osprey, 2008), 29.

chisel away" on that very night),[48] in a combination of catharsis, tourist glee, and commercial exploitation: some people hacked away to destroy a hated instrument of repression, others to take home pieces or sell them as souvenirs, and others were trying to carve out actual points of passage. Larger sections were eventually removed intact and sold in auctions to private companies and individuals, or given to museums and public offices in and outside of Germany.[49] The cultural and political symbolism of these actions was exploited as news media captured and broadcast scenes of the fall of the Wall repeatedly, from crowds waiting to cross Checkpoint Charlie to people climbing up the thick Wall section near the Brandenburg Gate to ecstatic and emotional East and West Germans embracing each other and celebrating.[50] But, as Brian Ladd points out, "only at a few tourist sites, such as Checkpoint Charlie, did the popular onslaught come close to obliterating the concrete wall. Most of the hundred miles of border fortifications remained largely intact for months."[51] The remaining sections of the Wall were, for the most part, not as photogenic or recognizable as the graffiti-covered portions in Potsdamer Platz. Made up of gray, prefabricated segments of reinforced concrete, they were gradually and unceremoniously removed, and then recycled. According to Hans-Hermann Hertle, over 40,000 segments of the Wall were crushed "for use as granules in road building," while others "are still to be found in cement works where they now separate different sorts of gravel from one another—instead of people."[52]

If much of the concrete remained then, and some of it still does now, the Wall was gone; as Ladd puts it, "What had disappeared . . . was the symbolic Wall—which meant that the concrete and the symbol were no longer the same thing."[53] Ladd published his cultural analysis of Berlin in 1997; less than ten years after the fall of the Wall, the impulse to rebuild a unified city and eliminate the remnants of the border fortification was a major force in urban planning, despite early calls to preserve at least portions of the Wall. Ten years' time, in urban planning and social events, can be a relatively short period. The differences between East and West Germans, and even East and West Berlin as urban settings, were still palpable and felt in the everyday.[54] The Wall survived in people's heads, notoriously, as the "Mauer im Kopf," as predicted by West German novelist Peter Schneider in his

---

48. Patrick Major, *Behind the Berlin Wall: East Germany and the Frontiers of Power* (Oxford: Oxford University Press, 2010), 254.

49. Ibid., 256; Ladd, *Ghosts of Berlin*, 8–9; Melanie van der Hoorn, *Indispensable Eyesores: An Anthropology of Undesired Buildings* (New York: Berghahn Books, 2009), 154–55.

50. Sunil Manghani analyzed media coverage and visual representations of the event in *Image Critique and the Fall of the Berlin Wall* (Bristol: Intellect Books, 2008).

51. Ladd, *Ghosts of Berlin*, 10.

52. Hans-Hermann Hertle, *Berlin Wall: Monument of the Cold War* (Berlin: Christoph Links, 2008), 163. Scenes of the crushing of Wall segments for use as road-building material can be seen in the documentary *Berlin Babylon*, directed by Hubertus Siegert (Germany, 2001).

53. Ladd, *Ghosts of Berlin*, 10.

54. Dirk Verheyen, *United City, Divided Memories? Cold War Legacies in Contemporary Berlin* (Lanham, MD: Lexington Books, 2010), 220–21.

prescient novel *The Wall Jumper*, published in 1983.[55] So the memory of division, and of the Wall as a structure of oppression and violence, was still fresh, precluding comprehensive attempts at preserving large portions of it on site.

But now, a quarter of a century after the fall of the Wall, historical distance—and perhaps increasing scarcity of remains—means that the Wall is back, this time as a monument. At first, efforts to preserve remains of the Wall, or its memory through installations or exhibitions, were small in scale and scattered (some even conducted by private initiatives).[56] Most of the Wall within the city was removed, except for three sections, which together add up to about a mile;[57] eventually, still in the late 1990s, ground markers for the former path of the Wall consisting of cobblestones and metal plaques were installed in central areas of the city.[58] In 1994, the city organized a competition for a memorial on Bernauer Straße—a street infamous not only because the Wall ran there, separating the western district of Wedding from the eastern neighborhoods of Mitte and Prenzlauer Berg, but also because the border fortifications included apartment buildings. This is because "the street itself was in West Berlin" and "the apartments were in East Berlin."[59] Before the windows and doors of these buildings were eventually boarded and bricked up, they served as literal springboards for East Berliners who tried to escape by jumping off (some succeeded).

The 1994 competition for a memorial on Bernauer Straße was won by two Stuttgart-based architects, Claudia and Sven Kohlhoff of Kohlhoff & Kohlhoff Architects.[60] The Memorial took advantage of a considerable length of Wall that was still in place there, thanks to a decision by the East Berlin magistrate on October 2, 1990 (one day before German unification), to declare those sections of Wall on

---

55. Peter Schneider, *Wall Jumper* (New York: Pantheon, 1983); originally published as *Der Mauerspringer: Erzählung* (Darmstadt: Luchterhand, 1982). On the expression *Mauer im Kopf*, see, among many others, Alexandra Tacke, "Die Mauer im Kopf: Mauerbau & -fall im kollektiven Gedächtnis," in *NachBilder der Wende*, ed. Inge Stephan and Alexandra Tacke (Cologne: Böhlau, 2008), 301–18; Mary Beth Stein, "The Present Is a Foreign Country: Germany after Unification," *Journal of Folklore Research* 30, no. 1 (1993): 29–43; Dieter Herberg, Doris Steffens, and Elke Tellenbach, *Schlüsselwörter der Wendezeit: Wörter-Buch zum öffentlichen Sprachgebrauch, 1989–90* (Berlin and New York: De Gruyter, 1997), 193.

56. Ladd, *Ghosts of Berlin*, 35–36; Jennifer Cohoon McStotts, "The Second Fall of the Berlin Wall: Examining the Hildebrandt Memorial at Checkpoint Charlie," *Future Anterior* 3, no. 1 (Summer 2006): 36–47.

57. Elizabeth Golden, "Following the Berlin Wall," in *Terrain Vague*, 220.

58. Claire Colomb, *Staging the New Berlin: Place Marketing and the Politics of Urban Reinvention Post-1989* (New York: Routledge, 2012), 253.

59. W. R. Smyser, *Kennedy and the Berlin Wall* (Lanham, MD: Rowman & Littlefield, 2009), 109.

60. "Gedenkstätte Berliner Mauer—Die Verzögerung," *Bauwelt* 29 (1997): 1616, http://www.bauwelt.de/sixcms/media.php/829/1997_29_klein.pdf. For critical analyses of the 1994 memorial, which I will not discuss here, see Golden, "Following the Berlin Wall"; Gerd Knischewski and Ulla Spittler, "Remembering the Berlin Wall: The Wall Memorial Ensemble Bernauer Strasse," *German Life & Letters* 59, no. 2 (April 2006): 280–83.

Bernauer Straße a historic monument.[61] The Memorial was dedicated in 1998; a year later, the Documentation Center of the Berlin Wall opened across the street, in a small, unassuming repurposed building originally dating from 1965. That is, instead of a glitzy new structure commissioned to a starchitect—as was the practice elsewhere in Berlin during that time, both for private enterprises and for public and cultural institutions—the Documentation Center was housed in relatively modest quarters, and presented an exhibition that was for the most part austere (if informative and well curated). Judging from resource allocation, the Wall as an object of musealization, exhibitions, and memorialization was still peripheral to other issues (for example, the Holocaust). Adding to the relative invisibility of the Documentation Center and Memorial, this particular area of Berlin on Bernauer Straße, at the time still untouched by gentrification, was also marginal to the boom of tourist attention, private investment, and new residents experienced just a few blocks south and east of there, in Mitte and Prenzlauer Berg.

According to Dirk Verheyen, "As the 1990s evolved, commentators noted that the 'loss' of the Mauer was having a profound impact on the city," mostly because of tourists who came searching for it, but also because of local sentiment.[62] At the end of the 1990s, the government took measures to centralize memorialization efforts in a more concerted way, and increasingly placed sites, vestiges, and even objects under protection as pieces of historical and archaeological value: "metal fences, lanterns, and even some bricked-up windows."[63] Beginning in 2002 the city began to mark the path and stations of the Berlin Wall Trail, which can be followed by foot or bicycle as it cuts through the city and goes around the perimeter of Berlin, combining a favorite Berlin activity and transportation means (biking) with historical exploration.[64] And in 2007, the city again turned its attention to Bernauer Straße. By then, the street held a loose-knit constellation of Wall-related sites: the Documentation Center, the Memorial, and the Chapel of Reconciliation. The latter is a commemorative chapel erected in 2000 on the site of the Church of Reconciliation, an 1894 building that ended up in the "no-man's-land" of the Wall fortifications, and was demolished by the GDR in 1985. The street was also home to other remnants of the border: the long section of Wall that had been placed under preservation by the East German government in 1990, stretching far beyond the Memorial; and the Nordbahnhof subway station, which was closed between 1961 and 1990 as one of East Berlin's notorious "ghost stations" (stations where West Berlin subway trains ran through without stopping).

---

61. "History of the Memorial," Berliner Mauer Gedenkstätte, http://www.berliner-mauer-gedenk staette.de/en/history-of-the-memorial-211.html.

62. Verheyen, *United City*, 222–23.

63. Ibid., 223. See also Landesdenkmalamt Berlin Datenbank for complete listings of Wall remains, sites, and associated structures under protection at http://www.stadtentwicklung.berlin.de/denkmal/ liste_karte_datenbank/de/denkmaldatenbank/index.shtml.

64. "Berliner Mauerweg," Berlin.de, http://www.berlin.de/mauer/mauerweg/index/index.de.php.

In 2007, a competition was held to reshape this area, tying together the loosely strung remains of the Wall border apparatus and its adjacent open land into a sharp and cohesive landscape design, and providing a Visitors Center at the southern end of Bernauer Straße, across from the Nordbahnhof station. The site of the Visitors Center is much closer to the bustling Mitte district than the Memorial and Documentation Center located several blocks farther north. The competition program not only called for a more visible and accessible nexus for the site, in terms of both location and architectural novelty, but also for combining the other memorial and documentation structures in the area into a larger, overarching plan, which I will refer to from now on as the Berlin Wall Memorial Grounds (this is also what the Berlin Wall Foundation, which is responsible for the site, calls the area). This plan, most of it implemented by now, spans a little under a mile (1.3 km) and 4.4 hectares along Bernauer Straße, from Nordbahnhof on the south all the way up to the Mauerpark. The Mauerpark, at the north terminus of the area, is not formally part of the plan or of the Berlin Wall Foundation, but it connects functionally, thematically, and visually with the linear exhibition path—unsurprisingly, since the Mauerpark was also built on the no-man's-land strip along the former path of the Wall. It was designed in 1994 by Hamburg-based architect Gustav Lange, in an initiative that was "part of a bid for the Olympic Games."[65] The open field of the Mauerpark had already been taken over by wild plants and local inhabitants after the Wall was demolished there; Lange's design tamed the landscape, and highlighted visible vestiges of the border, such as foundations embedded on the ground.

The 2007 competition for the larger plan for the Berlin Wall Memorial Grounds was won by the office of Mola + Winkelmüller (responsible for the architectural and urban design of the area, including the building for the new Visitors Center) in collaboration with ON Architektur (which designed the open-air exhibition elements) and sinai (responsible for the landscaping).[66] The whole area now gathers open spaces, buildings, and memorial structures, marked with permanent plaques, displays, and signs. The Memorial Grounds encompass four different thematic zones, which visitors can experience and understand through the open-air exhibition elements (fig. 26). While zones A ("The Wall and the Death Strip"), B ("The Destruction of the City"), and C ("The Building of the Wall") take advantage of the wide-open linear field that used to be the no-man's-land strip of the Wall, area D ("It Happened by the Wall") is a more spatially limited exhibition, restricted to the sidewalk along the street. In that area, the former no-man's-land is not incorporated into the Memorial Grounds because it was sold to a private developer, who later leased it for 199 years to the new occupants—architects and designers who

65. Edward Hollis, *The Secret Lives of Buildings: From the Ruins of the Parthenon to the Vegas Strip in Thirteen Stories* (New York: Metropolitan Books, 2009), 249.

66. Mola + Winkelmüller, http://www.mw-arch.de/; "Erweiterung der Gedenkstätte," Berliner Mauer Gedenkstätte, http://www.berliner-mauer-gedenkstaette.de/de/erweiterung-523.html.

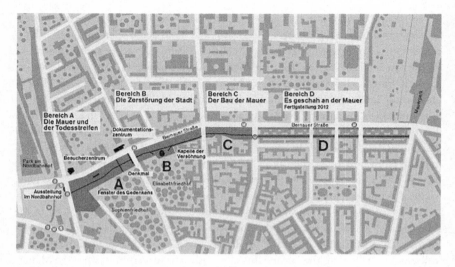

Figure 26. Berlin Wall Memorial Grounds, site plan. Each letter represents a thematic and spatial zone of the Memorial Grounds. A: Wall and Death Strip; B: The Destruction of the City; C: The Building of the Wall; D: It Happened by the Wall.
© Stiftung Berliner Mauer, Berthold Weidner

cooperatively built a group of architecturally innovative townhouses there between 2008 and 2013.[67]

The presence of Wall remnants in the area prompted design and curatorial decisions on the treatment and display of ruins, fragments, and decay. But while signs of ruination abound—crumbling concrete, rusting metal, broken pieces, wild plants—the incorporation of ruins into the new design is not an example of counterpreservation as I have defined it. And for this reason, it is a fitting conclusion to this book, as a contrasting case study to support my point that counterpreservation as an urban and architectural concept cannot be reduced to the material and aesthetic conditions of decrepitude, but rather must be understood always at the same time with relation to social, political, and cultural processes. This is not to say that the Berlin Wall Memorial Grounds are poorly designed, but rather that they represent a different way of appropriating ruins.

In order to make this clearer, we can begin at the intended starting point for visitors: the Visitor Center and open-air exhibition across from Nordbahnhof (the station is also part of the Memorial Grounds, with an exhibition on the GDR-era

67. Berliner Mauer Gedenkstätte, http://www.berliner-mauer-gedenkstaette.de/en/berlin-wall-memorial-12.html and http://www.berliner-mauer-gedenkstaette.de/en/memorial-grounds-548.html. On the new townhouses on the former no-man's-land strip, see Nick Amies, "Life without Walls," *New York Times*, September 11, 2013, http://www.nytimes.com/2013/09/12/garden/life-without-walls.html?_r=0.

subway ghost stations). The Visitor Center is composed of two stacked rectangular volumes, the lower one aligned with the street and the former path of the Wall, and the upper volume rotated to face the Memorial Grounds. The rotation affords wide views of the area to visitors in the building's upper floor, whose façade is generously glazed, creating a privileged viewing point that aims to connect the building to the area through sightlines. From afar, the rotation was also intended to join together the building and the open-air exhibition area, a long rectangle of grass and cement that sits on the other side of the wide lanes of Bernauer Straße. As the street curves slightly, the rotated volume turns intentionally to the open field on the other side—a gesture on the part of the architects, although not necessarily one that every passerby might perceive.[68]

The connection between the Visitor Center building and the open-air exhibition field is evinced more clearly through another formal device: the saturated rusted-red color that marks both the façade of the building and the metal fence on the perimeter of the open-air exhibition grounds. Both the building façade and the metal fence are made of Corten steel—also known by its trademark name COR-TEN steel or by the generic name weathering steel. Corten steel is alloyed in such a way as to allow for its outer layer to rust intentionally; the rusting of the exterior surface eventually slows down and hardens, protecting the structural integrity of the interior. The rusting effect is not only protective, but it is also purposefully "decorative with nice colours."[69] The intense, matte red of the Corten steel brings together the Visitor Center building and the metal fence on the exhibition field, and highlights them against the prevailingly gray background of this particular street (fig. 27).

The fence around the open-air exhibition is not meant to block passage, as the Wall once did along the exact same path. It is a series of thin, tall steel rods placed at varying distances from each other, forming a wispy boundary that serves both to delimit the space of the exhibition and to mark the former path of the Wall. In fact, the rods pick up where the Wall leaves off—where the remaining sections of crumbling Wall end or falter along Bernauer Straße. The use of Corten steel with its inevitable rust should not go unnoticed in this context. The sections of Wall that survived after 1989, especially the long-lasting ones—not only along Bernauer Straße, but elsewhere in the city, including, for example, on Niederkirchnerstraße along the Topography of Terror site—did not endure intact. At first they were picked at; and after they were placed under protection, even if they could not be mined anymore, they still weathered and deteriorated.

The Wall in its last incarnation was made of prefabricated sections of reinforced concrete, a material that demands maintenance to keep its integrity against the effects of heat, cold, humidity, and corrosion. But the Wall sections were not maintained—they were left exposed, their erosion aided by the initial hacking that

---

68. Mola + Winkelmüller, http://www.mw-arch.de/.
69. Einar Bardal, *Corrosion and Protection* (London: Springer, 2004), 196.

Figure 27. Berlin Wall Memorial Grounds, Corten steel rods marking the path of the Wall (2010).
© Daniela Sandler

broke the smooth surface of concrete. The surviving portions were crumbling, at points showing the concrete aggregate, and revealing the metal rebars—which, once exposed to air and humidity, began of course to rust. Although their rust is not as intensely red as that of the carefully contrived Corten steel rods, their deterioration is clearly visible. At points of the Wall remnants, the rebars peek out from under the concrete, barely uncovered; at other points, the rebars are all that remains, their lace-like coils creating windows on the Wall. The Corten steel fence of the new exhibition grounds alludes to this both indirectly (as a reinterpretation of the corroded rebars) and directly, as the fence fills in the gaps of the surviving Wall sections. The competition jury was well aware of this connection, as stated in the report of their second meeting to discuss the winning entry, and so were the architects.[70]

Elizabeth Golden describes the Corten steel fence as one of the elements that earned the designers first place in the competition, because of the play between

---

70. *Erweiterung der Gedenkstätte Berliner Mauer: Ergebnisprotokoll zur 2. Preisgerichtssitzung vom 12.12.2007*, digital document (Berlin: Senatsverwaltung für Stadtentwicklung, 2007), 9, https://www.competitionline.com/upload/downloads/7xx/723_08366_Protokoll_121207.pdf; Henner Winkelmüller, interview via e-mail, September 23, 2014.

transparency and opacity that allows the fence both to recreate the Wall and to dissolve it at the same time, making it permeable and therefore useless as a restrictive
border: "Thin rods of rusted metal . . . are positioned to recreate the scale and the
path of the Wall when viewed from the side, while becoming almost completely
invisible when viewed from the front."[71] The metal rods do not really become invisible, but they do create different levels of visibility depending on one's angle,
and they certainly convey the idea of a visual and material presence that can be
penetrated and trespassed at most points. As Regula Lüscher, the Senate building
director for Berlin, put it in her public announcement of the competition results,

> What is special about this project is that the designers had the courage to rebuild the
> Wall, but this time as a kind of curtain. I believe that this curtain, which is perme-
> able, is at once a sign of hope and of liberation. . . . One can see the former dimensions
> of the Wall, but one can at any point cross this curtain from one side to the other.[72]

This aspect of the fence was a response to one of the mandates of the competition,
which "was to reveal the physical remains of the Wall and to create a place that
would permit the viewer to see it as it once stood—without recreating what no longer exists."[73] The fence does not simply memorialize the Wall as it stood during the
years of division, but also commemorates its fall and afterlife as a crumbling, permeable structure. This is not quite counterpreservation, but a creative interpretation of the slowly eroding condition of the Wall.

The Memorial Grounds are clearly a departure from the kind of reenactment
sought, and offered, at Checkpoint Charlie—a more famous Wall location, thanks
not only to its role as a crossing point during the Cold War, but also to the epony-
mous museum created there by Rainer Hildebrandt, which became (and remains)
a tourist attraction. In November 2004, Hildebrandt's widow, Alexandra, built a
temporary memorial across from the Checkpoint Charlie museum that reproduced
the Wall—a full-size replica built with 120 Wall sections that "lacked provenance,"
and which did not follow the original path of the Wall exactly, as Jennifer McStotts
reports.[74] The pieces were plastered and whitewashed to create a smooth, unified
appearance, because the Wall sections used for the Memorial had been hacked away
and graffitied, and were therefore of uneven color and surface. Although the reconstruction was inaccurate (and heavily criticized for this), it was also "a source of
confusion for visitors," not all of whom could have been expected to be aware of the
Wall's exact original path or of issues of provenance and authenticity.[75] Although

71. Golden, "Following the Berlin Wall," 226.

72. Speech reproduced in Wolf-Sören Treusch, "Schlachtfeld Denkmal," *Deutschlandradio Kultur*,
January 30, 2008, http://www.deutschlandradiokultur.de/schlachtfeld-denkmal.1001.de.html?dram:
article_id=156470.

73. Golden, "Following the Berlin Wall," 225.

74. McStotts, "The Second Fall," 40.

75. Ibid.

it was labeled by Alexandra Hildebrandt as an "art installation" to justify such interpretive licenses in the reconstruction, the language of the Memorial—with its full-size dimensions, appearance of material integrity, and intention to recreate the original impression one might have had when walking by the Wall—earned it the predictable criticism of being a Disneyfied version of history.[76]

The whole Checkpoint Charlie area, with actors dressed up as border guards and a fake crossing-point station,[77] now stands as the antithetical model against which the Berlin Wall Foundation set its curatorial goals. In the Memorial Grounds, this translates in outstanding care to differentiate the contemporary interventions (the building, the fence, the exhibition displays) from the material vestiges of the border. For the foundation, whichever elements were lost—pieces of Wall, apartment buildings, the Church of Reconciliation—should be remembered indirectly, through visual or graphic means, making their irretrievable absence clear; nowhere should there be confusion as to the authenticity of an artifact or remain.[78] The Corten steel was elevated by the competition jury as a "commentary-material," a signature of the contemporary intervention applied not only to the Visitor Center building and to the fence, but also to other elements, notably those in the open-air exhibition displays: multimedia information kiosks, plaques, an urban model, and the "Fenster des Gedenkens" (Window of Remembrance, referred to in the jury report as Fenster der Erinnerung), a twelve-meter-long wall with portraits of 136 victims of the Wall (i.e., those who died trying to cross it). All of these various furnishings are made of Corten steel.

As a result, the Memorial Grounds appear very clearly as a contrived intervention that treats its site with such respect that it does not dare touch it. There are original remains incorporated at several points: an archaeological excavation of the foundations of an apartment building that used to be part of the border; pieces of urban infrastructure such as pipes and cables, found on the grounds of the open-air exhibition field; and of course the surviving sections of the Wall. The contemporary design frames these elements respectfully, following the mandate to preserve them as "documents" and "original witnesses":[79] an elegant roof protects the apartment building foundations; railings surround the infrastructural fragments; and the Corten steel rods stop short of the Wall sections with which they align.

At first glance, or stroll, one might think that these Memorial Grounds represent the victory of counterpreservation, the elevation of ruins and decay into the official, planned, neatly presented discourse of government memorials and museums. But the careful treatment of these elements as, really, museum pieces—an

---

76. Ibid., 40, 44.

77. Tony Paterson, "Berlin's Checkpoint Charlie Becomes Tourist Trap," *The Telegraph,* August 16, 2008, http://www.telegraph.co.uk/news/worldnews/europe/germany/2570286/Berlins-Checkpoint-Charlie-becomes-tourist-trap.html.

78. *Erweiterung der Gedenkstätte Berliner Mauer*, 8–10.

79. Henner Winkelmüller, interview via e-mail, September 23, 2014.

understandable reverence that reacts against the disappearance of most of the Wall—is the opposite of the dynamic, open-ended, and potentially destructive stance of counterpreservation. The Corten steel fence that so captivated the jury remains vehemently distinct from the Wall. The fence begins where the Wall stops; it offers a metaphor for it, but it takes great care not to mix with it. This is a very different approach from, say, Daniel Libeskind's flooding of SS-barracks ruins in Oranienburg, where the contemporary intervention would have embraced, mingled with, and transformed the ruins. It is also different from the inhabitation that inevitably touches, changes, and fuses with the inhabited structure—be it the decrepit apartment buildings of *Hausprojekte* or the gutted ruin of the Palace of the Republic.

Given the sense of urgency in salvaging the few remaining sections of the Wall—especially a relatively long stretch of Wall in a central, inner-city area such as Bernauer Straße, considered an exemplary area to experience a sense of the divided city[80]—it is not surprising that the whole site was treated as an urban-sized museum. And while at points the Memorial Grounds resemble, in architectural critic Friederike Meyer's words, a Wall "theme park,"[81] with spatially organized stations along which a visitor is supposed to move (a site model, info-kiosks, the Window of Remembrance, ground-level "archaeological windows"), overall the Memorial Grounds fulfill their mission of safeguarding the remains of the border within an informative and historically accurate framework. Visitors have plenty of occasions to learn about the history of the Wall in its physical, social, and cultural dimensions through a variety of media, both within and outside of the Visitor Center building; not only is the path of the Wall highlighted, but the "urban hole" caused by the no-man's-land strip is also preserved as an open field.

There are also opportunities for more personal or introspective moments of commemoration, more emotional and subjective, such as the Window of Remembrance and the previously existing 1994 Kohlhoff & Kohlhoff memorial and Chapel of Reconciliation (they are all linked as part of the Memorial Grounds through the intermittent Corten steel fence). Some of the installations verge on kitsch—this is the case with an arrangement of Wall sections in a row, in the open-air exhibition field, with allusive graffiti of what appears to be an angel. The Wall sections are unbalanced and askew, forming a kind of "fanned" linear monument, partly covered with plants and weeds. The arrangement looks a little arbitrary, even if it is clearly a creative interpretation and not an attempt at reconstruction. While the plants overtaking the inclined Wall segments suggest the process of overcoming the hated structure, the allusion to a vegetal reclaiming of the Wall is problematic in its naturalization of historical processes (a narrative contrary to the mission of the Memorial Grounds as described above). But overall the Memorial Grounds

80. Friederike Meyer, "Erweiterung der Gedenkstätte Berliner Mauer," *Bauwelt* 3 (2008): 11.
81. Ibid.

perform their function dutifully, in the zealous way with which Berlin treats itself as a city of memory.

Yet, for all the curatorial planning and architectural efforts, the most striking element along the path of the Memorial Grounds is still the vast expanse of crumbling Wall that survives (fig. 28). Walking along the southern sidewalk of Bernauer Straße, one could—and still can—experience the strange blankness of the Wall as an urban background. This is at once brutal and banal. After all, many streets in Berlin and beyond have large blocks lined by blank, impassable walls, perhaps bordering industrial lots or warehouses. The banality of the Wall, its bland and technocratic functionality, make the brutal side all the more striking. For of course, in the divided city, no one could have mistaken this for a normal urban wall. Then, one would have seen the bricked-up walls of the apartment buildings that fell in the Wall's path, the point of separation between East and West Berlin—and, once these buildings were bulldozed by the East German government to make way for a stronger Wall, one would have remembered them and perhaps missed them; one would have seen the cityscape through the memory of what once was there. One would have known that the stretch of Wall visible within a pedestrian's limited horizon was not the perimeter of some factory grounds, but a fraction of

Figure 28. Extant section of the Wall on Bernauer Straße (2009).
© Daniela Sandler

an impregnable, continuous boundary that looped around West Berlin, and which imprisoned East Germans. And one would have had the sense of finality, of an end point, that the Wall engendered not only as a physical structure (which one might or might not experience up close on an everyday basis) but as a political instrument and social barrier—a sociocultural force that was so powerful as to cause a psychological ailment, the Berlin Wall Sickness (*Berliner Mauer-Krankheit*).[82]

Arguably, all of this can be learned intellectually, in bits and pieces, in the Visitor Center, the Documentation Center, the open-air exhibition. But the remains of the Wall along Bernauer Straße conjure up this complex history in a spatial way, illustrating it more powerfully than any set of info-kiosks and creative monuments could. And because these remains are not intact, they do not obfuscate their history as the Hildebrandt memorial did. The decay visible on the surviving Wall sections incorporates the ongoing flow of events since 1989: the fall of the Wall, the hacking away, preservation attempts, and even advancing gentrification (visible not only through the revamped Memorial Grounds but also in new or refurbished housing and business, such as the townhouses built on the no-man's-land across from the Mauerpark mentioned above). One might say that this multivalent, decayed Wall section represents counterpreservation at work, but it only does so unintentionally. The Wall survived there only because of a preservation act, and it continues to be safeguarded by preservation and curatorial approaches of the Berlin Wall Foundation. The Wall section there is kept as an urban document, a preserved ruin—not a counterpreserved one.

Or it might be, after all, that in some cases counterpreservation really is in the eye of the beholder, despite my earlier claim to the contrary. With this I do not mean to suggest a license to read counterpreservation freely in just any blighted structure. What I mean is that spaces can be transformed not only by design (whether a top-down official design such as the Wall Memorial Grounds, or a bottom-up gradual design such as the *Hausprojekte*), but also by use: walking, inhabiting, perceiving, debating. This argument was made, of course, by Henri Lefebvre, Michel de Certeau, and most recently by many urban scholars. For instance, Melanie van der Hoorn investigates precisely the consumption of buildings as productive of social meaning and architectural form in her book *Indispensable Eyesores*, which includes Berlin among other case studies.[83] If counterpreservation empowers alternative approaches to buildings and cities, which—as I defined them—may be piecemeal, small in scale, temporary, or makeshift, then the experience of space, its use or consumption, social perceptions, and representations also play a formative (and not merely reflective) role.

---

82. Dietfried Müller-Hegemann, *Die Berliner Mauer-Krankheit: Zur Soziogenese psychischer Störungen* (Herford: Nicolaische Verlagsbuchhandlung, 1973).

83. Van der Hoorn, *Indispensable Eyesores*.

Peter Schneider—the author of *Wall Jumper*—has this to say about the memorialization of the Wall, in a recent collection of essays published in English as *Berlin Now*:

> Perhaps the most vibrant memorial [to the Wall] is the so-called Mauerpark. . . . All that remains of the Wall here is a roughly two-hundred-yard long section of the Hinterlandmauer—the wall that fugitives from East Germany had to scale in order to reach the cordon sanitaire of the actual Wall. This stretch of wall has since been plastered entirely with graffiti in flashy colors.
>
> If nothing else, it's a sign of life that the area around the former death strip has turned into an enormous green playground for a mostly young public. These days, a flea market, amphitheater, climbing wall, puppet theater, music groups, and playgrounds attract thousands of visitors every weekend. The pop remnant of the wall has become a recreational ghost, as it were, protectively watching over the colorful goings-on. . . . You could even say that Mauerpark has become the Tiergarten—Berlin's version of Central Park—for a young public.[84]

Schneider, of course, is a longtime chronicler of Berlin, beyond his "Mauer im Kopf" contribution from the *Wall Jumper*. With Margarethe von Trotta he cowrote the script for her movie *The Promise* (*Das Versprechen*, Germany, 1995), an epic story where two star-crossed—or, better, Wall-crossed—lovers have their lives shaped, twisted, and transformed by the erection of the Wall and then by its fall. Schneider also wrote the novel *Eduard's Homecoming*,[85] which follows the return of the expatriate protagonist Eduard from the United States to his native Germany when he inherits a decrepit apartment building in former East Berlin (which, when he arrives, is occupied by squatters). Eduard witnesses the city in the throes of its urban rehauling following unification.

In *Berlin Now*, Schneider's description of the lively scene at the Mauerpark conjures up a youthful, diverse, dynamic place, which is a bit unruly (he talks about the trash left in the aftermath of concerts), and also rich with social engagement (local citizens organized themselves to pick up the trash and clean up the park); a place that mixes historic fragments and contemporary additions that do not respect temporal boundaries of authenticity, such as the graffiti added to the Wall remains after 1989. His description has an affinity with my own definition of counterpreservation as a lively practice grounded in the present, incorporating history in a dynamic and sometimes iconoclastic way. Perhaps this is because Lange's design for the Mauerpark was not a contrived effort at dramatizing the historical scene of the

---

84. Peter Schneider, "What Happened to the Wall Anyway?," in *Berlin Now* (New York: Farrar, Straus and Giroux, 2014), 156.

85. Peter Schneider, *Eduards Heimkehr* (Berlin: Rowohlt, 1999), published in English as *Eduard's Homecoming* (New York: Farrar, Straus and Giroux, 2000).

Wall as concertedly as the Memorial Grounds do—the Mauerpark left room for new meanings and interventions.

Instead of a site, however, I will conclude with what I see as the most fitting appropriation of the Wall as a ruin—that is, an example of counterpreservation—which is also one of the most effective examples of preserving the history and memory of the Wall. This is not a building, nor is it a site or a memorial. It is an extensive documentation project that lives as a digital, online, public-access resource called Denkmallandschaft Berliner Mauer, or Berlin Wall Memorial Landscape (http:// denkmallandschaft-berliner-mauer.de/). The website offers an interactive map of Berlin displaying the location of Wall sections, remnants, and vestiges, including security structures placed far afield from the Wall (eventually it will also include other supporting structures, such as barracks where border guards were housed). The map also marks locations of Wall sections worldwide—that is, where they were sent after they were removed from Berlin. This project suggests that counterpreservation might be not only a spatially situated practice, but also a mode of representation that can nonetheless shape and transform built environments.

The project was a reaction to the disappearance of the Wall after 1989—as the project authors put it on the website, "an attempt was made to suppress and forget" it after unification. The task was immense, and it was conceived and carried out by a group of researchers and students in historic preservation at the Technical University of Brandenburg in Cottbus, under the leadership of Professor Leo Schmidt. The project was based on fieldwork from 2007 and 2008 (with later updates), and on a photographic documentation of the Wall from 1988 to 1989. The website, which is now maintained by the Berlin Wall Foundation (the same responsible for the Memorial Grounds on Bernauer Straße), was built using geoinformation systems (GIS), which allow for the map to display the location of objects or elements according to precise geographical data, and for users to search and navigate the map according to different types or layers of information (for example, one can search for "lighting fixtures" or "watchtowers" or "other border elements" in addition to Wall segments).

The digital mapping of the ruins of the Wall is a way of documenting and publicizing the spatial history of the Wall in its totality—a task that would have been impossible for any one memorial or monument to accomplish (although the Berlin Wall Trail approximates this). The bird's-eye perspective of the map affords a sense of the extension and former path of the Wall, while the scattered labels showing the location of fragments and remains are a constant reminder that most of the Wall substance has been lost. The ruins are displayed, and made eloquent as memorial notations on the screen.

One may use this map in different ways: as a history lesson from one's desktop, as a map for actual forays into the city, as a springboard for further research. While the project takes an objective and scientific approach to data collection and presentation, it is also sensitive to complex cultural questions, which it raises very clearly—this is an effort that sees the memory of the Wall, and whatever remains of its physicality, as worthy of preservation. The Berlin Wall Landscape, as the project is titled, is a real landscape, not a virtual one. The map, both as a visual record and as a guide, manages at once to preserve its object and to foreground its disappearance. It is this grappling with the material and memorial losses inevitably incurred in a dynamic urban context—a grappling that sometimes will retain the historic object fiercely, and sometimes will let it go; that will recognize the irreducible transience of architecture and of memory even as these two activities motion toward permanence—that represents the impulse behind counterpreservation.

Conclusion

Toward an Architecture of Change

The case studies examined in this book represent a time- and site-specific response to very particular urban and cultural circumstances. The city of Berlin after unification offered unique possibilities (and hurdles) not often encountered elsewhere. First, it had the unusual condition of having been a city divided by a wall for forty-five years. There exist, or existed, certainly other segregated cities and regions: from Belfast to apartheid-era Johannesburg, from Beirut during the Lebanese civil war to the Israeli West Bank. What made Berlin a special case was both the ideological resonance of the Berlin Wall as a metonym for the Iron Curtain, and the extensive and pervasive physicality of the Wall as an urban structure. This had many implications for the postunification city in general, and for counterpreservation in particular. The urban implications involved the task of reconnecting infrastructure into a single cohesive whole; reorienting the city so that the German capital could have a main focal point or center; and addressing the ruptures caused in the city fabric by the path of the Wall fortifications, whose widths ranged from twenty to several hundred feet. These challenges meant that after 1989 the city embarked on a vast urban and architectural refurbishment that was both intense and extensive, so exceptional in scale and ambition that it often elicited commentaries about Berlin as a "city of cranes" or as "the largest construction site in the world."[1] The revamping of Berlin figures in the narrative of counterpreservation as the mainstream urban force against which counterpreservation examples set themselves, especially as they attempted to resist the processes of gentrification and upgrading of cultural structures, and the implicit or explicit rewriting of historical narratives and representations.

Second, and as a consequence of the first condition (the division of the city), was the seclusion and marginalization of certain neighborhoods in both East and West Berlin. Proximity to the Wall meant that neighborhoods were not desirable or even possible to live in. In West Berlin, for example, border districts such as Wedding, Kreuzberg, and Neukölln were left at the periphery of public and private investment for most of the postwar era; middle- and upper-class residents preferred to live elsewhere. Granted, these three districts already had a working-class demographic even before the war, but the presence of the Wall and the sense of being at the "end" of the city did not help. The familiar cycle of disinvestment, vacancies, lower revenues, and physical deterioration of buildings and public spaces kept rents affordable, so that these neighborhoods also became centers for new immigrants, such as Turkish workers. The housing stock, mostly from the nineteenth century, was already problematic, as the apartment buildings (*Mietskasernen*) had been built densely, without enough ventilation, sanitation, or access to sunlight. Physical decay and lack of maintenance did not help. When the government invested in the area, it did so following the 1960s principles of urban renewal, now much maligned, by destroying the fine-grained texture of the city with wide roads and overdimensioned apartment buildings, which were too big and repetitive, respecting neither the scale of the block (therefore disrupting the city) nor the scale of the private dwelling (therefore disrupting familiar patterns of identification and inhabitation).

The path of the Wall caused further urban changes, especially where it snaked left and right in sharp angles, surrounding neighborhoods on three sides (this was the case with the easternmost portion of Kreuzberg, for example). This sense of seclusion, of being separated from the rest of the urban fabric, further contributed to devalue these districts. At the same time, it was this very sense of seclusion that made some of these areas attractive to new groups of citizens—*Autonomen*,

1. References to "the largest construction site in the world" and to a horizon taken over by cranes were sometimes applied to Potsdamer Platz, and sometimes to the whole city. They appear in news stories, promotional materials for tourism, documentary movies, scholarly books and articles, novels and other literary works, and blogs—this was a trope widely shared across different cultural environments and media. See, for instance, Anthony Grafton, "Hello to Berlin," *New York Review of Books,* August 14, 1997, http://www.nybooks.com/articles/archives/1997/aug/14/hello-to-berlin/; Gerald R. Blomeyer, "Letter from . . . Berlin," *Architectural Review* 207 (March 2000): 30; Brigitte Werneburg, "Rebuilding Berlin," *Art in America* 83 (November 1995): 83; Lewis Joachim Edinger and Brigitte Lebens Nacos, *From Bonn to Berlin: German Politics in Transition* (New York: Columbia University Press, 1998), 252; Dan Fesperman, *The Small Boat of Great Sorrows* (New York: Knopf, 2003); Peter Schneider, *Eduards Heimkehr* (Berlin: Rowohlt, 1999); *Nach dem Fall*, directed by Eric Black and Frauke Sandig (Germany, 1999); *Berlin Babylon*, directed by Hubertus Siegert (Germany, 2001), among many, many others.

dropouts, conscientious objectors to the German military draft and to the West German state, beatniks, hippies, punks, students, and artists. These groups could be seen as part of larger countercultural movements that went beyond Berlin and Germany (and who, unsurprisingly, also flocked to affordable and decayed neighborhoods elsewhere in the world), but, in Berlin, they found an almost perfect spatial incarnation of their attempt at an alternative society. In Kreuzberg, they could live for the most part outside of mainstream society and of the rest of the city (this seclusion has been reenacted with different degrees of violence every May 1, when the neighborhood is famously taken over by street riots, barricades, and burning cars). This is the third distinctive condition of Berlin: the longtime presence of an alternative culture, a condition inseparable from the first two (division, and marginalization or seclusion of neighborhoods).

In East Berlin, the situation was comparable, even though the forces of the private real estate market were not at play. Living close to the Wall was first and foremost restricted by the government so as to improve patrolling and decrease the chance of escapes to the West, so most citizens were pushed away forcefully from the border areas in Mitte, Prenzlauer Berg, and Friedrichshain. In addition, when it came to investing in housing, the government turned its attention away from the center, and instead built vast new neighborhoods at the margins of Berlin, in districts such as Marzahn and Hohenschönhausen. When the GDR government built in the center, it demolished old buildings and replaced them with modernist towers and blocks; the investment in recuperating historic buildings was, for the most part, little and late.[2] As a result, the center of East Berlin was a combination of war-damaged areas (certain blocks in Mitte, in areas such as the Nikolaiviertel and the Fischerinsel, remained in ruins until as late as the 1980s) and densely built, deteriorated nineteenth-century apartment buildings, similar to those in Kreuzberg, Wedding, and Neukölln. These buildings lacked private bathrooms; the heating had to be done with laborsome, fuliginous coal; and the built substance was often falling apart. Broken stucco, peeling paint, wartime pockmarks, and exposed masonry weathered under the smoke of coal ovens and Trabis; this, of course, is the aesthetics of "ruinous charm," later embraced by counterpreservation. Most well-adjusted, well-behaved East German citizens flocked to the comforts of the new modernist neighborhoods, while Prenzlauer Berg developed as the eastern counterpart to Kreuzberg, attracting dissidents, artists, bohemians, and punks.

The paragraphs above recap three related conditions: the division of the city (and the task of reconnecting it after unification); the marginalization and seclusion of certain neighborhoods; and the flowering of vibrant, countercultural social scenes and practices within these neighborhoods. All of this meant that after unification, whole swaths of the city offered a very particular and propitious field for

---

2. Florian Urban, *Neo-Historical East Berlin: Architecture and Urban Design in the German Democratic Republic, 1970–1990* (Farnham, UK, and Burlington, VT: Ashgate, 2009).

counterpreservation. This was a field not only of decayed housing stock—which had its problems as well as its aesthetic charms—but also of an established tradition of alternative practices: squatting, communal living projects, self-build initiatives, noncommercial bars and concerts, independent art spaces, unconventional street fashions. These practices both inscribed and displayed a kind of urban text whose signs and signifiers would have been shared and understood widely, even by those who were not a part of these alternative social groups. When the Wall came down in 1989, it was in a sense inevitable that something like counterpreservation would emerge. Aided by vacancies and unclear ownership, and caught in the middle of the sea change of rebuilding the city—a time of transition, plans for the future, revisions of the past—groups from both East and West Berlin, and often beyond, expanded the alternative attitudes of the divided city to empty buildings in Mitte, Prenzlauer Berg, Friedrichshain, and other neighborhoods.[3]

The question that follows from these considerations, which is the question of this concluding chapter, is, Was counterpreservation first and foremost a socio-architectural phenomenon specific to Berlin during the *Wende*, even if it could be applied to other places? In the first chapter of this book I argued that examples of counterpreservation can be found in many other cities in Germany and beyond. The appropriation of architectural decay for unorthodox lifestyles, contestatory political projects, and alternative art and cultural centers has occurred in Copenhagen, New York, Dresden, Providence, Budapest, Melbourne, and Hamburg, to name just a few cities. If Berlin was different, it was so in the extent of counterpreservation examples (aided by the unique urban conditions of division outlined above), and in the particularly complicated past that charged seemingly every building or urban site with memorial significance and historical conflict. But if these two intensifying factors are to be put aside, then hypothetically Berlin can be compared to broader urban and social trends associated not only with the rise of a visible, active counterculture in wealthy urban centers since the 1960s, but also with the more recent processes of gentrification, globalization, and urban upgrading that both displaced these countercultures and paradoxically revived them by eliciting responses and protests on their part.

If we are to follow the reasoning of the preceding paragraph—and we should do so only in a provisional and exploratory way, for the sake of deepening a theoretical conclusion—then counterpreservation should be defined as a specific historical phenomenon, temporally and spatially situated, present to different degrees in major cities of the developed world, places where architectural decay can be turned into a signifier of lively social contexts as opposed to destitution or lack of alternatives. In this picture, Berlin figures as a particularly prolific example, and only a circumstantial "place of origin" for the term. There would be nothing wrong

---

3. See the website Berlin Besetzt for an interactive map (http://berlin-besetzt.de/#!).

with circumscribing the concept of counterpreservation in this way, if that were the case, but it would certainly limit its scope to a moment that possibly—given the ineluctable pace of gentrification, private-market forces, and property laws—is well past its zenith. Counterpreservation would be—would have been—a sign of a particular time.

I propose, however, that counterpreservation is more than that. It is more because counterpreservation is not merely a description and analysis of existing practices. It is also an attempt (my attempt) to develop a larger conceptual framework that both learns from existing practices and tells them something new; that draws not only from fieldwork observation but also from a dialogue with theories of memorialization, preservation, and urbanism. This is not a static, one-way process (from case studies to theoretical discussion, or vice versa), but a mutually informative and constitutive relationship. The end result is *not* a generalizable theory illustrated by case studies, to be later applied immutably to other case studies, as in "Is this counterpreservation?" "Is that building counterpreserved?" Rather, it is a concept that aims to change ways of thinking about architecture, preservation, and historical representations in the built environment. It is, in a sense, a philosophical inquiry, one that reaches out to preservation theory as a whole; and it is also an idea that can speak to multiple urban situations, not just beyond Berlin, but also beyond the turn-of-the-century time frame of the case studies in this book. Counterpreservation might not always have the same visage, the same crumbling masonry walls or rusted railings or grimy façades. To think that these material signs are automatic visual signifiers of counterpreservation is to reduce the concept to a set of aesthetic principles, a preconceived formal mold that is anathema to the social commitments of all counterpreservation examples presented in this book. To restate my definition of counterpreservation: it is an appropriation of decayed buildings that is always rooted in social engagement or activism of some kind, and that is open-ended in both form and meaning—even if this means that it is also often provisional, temporary, fragile, or makeshift. Such an appropriation might take different forms, and the Zwischenpalastnutzung Initiative should serve as an example, with its flooded floors and plastic mountains, that the means and formal expressions of counterpreservation are multifarious. Because this book is not a design primer, it is not its task to describe or create the many possible concrete forms that counterpreservation might take; if counterpreservation is really a socially grounded practice, then these forms could not possibly be determined a priori.

As I noted earlier in this book, counterpreservation has an affinity with John Ruskin's views on architectural preservation, especially his valuation of the imprints of time, not only as romantic signs of weathering but also as diachronic registers of events and social actions that should be reckoned with, not whitewashed. Counterpreservation pushes these ideas further in its embrace of decay, radical changes, and even disappearance; this, I argue, is not a mere matter of degree separating counterpreservation from Ruskin, but also a qualitative difference. For the radical embrace of change is in most ways antithetical not just to the mission of preservation, but also to that of architecture in general, and not just because of the Vitruvian triad of *firmitas, utilitas, venustas* (permanence, usefulness, beauty) as defining factors of architecture. Yet there have been many attempts to search for an architecture of change, from the Futurists' call that "every generation should build its own cities" to the Metabolists' plans for buildings with replaceable parts to be upgraded as technological conditions advanced (not to mention nomadic architecture, but this introduces another factor—change in space—whereas here I will limit myself to change in time).

Can there be an architecture of change, of transience, alongside the impulse to build stable and enduring cities and buildings? Counterpreservation is a step toward a conceptual exploration in this direction, even if it cannot account for all of the aspects of an architecture of change, which would involve issues that go beyond historic structures. Here I can only sketch what such a broader investigation might look like, beyond the specificities of my case studies, so the following pages should be taken as preliminary explorations that point to a direction where the present study might unfold.

Transience

The self-destructive potential of counterpreservation is inseparable from the idea of growth, life, and construction. One way to understand this paradox may be to focus on the process of change, that is, the idea of transformation and dynamism, instead of fixating the analysis on the end result of this process, that is, extinction. This may be especially appropriate to the topic, since counterpreservation's penchant for chance and accident is more closely related to a constant process than to the planned achievement of a final goal. If we were to understand transformation merely in terms of destruction, this would mean focusing only on what is lost in the process instead of embracing the new. This focus on the lost object involves difficulty in mourning in the Freudian sense. The incorporation of transformation in architecture finds a parallel in Sigmund Freud's exploration of transience (*Vergänglichkeit*) and its relationship to both death and mourning.[4]

In the short piece "On Transience," Freud describes a conversation with a young poet and a "taciturn friend" who were disturbed by the finiteness of beauty in both nature and art. The sense that beauty would perish prevented its fruition, as if diminishing the value of things. Freud does not partake in this sentiment—but not because he disagrees with the perception of transience. He claims that transience is an inevitable part of reality, and as such cannot be denied. But it does not detract

---

4. Sigmund Freud, "On Transience," in *The Standard Edition of the Complete Psychological Works of Sigmund Freud*, trans. and ed. James Strachey (London: The Hogarth Press and the Institute of Psycho-Analysis, 1957), 14:303–7.

from the value, beauty, or enjoyment of the world. The awareness of transience, Freud claims, indeed adds to this value precisely because enjoyment is limited, in the same way that precious stones derive their value from rarity:

> But this demand for immortality is a product of our wishes too unmistakable to lay claim to reality: what is painful may nonetheless be true. I could not see my way to dispute the transience of all things, nor could I insist upon an exception in favour of what is beautiful and perfect. But I did dispute the pessimistic poet's view that the transience of what is beautiful involves any loss in its worth.
>
> On the contrary, an increase! Transience value is scarcity value in time. *Limitation in the possibility of an enjoyment raises the value of the enjoyment.* It was incomprehensible, I declared, that the thought of the transience of beauty should interfere with our joy in it.[5]

The passage above underscores the meaning of transience as limited duration, or "scarcity value in time." In this sense, the idea of transience with relation to architecture would seem paradoxical. The craft of building has historically been characterized by fixity, durability, and permanence. Buildings are laid on foundations set on firm ground; constructors choose materials that better resist conditions such as weather, human action, structural stresses, and accidents; and the very cost involved in construction demands a longer life span for edifices than that of individuals or generations. Buildings are enjoyed over long periods; it is hard to associate long-standing structures with "scarcity value in time." Moreover, up until the modernization of construction techniques that started in the Renaissance, major undertakings such as palaces and cathedrals often took generations to complete. These buildings were not ancestral inheritances, but ongoing construction works in which successive and overlapping generations were engaged. Each new generation of builders thus saw architecture as a task to be continually fulfilled toward completion. Their viewpoint projected architecture forward into the future, as opposed to the reverse outlook (looking "back" at past architecture from the present). This forward perspective informed the perception of buildings even after they were finished; that is, structures should be maintained and improved so as to last indefinitely. These structures were collective enterprises spanning long periods—an ongoing process rooted in the present, not the past. These buildings should last not (only) because of memorial or historical significance, but because of their present value. This value was twofold: it was symbolic inasmuch as every generation felt meaningfully engaged by the architectural forms; and it was concrete, since these generations had expended labor, time, and materials on the building.

Once it became easier to tear structures down or put them up, the economic incentive to make them last as long as possible diminished. This has of course been

---

5. Freud, "On Transience," 305; my italics.

a gradual process. Much as some of them might have wanted to, Renaissance architects did not tear all Gothic buildings down.[6] But they did transform the face of European cities through several major building undertakings whose number and dimension were possible only because of developments in architectural design, representation, and constructive methods. The Renaissance's symbolic attempt to create the world anew was matched by the material ability to produce this change. And yet the Renaissance reinvention of classicism was itself supposed to last and endure, like the all-controlling designs of baroque urbanism, the elaborately defined neoclassical buildings, or the utopian creations of the eighteenth-century visionaries.[7] These rational attempts to organize and refashion the world wanted to solve material or philosophical problems once and for all. It is only with the advent of modernity in the nineteenth century that architects questioned the universal and timeless validity of architectural forms, and ventured the idea of changing styles that would best express contemporary times. This questioning made way for radical propositions in the twentieth century, such as the Futurists' call for an endlessly renewing architecture. In his "Manifesto of Futurist Architecture," Antonio Sant'Elia writes:

> An architecture so conceived cannot give birth to any three-dimensional or linear habit, because the fundamental characteristics of Futurist architecture will be obsolescence and transience. "Houses will last less long than we. Each generation will have to build its own city."[8]

A few years later Frank Lloyd Wright incorporated change and movement in a different way, by proposing mobile units—hybrids of home and car—as the living space of Broadacre City.[9] Works like these, which have attempted to incorporate mobility or evanescence, draw attention precisely because they differ from traditional architectural conceptions.

Counterpreservation, unlike avant-gardist architecture, does not oppose architecture's fixity. Rather, it recognizes the limits of this fixity. Extensive repairs or restoration would mean a denial of transience. According to Freud, this is also a denial of reality, of the inevitable passage of time. Instead of counteracting transience, counterpreservation makes the most of it. It transforms a contingency into an advantage. In counterpreservation, there is no mutually exclusive opposition between transience

---

6. Donato Bramante, for example, was nicknamed "Bramante ruinante" (Bramante the destroyer) for the many buildings he tore down. See, for instance, Charles B. McClendon, "The History of the Site of St. Peter's Basilica, Rome," *Perspecta* 25 (1989): 49.

7. On the visionary architects Claude-Nicolas Ledoux, Étienne-Louis Boullée, and Jean-Jacques Lequeu, see Jean-Claude Lemagny, *Visionary Architects: Boullée, Ledoux, Lequeu* (Santa Monica, CA: Hennessey & Ingalls, 2002).

8. Antonio Sant'Elia, "Manifesto of Futurist Architecture," originally published in 1914; Ulrich Conrads, ed., *Programs and Manifestos on 20th Century Architecture* (Cambridge, MA: The MIT Press, [1970]), 38; the quotation marks are Sant'Elia's.

9. Robert Fishman, *Urban Utopias in the Twentieth Century: Ebenezer Howard, Frank Lloyd Wright, Le Corbusier* (Cambridge, MA: The MIT Press, 1982).

and fixity. The perception of change and transformation is possible only because some elements stay the same: the building still stands, solid, usable, on the same location; most of its built substance remains, so that a fallen chunk of plaster on the façade reveals the original bricks and mortar. Counterpreservation produces a tension between the permanent and the transient by introducing a vigilant historical conscience in discourse and practice. This historical conscience constantly reverts to the building's past as a point of reference, both symbolically and materially. While weathering and decay wash away visual signs of the past, the historical conscience tenaciously pushes these signs back up to the shore through the process of memory-work. Counterpreservation thus foregrounds not transience per se (that is, incessant, absolute change), but the embeddedness of transience and permanence. In counterpreservation, the meaning and interest of a building lie in the slow but constant change imprinted on fixed built matter. Without this fixed matter as a reference point, the change would be self-consuming, meaningless, even impossible to perceive.

For Freud, transience enhances the value of beauty—he described a field blooming in the summer, but he could have been talking about a building or object. His argument is that the enjoyment of these objects is intensified by the fact that they cannot be enjoyed forever. The crumbling apartment buildings in Mitte or Prenzlauer Berg, proudly displayed by their residents as points of resistance against gentrification, refuse nostalgia for their former architectural integrity. Their current state alludes to eventual, irreversible dissolution. But this sense of looming death does not impair the present use and appreciation of these buildings. In counterpreservation, the value of beauty also resides in transience itself. The gradual change of a building means that at any point something of its original or preceding state is lost or extinguished, and at any point new forms or meanings arise.

Freud's conception of transience is not the celebration of ongoing change per se and ultimate destruction. This is the key to differentiating counterpreservation from the meaningless and random dissolution of built substance. Freud's transience is inseparable from creation. Freud spells this out by associating transience with rebirth, new construction, and life at the conclusion of his text. And he does so by bringing up World War I, an event that had evoked the opposite reaction among his contemporaries—that is, despair and nihilism. Freud starts out by considering that the war damage went beyond burned villages and torn-up fields, but affected the optimistic faith in progress that had pervaded the Belle Époque:

> My conversation with the poet took place in the summer before the war. A year later the war broke out and robbed the world of its beauties. It destroyed not only the beauty of the countrysides through which it passed but it also shattered our pride in the achievements of our civilization, our admiration for many philosophers and artists and our hopes of a final triumph over the difference between nations and races.[10]

---

10. Freud, "On Transience," 306.

Freud binds physical destruction with a kind of loss of innocence. Modernity had been a promising succession of developments that improved the conditions of life. These developments included discoveries in medicine and sanitation, increased capacity for industrial production, improved transportation and telecommunications, breakthroughs in scientific knowledge, and the emancipation of thought (including, of course, the possibility for critical self-knowledge through psychoanalysis). World War I was not simply a retrograde event that antagonized these tendencies; to a large extent it was also the consequence of modern progress and technical development. Considered either as an irruption of irrational impulses not yet "tamed" by progress, or as the ultimate and rational outcome of modernity (and I will not go further into this question here), the first global, massive industrialized war laid bare the limitations of the teleological faith in human evolution through scientific and cultural advancements.

For some, the trauma was crippling, as Freud's studies on war neuroses show. In art, the experience of war informed pessimistic and negative works, from German expressionism to Dada. But for others, the shaken worldview prompted a self-critical revision directed at reconstruction. This was the case, for instance, with Walter Gropius, who had been fervently involved in the nationalistic Deutscher Werkbund, and as early as 1916 reflected on the need for a revised course of action in architecture—this time guided by Socialist and even utopian ideals, and decidedly international.[11] It is this constructive potential that Freud underscores as he concludes his appraisal of the impact of the war: "We shall build up again all that war has destroyed, and perhaps on firmer ground and more lastingly than before."[12] Thus transience is linked to the possibility not of restoration, but of new construction. "All that war has destroyed" can be rebuilt "on firmer ground." The legacy of the past is the basis for reconstruction, but reconstruction introduces new and improved elements. Freud's optimism is not fixated on the final objects (concrete or symbolic) that had been destroyed, but on the process of their creation; the same humanity that produced artworks and texts will be able to create artworks and texts again, though not exactly the same ones. The focus on creative potential is forward looking and life affirming, but it can develop only if loss is overcome. Thus Freud's exploration of transience is linked to the idea of mourning, as he explains:

> But have those other possessions, which we have now lost, really ceased to have any worth for us because they have proved so perishable and unresistant? To many of us this seems to be, but once more wrongly in my view. I believe that those who think thus, and seem ready to make a permanent renunciation because what was precious has proved not to be lasting, are simply in a state of mourning for what is

11. His writings and reflections at the time would become, three years later, the foundation for the Bauhaus manifesto, mission, and curriculum.

12. Freud, "On Transience," 307.

lost. Mourning as we know, however painful it may be, comes to a spontaneous end. When it has renounced everything that has been lost, then it has consumed itself, and our libido is once more free ... to replace the lost objects by fresh ones equally or still more precious. It is to be hoped that the same will be true of the losses caused by this war. When once the mourning is over, it will be found that our high opinion of the riches of civilization has lost nothing from our discovery of their fragility.[13]

The death and destruction brought about by World War I, the deadliest war to that point, did not invalidate the achievements of civilization. For those who truly cherished these values, the war destruction was an impulse to renew this appreciation and build civilization anew. Transience and perishability prompt renewal and rebirth, as long as mourning takes place and concludes. Conversely, the architectural incorporation of transience is inextricable from a constructive and renewing impulse. The Haus Schwarzenberg and the *Hausprojekte* are not dead or lost because their façades are crumbling. These buildings are integrated in the life of the city. The Schwarzenberg association introduces new, current uses: art studios, galleries, a movie theater, educational and research projects. The inhabitants of *Hausprojekte* not only live in these structures, but also use them to express a critical view on gentrification and real estate speculation. Daniel Libeskind's redesign for the Oranienburg SS-barracks area submerges the ruins in water as a symbol of overcoming, and restructures the land along a new strip of development for educational and productive activities. And the Zwischenpalastnutzung Initiative made the most of the doomed Palace of the Republic, infusing it with life and visions for a future city that have lasted beyond (and despite) the building's end point.

In each case the resonance with Freud's concept of transience goes beyond the idea of transformation and finiteness. All of these case studies also refer to a traumatic and violent history, which in the case of counterpreservation includes war, the Holocaust, national division, and a dictatorship. Freud links transience to the extreme destructiveness of war. Counterpreservation is inseparable from Berlin's own histories of destruction and belligerence. However, in neither case is destruction the inescapable focus. Transience for Freud, and counterpreservation for us, are the dynamic processes that overcome death and extinction by engendering the new. But it is the engagement with a difficult past (the two wars, the Nazi era, national division) that sets the process of transformation and renewal in motion. The alternative is the paralyzing melancholia that grips the poet in Freud's text, or the blind confidence that binds one to the fascinating spell of the past, as Adorno would put it.[14]

---

13. Ibid.
14. Theodor Adorno, "The Meaning of Working through the Past," in *Critical Models: Interventions and Catchwords* (New York: Columbia University Press, 1998), 89.

War is an extreme situation of destruction. But the cyclical alternation of life and death occurs beyond wars. Transience, both as a concept and as a quality of counterpreservation, is present in subtle but ubiquitous ways. Life demands constant renewal; it cannot be preserved, untouched and unchanged, as if frozen in time. Conversely, works of art, values, buildings, even the very idea of beauty, can only be kept "alive" and rooted in meaningful social practices insofar as individuals or groups continuously engage with them anew.[15] Even when objects remain the same, social relationships and attitudes toward them are transformed. The meaning and value of the Canterbury Cathedral, for instance, is not the same in contemporary touristic pilgrimage as it was in medieval religious pilgrimage. In the case of the Canterbury Cathedral, the "same" that is always present is transformed by gradual change. In Freud's consideration of the war, transience prompts the renewal (or reconstruction) of what existed before, although what is reconstructed is not exactly the "same" as the original. In both cases, permanence and transience are not antithetical to each other—rather, they are irrevocably linked. This relationship is essential for the constitution of an architecture of change, a concept that itself encapsulates a paradox. The sustained tensions between fixity and change, old and new, historical consciousness and openness to the future, remembrance and forgetting—these are the preconditions for counterpreservation. None of these elements can prevail without compromising the idea of counterpreservation and turning it into either conventional preservation or mere destruction.

Transience points to the impossibility of clinging to the past, to what is already known. Historic preservation and restoration, museums, archives, and research are to a certain extent a retrogressive attempt to reverse death and recover what has already passed, to salvage objects and events from forgetfulness and extinction. My own work, as I register the ongoing and often fleeting processes of spatial production that I call counterpreservation, is also part of this "retrogressive attempt" to stop time in its tracks and collect the debris. However, at the same time the reconstruction of history also entails new construction, as I strive to make sense of the disparate fragments of the past and thereby build new meanings. The idea of "preserving the past" not only masks the impossibility of the endeavor—the inevitable chasm between now and then—but also belies the imprint of our contemporary agendas.

---

15. Freud suggests that beauty or artworks or human achievements have no intrinsic value outside of the meaning imbued by emotional life: "A time may indeed come when the pictures and the statues which we admire today will crumble to dust, or a race of men may follow us who no longer understand the works of our poets and thinkers, or a geological epoch may even arrive when all animate life upon earth ceases; but since the value of all this beauty and perfection is determined only by its significance for our emotional lives, it has no need to survive us and is therefore independent of absolute duration." Freud, "On Transience," 307.

Every act of preservation or restoration is irrevocably embedded in current interests, values, and political stakes, as explored by Françoise Choay.[16] Conventional preservation and restoration, however, often elide these current uses under a cloak of neutrality. In other words, the restored historic artifact appears to speak only of its original incarnation, in the same way as a conventional museum display. Counterpreservation, on the other hand, evidences the actions and intentions of the present by drawing attention to the production and transformation of historical buildings, and to the social perceptions that surround them. Just as James Young's countermonuments are self-reflective memorials that recall their own coming-into-being, so counterpreservation points to the intentional and unintentional forces that shape architecture and the city over time. And just as the countermonument demands that its public perform the labor of memory-work, counterpreservation requires active and critical participation from the inhabitants, users, and designers of buildings, and from potentially every city dweller, visitor, or passerby.

The crumbling façades of the *Hausprojekte*, the eroding waterland of Project Mo**X**rning, and the temporary installations in the Palace of the Republic do not intend to comprise any kind of historical or semantic totality. They do not exhaust the task of remembrance, and they leave the production of historical meaning always open-ended. The façades of *Hausprojekte* or of the Haus Schwarzenberg may one day fall down; the SS-barrack ruins would have eventually dissolved under water; and the Palace of the Republic did, indeed, disappear. But none of this extinguished the memorial possibilities of these sites, which might live on, in different ways, with different meanings, even beyond themselves. Their architecture of transience is, in a way, just the beginning.

---

16. Françoise Choay, *The Invention of the Historic Monument* (Cambridge: Cambridge University Press, 2001).

Index

Page numbers in *italics* indicate illustrations.

CPSIA information can be obtained at www.ICGtesting.com
Printed in the USA
BVOW08*2041201016

465597BV00002B/5/P